Andrew Blyth and Gerald L. Kovacich

# Information Assurance

## Surviving in the Information Environment

 Springer

Andrew Blyth, PhD, Msc
School of Computing, University of Glamorgan, Pontypridd,
Mid Glamorgan CF37 1DL, UK

Gerald L. Kovacich, D.Crim, MSc, MA
ShockwaveWriters.com, Whidbey Island, WA, USA

*Series editor*
Professor A.J. Sammes, BSc, MPhil, PhD, FBCS, CEng
CISM Group, Cranfield University, RMCS, Shrivenham, Swindon SN6 8LA, UK

British Library Cataloguing in Publication Data
Blyth, Andrew
    Information assurance : surviving in the information
    environment. – (Computer communications and networks)
    1. Data protection
    I. Title  II. Kovacich, Gerald L.
    005.8
ISBN 185233326X

Library of Congress Cataloging-in-Publication Data
Blyth, Andrew, 1966-
    Information assurance : surviving in the information environment. / Andrew Blyth and
    Gerald L. Kovacich.
        p. cm. -- (Computer communications and networks)
    Includes bibliographical references and index.
    ISBN 1-85233-326-X
    1 Computer security.    2. Data protection.    I. Kovacich, Gerald L.    II. Title.    III. Series.
QA76.9.A25 B59 2001
005.8—dc21

                                                                    2001032780

Computer Communications and Networks ISSN 1617-7975

ISBN 1-85233-326-X  Springer-Verlag London Berlin Heidelberg
A member of BertelsmannSpringer Science+Business Media GmbH
http://www.springer.co.uk

Typesetting: Camera-ready by authors
Printed and bound at the Athenæum Press Ltd., Gateshead, Tyne and Wear
34/3830-543210  Printed on acid-free paper  SPIN 10768781

# Computer Communications and Networks

S
L
B
He
Ne
Bar
Hong Kong
Milan
Paris
Singapore
Tokyo

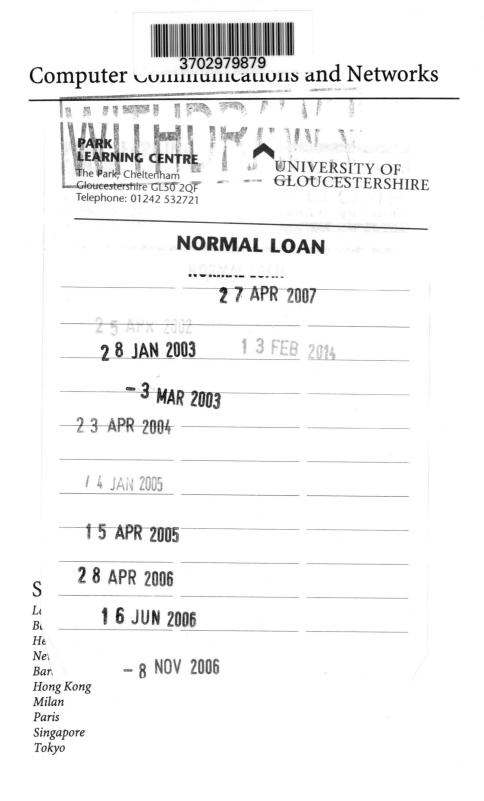

The **Computer Communications and Networks** series is a range of textbooks, monographs and handbooks. It sets out to provide students, researchers and non-specialists alike with a sure grounding in current knowledge, together with comprehensible access to the latest developments in computer communications and networking.

Emphasis is placed on clear and explanatory styles that support a tutorial approach, so that even the most complex of topics is presented in a lucid and intelligible manner.

*Also in this series:*

An Information Security Handbook
John M.D. Hunter
1-85233-180-1

Multimedia Internet Broadcasting: Quality, Technology and Interface
Andy Sloane and Dave Lawrence (Eds)
1-85233-283-2

The Quintessential PIC Microcontroller
Sid Katzen
1-85233-309-X

# Dedications

To my Wife, who is always there when I need her the most and without whose love and support, I would not have been able to complete this book.

Dr. Andrew J. C. Blyth
University of Glamorgan
United Kingdom

This book is dedicated to all those professionals in the world's government agencies and businesses who are responsible for providing leadership for the protection, integrity and availability of the sensitive information on which we all depend.

Dr. Gerald L. Kovacich, CFE, CPP, CISSP,
Whidbey Island, Washington
United States of America

# Quotations

"Our wish... is that... equality of rights [be] maintained, and that state of property, equal or unequal, which results to every man from his own industry or that of his fathers." --Thomas Jefferson: 2nd Inaugural Address, 1805.

"To take from one because it is thought that his own industry and that of his father's has acquired too much, in order to spare to others, who, or whose fathers have not exercised equal industry and skill, is to violate arbitrarily the first principle of association—'the guarantee to every one of a free exercise of his industry and the fruits acquired by it.'" --Thomas Jefferson: Note in Destutt de Tracy's "Political Economy," 1816.

# Foreword

When you first hear the term Information Assurance you tend to conjure up an image of a balanced set of reasonable measures that have been taken to protect the information after an assessment has been made of risks that are posed to it. In truth this is the Holy Grail that all organisations that value their information should strive to achieve, but which few even understand.

Information Assurance is a term that has recently come into common use. When talking with old timers in IT (or at least those that are over 35 years old), you will hear them talking about information security, a term that has survived since the birth of the computer. In the more recent past, the term Information Warfare was coined to describe the measures that need to be taken to defend and attack information. This term, however, has military connotations - after all, warfare is normally their domain. Shortly after the term came into regular use, it was applied to a variety of situations encapsulated by Winn Schwartau as the three classes of Information Warfare:

Class 1 - Personal Information Warfare.
Class 2 - Corporate Information Warfare.
Class 3 - Global Information Warfare.

Political sensitivities lead to "warfare" being replaced by "operations", a much more "politically correct" word. Unfortunately, "operations" also has an offensive connotation and is still the terminology of the military and governments. A term was needed that described the measures needed to safeguard the most precious asset in this modern, connected world - Information. The measures are much more than just security, encompassing the concepts of risk assessment, management and the protection of your information from compromise, theft, modification and lack of availability.

Information Assurance is ensuring that your information is where you want it, when you want it, in the condition that you need it and available to those that you want to have access to it - but only to them. In the past, information was recorded, stored and transported on paper, the methods of achieving security were developed over more than three thousand years, and had the distinct advantage that any action that was taken on the information could normally be easily observed. Now and increasingly in the future, information exists digitally and digital technology has only been in common use for less than 30 years. Add this shortage of time in which to gain experience in the best methods of protecting digital information to the fact that it can be moved from one place to another in a fraction of a second. Then add the facts that it can be stolen and yet remain unaffected in its original location; that vast quantities of it can be stored on increasingly small storage mediums and that you can no longer easily view, even with equipment to assist you, what is contained on the storage medium; and you begin to comprehend the problems of Information Assurance.

Modern day security specialists have an increasingly difficult problem to solve. In addition to the aforementioned factors, the technologies (both in hardware and software) are changing with increasing rapidity, making it even more difficult for even the most dedicated of professionals to gain and maintain the knowledge needed to allow them to effectively carry out their tasks.

The problem is compounded by the way in which we as a society organise ourselves. People who are involved in Information Assurance are mostly employed in the business of security and use the skills and knowledge that they have obtained to stop unauthorised users from gaining access to the information. As a result of this, they will tend not to share the information and knowledge that they have collected in order to protect the methods that have been used to acquire it. They will also tend not to advertise that they have suffered an attack to avoid embarrassment to their organisation and limit the damage that such an attack has caused. Those who attack information systems gain their knowledge by sharing and communicating with others of a similar persuasion in a culture of peer recognition and a shared goal.

We are all striving for a globally connected society where everyone is encouraged to make use of the information systems that are available, and those that cannot are considered to be disadvantaged. It is not surprising in this environment that we are seeing a growth in the level of a whole range of crimes that were previously seen in the paper based society migrating to this new medium. We have made it possible for a person who would wish to harm our interests to gain the three elements that they seek most – access to our valuables, the opportunity to remain anonymous and the potential to carry out the attack without having to physically visit the site of the attack – indeed, it is not even necessary to visit the country in which the attack is mounted.

Given that the problem is, in historical terms, very new and also global, it is not surprising that national legal systems are having difficulty in addressing the problem and that the international community, not renowned for its speed, is talking about the problem but not yet acting in response to it.

In the coming months and years, we will witness technological solutions to Information Assurance needs and comparisons will be seen with the way in which we handle the physical valuables of today. Strong-rooms that protect the physical environment will be matched by secured data warehouses and protected servers, couriers by encryption and digital signatures, locks on the doors by firewalls and security alarms and burglar alarms by Intruder Detection Systems in the virtual world. What of keys, oh yes, biometric devices and smart cards - whatever next?

**Andy Jones MBE BSc MBCS**
**Group Manager, Secure Information Systems; Defence Evaluation and Research Agency (UK)**

# Preface

In the late 1970s and early 1980s, information systems security began to gain in importance as more and more government agencies and businesses began to integrate computers into their processes. The 1990s was the decade of the massive integration of computers into corporate, national and international networks. The Internet became the backbone for the global networking of networks.

The information systems security profession was born and began to mature during this time. The concept of protecting computer systems and by doing so also protecting the information they processed, stored and transmitted was the norm. However, gradually another concept began to take hold, and that is the concept of information assurances (IA). IA is more than just information systems security or information security. The development of the concept of IAs is another step in the maturation of concepts, practices and processes needed to protect information, the vital asset of today's information-based, information-dependent nation-states and corporations.

As the threats, internal, national, and global to information grows, so is the need to develop new, more sophisticated holistic IA processes. However, before that can be accomplished successfully, one must understand the concept of IAs and surviving in the information environment. It is hoped that this book will assist in meeting those challenges.

This book aims to perform two very important functions:

- To bridge the gap between information assurance as a technical concept and IA as a business concept. Thus allowing information systems managers to effectively manage information systems' security in such a manner so as to facilitate the business process and contribute to the competitive advantage of the organisation.
- To provide information systems managers and students with a core text on assuring accurate information is available when needed to only those that need it. As the Internet continues to expand and more companies start conducting business on the Internet, electronic business, there is going to be a need for people who understand not only the IA concepts and best practices, but also the business, legal and technical aspects of conducting business online. It is hoped that this book provides some assistance in that endeavour.

The book is divided into four sections and a total of fifteen chapters as follows:

## Section 1 – An Introduction to Information Assurance
This section sets the context of the book, and talks about the need for all organisations to take IA seriously. It will also provide an introduction to IA and related topics. It will provide the reader with a baseline on which to build an understanding of the theories, philosophies, models, processes, management, and technical aspects of IA.

### Chapter 1. What is Information Assurance?

This chapter will define basic terms such as IA, information operations, information security, information systems security, and information warfare. It will also provide a short history of these concepts.

### Chapter 2. The World of Information

This chapter will discuss the global and national economic and political environment as it relates to conducting business and the increasing need for IA in this new global marketplace.

### Chapter 3. The Theory of Risks

This chapter will define and discuss threats, vulnerabilities, and risks. Also addressed will be the concepts of qualitative and quantitative risk analysis and risk management vis-à-vis IA.

### Chapter 4. The Information World of Crime

IA is required because of human error and because there are people in business and throughout the world who will use any legal and illegal means in order to obtain information for resale or to give others a competitive advantage. These issues will be discussed in this chapter based on theories of criminology, psychological profiling, and examples of actual cases will be analysed. Included will be a discussion of inquiries, investigations and examinations of incidents caused by these miscreants, to include a discussion of computer forensics. Included will be an introduction to cybercrime and the effect that it can have on organisations and businesses, e.g. public confidence in CITI-Bank.

### Chapter 5. IA Trust and Supply Chains

In this chapter, the idea of trust within organisations, processes, and systems will be discussed along with the idea of supply chains.

### Chapter 6. Basic IA Concepts and Models

Building on the above, this chapter will address the various IA related models such as: The Confidentiality-Integrity-Availability (CIA) Model; The Protect-Detect-React-Deter (PDRD) Model; The Need-to-Know (NTK) Model; and The Information Value (IV) Model.

## Section 2 – IA in the World of Corporations

This section will begin with a discussion of the corporate security officer, to include a description and discussion of their duties and responsibilities, and their IA role. This will be followed by a discussion of the corporate IA officer, and the functions of an IA organisation within a corporation.

### Chapter 7. The Corporate Security Officer

This chapter will identify and discuss the duties and responsibilities of a corporate security officer as it relates to IA and the protection of the corporate assets to include the protection of information and information systems.

### Chapter 8. Corporate Security Functions

This chapter will identify and describe security functions of a corporation to include those functions that are an integral part of any corporation's IA program.

### Chapter 9. IA in the Interest of National Security

This chapter will describe and discuss IA requirements in the national security environment of government agencies and defence-related businesses since many of the philosophies and processes can be adapted to meet the IA needs of corporations.

### Chapter 10. The Corporate IA Officer

This chapter addresses the position of the corporate IA officer. It describes the basic qualifications, duties and responsibilities required to lead an IA effort for a corporation into the 21$^{st}$ century.

### Chapter 11. IA Organisational Functions

This chapter will identify and discuss a corporation's IA organisational structure and its IA functions.

## Section 3 – Technical Aspects of IA

This section will discuss the technical aspects of IA as it relates to the storing, processing and transmitting of information.

### Chapter 12. IA and Software

This chapter will discuss the problems and possible solutions to the IA questions in the software and firmware environment of operating systems, databases, and applications software. Included will be a discussion of malicious codes.

### Chapter 13. Applying Cryptography to IA

This chapter will describe and discuss cryptography including when to use it, when not to use it, and the related political ramifications of cryptography in the global marketplace. Topics discussed include algorithms; public and private key; key management; digital signatures; and the world of PKI.

### Chapter 14. IA Technology Security

This chapter will discuss the technical equipment available and in use to protect or attack the IA processes including ADT, CCTV, biometrics, EMP weapons, HERF guns, TEMPEST, line filtering, and smart cards.

## Section 4 – The Future and Final Comments

This section will provide the authors' final comments, predictions and conclusions.

### Chapter 15. The Future, Conclusions and Comments

This chapter will summarise the main points of the book, draw some conclusions, and look into the future of IA as we enter the 21$^{st}$ century.

# Acknowledgements

To successfully take on and complete such a project as writing this book, one must rely on many people who freely give of their professional advice and assistance. We are grateful to the following friends and colleagues for their never-ending support and consultations: Andy Jones, William C. Boni, Perry G. Luzwick, Paul Zavidniak, Ed Halibozek, and Motomu Akashi.

A special thanks to John Meyer, Reed Elsevier's Advanced Technology Group, Oxford, England; and to Carola E. Roeder, Permissions, Butterworth-Heinemann, a member of the Reed Elsevier Group, Woburn, Massachusetts, USA; for their years of support and for granting permission to include relevant material from Dr. Kovacich's other books and articles published by them. Also to Ken Cutler, CISA, CISSP, Managing Director, Information Security Institute, for providing the "MIS Training Institute Swiss Army Knife"; and Keith Lawrence Buzzard, B.Sc, M.Sc., for a copy of his paper, "Computer Misuse Act 1990 - Loopholes and Anomalies".

Regardless of how much good advice we received from our colleagues, this book could never have been successfully published if it were not for Rosie Kemp of Springer-Verlag, our publisher, who was willing to risk signing a couple of "crazy doctors" to a book contract. Thanks Rosie!

Writing and publishing this book was truly a team effort. Other members of that team who made this all possible deserve a note of appreciation. They are: Karen Borthwick, Sally Tickner, and Joanne Cooling.

# Contents

# Section 1

# An Introduction to Information Assurance

This section sets the context of the book, and discusses the need for all organisations to take information assurance seriously. It will also provide an introduction to information assurance and related topics. It provides the reader with a baseline on which to build an understanding of the theories, philosophies, models, processes, management, and technical aspects of information assurance.

When introducing the topic of information assurance, it is important that the reader understand the basic terminology to avoid possible confusion later. Therefore, Chapter 1 defines the basic terms, beginning of course with the term information assurance. It will also provide a short history of basic information assurance related concepts. Chapter 2 discusses the basic global economic, political, and business environment where information is a vital asset and where information assurance is a vital necessity. With that understanding, Chapter 3 discusses risk theories; as well as risk assessment, risk management and the threats and vulnerabilities associated with risk.

Building on the first three chapters, Chapter 4 explains why there is a need for information assurance. Chapter 5 and Chapter 6 then go on to describe the basic philosophies that should be applied when developing information assurance processes and programs.

# Chapter 1

## What is Information Assurance?

When one hears the term, information assurance, what does one think of? What exactly is information assurance (IA)? Is it information systems security by another name? Is IA a subset of information security or is information security a subset of IA? These terms and other basic terms such as information operations, and information warfare will be defined and discussed.

## 1.1 Information Assurance and Its Subset – Information Security

Information assurance (IA) is about protecting your information assets from *destruction, degradation, manipulation and exploitation* by an opponent. The difficulty with achieving this is that one day a party may be collaborating on a project and therefore need access to confidential information, and the next day that party may be an opponent. In 1996 the United States (US) Department of Defence defined information assurance as:

*"Actions taken that protect and defend information and information systems by ensuring their availability, integrity, authentication, confidentiality and non-repudiation. This includes providing for restoration of information systems by incorporating protection, detection and reaction capabilities."*

Information security (InfoSec) can be defined as:

*"The protection of information against unauthorised disclosure, transfer, modification, or destruction, whether accidental or intentional"*

Information security and information assurance are concerned with both intentional and unintentional attacks. Information assurance covers areas not covered by information security, such as perception management. Information assurance can be considered at three levels: physical, information infrastructure and perceptual. These three levels are considered in Table 1.1

**Table 1.1   Characteristics of Information Assurance**

| Characteristics and Components | Security Measure |
| --- | --- |
| Knowledge and understanding in human decision space. | Physical and technical measures to maintain accurate, objective perception of the security state of the system and the information contained in the system. |
| | Personnel measures to maintain personnel security to protect from insider attacks, and to provide protection from psychological operations. |
| Information and data manipulation ability maintained in cyber-space. | Make use of cyber defensive techniques, such as encryption, intrusion detection, integrity analysis, etc. |
| Data and data processing activities that are managed and performed in the physical space. | Physical access controls and facility protection. |
| | Personnel management and security. |
| | Contingency planning and disaster recovery. |

In information security, an exposure is a form of possible loss or harm against an information asset. That information asset may be either logically based (i.e. 1's and 0's inside a computer), or physically based (i.e. paper, nuts and bolts or hardware). Examples of exposure include unauthorised disclosure of data, modification of data, or denial of legitimate access to the information asset.

## 1.1.1   Interruption, Interception, Modification and Fabrication

The following factors adversely impact Information Assurance (IA):

- *Interruption*: in an interruption an information asset of the system becomes unusable, unavailable or lost. For example, the physical theft or physical destruction of a computer system would be viewed as an interruption. The removal of information or software from an information system would also be viewed as an interruption.
- *Interception*: an interception means that some unauthorised party has gained access to an information asset. The party can be a program, computer system or person. For example, recording a telephone conversation or monitoring a computer network can be viewed as interception (see Figure 1.1).
- *Modification*: modification of an asset means that some unauthorised party tampers with the asset. For example, the unauthorised installation of monitoring software or hardware, or the unauthorised insertion, manipulation or deletion of information can be viewed as modification.

- **Fabrication**: fabrication of an asset means the counterfeiting of an asset. For example, an intruder may insert spurious transactions into a computer network.

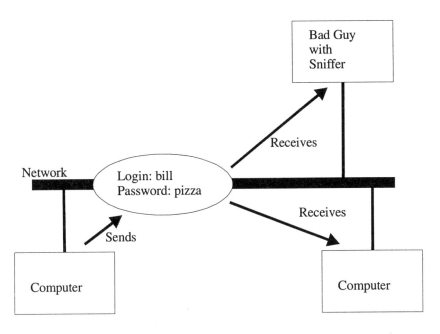

**Figure 1.1   Sniffing**

## 1.1.2   Information Assurance in Context

Financial losses attributed to malicious hacking, online corporate espionage and other computer crimes probably doubled in 1999, according to a survey by the Computer Security Institute (CSI). The survey covered 643 major corporations and public agencies that estimated their computer crime losses at $266 million in 1999. Based on that number, CSI estimates that total losses attributable to computer crime are around $10 billion annually, mostly from financial fraud and proprietary information theft. Based on the survey responses, 59% of the companies said the computer attacks initiated from the Internet, while 38% said they initiated from internal company computers.

Information assurance is sometimes referred to as information operations that protect and defend information systems by ensuring their availability, integrity, authentication, confidentiality, and non-repudiation. This includes providing for restoration of information systems by incorporating protection, detection and reaction capabilities. Information assurance is concerned with the containment of, and recovery from, an attack. It also defines how attacks are to be detected through the use of a set of indicators and warnings, and, how once an attack has occurred we should respond to the attack. In addition, information assurance deals with deterring attacks and the application of legislation designed to address issues of privacy, computer-related crime, computer forensics and the like. The term "information operation" is used to refer to actions taken to affect an opponent's information and information systems while defending one's own information and information systems.

Figure 1.2 depicts the various components and their relationships that function to set the concept of information assurance in context. The *owner* of the system is the organisation, group-of-individuals, or individual, that functions as the stakeholder of the security requirements. Stakeholders are defined as all those claimants within and without an organisation who have a vested interest in decisions faced by the organisation in adopting and utilising information technology. The *owner* possesses a set of *assets* that have *value* to the *owner*. The *owner* may be *aware* of a set of *vulnerabilities* that could lead to the loss of an *asset*. In order to protect the *asset* the owner *imposes* a set of protection and defensive *counter-measures* on the *asset* in the belief that by doing so that *owner* is protecting the *asset* from possible *loss, exploitation, abuse* or *damage* by a *threat-agent*. The *threat-agents* are the parties that *give-rise-to* the *threats* to the *assets* of the system. An *asset* of a system can be a physical component of a system such as a hard disk, or it can be a logical component of a system such as a file stored on a hard disk.

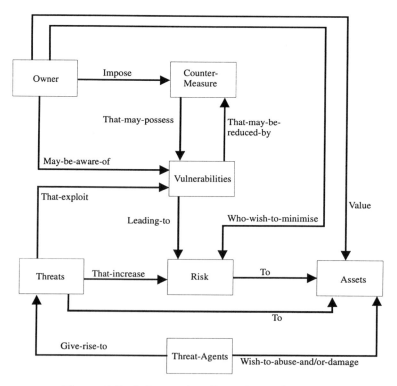

**Figure 1.2   Information Security in Context**

The objective of a counter-measure is to reduce the vulnerabilities contained in a system. However, it should be noted that no counter-measure is perfect and a counter-measure may have the effect of possessing a vulnerability of its own. A threat may wish to exploit vulnerability in order to gain access to the assets of a system. Thus, a threat has the effect of increasing the risk posed to an asset, and vulnerabilities have the effect of leading to a potential risk. The owner will wish to minimise the level of risk posed to the assets, which the owner values. In order to minimise the risk, and thus reduce the level of threat posed to the assets by a threat-agent, the owner of the assets may impose a set of security counter-measures.

## 1.2 Information Warfare (IW)

*"In the practical art of war, the best thing of all is to take the enemy's country whole and intact; to shatter and destroy it is not so good. So, too, it is better to recapture an army entire than to destroy it, to capture a regiment, a detachment or a company entire than to destroy them. Hence to fight and conquer in all your battles is not supreme excellence; supreme excellence consists in breaking the enemy's resistance without fighting." Sun Tzu*

Information warfare (IW) is not new, in fact it has been around for centuries. IW is also not unique to the human species. Within nature, many types of plants and animals rely upon some form of IW in order to ensure survival via the acquisition of key resources. In today's terminology, IW is about information dominance (see Figure 1.3)

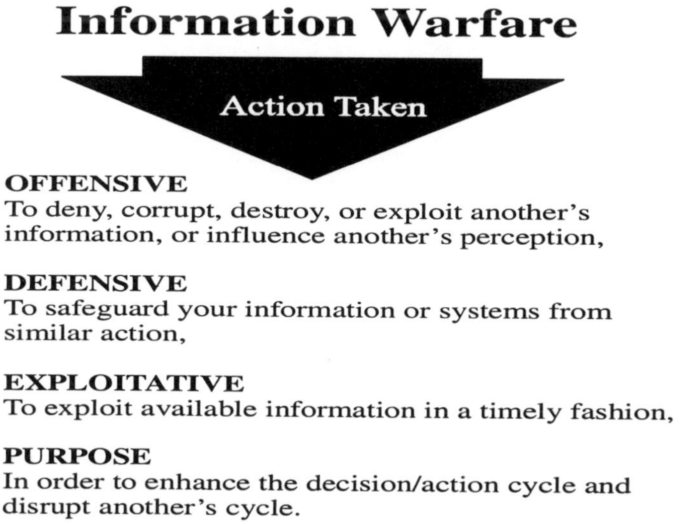

# Information Warfare

**Action Taken**

**OFFENSIVE**
To deny, corrupt, destroy, or exploit another's information, or influence another's perception,

**DEFENSIVE**
To safeguard your information or systems from similar action,

**EXPLOITATIVE**
To exploit available information in a timely fashion,

**PURPOSE**
In order to enhance the decision/action cycle and disrupt another's cycle.

**Figure 1.3  Information Warfare**

The offensive part of IW is referred to as information operations, and the defensive part of IW is referred to as information assurance[1].

Most countries today are making heavy use of information technology (IT) for the purpose of meeting commerce and government objectives. This heavy dependency on IT creates the ability for one country to cripple another without the use of deadly force. For example:

- In the Gulf War (1990-1991), the allied forces used modern IW techniques to cripple the ability of the Iraqi government to communicate with its armed forces. In addition, the United States (US) armed forces allegedly also became the victim of IW when a group of five Dutch hackers allegedly broke into US military computers. They allegedly stole information relating to the exact locations of US troops, the types of weapons they had, the capabilities of the Patriot missile, and the movement of warships in the Gulf region. According to Jim Christy, a program manager with the computer crime investigations and IW unit of the Air Force Office of Special Investigations, "They didn't, but they could have; instead of sending bullets to the Gulf, they could have sent toothbrushes".

This example illustrates the complex web of dependencies that are created when any organisation uses IT, and that if you disrupt one element in that complex web of dependencies then you can stop, or delay, an organisation achieving its objectives.

IW is defined in terms of three types of warfare, and these are:

- Type I involves the managing of the opponent's perception through deception operations and psychological operations. Within military circles this type of IW is often called Truth Projection.
- Type II involves denying, destroying, degrading or distorting the opponent's information flows in order to break down their organisation and their ability to co-ordinate operations.
- Type III gathers intelligence by exploiting the opponent's use of information systems.

In addition, IW can be decomposed down into three classes[2], and these are:

- Class 1 - Personal IW is waged against an individual's privacy.
- Class 2 - Corporate IW is waged against a business or corporation.
- Class 3 - Global IW is waged against industries, political spheres of influence, global economic forces, and entire countries.

---

[1] As with any "new" concepts such as IA, IW, IO, there is some disagreement as to their definitions and their order. For example: some believe InfoSec is a subset of IA while others believe it is just the opposite. When it comes to protecting information assets, does it really matter, except to the "information protection bureaucrats"? It is not the intention of the authors to get into a "what came first, the chicken or the egg" debate. We are presenting it one way while others may disagree. The real issue is information asset protection, however you want to view it.

[2] See Winn Schwartau's IW Web site at infowar.com and Dr. Kovacich's site at shockwavewriters.com for additional information.

The art of IW can be summed up as using an information infrastructure to break the opponent's resistance without fighting. Consequently, IW offers the ability for a smaller country to neutralise the offensive and defensive potential of a much larger country. In more detailed terms, we can define IW as follows:

*"The implementation of Information Warfare (IW) is the sequence of actions undertaken by all sides in a conflict to destroy, degrade, manipulate and exploit the information assets of their adversaries. Conversely, information warfare implementation also comprises all the actions aimed at protecting information assets against hostile attempts at destruction, degradation, manipulation and exploitation. It is very easy for any country, group, or individual to develop and deploy information warfare techniques. The term conflict is used to refer to fight or struggle between opposing forces. These forces could be national, corporate, or individual in nature."*

## 1.2.1　Perspectives on Information Warfare

Over the past few years various people have tried to define what IW means. These definitions tend to characterise it rather than define it. A definition of IW by Col. D. Hotard, Director of Information Warfare, US Office of the Assistant Secretary of Defence, Jan 1996 is:

*"Actions taken to achieve information superiority by affecting adversary information, information-based processes, information systems and computer-based networks, while defending our own information, information-based processes, information systems and computer-based networks."*

In addition, the Department of Defence in the US has also defined the military element of IW as:

*"Actions taken to achieve information superiority in support of national military strategy by affecting adversary information and information systems while leveraging and defending our information systems."*

Both of the above definitions talk about IW in terms of achieving information superiority with regard to the information-based activities of an adversary. In addition, they explicitly mention computer-based networks. It is interesting to note that the US view of IW does not directly mention psychological warfare, and does not define IW in terms of a nation-state. The view taken by the US is wider and attempts to encompass some of the commercial consideration.

The Russian view of IW is:

*"Information Warfare is a way of resolving a conflict between opposing sides. The goal is for one side to gain and hold information advantage over the other. This is achieved by exerting a specific information/psychological and information/technical influence on a nation's decision making systems, on the nation's populace and on its information resource structures, as well as by defeating the enemy's control systems and his information resource structures with the help of additional means."*

The Russian view of IW makes an explicit reference to psychological warfare and defines IW in terms of the nation-state. It defines IW with regard to a nation's decision-making systems, and the nation's population. Thus any IW attack against any part of Russia would be seen as an attack upon the Russian nation-state. The Chinese view of IW is:

*"Information Warfare is a transformation from mechanised warfare of the industrial age to a war of decision and control, a war of knowledge and a war of intellect."*

The interesting point to observe about the Chinese definition of IW is that they explicitly view IW about control and controlling the decisions and actions of an opponent. It refers to IW as a war of intellect and not a mechanised war. This is logical based on the Chinese view of warfare starting with Sun Tzu, Wei Liao and others. In addition, the Chinese definition makes no direct reference to the systems that may be targeted or the methods that may be used in order to achieve the control of an opponent.

## 1.2.2    Nature of the Threat

All a person needs to enter the world of IW is motive, means and opportunity. Motive is a function of the players concerns, commitments and beliefs. Means are determined capabilities and availability of technical, and information, based resources. Opportunity is a function of access and also includes other factors such as perception and belief. For example: an individual may believe in their cause so much that they are prepared to go to prison for it. However, most do not believe they will be caught.

Although anyone can engage in offensive IW, in general offensive players in the world of IW come in six types: insiders, hackers, criminals, corporations, governments and terrorists.[3]

- *The Insider*: insiders consist of employees and may also include former employees and contractors. If a company out-sources its IT functions, then the employees of the out-source company may also be considered as insiders. Studies have shown that this group is the biggest threat that any organisation faces. They act as information brokers selling information that belongs to the organisation to foreign governments, competitors, and organised crime. In addition, insiders can also intentionally, or unintentionally, damage or destroy information and equipment. For example: Volkswagen lost almost $260 million as the result of an insider scam that created phony currency-exchange transactions and then covered them with real transactions a few days later, pocketing the float as the exchange rate was changing. Four insiders and one outsider were subsequently convicted with the maximum jail sentence being six years.

---

[3] Although hackers, terrorists and other criminals can also be insiders, for our purposes we have distinguished between insiders and the others since they generally operate outside the business, or government agency.

- **The Hacker**: a hacker was once thought of as a "computer enthusiast". However, thanks to the news media, the hacker has become one who gains unauthorised access to or breaks into computer-based information systems. Often for this group of individuals the motives include thrills, challenges and power. There are however a growing number of hackers who are breaking into systems for financial reward.

- **The Criminal**: criminals target information that is of value to them, such as bank accounts, credit cards or intellectual property that can be converted into money. For example: the Pennsylvania State lottery was presented with a winning lottery ticket worth $15.2 million that had been printed after the drawing by someone who had browsed through the online file of still-valid unclaimed winning combinations. The scam was detected because the ticket had been printed on card stock that was different from that of the legitimate ticket. The main motivation in this case was money. Criminals will often make use of insiders to help them. They may be in collusion with the insiders or use such tactics as threats, blackmail and the like.

- **The Corporation**: corporations engage in offensive IW when they actively seek intelligence about their competitors or steal their sensitive information, e.g. trade secrets. Money, market position and competitive stance are examples of some of the corporate motivations for using IW tactics. In addition, corporations have always engaged in a form of IW even before the term was first used. This type of IW is called advertising and marketing.

- **Governments and Government Agencies**: most governments now recognise the need to protect the information assets that their country has created. These assets have a financial value for business and can have a value in terms of national security. Intelligence agencies seek the military, diplomatic, and economic secrets of foreign governments, foreign corporations, and foreign adversaries. They always have; however, they can now do it remotely and with less risk due to information systems vulnerabilities. In addition, intelligence and law enforcement agencies seek to protect the information assets of the nation by targeting the activities of criminals and foreign intelligence operatives. In times of war, a government may target the national infrastructure of another country in order to help it achieve its objectives. For example: in the Gulf War, the allied forces targeted and partially destroyed the national infrastructure (physical and information) of Iraq. In fact, in probably every war fought in the last hundred years, examples can be found of targeting the adversaries infrastructures.

- **Terrorists**: terrorists are of particular interest because of the damage that they can cause against the information infrastructure such as emergency services, utilities such as water and electricity, and financial services. Terrorists are politically motivated and have their own political agenda that they use to select targets. However, terrorists have been slow to use offensive IW tactics. Why? No one really knows for sure, but most agree that it is just a matter of time. For example: alleged terrorist, Usama bin Laden, has access to massive telecommunications systems, money, and other resources; however, it appears that most terrorists are still concerned with destroying people than destroying nation-state economies. Destroyed buildings and "blood in the streets" still seem to have more of a major propaganda value on the six o'clock news than showing a burned out computer.

# 1.3    Information Operations

Information operations (IO) are about manipulating the Global Information Environment (GIE) to achieve an advantage over one's competitors. It can include legal activities such as marketing and advertising, and illegal activities such as espionage and hacking. Information operations are performed in the context of a strategy that has a desired objective (or end state) that may be achieved by influencing a target (the object of influence). The following is a definition of information operations and is derived from the US Army military definition:

*"Continuous operations within the Global Information Environment (GIE) that enable, enhance and protect friendly organisations' ability to collect, process and act on information to achieve a competitive advantage across the full range of organisational operations; information operations include interacting with the Global Information Environment (GIE) and exploiting or denying an adversary's information and decision capabilities."*

The term "organisation" is used to refer to commercial, government and/or military organisations. The definition is intended to include the wide range of activities of both commercial and military perspective. As more organisations (both commercial and military) integrate their supply chains, so more organisations want to share information across supply chains. One of the consequences of this is that information security is much harder to achieve and maintain. The definition recognises that Information Operations function at three distinct levels, and these are: (1) physical space, (2) cyber-space and (3) the minds of humans (perception level).

## 1.3.1    The Physical Level

The lowest level is the physical level. This level includes computers, physical networks, telecommunications and supporting systems such as power, facilities and environmental controls. Also at this level are the people who manage the systems. Many organisations have a single system administrator who understands how the system functions. If this person is removed from the organisation, then the organisation will lose its ability to manage information systems and to recover from any potential disaster. The characteristics of the physical level are summarised in Table 1.2.

For example: a programmer, Michael John Lauffenberger, was convicted of logic bombing General Dynamics' Atlas Rocket Database. He had quit his job and hoped to be rehired at a premium when the logic bomb went off. However, another programmer discovered it.

This example illustrates the critical dependencies that can exist between the people who create and manage the system and the services offered by the system.

#### Table 1.2  Characteristics of the Physical Level

| Characteristics and Components | Attacker's Operations | Defender's Operations | Desired Effects |
|---|---|---|---|
| Data and data processing activities that are managed and performed in the physical space, including:<br><br>Data gathering equipment<br><br>Computers and data processing equipment<br><br>Storage<br><br>Networks<br><br>Electrical Power | Physical attack and destruction, including:<br><br>Electromagnetic (EMP) attack.<br><br>Visual Spying<br><br>Intrusion<br><br>Physical scavenging and physical removal<br><br>Wiretapping, including:<br><br>Covert Channel Analysis<br><br>Interference<br><br>Eavesdropping | Physical security (OPSEC), including:<br><br>TEMPEST | Technical<br><br>To affect the technical performance and capacity of the physical systems, so as to disrupt the capabilities of the defender to function at the physical level |

## 1.3.2   The Information Structure Level

The next layer is the information infrastructure layer, which includes the abstract information that accepts, processes, manages, and stores the information. This layer is most commonly considered to be the cyber-space level, at which malicious software and infrastructure exploitation (hacking) occurs. The effect of disrupting this level is to disrupt the functional behaviour of the system. The function of this level is to deliver meaningful information to humans so that they can make informed decisions, and control the objects in the physical level. Attacks at this level can have effects at both the perception and physical level. For example:

- In 1992 The "GP1" virus was found throughout many Italian judicial computer systems. Its effect was to award maximum security clearance to uncleared users.[4]
- In 1994 Vladimir Levin broke into the computers at Citibank and stole $10 million. Using a mis-configured modem, he was able to gain access to the electronic fund transfer system and he simply transferred money from a series of bank accounts to his own. This attack is limited to the information structure level as only information in the digital sense was manipulated.

---

[4] Although the cases sometimes cited are somewhat dated, they make the point and also indicate that many such incidents have been taking place for quite some time.

- In 1998, two crackers broke into a bank computer network and allegedly stole 260,000 yuan (US$31,400). The two crackers were Hao Jing-long, formerly an accountant at the Zhenjiang branch of the Industrial and Commercial Bank of China and his brother, Hao Jing-wen. The two opened 16 accounts under various names in a branch of the bank in September 1998, and later broke into the branch to install a controlling device in a bank computer terminal. They used the device to electronically wire 720,000 yuan in non-existent deposits into the bank accounts. Afterward, they successfully withdrew 260,000 yuan from eight different branches of the bank. All the money has since been recovered. The two crackers were captured by the Chinese police in 1998 and were found guilty and sentenced to death. This example illustrates how attacks at two levels can be combined. The two crackers attacked both the physical level and the information structure level.

The characteristics of the information structure level are summarised in Table 1.3.

**Table 1.3   Characteristics of the Information Structure Level**

| Characteristics and Components | Attacker's Operations | Defender's Operations | Desired Effects |
|---|---|---|---|
| Information and data manipulation ability maintained in cyber-space, including:<br><br>Data structures<br><br>Process and Programs<br><br>Protocols<br><br>Data content and databases | Cyber-based attack including:<br><br>Impersonation<br><br>Piggybacking<br><br>Spoofing<br><br>Network Weaving<br><br>Network Sniffing<br><br>Trojan Horse<br><br>Logic Bomb<br><br>Malevolent Worms<br><br>Virus Attacks<br><br>Trapdoors<br><br>Authorisation<br><br>Basic Active Misuse<br><br>Incremental Attacks<br><br>Denial of Service | Information security technical measures such as:<br><br>Encryption and key management<br><br>Intrusion detection systems and computer misuse detection systems<br><br>Anti virus software<br><br>Systems Auditing<br><br>Use of redundancy<br><br>Security assessment tools<br><br>The use of security Standards, such as:<br><br>ITSEC<br><br>BS7799 | Functional<br><br>Influence the effectiveness and performance of information functions supporting perception, decision making, and control of physical processes |

### 1.3.3  Perceptual Level

The next layer is the perception layer. This layer is abstract in nature and is concerned with the management of perceptions of a target. In particular, this layer is about influencing the perceptions of the people who are making the decisions. The goal is to get your opponent to make the decisions and to implement the actions that you want. This is achieved by controlling the information that your opponent accesses and knowing how the opponent will react after receiving that information – in a way favourable to you. The abstract components of this layer include objectives, plans, perceptions, beliefs and decisions. The golden rule at the perception layer is that information is power, and whoever controls the flow of information within a given environment will control the behaviour of various parties in that environment. For example:

- In 1991, a convicted forger serving a 33-year term was released from a Tucson, Arizona jail after a forged fax had been received ordering his release. A legitimate fax had been altered to bear his name.
- In 1992, during the Gulf War it was reported in the press that the US Government had released a virus into the Iraqi computer systems via a chip in dot-matrix printers that the Iraqi's had purchased. The virus was said to have been developed by the NSA and installed by the CIA. It was designed to disable Windows and mainframe computers. This was a hoax and designed to misinform the Iraqi government, an example of the psychological warfare aspects of IW, or possibly an urban legend (a tale or rumour that is spread through the Internet).
- Motivated mainly by greed, in September 1997, Theodore R. Melcher Jr., 51 was sentenced to a year in federal prison for conspiring to defraud investors in the System of Excellence Inc., a small Virginia computer company.

The characteristics of the perception level are summarised in Table 1.4.

## 1.4  Summary

This chapter introduced the concepts of Information Assurance, Information Security, and Information Warfare. These concepts are all inter-related and play major roles in the protection and defence of information systems and the information that the systems process, store and transmit. The definitions of these terms may vary somewhat; as well as which concept is a subset of the other. This "what came first, the chicken or the egg" issue is not important. What is important is that protection professionals focus on the threats, vulnerabilities and risks associated with the protection and defence of information and information systems, then develop a holistic program to protect and defend these valuable assets.

**Table 1.4   Characteristics of the Information Structure Level**

| Characteristics and Components | Attacker's Operations | Defender's Operations | Desired Effects |
|---|---|---|---|
| Knowledge and understanding in human decision space:<br><br>Perception<br><br>Beliefs<br><br>Reasoning | Psychological Operations, such as:<br><br>Deception<br><br>Blackmail<br><br>Bribery and corruption<br><br>Social engineering<br><br>Trademark and copyright infringement<br><br>Distortion and fabrication<br><br>Defamation<br><br>Diplomacy<br><br>Civil and public affairs<br><br>Creating distrust | Personnel Security, including:<br><br>Psychological Security<br><br>Profiling<br><br>Training and education of staff<br><br>Fake detection, including:<br><br>Biometrics<br><br>Watermarks<br><br>Public/Private Key<br><br>Passwords | Cognitive<br><br>Influence decisions and behaviour |

# Chapter 2

## The World of Information

We live in an information-dependent and information-driven world. A world where information and information systems are being used to drive the rapid changes in the global marketplace and which is having a major affect on the economic and political aspects of every modern nation. This chapter will discuss this phenomenon as it relates to information assurance.

## 2.1 What is Information?

For our purposes we will adopt the following definition:

*"Information is data endowed with relevance and purpose. Converting data into information thus requires knowledge. Knowledge by definition is specialised."*

## 2.2 Properties of Information

If an organisation is to be successful then there is a need for the data to be relevant and the processing to be meaningful in order for the information to be of value. The value of information itself cannot be guaranteed, but there are certain characteristics of information that must be present if the information is to be useful. Information should be *accurate, timely, complete, verifiable* and *consistent*.

- *Accurate*: naturally if decision makers go to the trouble of identifying some information that will help reduce the uncertainty in the decision environment, they will need to be confident of the accuracy of that information. Misinformation can be used to direct an opponent to make the decision that you want. For example: during World War II, British intelligence fed the Germans with incorrect information about the effectiveness of their flying bombs. The net result was that they fell short, thus saving London.

- *Timely*: for information to be effective it must be timely. For example: a former cost estimator for Southern Colour Lithographers in Athens, Georgia, was convicted of destroying billing and accounting data on a Xenix system, based on an audit trail linking the deleted commands to his terminal. The employer claimed damages of $400,000 in lost business and downtime, as key business information assets were not available. Another example: in 1987, a woman from Vancouver, British Columbia, visiting Honolulu, Hawaii, attempted to withdraw $1100 (Canadian) from her home bank using an ATM, which was controlled by a computer in the state of New Jersey, US. The satellite delays combined with a flaw in the supposedly atomic transaction protocol resulted in her account being debited without her getting the money. On seeing her monthly statement, she accused her fiancé of theft, and had him apprehended. It took a month to sort it all out.
- *Complete*: for information to be effective it must be as complete as possible. For example: on 5 July 1988, the USS *Vincennes*, a US ship of war, shot down an Iranian passenger airliner killing every person onboard. An inquiry concluded the decision to fire at the passenger airliner was in part based upon information that did not paint a complete picture of the situation.
- *Verifiable*: increasingly, managers are being asked to justify the decision that they have made. For example: Jean Paul Barrett, a convicted forger serving a 33-year term, was released from a Tucson, Arizona, jail on 13 December 1991, after a forged fax had been received ordering his release. A legitimate fax had been altered to bear his name.
- *Consistent*: for information to be effective it must be consistent. For example: in November 1998, a man in North Carolina, attempted to open a checking account at a BB&T branch by presenting relevant information, including birth date and social security number. One of the bank's tellers examined the paperwork, and she called the police after she realised that the information described her husband, who had died three weeks earlier. Police charged the suspect with two charges of obtaining property under false pretences.

## 2.3    The Information and Competitive Advantage

*"Information is power and they who control information and its flow control the world."*

Information is a national and corporate resource and has a real financial cost associated with it. It is through the correct application of information that value is added and wealth created (see Figure 2.1). Consequently any restrictions on the flow of information between departments will adversely affect the organisation. In essence there are four strategies that an organisation can adopt to achieve a competitive advantage. The term value-added can be used to mean:

- Reducing costs through the optimisation of the business process.
- Creating new business opportunities.

- Improving the competitive position of the organisation.
- Modifying the structure of the industry.

What are the strategies that an organisation could utilise in order to achieve success and what are the security implications? They are:

- Proprietary advantage.
- One step ahead.
- Discontinuity.
- Implementation.

## 2.3.1   Proprietary Advantage

Within the proprietary advantage strategy an organisation develops a distinctive technology, one that sets it apart from the rest of the industry. It then protects this lead, which is based of course on such things as barriers, e.g. patents, extraordinary investment, long lead times or rare skill base. The key factor to the success of this strategy is intellectual property. Many organisations invest large sums of money into research and development, which in turn creates new products and thus commercial success for the organisation. Because of the important role that research and development plays within this strategy, organisations will go to extreme lengths both to protect it, and to acquire it from a competitor.

## 2.3.2   One Step Ahead

The one step ahead strategy demands that an organisation continually releases new and improved technology. This ongoing innovation keeps it just ahead of the competition, despite the ability of rivals to duplicate particular aspects of the technology. Within this strategy an organisation needs to protect the new features that it will embed within its technology. If a competitor could release a piece of technology first that possesses these new features then that company could increase its market share at the expense of the developing company, and the development costs could be lost. For example: in the pharmaceutical industry all new developments have a lifetime of six months. That means that six months after their release a competitor will have created a similar drug. Thus, the majority of the research and development costs have to be recovered within six months of the release of a new product.

## 2.3.3   Discontinuity

Within the discontinuity strategy an organisation applies technology to produce a quick, decisive shift in the market it serves. For example: Citibank was the first bank in the US to install ATMs. Its widespread installation of ATMs reportedly almost tripled its market share.

### 2.3.4   Implementation

Within the implementation strategy an organisation applies commonly available technology uncommonly well. This strategy can offer a double pay-off, both delivering a competitive advantage in itself and improving the performance of other strategies. For example: the SWIFT network is an e-mail system owned by over 1000 banks, which use it to send payment instructions and other messages from one bank's computer to another through a network of encrypted leased lines. The technology that the banks are using is standard commercial encryption and networking systems. They have applied the technology uncommonly well to create a single robust and secure system that now supports most of the world's banks and commerce. The creation and deployment of this system has allowed banks to maintain a competitive advantage over their rivals in the commercial finance sector.

## 2.4   The Birth of the Internet and of Cyber-Crime

In 1965, the US Advanced Research Project Agency (ARPA) sponsored a study on networking technologies, and from this initial study the Internet was born. By January 1996, 20,000 .com domains had been registered and there was an estimated 9.5 million hosts connected to the Internet. In January 2000, 29.1 million .com domains had been registered and there was an estimated 72.4 million hosts connected to the Internet. The World Wide Web (WWW) was created by Tim Berners-Lee in 1991 and now accounts for most of the traffic on the Internet. In November 1996, Version 3.0 of the Secure Socket Layer (SSL) was released. SSL provides WWW clients and browsers with encryption and thus the ability to have a secure conversation via the Internet.

It seems that fraud has been perpetrated against every commerce system ever invented, from gold coins to stock certificates to paper cheques to credit cards. Information systems are no different; if that's where the money is, that's where the crime will be. The growth of the Internet has also allowed criminals to communicate and more effectively share information.

Commercial organisations have not been slow to embrace the ability of the Internet to communicate with users and engage users in business transactions. In 1990, the World-Comes-On-Line (world.std.com) became the first commercial provider of Internet dial-up access. In 1992, the World Bank (www.worldbank.org) was among the first banks to go online, and shopping malls appeared on the Internet in 1994. In 1994, a pizza company called Hut-Online allowed you to order a pizza on the Internet, First Virtual opened for business and became the first Cyber-Bank. On 22 February 1999, the First Internet Bank of Indiana, US, (firstib.com) became the first full-service bank available only on the Internet.

In 1995, the first official Internet wiretap was successful in helping the US Secret Service and Drug Enforcement Agency (DEA) apprehend three individuals who were illegally manufacturing and selling cellular telephone cloning equipment and electronic devices. In what may be the first instance of government-supported information warfare, an Irish Internet Service Provider recently accused Indonesia of attacking its computer servers. The Indonesian government denied the allegations. Connect-Ireland hosts the *.tp* country code domain for the disputed territory of East Timor, which has been under Indonesian occupation for almost 25 years. On 28 January 1998, the domain of East Timor (*.tp*) was removed from the internet when hackers broke into the Dublin, Ireland based Internet Service Provider (ISP) that was hosting the domain. The attacks against the ISP came from computer servers in Canada, the United States, Australia and Japan, and thus it was impossible to identify the individual(s) who perpetrated the attack. *"I believe the attack was sponsored by the Indonesian government,"* said Martin Maguire, Connect-Ireland's founder and managing director. *"I have lodged a complaint with the Indonesian Embassy in London."*

A study conducted by Deloitte & Touche on behalf of the European Commission estimates that international fraud has cost the European Union anywhere from 6-60 billion European currency units, with much of that fraud perpetrated over the Internet. "At its simplest, the Internet allows a fraudster to set up a site on the World Wide Web which claims to be the site of a reputable company or organisation. Victims are then induced to part with funds via credit-card payments, or induced to reveal valuable information. At least one major international bank is known to have suffered from this although details of losses are not available," says the study. And while encryption can help ameliorate some of the problems, it is a "double-edged sword" says the study, because it can also shield the nefarious doings of crooks on the Net. The study calls for international co-operation among governments in apprehending electronic fraudsters, and says the issue poses "huge" challenges to law enforcement and civil agencies: "The traditional sources of forensic and other evidence will become rarer, and a range of new types of evidence will need to be acceptable to the courts." (BNA Daily Report for Executives, 5 May 1997)

The Internet and sites on the Internet which engage in electronic commerce are now targeted for extortion.

- On Monday, 10 January 2000, the US newspaper, the *New York Times*, reported an extortion attempt involving credit card numbers stolen from online merchant CD Universe. Someone who called himself "Maxim" and claimed to be Russian said that he had copied 300,000 credit card numbers from their system, and that he would post them on the Internet unless he was paid $100,000. The article quoted the chairman of eUniverse, the company that operates the site, as confirming that Maxim did indeed have their data. eUniverse declined to pay the $100,000; Maxim posted 25,000 card numbers to a Web site. Several thousand people downloaded the file before it was removed.

- According to an article by Jon Ungoed-Thomas and Stan Arnaud in *The Sunday Times of London* for 16 January 2000, British hackers have compromised the source code for the Visa card system and have sought ransom for it. Excerpts from the story which were found online under the headline, "Hacker gang blackmails firms with stolen files'", follow: Visa confirmed last week that it had received a ransom demand last month, believed to have been for £10 million. "We were hacked into in mid-July last year" [despite layers of firewalls], said Russ Yarrow, a company spokesman. It is understood the hackers stole critical source code, and threatened to crash the entire system. Visa's system handles nearly £1 trillion of business a year from customers holding 800 million Visa cards.

A United Kingdom (UK) Government Audit Commission report published in February 1998, found that 45% of organisations in the UK now suffer from some type of computer fraud, and that one-quarter of all frauds were committed by staff in managerial positions. The report also stated that the loss of intellectual property relating to software cost the global software industry $11.2 billion.

## 2.5    The Power of Information

*"It is a matter of life and death, a road either to safety or to ruin. Hence it is a subject of inquiry, which can on no account be neglected." Sun Tzu*

In relation to the global nature of information the meaning of the above is clear, in business and war, information on an opponent's capabilities and tactics is the key to success.

Intellectual property rights deal with copyrights, patents, trademarks and designs. Basically intellectual property rights are the rights designed to provide remedies against those who steal the fruits of another person's ideas or works. An example of an intellectual property right is the right to execute a computer program. The effect of information in general is to create knowledge by allowing one to add value to a resource. That resource may be physical (such as a new cure for an illness), or it may be logical (such as a piece of information). The effect of adding value to a resource is to create wealth for the individuals and organisation that own it, and/or the users who consume it (see Figure 2.1).

For example: the growth of Silicon Valley in California, USA is largely based upon the concentration of expertise in the area of information technology. This expertise has created wealth for the companies that have located themselves in Silicon Valley, and used the skilled workforce to create intellectual property and consequently add value. The net effect is that if California were considered as a country, it would have the sixth largest Gross Domestic Product (GDP) of any country in the world.

The growth of the Internet currently allows organisations around the globe to communicate with each other in ways that have previously been unheard of. This ability to share information has transformed the marketplace and has become one of the major factors governing business success and competitive advantage. This ability to share information and the market pressures of a competitive world economy has driven many organisations to integrate their supply chain. This integration has allowed many organisations to react faster to the changing demands of the world marketplace, and to create strategic relationships with its customers.

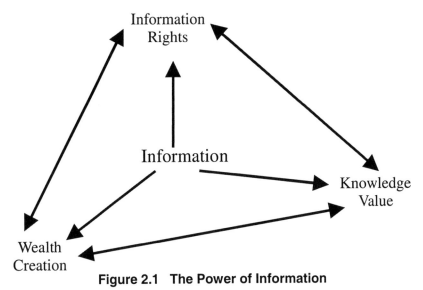

**Figure 2.1   The Power of Information**

The ability to integrate a supply chain using technologies such as the Internet has created commercial organisations that span the globe. The effect of these global organisations is that they can directly affect the state of a nation's economy. In addition, as governments have sought to achieve cost savings, they have made use of outsourcing certain functions such as information technology management. This has increased the dependency between commercial organisations and their associated government. Today, this dependency has reached such a state that in terms of IW, major global corporations face increased risks. If a large multinational organisation's information systems were destroyed, subsequently the loss of critical business information could have disastrous consequences for a government in financial and economic terms, global power, and public relations, just to mention a few.

Industrial espionage is when a competitor uses illegal means to obtain proprietary information. Typically this type of activity will have a detrimental effect on the victim, and could ultimately lead to bankruptcy. If enough of this activity was targeted against a nation-state, it could have a substantial effect on a nation's economy. For example:

- In November 1999, the online bookseller Alibris, admitted to snooping on emails intended for Amazon.com, after Amazon accused it of deliberately collecting intelligence on the market. Although Alibris pleaded guilty to the charges, CEO Marty Manley claimed the emails were not used for commercial profit or to breach confidential information.
- On 11 April 1999, the *Sunday Telegraph* reported that "Security experts in Germany have uncovered evidence of an American industrial espionage operation in Europe. German business is thought to suffer annual losses of at least £7 billion through stolen inventions and development projects."

- In 1999, two criminals in Sweden broke into a communication company's systems and downloaded their five-year plan for its cellular systems. They asked for $2 million to destroy the information. Fortunately, the company being extorted also owned a local ISP, and the hackers came in through that ISP – that provided much easier access to computer logs and telephone identification. The hackers turned out to be 17 and 15 years old.
- In June 1997, two private investigators were each jailed for industrial espionage. The two men were charged with stealing secrets from a Cypriot based pharmaceutical company. The two men were arrested while trying to board a plane to London after concealing documents from a customs' clearing office.
- In 1994, an EU report on electronic spying stated that US intelligence agencies that intercepted phone calls between Brazilian officials and the French firm Thomson-CSF used the information to swing a $1.3 billion radar contract to the US corporation Raytheon.

As we move into an information economy, so the ability to protect information from leakage to third parties and unwanted exploitation will undoubtedly increase. Increasingly, more companies are becoming the victims of industrial espionage; as well as Netspionage and economic espionage; and thus, more and more governments are introducing industrial/economic espionage laws.[1]

## 2.6 The Consumer-Provider Model of Information Usage

Figure 2.2 depicts the cyclic process that exists when parties act as information providers and information consumers. An information consumer can also act as a consumer for many information providers, and an information provider can also act as a provider to many information consumers. Within this model information security is concerned:

- *From the perspective of the provider*: that the information is flowing to the intended party and that the confidentiality, integrity and availability of the information have not been compromised.
- *From the perspective of the consumer*: that the confidentiality, integrity and availability of the information has not been compromised, and that the source of the information can be validated and is known to be reliable.

In terms of information warfare, its objective is to achieve information dominance over a rival. One method of achieving this is to control the information

---

[1] According to the US Federal Bureau of Investigation, industrial espionage is when one company spies on another; and economic espionage is when a nation spies on a company or assists a company on spying on another company, normally a foreign firm. Netspionage, according to Dr. Kovacich and William C. Boni, in their popular book, *Netspionage: The Global Threat to Information,* is defined as network-enabled espionage, e.g. using the Internet for espionage purposes.

providers that the rival has access to. Misinformation, through the pollution of information from an information provider can be used to control and direct the actions of an opponent.

- Misinformation can be used directly to corrupt the information base that an opponent is using to make decisions by calling into question a piece of valid information.
- Misinformation can be used to give a false impression of ones intentions.

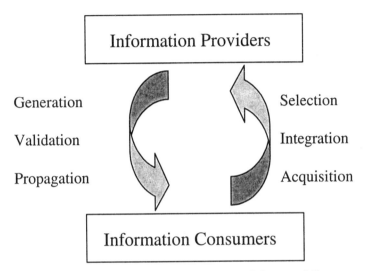

**Figure 2.2   A Model of Information Provision and Consumption**

Within a military context, this can be achieved by eliminating sources of information such as radar and radio installations. Within a commercial context this can be achieved by introducing misinformation into the information provider. In the Gulf War (1991), the Iraqi government was known to be using CNN as an information provider. Thus the US forces staged several amphibious exercises along the Saudi coast in front of CNN crews in order to trick Saddam into believing that the coalition planned an amphibious assault to flank Iraqi forces along the Kuwaiti border. The deception paid off as several Iraqi divisions were tied down defending the coast.

Within the commercial context the Internet is being increasingly used as an information provider. On 15 December 1999, a US federal prosecutor charged two men with posting false messages about a company on Internet bulletin boards in an effort to bolster the company stock prices. The pair was accused of posting false stories over a two-day period in November about NEI Web-World; a Dallas based printing services company. The published bogus postings pushed the NEI stock up from 13 cents to more than $15 per share.

## 2.6.1    Generation, Validation and Propagation

An information provider has to create or synthesise the information that an information consumer requires. This is achieved by observing the domain of interest of the information consumer. For example: in the Gulf War in 1990, CNN acted as an information provider for most of the world. In particular CNN acted as one information provider for the Iraqi government. This allowed the allied forces to feed misinformation to the Iraqi government.

In any organisation, if a person uses only one source of information in its decision making process, then it is at risk of acting on misinformation. Once an information provider has obtained a piece of information, then it should attempt to validate that information. This validation process can take one of two forms. It can either be validated through other information providers, or through observation and information that is already known to the information provider. Once the information has been validated, it can be propagated to the information consumers that require it.

## 2.6.2    Acquisition, Integration and Selection

In order for an information consumer to acquire information it has to know:

* what type of information is required; and
* where that information can be obtained.

Once that information has been obtained, then it has to be integrated with the rest of the information that the information consumer possesses. This process of integration also involves an element of validation. An information consumer may draw upon many information providers in an effort to identify the truth. Once the information has been integrated, then the information consumer can select and apply the information required. Once the information consumer has done this, then the information provider may, or may not, observe the affect that the information consumer is having on the world. This observation then feeds into the generation, validation and propagation process executed by the information provider.

# 2.7    The Intelligence Model of Information Usage

Intelligence, the information and knowledge about an adversary obtained through observation, investigation, or understanding, is the product that provides awareness. There are three major categories of intelligence products: strategic, tactical and operational. The objective of strategic intelligence is to understand the current and future status and behaviour of a domain of interest. A domain of interest is a term that is used to describe the subject of inquiry. It can include the current status of a nation state or the future state of a business competitor or marketplace. In military terms, tactical intelligence is used to refer to the real-time situation awareness of military units and the active behaviour of the battle-space. In business terms, tactical intelligence is used to refer to the indicators and warnings associated with the status of a business competitor or marketplace. In military terms, operational intelligence is used to refer to the indicators and warnings associated with the order of battle and possible future developments. In business terms, operational intelligence is used to refer to the real-time situation awareness of a business competitor or market.

The process that delivers strategic, tactical and operational intelligence is generally depicted in a cyclic form with six distinct phases (see Figure 2.3).

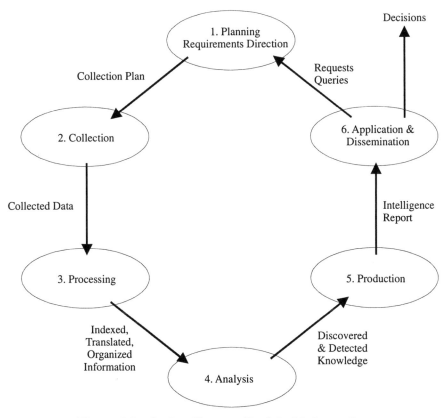

**Figure 2.3   An Intelligence Model of Information**

- *Planning, requirements and direction*: this stage involves determining the decision makers' requirements. The decision makers define the information that is required to make a) policy and b) decisions at the strategic, tactical and operation levels. The requirements are then analysed in order to identify the specific information elements that are required in order to create the correct understanding of the problem and thus make the correct decision. Once these information elements have been identified then specific collection methods can be identified and a collection plan constructed.

- **Collection**: following the collection plan, human and technical sources of data are used to collect information. The following shows the major intelligence categories and collection means.

### Table 2.1  Sources of Intelligence

| Source Type | Representative Sources |
| --- | --- |
| OSINT: Open Source Intelligence | Radio and television news sources. |
| | Printed material: books, magazines, periodicals, journals, sales literature. |
| | Internet news and discussion groups. |
| HUMINT: Human Intelligence | Messages from friendly third-party sources. |
| | Reports from agents located within the adversary. |
| | Reports from defectors from the adversary. |
| SIGINT: Signal Intelligence | Electromagnetic signals monitoring, such as EM radiation given off by VDU screen. |
| | Communications traffic monitoring for internal and external traffic, such as telephone tapping and electronic surveillance. |
| NETINT: Network Intelligence | Network analysis and monitoring. |
| | Network message interception and traffic analysis. |
| | Computer intrusion, penetration and exploitation. |
| IMINT: Imagery Intelligence | Surveillance imagery. |

- **Processing**: in general, the processing is the conversion of collected information into a form suitable for analysis. The collected data is indexed and organised in an information base, and progress on meeting the requirements of the collection plan is monitored.
- **Analysis**: the organised information is processed using deductive inference techniques that fuse all the sources of data in an attempt to answer the requester's questions. At this stage, attempts are made to remove and reduce errors and omissions in the analysed information.
- **Production**: the analysed data is taken and an intelligence report is produced. This report directly attempts to answer the questions raised by the consumers of the intelligence. In essence, there are three types of intelligence reports:
  - Current intelligence reports that are like news reports that describe recent events, indicators and warnings.
  - Basic intelligence reports that attempt to provide a complete description of a particular situation or question.
  - Intelligence estimates that attempt to predict feasible future outcomes as a result of current situations, constraints and possible influences.

- *Application and Dissemination*: the intelligence report is disseminated to the user, providing answers to specific questions. The goal of the application and dissemination of the intelligence report is to allow the user to achieve some form of dominance and/or competitive advantage over a competitor/adversary. In term of information warfare, the role of intelligence is to aid the achievement of information dominance.

## 2.8 Summary

Information, to be useful, must be accurate, timely, complete, verifiable, and consistent. One that has useful information *and* knows how to use it can gain an advantage over its competitors – whether they are nation-states or businesses. The Internet is a useful tool to gain an advantage but it is also the tool of fraudsters and other criminals who prey on businesses and government agencies. In this information age, information is power. To be successful, one must know how to get the information needed. There are information providers who make a business of fulfilling that need for information. Some resort to economic, industrial and/or Netspionage to obtain information.

# Chapter 3

# The Theory of Risks

Information assurance is more of a goal than a reality today. IA is all about mitigating risks to information and information systems. This chapter will define and discuss the theory of risk, risk assessment, risk management, threats, and vulnerabilities and integrating risk concepts into an IA program.

## 3.1 Threats, Vulnerabilities, and Risks

The concept of risk management is often neglected and often turned into a manual or automated nightmare. Thus, this basic concept, which is an integral part of IA, InfoSec, IO, and defensive IW programs, is often ignored.

The fundamentals of identifying the current threats, the processes' and information systems' vulnerabilities, and their associated risks must be conducted if one is to have a cost-effective information protection and defence program.

## 3.2 Threats and Threat Agents

Within the context of information assurance a threat to a system can be defined as:

*"A circumstance or event that has the potential to cause harm by violating security"*,

and a threat agent can be defined as:

*"Those parties that would knowingly seek to make a threat manifest"*.

In today's networked environment, organisations are connecting their information infrastructures together in a bid to achieve a competitive advantage over their rivals. Figure 3.1 illustrates the extent of the interdependence that now exists. With the drive for more organisations to engage in electronic commerce so the interdependence between systems is further increased. For example: on 28 January 1998, the root level domain name servers for the East Timor (*.tp*), were attacked and the entries for East Timor where deleted. The result was that sites with a *.tp* suffix were removed from the domain-name lookup system used by the Internet. The overall result of this was that you could not connect to sites located in the *.tp* domain by using their domain name. In effect, East Timor had been removed from the Internet. Thus one could not engage in electronic commerce with sites with a *.tp* suffix.

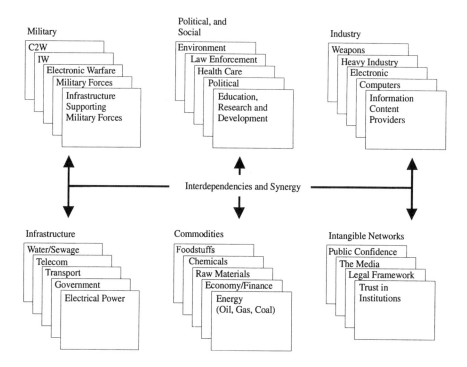

**Figure 3.1   The Infrastructure**

In general, information will flow via some medium from an information source to an information destination.   The medium through which information flows can be physical such as transcribed on a piece of paper, or it can be logical such as 1's and 0's used to encode information into a digital form.

In essence there are four types of events that can manifest themselves with regard to the flow/processing of information, and these are depicted in Figure 3.2.

- *Interruption*: this term refers to an asset of a system that is destroyed or becomes unavailable. This type of threat is a direct attack upon the availability of a system.
- *Interception*: this is when an unauthorised party gains access to an asset. This type of threat is a direct attack upon the confidentiality of a system.
- *Modification*: this type of threat is when an unauthorised party not only gains access to, but also modifies the asset. This type of threat is a direct attack upon the integrity of a system.

- *Fabrication*: this is when an unauthorised party inserts a counterfeit asset into the system. This type of threat is a direct attack upon the authenticity of a system.

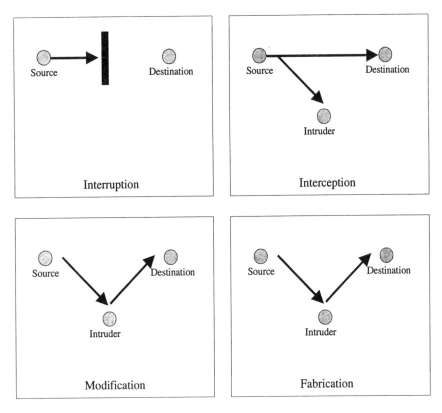

**Figure 3.2  Types of Events**

Threat agents can take many forms, but in general we can classify threats into three broad categories: natural, unintentional and intentional (see Figure 3.3).

## 3.2.1  The Natural Threat Agents

The natural threat agents include things such as fire, floods, power failures, rock movements (such as mudslides). The *other* is a catch-all term used to refer to all of the natural threat agents not covered in the list, such as ambient interference and small animals. For example: on 29 May 1989, a squirrel shorted out the power for US-based SRI International. The power remained off for nine hours, and many computers remained down after that time. Some of the computers had had their monitors burned out by the power surge created when the squirrel stepped in a high voltage isolation point. Needless to say, the squirrel also was the victim of a power surge!

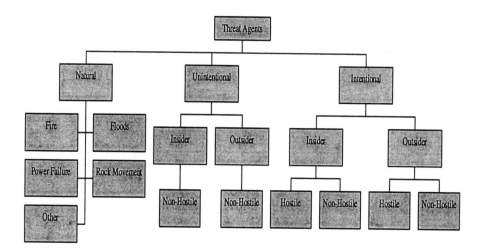

**Figure 3.3  Types of Threat Agents**

Fire and floods can pose a serious threat to information assurance. The following are examples of these natural threat agents:

- On 8 May 1988, a fire and the ensuing water damage in the US town of Hinsdale, Illinois, seriously affected computers and communications throughout the area. Some 300 ATM machines where rendered inoperative. In addition, 35,000 telephone subscribers were out of operation and a new telephone switch had to be brought in to replace the old one.
- In May 1988, the US-based Dreyers Ice Cream plant fire destroyed all of the secret formulae for ice-cream flavours. The flavour team had not completed the computer back-ups and many flavours were lost in the fire. The result of the fire was a loss of competitive advantage for Dreyers Ice Cream.

## 3.2.2   The Unintentional Threat Agents

The unintentional threat agents are parties that without direct intent cause damage or loss of service. For example: in 1990, the AT&T network slowdown was caused by a flaw in the software implementation of a crash recovery algorithm in 114 switches. The network slowdown was a nine-hour nationwide blockage of long-distance calls.

Unintentional threats can be from employees of the organisation, or external to it. For example: an AT&T crew removing an old cable in Newark, New Jersey, accidentally severed a fiber-optic cable carrying more than 100,000 calls. Starting at 9.30 a.m. on 4 January 1991, and continuing for much of the next day, the effects included:

- Downtime of the New York Mercantile Exchange and several commodities exchanges.
- Disruption of Federal Aviation Administration (FAA) air-control communication in the New York metropolitan area.
- Lengthy flight delays into, and out of, the New York area.
- Blockage of 60% of the long-distance telephone calls into, and out of New York City.

The largest component of the unintentional threat agent arises from the use of software. The problem is that software can never be exhaustively tested for bugs, and the larger the piece of software the greater the chance of encountering a bug when using the software. The following are examples of unintentional threats:

- The Bank of New York (BoNY) experienced a $32 billion overdraft as the result of the overflow of a 16-bit counter that went unchecked. BoNY was unable to process the incoming credits from security transfers while the New York Federal Reserve automatically debited BoNY's cash account. BoNY had to borrow $24 billion to cover itself for one day (until the software was fixed); the interest on which was about $5 million. Many customers were also affected by the delayed transfer completions. The net result of this was a loss of business prestige, trust and confidence in the company.
- The Northeast Air Traffic Control Centre in Nashua, New Hampshire, reverted to the old voice-and-paper-slip back-up system for 37 minutes on 19 August 1998, because of a computer failure. A total of 350 planes were being handled at the time. The system also failed again the next day. William Johannes, president of the National Air Traffic Controller's Association, said, "It's like a Chevy with 485,000 miles on it and you are trying to stretch it. The longer it goes, the more times we are going to have failures."

### 3.2.3   The Intentional Threat Agents

The intentional threat agent is a party that knowingly sets out to cause damage or loss to a system. The hostile component of the intentional threat can cause serious damage or financial loss to a company. The following are examples of the intentional threat:

- In 1999, a hacker called Maxim broke into an online electronic commerce company by the name of CD-Universe. The hacker stole details belonging to 300,000 valid credit cards. He then demanded $100,000 in return for him destroying all his information. When the company refused to pay the blackmail the hacker started posting the credit cards to the Internet.
- Volkswagen lost almost $260 million as the result of an insider scam that created phony currency-exchange transactions and then covered them with real transactions a few days later. Four insiders and one outsider were convicted and jailed for six years.

The non-hostile component of the intentional threat agent refers to the fact that the actions of an intentional threat agent may have consequences other than those intended by the threat agent. For example, in Clifford Stoll's book called *The Cuckoo's Egg*, he noted that German hackers had broken into a computer that was being used to control radiotherapy for cancer victims. In their search for information the actions of the hackers could have had dire consequences for the cancer suffers, but the hackers were unaware of the medical use of the computer. The following is a refinement of the threat agent category:

### Table 3.1   Threats

| Threat Type | Threat Description |
|---|---|
| Foreign agents | These are people who professionally gather information and commit sabotage for governments.<br><br>• They are highly trained and highly funded.<br><br>• They are backed by substantial scientific capabilities, directed towards specific goals, and skilful in avoiding detection.<br><br>• They can be very dangerous to life and property. There is limited evidence to support the assertion that this threat agent is real and it is predicted that its use will not become widespread until after 2005. |
| Industrial or economic espionage | Corporate or Industrial Espionage involves operations conducted by one corporation against another for the purpose of acquiring a competitive advantage in domestic or global markets. There is ample evidence to support the assertion that this threat agent is real and that its use is widespread. |
| Terrorists | Terrorists use attacks to inflict fear and to achieve either social or political change.<br><br>• The FBI defines terrorism as "the unlawful use of force or violence against a person or property to intimidate or coerce a government, the civilian population, or any segment thereof, in furtherance of political or social objectives."<br><br>• They can be very dangerous to life and property. There is limited evidence to support the assertion that this threat agent is real and it is predicted that by 2005 its use will be widespread. |
| Organised crime | The threat from organised criminals arises as organised crime has realised that information has a distinct financial value attached to it, and information technology can be used to hide criminal activities. There is evidence to support the assertion that this threat agent is real and it is predicted that by 2005 its use will be widespread. |

| Insiders | The biggest threat that any organisation faces is from its own employees. There are many documented cases where employees have sabotaged, modified or stolen information belonging to their employing organisation. One of the key aspects to the insider threat is that the insider may have legitimate access to the information. There is ample evidence to support the assertion that this threat agent is real and that its use is widespread. |
|---|---|
| Hackers and crackers | This class of threat is often referred to as cyber-vandals. The image is generally that of a teenager breaking into a system for the fun of it, and the recognition of his peers. However, we are now starting to see hackers selling their services as the cyber warrior equivalent of a soldier-of-fortune. There is ample evidence to support the assertion that this threat agent is real and that its use is widespread. |
| Political dissidents | These are people who are attempting to use information and information technology to achieve a political objective.<br><br>• They are using information technology to inform the civilian population and other organisations or individuals about the alleged activities of their government.<br><br>• They are using information technology to gather (via legal, or illegal means) information relating to the activities of their government.<br><br>• They are using information technology to disrupt or undermine the activities of their government.<br><br>There is ample evidence to support the assertion that this threat agent is real and that its use is widespread. |
| Vendors and suppliers | Vendors and suppliers are now integrated into the fabric of most organisations. For example: when we outsource IT functions to a third party, the security of the outsourcing organisations become critically dependent upon the security of the third party. The same dependency is true when organisations integrate their supply chain using information technology. Evidence exists to demonstrate that this type of threat agent already exists and is growing. |

## 3.3 Vulnerabilities

Within the context of information assurance, a threat to a system can be defined as:

*"Some weakness of a system that could allow security to be violated"*.

Vulnerability assessments are concerned with the identification of the weakness that may be exploited. In general, vulnerabilities exist throughout the information systems processes, software, hardware, and information. Software can be vulnerable to interruption of execution, deletion, interception of software in transit, and modification. Hardware is vulnerable to theft and interruption of service. Finally, information is vulnerable to interruption (loss), interception, modification and fabrication. In essence, there are seven types of vulnerabilities that can exist in any system, and these are:

- *Physical Vulnerabilities*: intruders can break into computing facilities. Once in they can sabotage and vandalise computers, and they can steal hardware, diskettes, printouts etc.
- *Natural Vulnerabilities*: computers may be vulnerable to natural disasters and to environmental threats. Disasters such as fire, flood, earthquakes and power loss can wreck your computer and destroy information.
- *Hardware/Software Vulnerabilities*: certain kinds of hardware and software failures can compromise the IA of a computer system. Software failures of any kind may cause systems to fail, and may open up systems to penetration, or make systems so unreliable that they can't be trusted.
- *Media Vulnerabilities*: disk packs and tapes can be stolen or damaged by such mundane perils as dust and ballpoint pens.
- *Emanation Vulnerabilities*: all electronic equipment emits radiation that can be intercepted.
- *Communication Vulnerabilities*: if your computer is attached to a network then its message can be intercepted, and possibly modified or misrouted.
- *Human Vulnerabilities*: the people who administer and use your computer facilities represent the greatest vulnerability of all. They may be vulnerable to greed, revenge, blackmail and the like.

These vulnerabilities can manifest themselves via the following types of misuse (Tables 3.2 to 3.10).

### Table 3.2   External Misuse

| Mode of Misuse | Description |
|---|---|
| Visual Spying | Observation of keystrokes or screen. |
| Misrepresentation | Deceiving operators and users. |
| Physical Scavenging | Dumpster diving for printouts, floppy disks, etc. |

External misuse of an information system is related to the creation, manipulation and destruction of information by a user within the organisation. This type of misuse forces one to examine how, when, where and by whom information is created, manipulated and destroyed. This type of analysis is primarily concerned with the physical environment within which the users execute the business processes.

Generally non-technological and unobserved, external misuse is physically removed from computer and communications facilities. It has no direct observable effects on the systems and is usually undetectable by the computer IA systems. Types of external misuse include:

- *Visual spying*. For example: remote observation of typed key strokes or screen images.
- *Physical scavenging*. For example: collection of waste paper or other externally accessible computer media - so-called Dumpster Diving.
- *Deception*. Various forms of deception external to computer systems and telecommunications. For example: social engineering (having one act in a manner conducive to another's needs, e.g. release their password).

### Table 3.3  Hardware Misuse

| Mode of Misuse | Description |
|---|---|
| Logical Scavenging | Examining discarded/stolen media. |
| Eavesdropping | Intercepting electronic or other information. |
| Interference | Jamming, electronic or otherwise. |
| Physical Attack | Damaging or modifying equipment or power. |
| Physical Removal | Removing equipment and storage media. |

Hardware misuse of an information system is primarily concerned with the IA of the physical devices that form the physical infrastructure of the organisation's information system. It is important to note that this type of misuse also includes theft of removable storage media such as printout and electromagnetic tapes, and other electronic, removable media. In essence there are two types of hardware misuse: passive and active.

- *Passive Hardware Misuse*. This tends to have no immediate side-effect on hardware or software behaviour, and includes:
  - logical scavenging (such as the examination of discarded computer media);
  - electronic or other types of eavesdropping that intercept signals, generally unbeknownst to the victims. For example: picking up emanations, known as TEMPEST; and
  - planting a spy-tap device in a terminal, workstation or mainframe, or other hardware sub-system.
- *Active Hardware Misuse*. This generally has noticeable effects and includes:
  - theft of computing equipment and physical storage media;
  - hardware modifications, such as internally planted Trojan horse hardware devices; and
  - physical attacks on equipment and media, such as interruption of power supplies. This type of attack can also make use of electro-magnetic pulse (EMP) weapons.

### Table 3.4  Masquerading

| Mode of Misuse | Description |
|---|---|
| Impersonation | Using false identities external to the computer system. |
| Piggybacking Attacks | Usurping communication lines and workstations. |
| Spoofing Attacks | Using playback, creating bogus nodes and systems. |
| Network Weaving | Masking physical whereabouts or routing. |

Masquerading misuse of an information system is primarily concerned with the authentication of information, its source, its destination, and its users. Masquerading attacks include:

- *Impersonation of the Identity of Some Other Individual or Computer Subject*. For example: using a computer identifier and password to gain access to a computer system. The computer identifier and password may belong to a person or a computer demon.
- *Spoofing Attacks*. For example: using the identity of another machine on a network to gain unauthorised access. Types of attacks include a) IP spoofing, b) machine spoofing, and c) demon spoofing.
- *Piggyback Attacks*. For example: an unauthorised user may hijack a communication channel to a computer.
- *Playback Attacks*. For example: the playback of network traffic in the attempt to recreate a transaction.
- *Network Weaving to Hide Physical Whereabouts*. This is where a person will connect through several machines to a target machine.

### Table 3.5  Pest Programs

| Mode of Misuse | Description |
|---|---|
| Trojan Horse Attacks | Implanting malicious code, sending letter bombs. |
| Logic Bombs | Setting up time or event bombs. |
| Malevolent Worms | Acquiring distributed resources. |
| Virus Attacks | Attaching to programs and replicating. |

Pest programs are primarily concerned with the availability of information systems services, and the expected behaviour of services.

- *Trojan Horse:* a Trojan horse is an entity (typically a program, but not always) that contains code or something interpretable as code which, when executed, will have undesirable effects, such as the clandestine copying of information or the disabling of the information system.

- *Logic Bomb:* a Logic Bomb is a Trojan horse in which the attack is detonated by the occurrence of some specified logical event such as the first subsequent login by a particular user.
- *Time Bomb:* a Time Bomb is a Logic Bomb in which the attack is detonated by the occurrence of some specified time-related logic event, e.g. the next time the date is 18 December.
- *Letter Bomb:* a Letter Bomb is a peculiar type of Trojan horse attack whereby the harmful agent is not contained in a program, but rather is hidden in a piece of mail or information. The harmful agent usually consists of special characters that are only meaningful to a particular mail agent. This bomb is triggered when it is read as a piece of electronic mail.
- *Virus:* viruses and worms often attack the Internet and other networks. For example: in May 2000, the *"I Love You"* e-mail virus was released. When the worm executes, it will search for certain types of files and make changes to those files depending on the type of file. For files on fixed or network drives, it will take the following steps:
  - Files with the extension *vbs* or *vbe* are overwritten with a copy of the virus.
  - Files with the extension *mp3*, *mp2*, *js*, *jse*, *css*, *wsh*, *sct*, *jpg*, *jpeg* or *hta* are overwritten with a copy of the virus and the extension is changed to *vbs*.

Since the modified files are overwritten by the worm code rather than being deleted, file recovery is difficult and may be impossible. By 10 May 2000, it was estimated that the viruses had infected 600,000 machines in the US alone and had cost American business $2.5 billion in damages and lost income.

### Table 3.6   Bypasses

| Mode of Misuse | Description |
| --- | --- |
| Trapdoor Attacks | Utilising existing flaws in the system and mis-configured network programs. |
| Authorisation Attacks | Password cracking etc. |

Bypasses is a type of misuse of an information system primarily concerned with authorisation and configuration management. A *trapdoor* is an entry path that is not normally expected to be used. There are several types of trapdoors:

- Inadequate identification, authentication, and authorisation of users, tasks and systems, e.g. the sendmail debug option that was used by the Internet Worm.

- Improper initialisation. Many bypasses are enabled by systems being incorrectly configured, so that when they are initialised IA features can be bypassed.
- Improper finalisation. When a program terminates it must ensure that it disposes of all secure information properly. If not, improper finalisation occurs.
- Incomplete or inconsistent authentication and validation can be caused by improper argument validation, e.g., the Internet Worm used a bug in the *get* function located in the finger demon to gain root access. The bug was that the *get* function did not do a bounds check on the number of arguments.
- Improper encapsulation of the internals of a system can allow a user to access information or functions that they are not authorised to access.

### Table 3.7  Active Misuse

| Mode of Misuse | Description |
| --- | --- |
| Basic Active Attack | Creating, modifying, entering false or misleading information. |
| Incremental Attack | Using salami attacks. |
| Denial of Service | Perpetrating saturation attacks. |

Active misuse of an information system is primarily concerned with modifying information, or entering false or misleading information. The following are also examples of active misuse:

- A box office supervisor cancelled tickets, which had been sold, and then later resold the tickets, keeping the cash. The box office supervisor falsified the audit trail, but this was detected after problems with the software were investigated. The employee was prosecuted and given six months imprisonment.
- The World Wide Web provides a vehicle through which organisations and people can communicate and disseminate information. Hundreds if not thousands, of businesses and government agencies have had their Web sites attacked. The general effect of unauthorised alteration of a Web site is a loss of public confidence in the agency's ability to protect its information systems, and often a public relations nightmare.

In addition, this type of misuse is concerned with the denial of service. For example, a company that specialises in trading on the Internet is exposed to the threat that if the Internet connection is lost then the ability for the company to conduct business is lost and the supply chain is broken.

**Table 3.8   Passive Misuse**

| Mode of Misuse | Description |
| --- | --- |
| Browsing | Making random and selective searches. |
| Inference, aggregation | Exploiting database inferences and traffic analysis. |
| Covert Channels | Exploiting covert channels or other information leakage. |

Passive misuse of an information system is primarily concerned with exploiting the information within the system so as to conduct analysis and make inferences about the existence of sensitive information.

**Table 3.9   Inactive Misuse**

| Mode of Misuse | Description |
| --- | --- |
| Inactive Misuse | Wilfully failing to perform expected duties, or committing errors of omission. |

Inactive misuse of an information system is primarily concerned with wilfully failing to perform expected duties, or committing errors of omission.

**Table 3.10   Indirect Misuse**

| Mode of Misuse | Description |
| --- | --- |
| Indirect Misuse | Preparing for subsequent misuses, as in off-line pre-encryption matching, factoring large numbers to obtain private keys, auto-dialer scanning. |

Indirect misuse of an information system is primarily concerned with preparing for subsequent misuses, as in off-line pre-encryption matching, factoring large numbers to obtain private keys, auto-dialer scanning.

# 3.4   Risk and Risk Management

Risk management is concerned with the assessment of risk and the implementation of procedures and practices designed to control the level of risk. Figure 3.4 depicts the various components that comprise a risk management strategy.   Risk assessment is concerned with:

- the identification of the risk;
- the analysis of the risk in terms of performance, cost and other quality factors; and

- risk prioritisation in terms of exposure and leverage.

    Risk control is concerned with:

- management planning in terms of risk avoidance, transfer and reduction;
- risk resolution, in terms of prototyping and simulation; and
- risk monitoring.

Risk Management
- Risk Assessment
  - Risk Identification
    - Checklists
    - Decision Driver Analysis
    - Assumption Analysis
    - Decomposition
  - Risk Analysis
    - Performance Models
    - Cost Models
    - Network Analysis
    - Decision Analysis
    - Quality Factor Analysis
  - Risk Prioritisation
    - Risk Exposure
    - Risk Leverage
    - Comp-Risk Reduction
- Risk Control
  - Risk Management Planning
    - Buying Information
    - Risk Avoidance
    - Risk Transfer
    - Risk Reduction
    - Risk Element Planning
    - Risk Plan Integration
  - Risk Resolution
    - Prototypes
    - Simulations
    - Benchmarks
    - Analysis
    - Staffing
  - Risk Monitoring
    - Milestone Tracking
    - Top 10 Tracking
    - Risk Reassessment
    - Corrective Action

**Figure 3.4   Risk Management**

The process of IA risk management in the context of information assurance and InfoSec is about identifying the level of risk that is acceptable, and then putting procedures in place to ensure that that level of risk is maintained and managed.

The process of IA risk management is shown in Figure 3.5 as a constant iterative process. The first stage of risk management begins with an assessment of the threats and their associated capabilities. For a vulnerability assessment one would identify all of an organisation's assets, and their known vulnerabilities. The process of IA risk management is a constant process because the nature and capability of the threat is always changing, and the list of known vulnerabilities is always growing.

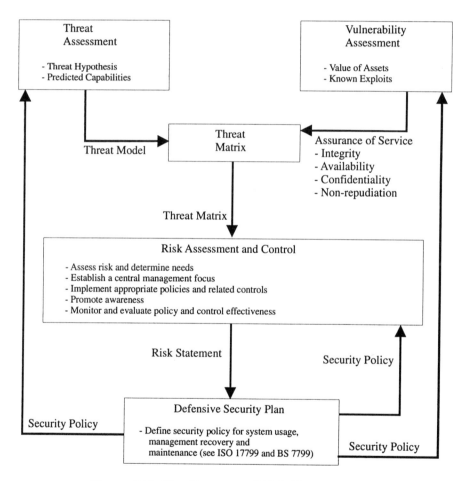

**Figure 3.5   The Process of Risk Management**

The vulnerability and threat assessments are used to create a threat matrix and the threat matrix is used to define and direct the process of risk assessment and mitigation. This process is concerned with identifying how the risk is to be controlled and then putting methods in place to manage the risk evaluated. The output of risk assessment and control is a risk statement. This statement is used to create an IA plan that defines:

• how the system is to be managed/maintained; and
• what methods will be used to recover from a IA incident.

Once an IA plan has been created then the whole process of risk management can begin again. In fact the process of monitoring threats and vulnerabilities, and updating policies and procedures when changes occur in the level of threat or vulnerability, is a constant one

## 3.4.1   Threat Matrix

A threat matrix is a matrix where the IA capabilities of a threat are set against the type of vulnerabilities that can exist for a given asset. The vulnerability assessment defines a set of assurance levels for each asset in terms of confidentiality, integrity, availability and non-repudiation.  A cell of a threat matrix is illustrated in Figure 3.6.

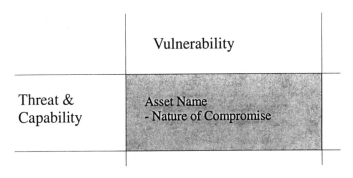

**Figure 3.6   A Threat Matrix**

The nature of the compromise is used as part of the risk assessment and risk control process. For each asset identified in a threat matrix, one can examine how the nature of the compromise affects the ability of the organisation to conduct business. This analysis is performed by focusing upon the role of the asset in the business process from a particular perspective:

- *Performance Perspective*: this analysis examines the role of the asset in determining the performance of the business process.
- *Cost Perspective*: this analysis examines the cost of recovering from the loss or corruption of the asset.
- *Decision Making Perspective*: this analysis examines the role of the asset in the organisation's process of decision making. In particular it focuses upon the cost of the corruption and deletion of the asset.

### 3.4.2   Risk Management

Risk management is the process of assessing risk, taking steps to reduce risk to an acceptable level, and maintaining that level of risk. Managers analyse risks for many aspects of their business; they consider alternatives and implement plans to maximise returns on their investments. A risk management process for information systems enables managers and their organisations to build an in-depth knowledge about their systems and how they are interrelated. Risk management is a vital element of a comprehensive IA program.

### 3.4.3   Five Principles of Risk Management

The five principles of risk management are as follows:

- Assess risk and determine needs.
- Establish a central management focus.
- Implement appropriate policies and related controls.
- Promote awareness.
- Monitor and evaluate policy and control effectiveness.

  The successful organisation will apply these principles by linking them into a cycle of activity that enables the organisation to address risks in a continuous process. The success of IA programs depend upon the recognition and understanding of the senior executives that their information systems are subject to risks and that these risks affect their business operations. After assessing the risks of their business operations, the organisation should:

- establish policies and selected controls;
- increase awareness of users to the policies and controls ;
- monitor the effectiveness of the policies and controls ;and
- use the results to determine if modifications of policies and controls are needed.

  All organisations studied said that risk considerations and related cost-benefit tradeoffs were a primary focus of their IA-related programs. IA is not an end in itself, but integrated into business processes, e.g. set of policies and controls designed to support business operations.

## 3.4.4    Sixteen Successful Practices

### 3.4.4.1    Principle: assess risk and determine needs

- *Practice 1. Recognise information resources as essential organisational assets that must be protected*: the efforts of high-level executives to understand and manage risks help to ensure that IA is taken seriously at lower levels in the organisation and that IA programs have adequate resources. IA specialists should keep managers at all levels informed of developing IA issues.
- *Practice 2. Develop practical risk assessment procedures that link IA to business needs*: for example: an organisation can make use of automated checklists in risk assessment.
- *Practice 3. Hold program and business managers accountable*: organisations should hold business managers accountable for managing the IA risks associated with their operations, just as they are held accountable for other business risks. IA specialists in these organisations can have an advisory role, including keeping management informed about risks.
- *Practice 4. Manage risk on a continuing basis*: organisations should emphasise a continuous attention to IA. Continuity of attention can help to ensure that controls are appropriate and effective, and that individuals who use and maintain information systems comply with the organisational policies.

### 3.4.4.2    Principle: establish a central management focal point

- *Practice 5. Designate a central group to carry out key activities*: a central IA group can serve a catalyst for ensuring those IA risks are considered in planned and ongoing operations. This group can provide advice and expertise to all organisational levels and can keep managers informed about IA issues. They can develop organisation-wide policies and guidance; educate users about IA risks; research potential threats, vulnerabilities and control techniques; test controls; assess risks; and identify needed policies.
- *Practice 6. Organisations should provide the central group with ready and independent access to senior executives*: IA concerns can be at odds with the desires of business managers and system developers. Elevating IA concerns to higher management levels can help to ensure that the risks are understood and taken into account when decisions are made.
- *Practice 7. Designate dedicated funding and staff*: organisations should define budgets that will enable them to plan and set goals for IA programs. The budgets should cover central staff salaries, training, and IA software and hardware. IA responsibilities should be clearly defined for the groups carrying out the IA programs, and dedicated staff resources should be provided to carry out these responsibilities.

- *Practice 8. Enhance staff professionalism and technical skills*: organisations should take steps to provide personnel involved in IA programs with the skills and knowledge that they need. Staff expertise should be updated frequently to keep skills and knowledge current. Staff members should attend technical conferences and specialised courses, and should review technical literature and bulletins. Special training courses should be provided for system administrators who are the first line of defence against IA intrusions and are often in the best position to notice unusual activities.

### 3.4.4.3   Principle: implement appropriate policies and related controls

- *Practice 9. Link policies to business risks*: organisations should stress the importance of up-to-date policies that make sense to users and others who are expected to understand them. A current and comprehensive set of policies is a key component in an effective IA program. These policies must be adjusted on a continuing basis to respond to newly identified risks. In today's interconnected network environment, users can accidentally disclose sensitive information to many people through electronic mail or introduce damaging viruses that are then transmitted to other computers in the organisation's networks. For example: one of the methods that the Love-Bug uses to propagate itself is through users reading e-mail and executing an attachment.
- *Practice 10. Distinguish between policies and guidelines*: policies generally outline fundamental requirements that managers consider to be mandatory, while guidelines contain more detailed rules for implementing the policies. By distinguishing between the two, the organisation should emphasise the most important elements of IA while providing flexibility to unit managers in implementing policies.
- *Practice 11. Support policies through the central IA group*: organisations should have a central IA management group who are responsible for writing policies in partnership with other organisational officials. The central group provides explanations, guidance, and support to the various units within the organisation. This practice encourages business managers to support centrally developed policies that address organisational requirements and are practical to implement.

### 3.4.4.4   Principle: promote awareness

- *Practice 12. Continually educate users and others on risks and related policies*: the central IA management group should work to improve everyone's understanding of the risks associated with information systems and of the policies and controls in place. They should encourage compliance with policies and awareness on the part of users of the risks involved in disclosing sensitive information or passwords.

- *Practice 13. Use attention-getting and user-friendly techniques*: the techniques used can include intranet Web sites that explain policies, standards, procedures, alerts and special notices; awareness videos with messages from top managers about the IA program; interactive presentations by IA staff with various user groups; IA awareness days; and products with IA related slogans.

### 3.4.4.5   Principle: monitor and evaluate policy and control effectiveness

- *Practice 14. Monitor factors that affect risk and indicate IA effectiveness*: organisations should test the effectiveness of their controls.   Most organisations rely primarily on auditors to carry out this function. This enables the IA organisations to maintain their role as advisors. A central IA management group should keep track of audit findings and the organisation's progress in implementing corrective actions. In some cases, the central IA management group should conduct their own tests, and some organisations allow designated individuals to try to penetrate systems.   The testing of controls enable the organisations to identify unknown vulnerabilities and to eliminate or reduce them. Organisations should monitor compliance with policies, mostly through informal feedback to the central IA group from system administrators. Organisations should keep summary records of actual IA incidents to measure the types of violations and the damage suffered from the incidents.   The records are valuable input for risk assessments and budget decisions.
- *Practice 15. Use results to direct future efforts and hold managers accountable*: organisation officials have stated that monitoring encourages compliance with IA policies, but the full benefits of monitoring are not achieved unless results are used to improve the IA program.  Results can be used to hold managers accountable for their IA responsibilities.
- *Practice 16. You should constantly be on the lookout for new monitoring tools and techniques*: if one does not keep up with new versions of IA-related products and use software patches as soon as they are available, the organisation's information systems will soon be more vulnerable than had previously been the case.

## 3.5   Summary

The risk management processes are an integral part of any IA program. One should begin by identifying the current threats to information systems and match those threats to the corporation's information systems' vulnerabilities. Then through a risk assessment process, one can begin to develop a cost-effective IA program.

# Chapter 4

# The Information World of Crime

IA is not a luxury but a necessity because intentional and unintentional acts are constantly occurring that place information at risk. With the advent of the global information infrastructure based on the Internet, more people have more access to more systems and more information than at any other time in our history. Many of these individuals make human errors that adversely impact information. There are also a small but growing group of people who have taken advantage of the vulnerabilities of these systems to steal, modify, destroy, or deny use of them and the information that they store, process and transmit. This chapter will address this world of crime; as well as the conduct of inquiries, investigations and forensic examinations.

## 4.1 Introduction

The term "cyber-crime" is used to denote any crime that involves information systems and networks, including crimes that do not heavily rely on information systems or networks. For example: the following would be classified as a cyber-crime:

- On 22 April 1996, in Greenfield, California, a woman contacted the local police and reported that Ronald Riva, the father of the host, had molested her six-year-old daughter during a slumber party. Additionally, a ten-year-old girl at the party reported that Riva and his friend Melton Myers used an information systems to record her as she posed for them. Riva and Myers led investigators into an international ring of child abusers and pornographers that convened in an Internet chat room called the Orchid Club. As a result of an international investigation, 16 men from Finland, Canada, Australia, and the United States were arrested and charged with various sex offences. The investigation into the Orchid Club led law enforcement agencies to a larger group of pornographers and paedophiles called the Wonderland Club. After more than two years of investigation 200 people from 14 countries had been arrested and charged.

- Over a period of two years, a member of staff in a UK government agency altered information systems records to which she had legitimate access to produce false payments, which were collected and cashed by a member of her family. The perpetrator was very experienced and trusted and, as a result, her line manager conducted no checks on her work, Significantly, she took little leave and when she did so, she insisted that no one need cover her work as she would catch up on her return. The fraud came to light when an amendment to one of the payments triggered a special check. The perpetrator was prosecuted and sentenced to 18 months imprisonment.

The term "information systems crime" is used to denote a crime that takes place "on" an information systems, such as theft of software or data, or unauthorised access-of/modification-to information. For example: the following would be classed as an information systems crime:

- Following the failure of regular early morning processes, IT staff at a UK local government authority found that there had been unauthorised amendments and deletions to a number of information systems files the previous evening. The extent of the damage was unclear and hardware and software suppliers were asked to come on-site to perform a system audit. They found that all permissions had been removed for a particular library of files and that this could lead to problems with the loading and processing of information. The sophisticated nature of the security breach required particular expertise and local knowledge, and suggested the involvement of the former operations manager who had resigned one month before. Further investigations by IT staff identified a malicious program which, had it been run, would have created a major disruption to the organisation's systems and services. It was later discovered that the program had been compiled two days before the operations manager left. A police investigation found that the operator on duty had allowed the former operations manager access to the master operator terminal at the time. The former manager was successfully prosecuted under UK Law (the *Information Systems Misuse Act 1990*).

The difference between information systems crime and cyber-crime is based on the concept of authorised access. If a person has authorised access to an information systems and the information contained on that information systems, and uses the information systems or modifies the information on the information systems to commit a crime, then that would be classed as cyber-crime. If, however, the person does not have authorised access to an information systems or the information contained on that information systems, and uses the information systems or modifies the information on the information systems to commit a crime, then that would be classed as information systems crime. [1]

---

[1] One must remember that the definitions noted are not accepted worldwide. Generally, the definitions would be based on the definitions noted in the criminal laws that applied.

## 4.2   Information Systems and Crime

We can classify how information systems are involved in crime in the following ways:

- An information systems can be the *object* of a crime. When the criminal act has an affect on an information systems, then the information systems is the object of crime (e.g. when an information systems is stolen or destroyed).
- An information systems can be the *subject* of a crime. When an information systems is the enviroment in which the crime is commited, it is the subject of the crime (e.g. when an information systems is infected with a virus, or the functioning of the information system is impaired in some manner such as a Trojan horse or logic bomb).
- An information systems can be used as the tool for conducting or planning a crime. For example: when an information systems is used to forge documents, create/manipulate illegal images or to break into another information systems, then it is the *instrument* of the crime.
- The *symbol* of the information systems can be used itself to intimidate or deceive. For example: a stockbroker tells his clients that he was able to make huge profits on rapid stock option trading by using a secret information systems program. Although the stockbroker had no such program, hundreds of clients were convinced enough to invest a minimum of $100,000 each.

## 4.3   *Modus Operandi*

The term "*modus operandi*" is Latin and it means "a method of operating". A criminal's *modus operandi* (MO) is comprised of learned behaviours that can evolve and develop over time. As time passes and the criminal becomes more experienced, sophisticated and confident the MO of the criminal will change to reflect this. The *modus operandi* of a criminal will function to serve one or more of three purposes:

- To protect the offender's identity.
- To ensure the successful completion of the crime.
- To facilitate the offender's escape.

With regard to the Internet, examples of *modus operandi* behaviours include:

- Amount of planning before a crime, evidenced by behaviour and materials (i.e. notes taken in planning stage regarding location selection and potential victim information, found in e-mails or personal journals on a PC).
- Materials used by the offender in the commission of the specific offence (i.e. system type, connection type, software involved, etc.)

- Presurveillance on a discussion list, learning about a potential victim's lifestyle or occupation on their personal web-site; contacting a potential victim directly using a friendly alias or a pretence, etc.
- Offence location selection (i.e. a threatening message sent to a Usenet newsgroup, a conversation in an IRC chat room to groom a potential victim, a server hosting illicit materials for covert distribution, etc.).
- Use as a weapon during a crime (i.e. harmful virus or Trojan program sent to a victim's PC as an e-mail attachment, etc.).
- Offender precautionary acts (i.e. the use of an alias, stealing time on a private system for use as a base of operations, IP spoofing, etc.).

In the following example, the MO consists of manufacturing and marketing child pornography to other distributors using enhanced digital imaging technology and the Internet. Contact with the buyers was first made through the use of IRC chat rooms. The materials were then distributed on CD-ROM.

- In August 1997, a Swiss couple, John (52 years old) and Buntham (26 years old) Grabenstetter, were arrested at the Hilton in Buffalo, New York, and accused of smuggling into the United States thousands of information systemised pictures of children having sex. The couple were alleged by authorities to have sold wholesale amounts of child pornography through the Internet, and carried with them thousands of electronic files of child pornography to the United States from their Swiss home. They were alleged to have agreed over the Internet to sell child pornography to US customs agents posing as local US porn shop owners. They were alleged to have agreed to sell 250 CD-ROMs to US investigators for $10,000. According to reports, one CD-ROM had over 7000 images. It is further alleged that their two-year-old daughter, who was travelling with them at the time of their arrest, was also a victim. Authorities claim that photographs of their daughter are on the CD-ROMs her parents were distributing.

## 4.4   Information Systems Crime Adversarial Matrix

This matrix (Table 4.1) was first developed by the US Federal Bureau of Investigation (FBI), and describes a number of different information systems criminals and their characteristics. The matrix categorises offenders into three types:

- *Crackers*: many of this type of adversary are teenagers. Despite their tender years, they have broken into banks, companies that manufacture games, traditional corporate machines, and military systems. In one reported case, a 14-year-old boy broke into the information systems that position US Air Force satellites. Despite their intelligence many teenagers do poorly at school and have few friends. Their major form of human interaction is via BBS, IRC and e-mail, where they share information and stories with their other cracker friends. Typically this type of adversary break into systems for the intellectual challenge, however some see themselves as a Robin Hood type character fighting for truth, justice and freedom. In recent years many crackers have become a good deal more professional.

- *Information Systems Criminals*: this type of adversary can be subdivided into espionage and fraud/abuse. A nation-state or an industrial competitor typically backs the espionage adversary. The drive for this crime is for a nation-state or industrial competitor to gain a competitive edge over its rivals. The fraud and abuse adversary is typically either an individual or a criminal organisation. Major criminal organisations are now moving into information systems crime as a direct source of illegal income generation and intelligence gathering.

- *Vandals*: this type of adversary can be subdivided into users and strangers. Typically this type of adversary does not commit crimes for profit or the intellectual challenge. In general they are motivated by anger directed at an individual, organisation, or life in general. The user group is the category of individuals who have authorised access to the system, but perform unauthorised actions. Typically, a user is a person who feels wronged in some way and wants to retaliate. The stranger group is the category of individuals who do not have authorised access to the system at all and break into a system in order to do damage. Outside vandals are rare, most often the stranger who breaks into a system is a cracker or a true criminal.

The aim of the matrix is to create a profile of the adversary from four perspectives:

- Organisational.
- Operational.
- Behavioural.
- Resource.

## 4.4.1   Organisational Characteristics

Organisational characteristics describe the ways in which some information systems criminals group themselves. It describes the group structure, and social hierarchy, and motivational factors that govern the group.

**Table 4.1   Organisational Characteristics**

| Organisational Characteristics | | | |
|---|---|---|---|
| **Categories of Offenders** | **Organisation** | **Recruitment & Attraction** | **International Connections** |
| **Crackers** | | | |
| Group | Unstructured organisation with counterculture orientation. | Peer group attraction. | Interacts and corresponds with other groups around the world using tools such as IRC and e-mail. |
| Individual | None.   These people are true loners. | Attracted by intellectual challenge. | Subscribes to cracker journals and may interact with other group and/or individuals around the world using tools such as IRC and e-mail. |
| **Criminals** | | | |
| Espionage | Supported by hostile organisation. | In most cases, money; some cases of ideological attraction; attention. | Uses information systems networks to break into target information systems around the world. |
| Fraud/Abuse | May operate as small organised crime group or as a loner. | Money; power. | Uses wire service to transfer money internationally. |
| **Vandals** | | | |
| Strangers | Loner or small group. May be quite young. | Revenge; intellectual challenge; money. | Use of information systems networks and phone systems to break into target information systems. |

| Users | Often employee or former employee. | Revenge; power; intellectual challenge; disgruntled. | None. |
|---|---|---|---|

## 4.4.2  Operational Characteristics

Operational characteristics describe the ways in which information systems criminals actually carry out their crimes. This characteristic describes how much care they take when planning their crimes, their skill level, and the typical techniques that they will use when performing the crime.

**Table 4.2  Operational Characteristics**

| Operational Characteristics | | | |
|---|---|---|---|
| **Categories of Offender** | **Planning** | **Level of Expertise** | **Tactics and Methods used** |
| **Crackers** | | | |
| Groups | May involve detailed planning. | High | Enter target information systems via information systems networks. Exchange information with other crackers and groups. |
| Individuals | Study networks before attempts are made. | Medium to high. Experience gained through social networks. | Enter target information systems via information systems networks. If skill level is low, then more likely to use trial and error online than to do careful research and planning. |

| Criminals | | | |
|---|---|---|---|
| Espionage | May involve detailed planning. | High. | May make use of crackers to perform information operation. |
| Fraud/Abuse | Careful planning prior to crime. | Medium to high, although is typically more experienced at fraud than at information systems programming. | May use more traditional intrusion methods such as wiretapping and trapdoors. Will break into systems using asic methods. |
| Vandals | | | |
| Strangers | Not much planning, more a crime of opportunity. | Varies. | Looks around until able to gain access to system. |
| Users | May involve detailed planning and execution. | Varies. May have high level of expertise. | Trapdoor and Trojan horse programs. Data modification. |

## 4.4.3    Behavioural Characteristics

Behavioural characteristics describe the information systems criminals themselves. They define what motivates them and what their personal characteristics are. In addition, they define any potential weaknesses that the information systems criminal may possess that may be exploited by those who investigate their crimes.

### Table 4.3    Behavioural Characteristics

| Behavioural Characteristics | | | |
|---|---|---|---|
| Categories of Offenders | Motivation | Personal Characteristics | Potential Weaknesses |
| Crackers | | | |
| Groups | Intellectual challenge; peer group fun; in support of a cause. | Highly intelligent individuals. Counterculture oriented. | Do not consider offences crimes. Talk freely about actions. |

| Individuals | Intellectual challenge; problem solving; power; money; in support of a cause. | Moderate to high intelligence. | May keep notes and other documentation on actions. Those of high intelligence will typically encrypt these notes. |
|---|---|---|---|
| **Criminals** | | | |
| Espionage | Money and a chance to attack the system. | May be cracker operating in a group or as an individual. | Becomes greedy for more information and may then become careless. |
| Fraud/Abuse | Money or other personal gain; power. | Same characteristics as other fraud offenders. | Becomes greedy and then makes mistakes. |
| **Vandals** | | | |
| Strangers | Intellectual challenge; money; power. | Same characteristics as crackers. | May become too brazen and make mistakes. |
| Users | Revenge against an organisation; problem solving; money. | Usually has some information systems expertise. | May leave audit trail in information systems logs. |

## 4.4.4   Resource Characteristics

Resource characteristics describe what resources the information systems criminal requires. In particular, it focuses upon the training required, the equipment required, and the support structure required in order to perform the crime.

**Table 4.4  Resource Characteristics**

| Resource Characteristics | | | |
|---|---|---|---|
| **Categories of Offenders** | **Training Skills** | **Minimum Equipment Required** | **Support Structure** |
| **Crackers** | | | |
| Groups | High level of informal training. | Basic information systems equipment with modem. | Peer group support. |
| Individuals | Expertise gained through experience. | Basic information systems equipment with modem. | Information exchange mechanisms such as BBS, IRC, e-ail, etc. |
| **Criminals** | | | |
| Espionage | Various levels of expertise. | Basic information systems equipment with modem. In some cases may use more sophisticated equipment. | Support may come from sponsoring organisation. |
| Fraud/Abuse | Some programming experience. | Information systems with modem or access to target information systems. | Peer group; possible organised crime enterprise. |
| **Vandals** | | | |
| Strangers | Range from basic to highly skilled. | Basic information systems equipment with modem. | Peer group support. |
| Users | Some information systems expertise. Knowledge of programming ranges from basic to advanced. | Access to target information systems. | None. |

# 4.5    Motives of the Cyber Criminal

*"What does he do, the man you want?"*
*"He kills–"*
*"Ah–" he said sharply, "That's incidental. What is the first and principal thing he does, what need does he serve by killing?"*
                    *Hannibal Lector to Agent Starling (Silence of the Lambs, 1989)*

The term "motive" refers to the emotional, psychological, or material need that impels, and is satisfied by, behaviour. In general terms there are five types of behaviours that an intruder will engage in, and these are:

- Power assurance.
- Power assertive.
- Anger retaliatory.
- Sadistic.
- Profit oriented.

## 4.5.1    Power Assurance (aka Compensatory)

There are criminal behaviours that are intended to restore the criminal's self-confidence or self-worth through the use of low aggression means. This type of behaviour suggests that the criminal has an underlying lack of self-confidence and personal inadequacy. This type of criminal will often engage in cyber-stalking. For example: times have changed. People no longer have to leave the confines and comfort of their homes to harass somebody. (Oakland County Assistant Prosecutor Neal Rockind, 1996). In 1996 Mr Archambeau, 32, was charged with a misdemeanour for cyber-stalking a woman from Farmington Hills. He met her through an information systems dating agency. After they had met in person a couple of times, she dumped him by e-mail. He continued to leave phone messages and e-mail messages, even after a police warning. He was arrested and charged under the state's stalking laws in May 1994.

### 4.5.1.1  MO Behaviour
- Targets an individual who typically lives alone or with a small child.
- Selects victims who live in the same general area, often near offender's home, work or other places where they feel comfortable.
- They will engage in surveillance of the target in advance of the crime in both the physical world and in cyber-space.

### 4.5.1.2  Signature Behaviour
- They will keep records/journals of the attack.
- Engage in voyeuristic behaviour of the victim before and after the attack.

## 4.5.2  Power Assertive (aka Entitlement)

These include offender behaviours that are intended to restore the offender's self-confidence or self-worth through the use of moderate- to high-aggression means. These behaviours suggest an underlying lack of confidence and a sense of personal inadequacy that are expressed through control, mastery, and humiliation of the victim, while demonstrating the offender's sense of authority. Offenders evidencing this type of behaviour may grow more confident over time, as their egocentricity may be very high. They may begin to do things that can lead to their identification. Law enforcement may interpret this as a desire by the offender to be caught. In fact, this is not true as the offender has no respect for law enforcement. This type of behaviour does not indicate a desire to harm the victim, but rather to possess the victim. Demonstrating power over their victims is their means of expressing mastery, strength, control, authority, and identity to themselves. The attacks are therefore intended to reinforce the offender's inflated sense of self-worth, self-value and self-confidence. In the perception of the intruder they are entitled to the fruits of their attack by virtue of being superior. For example: on 23 March 2000, police in Wales arrested Curador, a hacker suspected of stealing thousands of credit cards from nine e-commerce sites and posting many of them on the Web. On 8 March 2000, Curador took part in an interview for Internet-Radio News. During the interview Curador taunted police, saying he didn't think they would be ever able to catch him, and even if they did there was no prison in the world that could hold him.

### 4.5.2.1  MO Behaviour
- The victim is pre-selected or opportunistic (too good an opportunity to pass up).
- The victim is chosen by availability, accessibility and vulnerability.
- The intruder will engage in surveillance and intelligence gathering against the victim.
- The attacker will take a trophy to prove superiority; however, the attacker will usually not keep a detailed journal of the attack.

### 4.5.2.2  Signature Behaviour
- Demeans and humiliates the victim demonstrating the offender's power of control over the victim.
- Offender's pleasure is primary as it reinforces the offender's belief in his invulnerability.
- Offender may demonstrate a lack of care with regard to covering of his tracks/evidence.
- The victim is a prop only to support the offender's belief in his invulnerability.

### 4.5.3 Anger Retaliatory

These include criminal behaviours that suggest a great deal of rage, either towards a specific person, group, institution, or a symbol of either. These types of behaviours are commonly evidenced in stranger-to-stranger sexual assaults, domestic homicides, work related homicides, harassment, and cases involving political or religious terrorism. Anger retaliation is just what the name suggests – the offender is acting on the basis of cumulative real or imagined wrongs from those that are in their world. The victim may symbolise that person to the offender in occupation, or other characteristics. The main goal of the behaviour is to service their cumulative aggression. They are retaliating against the victim for wrongs or perceived wrongs. The offender may believe that they are correcting some injustice.

- During December 1996, a hacker group called PHAIT (Portuguese Hackers Against Indonesian Tyranny) broke into various Indonesian Web sites and defaced them with political anti-government messages. In addition, they also erased data on a variety of government servers such as the Directorate for the Human Settlement and Environmental Technology server (huset.pt.bppt.go.id).
- On 11 February 1997, a hacker by the name of Toxyn broke into the Web server of the East Timor Government and defaced it with anti-Indonesian government pictures and text messages.

#### 4.5.3.1 MO Behaviour
- Attack is unplanned; a result of an emotional reaction on the part of the offender.
- Attack is skilfully planned and focused on a particular victim or victim population.
- Offences appear sporadic over time, occurring at any location, at any time of day or night (whenever the offender gets irritated or whenever a particular victim type is accessible).
- If planned, the offender will make excessive preparation.
- Offender knows the victim, or the victim symbolises something specific to the offender.

#### 4.5.3.2 Signature Behaviour
- There is a lot of anger directed towards the victim.
- Collateral victims in the crime scene are a result of anger and lack of planning. Collateral victims are guilty by association.
- The attack is directed towards a particular person, group, institution or organisation.

## 4.5.4   Sadistic

These include criminal behaviours that evidence offender gratification from the pain and suffering of others. The primary motivation for this behaviour is sexual; however, sexual expression for the offender is manifested in physical aggression, or torture, towards the victim. The offender wants the victim to suffer and wants to see the victim suffering. The goal of this behaviour is total victim fear and submission for the purposes of feeding the offender's sexual desires. The result is that the victim must be physically or psychologically abused and humiliated for the offender to become sexually excited and subsequently gratified. Any example of sadistic behaviour must include evidence of sexual gratification that an offender achieves as a result of directly experiencing the suffering of their conscious victim.

### 4.5.4.1   MO Behaviour
- The offender chooses or impersonates an occupation that allows them to act as an authority figure, placing them in a position to identify and acquire victims.
- Offences planned in exacting detail.
- Offences executed methodically.

### 4.5.4.2   Signature Behaviour
- The attacks can last for an extended period of time.
- Offender is good at presenting the image of a loving and sincere individual.
- Victims are strangers to the offender.

## 4.5.5   Profit Oriented

These include criminal behaviours that evidence an offender motivation oriented towards material or personal gain. These can be found in all types of homicides, robberies, burglaries, mugging, arson, bombing, kidnapping, and fraud to name just a few. This type of behaviour will not necessarily satisfy psychological and emotional needs. In terms of information systems crime and cyber-crime this type of profile is one of the most common.

- In 1987 Volkswagen lost almost $260 million as the result of an insider scam that created phony currency-exchange transactions and then covered them with real transactions a few days later. Four insiders and one outsider were convicted and jailed for six years.
- In 1994 Vladimir Levin broke into Citibank information systems and stole $10.6 million. This crime was committed by the Russian Mafia and Vladimir Levin was only a small part of the operation. They gained access to the Citibank network via a mis-configured modem, and from there broke into the VAX information systems that controlled the transfer of money on the banking network. From there levin transferred money from Citibank customers to accounts controlled by the Russian Mafia in Finland, the Netherlands, Germany, Israel and the United States. He is now serving time in a US prison.

- In mid July 1999, a British group of hackers broke into the information systems of VISA and stole confidential files. The group then issued a ransom demand for £10million and is also suspected of hiring out its services. In addition, in January 2000 a company called CD Universe confirmed that it had called in the FBI after being blackmailed by a hacker who had copied more than 300,000 of its customer credit card files.

### 4.5.5.1 MO Behaviour

- Shows interest in completing an offence as quickly as possible, and disinterested in activities that may prolong the offence.
- Depending on the skill and ability of the offender, they may attempt to gather intelligence on the victim in the belief that this will aid them in the successful execution of the crime.
- Depending on the skill and ability of the offender, they may attempt to cover their tracks by corrupting/destroying evidence.

### 4.5.5.2 Signature Behaviour

- This type of offender usually does not keep trophies or journals associated with the crime.
- Special materials are brought to the scene of the crime to aid in the execution of the crime.
- The offender will attempt to minimise their length of exposure to the victim in order to minimise the chance of being caught.

## 4.6 A Model of Information Systems Intrusions

Hackers operate in a characteristic fashion, performing a set of analytic, probing and exploiting behaviour with information systems or networks. This behaviour is identifiable and, to an extent, predictable. Within this element of the work package, the authors have constructed a general-purpose model of hackers' activity – a model which can be applied not simply to the recreational, low-skill "Kiddie Script" hacker aimlessly exploring information systems networks, but also to the more determined "professional" criminal.

Central to this model is the recognition of a sequence of activities, but crucially incorporating a sense of *expenditure* on the part of the intruder in terms of time, equipment, finance and commitment. Using this model, we can address the most fundamental of our questions for consideration: *"How do hackers penetrate information systems networks and systems?"* The diagram (Figure 4.1) provides one example of a flowcharted model for the individual decision points and activities that are common to intrusion attempts. The model is a simple, general-purpose one, in which hackers of any persuasion perform a series of increasingly refined actions against an increasingly focused set of target information systems.

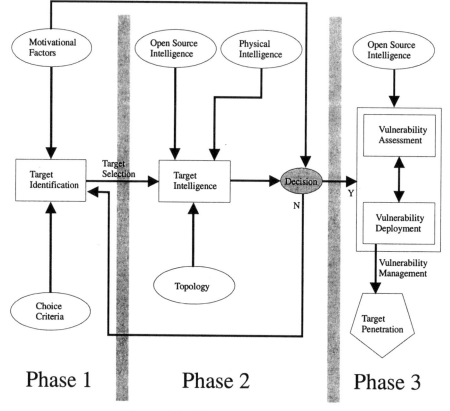

**Figure 4.1   The Hacking Process**

Figure 4.1 shows the basic process that an intruder would go through when penetrating a system. This process is divided into three distinct phases:

- The first phase is concerned with the processes by which an intruder identifies and selects the machine(s) and network(s) to be penetrated.
- The second phase is concerned with the processes by which an intruder would gather intelligence about the machine(s) and network(s) to be penetrated.
- Phase three is concerned with the processes by which an information systems system is penetrated. This phase involves the selection and deployment of a vulnerability against a set of target machine(s) and network(s).

## 4.6.1   Target Identification

The world contains untold millions of information systems, each of which might be a potential target for a hacker, depending upon the criteria which the hacker applies in selecting information systems for attention. For some hackers, every one of these millions of systems is indeed a potential target. They are as likely to attack any one as any other, with a selection criterion that is essentially opportunistic. For others, the total set of systems can be more finely subdivided, into systems which do not interest them and systems in which they have a very specific interest and a determination to perform a more focused sequence of activities.

In the target identification section of the model, we uncover the decisions and activities that have been applied by the hacker in uncovering the specific types of information systems of interest to them. All government information systems belonging to animal testing organisations; Irish Republican newspaper sites; all banking information systems networks, etc. This represents a sub-division of the universal set of information systems, with decisions made by the hacker based on two important elements:

- Their determination to penetrate the information systems.
- The specific criteria to be applied. These are the two important aspects in constructing a profile of the hackers' activity – the footprint.

## 4.6.2   Motivational Factors

The motivational factors are the specific real-world elements that drive a hacker to consider penetrating an information systems system. Analysis of information systems criminals suggests that the primary motivations include the following, sometimes in combination:

- The need to resolve intense personal problems such as job related difficulties, mental instability, debt, drug addiction, loneliness, jealousy, and the desire for revenge.
- Peer pressure and other challenges, for example: among malevolent hackers.
- Idealism and extreme advocacy, for example: by espionage agents and terrorists.
- Financial gain.

There are a variety of features that are worth considering in the question of motivation.

- Firstly, motivation provides the *impetus* for the hacking attempts.   It determines how persistent the hacker will be in his attempts. It determines how much effort (time, money) the hacker is prepared to expend on the attempt. It determines, in short, just how much one should be concerned about the hacker. This aspect is examined further below.
- A second feature of importance in motivation is the *continuity* that it implies. A strong and focused motivation – say in pursuit of animal rights or Irish liberation – will suffuse much of the individual's offensive activity. A recreational motivation will lead predominantly to a recreational approach to hacking attempts – though it is of course important to understand that recreational motivations can easily translate under certain circumstances, such as duress, into more sinister activities.
- This indeed leads to the third important feature of the motivation, which we can classify as its *flavour*. For example: is the hacker motivated by the opportunity for financial gain? Is the motivation ideological, personal or even

trivial in nature? Is the hacker perhaps motivated by external coercion? This flavour of motivation is important because it has a bearing on persistence, but also because it has a bearing on the selection criteria that the individual will apply.

Motivational factors in and of themselves cannot be *detected* by IDS technology – at least, not with the current state of the art. However, important motivational elements can be observed in the records that are collected and maintained by a variety of network IA systems, they represent important information that can and should be analysed. Abstracting such profiles is part and parcel of the objective of this new-generation IDS technology, allowing confident identification of individuals to be supported.

### 4.6.3    Choice Criteria

Driven by the motivation factors, hackers will apply their individual choice criteria to the universal set of information systems, abstracting the (possibly still large) set of targets in which they have an interest.

The choice criteria have several aspects to them:

* First of all, there is the question of criteria *freedom*; does the hacker in fact have any say in the specific criteria applied, or is the choice pre-determined by an external agency? Again, this element of target selection can be observed as a feature which we can think of as *persistence*: how determined does the intruder seem to be in the face of real or perceived IA measures?

* Secondly, there is the question of criteria *flexibility*: will the selected set of targets evolve over time, perhaps compromising choice as the difficulty of hitting specific targets becomes obvious? Or are the criteria immutable?

* Thirdly, what is the criteria breadth? How many systems are considered? Where are they located? How are the choice criteria effectively articulated?

Self-evidently, there is an interaction between motivational and choice aspects, leading to the determination, the persistence, the precision, etc, with which the hacker approaches the subsequent stages of his activity. The target identification stage provides the hacker with a set of potential victims to be considered: a set from which the specific targets are then selected.

### 4.6.4    Target Selection and Intelligence

The selection of specific targets from the broad set of potential victims is driven by a variety of elements. First and foremost, obviously there is an opportunistic element to even the most highly-focused attacks: a range of systems might be scanned in a particular order; or a more intelligent set of choices might be made, based on what intelligence can be gathered about the system on the part of the hacker. Some of this intelligence is also available to the *defender* of the system, although it is unlikely that more than a subset of this will be feasibly obtained by the IDS itself.

## 4.6.5   Open Source Intelligence (OSI)

Hackers will attempt to perform a review of open source material in an attempt to gather intelligence on the network topology for a target organisation or network. This can include such diverse elements as newsgroup postings referring to problems operating a particular type of information systems; evidence showing with whom the employees of the target normally communicate; and Computer Emergency Response Team (CERT) notices.[2] For example: a hacker could:

- Perform web searches on related names and terms using web search engines, such as:
  - ➢ http://www.altavista.digital.com
  - ➢ http://www.lycos.com
  - ➢ http://www.yahoo.com
  - ➢ http://www.google.com
- Analyse postings by users of target systems and target organisations on Usenet, such as:
  - ➢ http://www.altavista.digital.com
  - ➢ http://www.dejanews.com
- Analyse various open source exploit databases, such as:
  - ➢ http://www.securityfocus.com
  - ➢ http://packetstorm.security.com
  - ➢ http://www.technotronic.com
- Analyse various other open source material, such as:
  - ➢ http://www.opensource.org
  - ➢ http://www.phrack.com
  - ➢ http://www.ripe.net/db
  - ➢ http://catless.ncl.ac.uk/Risks
- Use remote DNS mining tools such as http://www.netsys.com/nslookup.html
- Connect to various information systems underground servers and acquire the password file for the target system.

It should be noted that from the perspective of an outsider penetrating an information systems network, a review of open source literature is an activity that an Intrusion Detection System is unlikely to detect. However, from the perspective of an employee within an organisation, it is possible that by logging all out-bound traffic one will be able to identify an insider accessing various types of open source intelligence. This type of analysis of traffic generated by employees within a system can be used as an early-warning system.

---

[2]   CERT announcements are an excellent source of information about systems' vulnerabilities; however, the system defenders are usually very slow to learn about the new vulnerabilities and make the needed IA changes. However, hackers are not!

## 4.6.6   Topology

The topology of the target information systems network includes a variety of elements:

- the type and distribution of information systems;
- the nature of the network;
- the geographic coverage of the network; and
- the personnel responsibilities within each office, etc.

In a classic sense, network topology is uncovered by hackers using a variety of easily obtained scanner tools, or through the open-source intelligence available to them, etc. In more determined attacks, though, topology can be as readily determined through subversion of personnel, through physical intelligence gathering, or through access to trusted third parties. Once the topology of the network is understood, a realistic assessment of the target's potential to the hacker can be produced, and based on that, a decision point is reached.

## 4.6.7   The Deployment Decision

The decision whether or not to engage in an attack will be based upon the motivation factors of the intruder. The decision is based upon the following factors:

- How much it will cost to penetrate the machine and achieve the objective?
- What are the risks of penetrating the machine?
- How much profit to be made if the intruder is successful?

The cost and risks associated with penetrating a machine will then be set against how much benefit the intruder will derive if successful. The intruder will then simply make a decision based upon cost-benefit analysis. If the intruder is motivated by greed, then the decision will be based upon financial factors such as how much money it will cost to achieve the objectives, and how money will be made when the objective is achieved. If on the other hand, an intruder is motivated by political or ideological factors, then the decision is based upon the ideological beliefs and experiences of the intruder; and the peer recognition and acceptance of a group.

## 4.6.8   Vulnerability Management

This is the phase of activity when the intruder identifies a vulnerability on a target machine and then attempts to exploit that vulnerability to gain unauthorised access. An intruder may have to use several vulnerabilities in order to penetrate a system, and once that is achieved an intruder may have to use several exploits to achieve their objective. Thus the assessment and deployment of a vulnerability in order to achieve an objective will form a time-line that will form part of the intruder's footprint.

The time-line associated with an attack, and activity on that time-line that is created by the process of an intruder attacking a system, will be virtually unique to every intruder. The reason for this is that the time-line will represent the decision process that an intruder executed when penetrating a system. It will also present the knowledge, in term of vulnerabilities known, that an intruder possesses. The status of an intruder's knowledge will give us the ability to access the level of threat posed by that intruder.

The decision process that an intruder executes when penetrating a system will also be influenced by the motivational factors that drive a person's behaviour. For example: a criminal that is driven by financial reward will be making decisions based upon how much an object is worth versus how much it will cost to obtain. In addition, a political activist may have little in the way of technical skill, but be prepared to spend a lot of time and money in order to achieve an objective. For both of the examples, the objectives could be the same, but the set of IA countermeasures one would deploy against each threat may be different.

The reason for this is that each incident will have its own time-line that is dependent upon the decisions that the intruder has made in order to penetrate a system. One of the contributing factors to the decision process of any individual is the political and social belief system of that individual. Consequently the footprint of an intruder will provide us with the ability to suggest the motivational factors governing an intruder's actions; and recommend a set of countermeasures to counter the activity of the intruder.

## 4.7  Summary

Information systems-related crimes or computer crimes can be classified according to the impact on the computer, e.g. object of the crime, subject of the crime, tool of the crime, and/or symbol of the crime. The offender's modus operandi may vary but functions to protect the offender, support a successful crime and facilitate an escape. An offender's profile can be viewed by organisational, operational, behavioural and resource characteristics.

Motives include power assurance, power assertive, anger retaliatory, sadistic, and profit-oriented. A model for information systems intrusion includes target identification, motivational factors, choice criteria, target selection and intelligence, topology, deployment decision and vulnerability management.

# Chapter 5

## IA Trust and Supply Chains

In today's information-driven and information-dependent organisations, trust and supply chains are key elements. In this chapter, the concept of trust will be explored, in particular within organisations, processes, and systems. In addition, the critical dependencies that now exist for most organisations using information systems to manage and coordinate a supply chain will be analysed and discussed.

## 5.1    Introduction

Over the past two decades, communications technology has developed to a point where new methods of working and approaches to commerce are exponentially changing. While such technology has the potential to revolutionise the way that people do business, both individuals and organisations remain very sceptical about their applicability, use and ability to protect information. If the technology is to realise its potential, then ways need to be identified that will help to facilitate its uptake and use. It has been suggested that:

*"Participants in collaborative work relationships are likely to vary in the knowledge they possess, and must therefore engage each other in dialogues that allow them to pool resources and knowledge, and negotiate their differences to accomplish their tasks."*

Organisations function because people co-operate with each other. A successful organisation is one with constantly evolving trust relationships. If two people are to communicate to solve a problem then there has to be an element of trust. In fact, virtually all transactions in every domain of human endeavour are built upon the concept of trust to such an extent that without it society and organisations could not function. Ron Chernow summarised this nicely when he wrote in the book *The House of Morgan*:

*"Utermyer:     Is not commercial credit based primarily upon money and property?*
*Morgan:      No, sir, the first thing is character.*
*Utermyer:     Before money and property?*

*Morgan:*          *Before money or anything else. Money cannot buy it. Because a*
                   *man I do not trust could not get money on all the bonds in*
                   *Christendom."*

Organisations are networks of people who co-operate in order to achieve a variety of goals, and the social networks within them are built upon trusting relationships. Evidence shows that when people have too little, or too much, trust within an organisation then that organisation can fail to function. Modern management now recognises the importance that trust plays in the governing and managing of people's behaviour. In short, trust properly developed is the glue that binds organisations together and allows them to function.

Within organisations that make extensive use of an information technology (IT) infrastructure, IA plays a vital role in the creation and mediation of trust, and consequently of doing business. For example: if two organisations are using electronic mail to engage in contract negotiations then it is vital that the confidentiality, integrity and availability of the electronic mail messages be guaranteed. If any of these were to breakdown, then it would adversely affect the relationship and could ultimately result in loss of a business relationship.

Where IA and trust really come together is in the area of electronic commerce. When people are engaging in commercial transactions across the Internet it is vital that a trustworthy image be created and maintained. For example:

- In July 1995, Amazon.com opened its virtual doors with a mission to use the Internet to transform book buying into the fastest, easiest, and most enjoyable shopping experience possible. It knew that in order for it to succeed it would need to create an image so that its customers could trust it to deliver what was ordered and to keep their information in a private and secure manner. To this end they created a privacy policy which explicitly told its customers what information they would gather and how they would treat this information. It also spelt out exactly what Amazon would accept responsibility for and what its customers are responsible for.
- On Friday, 26 November 1999, a security hole forced the Halifax Building Society to shut its online share shop after a breach of security allowed customers to view other people's accounts. The effect of this incident along with other incidents such as security breaches at Visa (January 2000), and Power-gen (July 2000), is to undermine the trust that people place in doing business online.

In short, IA is the oil that lubricates the workings of trust in an IT environment. Without IA it is impossible to create trust and consequently impossible to do business.

## 5.2    Developing a Conceptual Model of Trust

Over the past decade, various researchers have attempted to define and model trust. Each of these has drawn upon a particular area of concern, such as sociological, business, organisational and technological. Each of these attempts to define trust within a particular domain, and thus the lessons learned from applying each of the models is not transferable.

What is required is a general model of trust that is transferable across multiple application domains, and that has the ability to make use of benchmarks. The conceptual model of trust presented is a meta-model of trust that attempts to draw together the various strands of research, and to create a model of trust that has a general scope of application. In short, it aims to provide people with a tool that can be used to understand and measure trust within and between organisations and people.

## 5.2.1   The NICE Model of Trust

This conceptual model of trust has four distinct components that are defined as follows:

### 5.2.1.1   Need

The concept of "need" is one of the four, distinct components. For example: I can trust you because I know you need the deal to take place, you are aware of serious penalty clauses, a time limit on your side is close, or you could trust me since I am the one in trouble. I may also need to trust someone as an article of faith, perhaps because I cannot accept a situation without it (e.g. trust in a doctor or a priest, irrespective of whether they can do anything or not). This is a predominantly tactical and calculating approach. A patient may trust a health care provider because they need to feel that they will get better, and that they are not prepared to consider the alternatives.

The need to trust can also be based on the motivation factors governing the behaviour of a person. It is important to note that motivation factors for trusting will always relate to people and never to an information system. The motivation factors can include the following set of needs a) physiological, b) safety, c) love, d) esteem, and e) self-actualisation.

### 5.2.1.2   Identification

The concept of "identification" is another of the four, distinct components. This parameter is more strategic than the previous one and more openly subjective. For example: I trust you because I believe we share a common set of values, mission, vision, roles, culture etc.

The common set of values can be derived from the following:

- Membership in a social club or society, such as supporting the same football team.
- Membership in a political party.
- Membership in a religious organisation.
- Membership in a particular division within an organisation.
- Performance in a particular role or activity.

One example of this type of trust could be that a patient is only willing to talk to or accept-treatment-from the patient's own doctor. The justification that a patient could give for this behaviour is that the doctor understands the social environment that the patient lives in as the doctor lives in the same social environment and is a member of the community.

### 5.2.1.3   Competence

Competence is the third component. For example: I trust you because your processes are visibly good and your skills are accredited. A person wishing to instil trust in another may say "Trust me because I am an expert".

In particular, competence based trust can be established through:

- Qualification from recognised bodies or agencies.
- Supervision by a recognised body or agency.
- Knowledge of the business process and value chains that are at work within the organisation.

Medical doctors can be seen to possess competence-based trust because of the Royal College of Physicians (RCP) that accredits their qualifications in the UK. Thus, one can have competence-based trust because of the qualification. In addition, the General Medical Council (GMC) in the UK monitors the behaviour of doctors and there is a process by which one can complain about a doctor. If a person was to complain about the behaviour of a doctor, and that complaint was upheld, then the doctor could be stopped from practising medicine. Consequently, one can have competence-based trust in a doctor because one knows the business process and value chains which govern the evaluation of the behaviour.

### 5.2.1.4   Evidence

Evidential based trust is based upon an individual having evidence, the fourth component, to support the assertion that they or another individual are trustworthy. Evidence based trust comes in various forms. These include:

- First hand-evidence– you have direct experience of how another party behaves and so can decide how they will behave in a given situation.
- Second-hand evidence– you have indirect experience of how another party behaves. A person that you know and have contact with has the direct experience of how the other party behaves.  The question with second-hand evidence is:
  - How trustworthy is the person who has the direct experience of the behaviour of the other party?
- Third-hand evidence– you have indirect experience of how another party behaves. In conversational terms we may say "a friend of a friend" has the direct experience of how another party behaves. The questions with third-hand evidence are:
  - How trustworthy is the person who has the direct experience of the behaviour of the other party?
  - How trustworthy are the people in the social network that leads from the first-hand knowledge to you?

This progression from first-hand to third-hand evidence leads on to nth-hand evidence, where with nth-hand evidence there are n-1 people in the social network from you to the other party performing the trusted action.

## 5.2.2 The Trust Footprint

The four components of the trust model can be used to create a footprint of a trusted relationship, and this footprint can be used to benchmark the current and future status of the trust relationship. The purpose of the footprint is to allow us to analyse the trusted relationship and to identify the factors that facilitate the creation of trust, and the factors that destroy trust. The footprint model provides a visual mechanism for analysing and benchmarking the trust relationship.

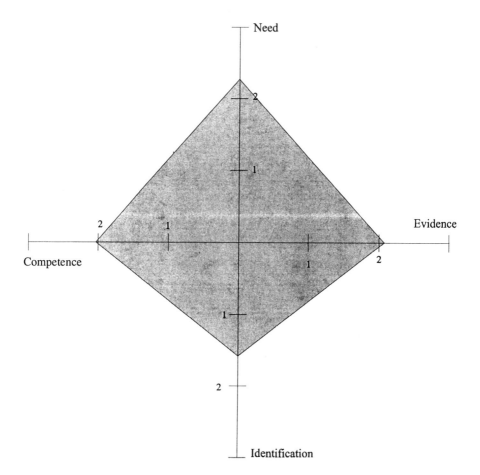

**Figure 5.1  The Trust Footprint**

In Figure 5.1, the scales that are used on the axes are as follows: a) +1 denotes compete trust, b) -1 denotes complete mistrust, and c) 0 denotes no-trust. The term no-trust is used to indicate that an individual is neutral about trusting another individual. Some factors in the environment will act to reduce the area of the footprint, by reducing the values on the axes. For example, if a doctor misdiagnosis a patient and the patient finds out, then this will have the effect of reducing the competence component of the trust model. If a doctor makes an early diagnosis of an illness for a patent, and the diagnosis is correct and saves the patient's life, then that is going to increase the competence component of the trust model. Consequently, the trust footprint allows us to examine the possible effect that a breakdown in IA will have upon a relationship.

The footprint model is a graphical representation of how much trust the maker of the footprint feels towards the target of the footprint. Figure 5.1 tells us that:

- The owner of the footprint has an element of mistrust towards the individual who is the target of the footprint because there is a negative element of identification between the individuals (the value of identification axis is negative).
- The owner of the footprint trusts the target to be a competent individual (the value of competence axis is positive).
- The owner of the footprint has an element of limited trust towards the target because the owner believes that the target needs the transaction to take place (the value of need axis is a small positive).
- The owner of the footprint has an element of no trust towards the target as there is no, or limited, historical data to support the assertion that the target is trustworthy (the value of evidence axis is zero).

This visual representation gives the ability to analyse the component of trust that is weakest, and to identify the actions required to improve that value which would have the greatest reward on the overall value of the trust between the owner and the target of the footprint. For example:

- In May 1999, UK Internet savings bank, Egg, owned by Prudential, rushed to close a security flaw that allowed some users to see other potential savers' confidential financial information.
- In July 2000, the UK electricity and gas supplier, Powergen, confirmed a security breach in which thousands of customers may have had their banking details revealed.

The result of both of these incidents is a loss of competence in the ability of organisations to manage e-commerce systems in a secure manner; and the creation of evidence that supports the assertion that the Internet is not a safe place to do business. Consequently, the net result of the incidents is a loss in area of the trust footprint.

## 5.3   Supply Chains

The term supply chain encompasses all activities associated with the flow and transformation of goods from the raw materials stage, through to the end user, as well as the associated information flows. Materials and information flow both up and down the supply chain. A supply chain includes the management of information systems, sourcing and procurement, production scheduling, order processing, inventory management, warehouse, customer service, after sales support, etc. Supply networks consist of all the organisations that provide inputs, either directly or indirectly to the organisation. If we consider an individual firm that makes hard disks for computers, then when examining the supply chain for that company, we must examine both its upstream supplier network and its downstream distribution channel. The company has to order parts/services from its suppliers and manage that process, and supply parts/services to its customers and manage that process. In essence, a supply chain is a series of linked suppliers and customers; every customer is in turn a supplier to the next downstream organisation until the finished product/service reaches the ultimate end user. Figure 5.2 illustrates a supply chain.

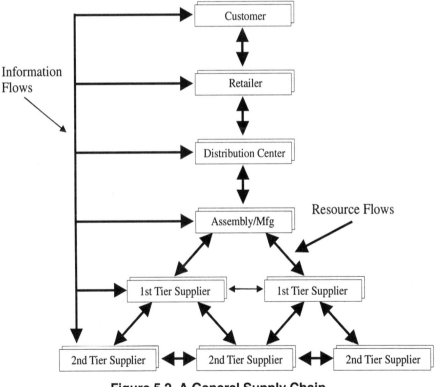

**Figure 5.2  A General Supply Chain**

The $2^{nd}$ tier supplier supplies goods/services to the $1^{st}$ tier suppliers who then in turn supply goods and services to a manufacturing organisation. The term manufacturing organisation is used to denote any organisation that creates or makes a product or service. For example: the new provider CNN (Cable Network News) can be seen as a manufacturing organisation with the news agency Reuters acting as a $1^{st}$ tier supplier. The manufacturing organisation distributes its product/services via a distribution centre to a retailer. The retailer then sells the product/services to the ultimate end user known as the customer. On the Internet, an Internet service provider (ISP) functions as the distributor.

In today's modern world, many organisations have adopted the just-in-time supply chain management (JiT) philosophy. This means that they only hold the stock that they require for a few days, thus organisations minimise the amount of storage space required and have more deliveries of stock on a regular basis. This supply philosophy however assumes that the supply chain is functioning. If a supplier runs out of stock then this can have severe consequences for organisations further down the supply chain. For example: in September 2000, a group of people blockaded a fuel depot and distribution points within the UK. Within two to three days, people were running out of fuel. The consequences were that people could not get to work, and that distributors could not distribute goods to the retailers. Thus, shops started to run out of commodities such as bread, milk and toilet roll. Had the fuel blockade not been lifted when it was, it may not have been long before companies were forced into liquidation due to the lack of supplies. The other interesting point to note about the fuel blockade was that as a result of the blockade and the inability of the government to deal with the people manning the blockades, many people lost their trust in the government and its ability to govern fairly and respond to the needs of the people.

Supply chains are made even more complex when one considers the complex interrelationships that exist between organisations. Figure 5.3 illustrates the many faceted relationships and dependencies that exist with the modern commercial environment. For example: most organisations make use of water, electricity and telecommunications, and there are numerous examples of what can happen to computer systems when the power fails.

The following illustrate the complex relationships that exist between many different services in a supply chain:

- On 2 October 1984, a power failure resulted in millions of customers in 10 western US states being without power. The problem was traced to a computer error in an Oregon substation.
- A former cost estimator for Southeastern Color Lithographers in Athens, Georgia, was convicted of destroying billing and accounting data on a XENIX system. The lost data had the effect of disrupting the supply chain for the organisation. The conviction was based on an audit trail linking the delete commands to his terminal (but not necessarily to him). The employer claimed damages of $400,000 in lost business and downtime.
- On 29 May 1989, a squirrel shorted out a power supply at SRI in California. The power was off for nine hours and many computers remained down after that time – some with their monitors burned out.

- An AT&T crew removing an old cable in Newark, New Jersey accidentally severed a fiber-optic cable carrying more than 100,000 calls. Starting at 9.30a.m. on 4 January 1991, and continuing for much of the next day, the effects included:
  - Downtime of the New York Mercantile Exchange and several commodities exchanges.
  - Disruption of Federal Aviation Administration (FAA) air-control communication in the New York metropolitan area.
  - Lengthy flight delays into, and out of, the New York area.
  - Blockage of 60% of the long-distance telephone calls into, and out of, New York City.

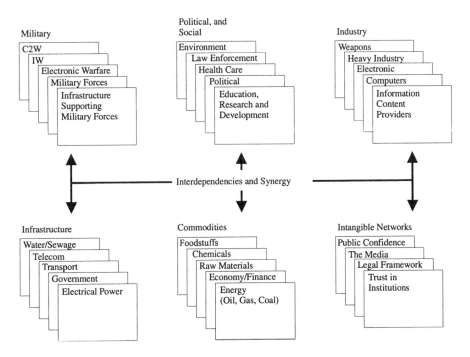

**Figure 5.3  Complex Relationships**

The manipulation of supply chains is not new and has been used to devastating effect in 1943. In the summer of that year, the British Navy and Coastal Command managed to sink seven out of eight supply boats sent to re-supply the German U-boats. In essence, what they did was to disrupt the supply chain for the German U-boats. This disruption allowed the British and Americans to win the war of the Atlantic and thus establish and supply a second front in World War II.

Modern information technology can introduce extremely complex dependencies. During the Gulf War, computer vandals cracked into US government computers at 34 military sites to steal information about troop movements, missile capabilities, and other secret information. They then offered it to the Iraqis, but the Iraqis rejected it because they considered the information a hoax. Dr. Eugene Schultz, former head of computer security at the US Department of Energy, has told the British Broadcasting Company: "We realised that these files should not have been stored on Internet-capable machines. This was a huge mistake".

The lessons that we learn from this are that in terms of information assurance, an organisation is extremely dependent upon its supply chain, and physical security is an important part of IA. In terms of IA, the dependencies that govern the flow of information around an organisation are crucial to business success.

These dependencies can become critical when one examines the extent to which a lot of organisations are now outsourcing the provision and support of an information system and an information systems infrastructure. Let us consider a fictitious organisation called Blyths Books. This company is located in Cardiff, Wales, and sells rare books on the Internet via online auctions. It is considered to be one of the best online bookshops on the Internet and has one of the largest databases of rare books' rare book sellers and customers in the world. It has a large WEB presence (www.blythsbooks.com) and makes use of a single local Internet service provider (ISP) called Welsh ISP Ltd. (www.wisp.com).

In addition, Blyths Books has also outsourced its information services provision to another local company called Welsh-Net Inc., which also manages and supports the Blyths Books Web site. Blyths Books has also outsourced its responsibility for physical security and cleaning of its offices to another local company called Group-101. The objectives of Blyths Books when making use of outsourcing/facilitates-management companies are to minimise costs and maximise profits. The consequence of this is that any of the outsourcing companies has potential access to some/all of Blyths Books corporate information. The loss of any corporate information for Blyths Books could have devastating consequences for the company.

When using a supply chain to control/support a critical organisation function one is only secure as the weakest link in the chain. Consequently, many organisations are now demanding the organisations in their supply chain take IA seriously and meet certain minimum standards.

## 5.4    Analysis of Supply Chains

Analysis of supply chains can be conducted using the Porter Value Chain Model. This model describes the various components that make up an organisation and its supply chain.

Value chain analysis has been widely used as a means for describing the activities within and around an organisation, and relating them to an assessment of the competitive strength of an organisation. Value chain analysis was originally introduced as an analysis tool that was designed to shed light on the "*value added*" of separate steps in complex manufacturing processes, in order to determine where cost improvements could be made and/or value creation improved.

One of the key aspects of value chain analysis is the recognition that organisations are much more than a random collection of machines, money and people. These resources are of no value unless deployed into activities and organised into routines and systems which ensure that products or services are produced which are valued by the finer customer/user. In other words, it is these competencies to perform particular activities and the ability to manage linkages between activities, which are the source of competitive advantage for organisations. It is also these manage linkages that create the potential for the activities of one organisation to affect the performance of another. Thus, when sharing information across a supply, the rule is that one only is as secure as the weakest link in the supply chain. Consequently, some organisations with large and complex supply chains are starting to mandate that suppliers, distributors and resellers comply with security standards such as BS7799.

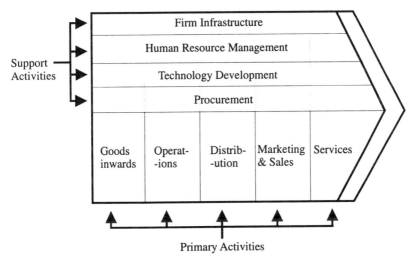

**Figure 5.4 The Value Chain**

An understanding of critical dependencies within a supply chain must start with an identification of the value activities that an organisation performs. Figure 5.4 is a schematic representation of a value chain within an organisation. Value chains are a way of modelling the organisation in order to answer questions activity by activity. In order to answer these questions, the organisation must study the primary activities that get the product, or service, to the customer and the support activities that facilitate that. In addition, there are linkages between these activity processes. Increasingly, it is with improvements to these linkages that information systems can offer the most support and help an organisation achieve a competitive advantage.

The *primary activities* of the organisation are grouped into five main areas:

- Inbound logistics.
- Operations.
- Outbound logistics.

- Marketing and sales.
- Service.

Each of the primary activities is linked to *support activities*. The *support activities* can be divided into four areas:

- Procurement.
- Technology.
- Development.
- Human resources.
- Management.
- Infrastructure.

## 5.4.1   Primary Activities

There are five basic activities that apply to supply chains. They are:

- *Inbound Logistics* are the activities concerned with receiving, storing and distributing the inputs to the product/service. These include materials handling, stock control, transport, etc.
- *Operations* transform these various inputs into the final product or service, for example: matching, packaging, assembly, testing, etc.
- *Outbound Logistics* collect, store and distribute the product to the customers. For tangible products this would involve warehousing, materials handling, transport etc. In the case of services, it may be more concerned with bringing customers to the service if it is at a fixed location.
- *Marketing and Sales* provide the means whereby consumers/users are made aware of a product/service and are able to purchase it. This would include sales administration, advertising, selling etc.
- *Service* covers all those activities which enhance or maintain the value of a product/service, such as installation, repair, training, spares, etc.

## 5.4.2   Support Activities

There are four basic activities that apply to support activities. They are:

- *Infrastructure*: the systems of planning, finance, quality control, etc. are crucially important to an organisation's strategic capabilities in all primary activities. Infrastructure also consists of the structures and routines of the organisation which sustain its culture.
- *Human Resource Management*: this is a particularly important area which transcends all primary activities. It is concerned with those activities involved in recruiting, training, developing, and rewarding people within the organisation.
- *Technology Development*: all value activities have a technology, even if it is simply "know-how". The key technologies may be concerned directly with the product, a process, or with a particular resource.

- **Procurement**: this refers to the process for acquiring the various resource inputs to the primary activities.

## 5.4.3   Industry Value Chain Showing Strategic Alliances Between Organisations

One of the key features of most organisations is that very rarely does a single organisation undertake all of the value activities from the product design through to the delivery of the final product or service to the final consumer. There is usually specialisation of the role and any one organisation is part of the wider value system, which creates a product or service. Figure 5.5 begins to illustrate just how easily a complex web of interdependencies can be created.

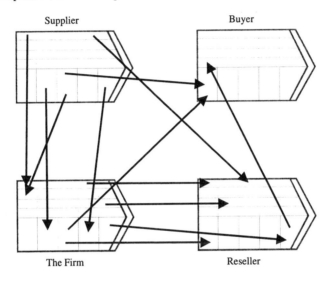

**Figure 5.5  Strategic Alliances between Organisations**

In understanding the basis of an organisation's capability, it is not sufficient to look at the organisation's internal position alone. Much of the value creation will occur in the supply and distribution chains, and this *whole process* needs to be analysed and understood. For example: the quality of an automobile when it reaches the final purchaser is not only influenced by the activities, which are undertaken within the manufacturing company itself; the quality of components and the performance of the distributors also determine it.  The ability of an organisation to influence the performance of other organisations in the supply chain may be crucially important in competence and of course in competitive advantage.

Some organisations have integrated their supply chain to such an extent that it is very difficult to tell the difference between the suppliers, distributors and resellers. For example:

- The Analytical Systems Automotive Purchasing (ASAP) system helped customers of the American Hospital Supply Corporation (AHSC) automate the ordering part of their stock control by placing order entry terminals in their hospitals. This elimination of effort for the customer was, inevitably, popular with all of AHSC customers. This system grew out of a supply system that was installed between AHSC and the Stanford Medical Center. In order for AHSC to maintain its market share, the ASAP has been continually enhanced and supported.

- Federal Express was started-up in 1973 as an overnight delivery service. From the very beginning, the company invested in IT and integrated it into its supply chain. Through the use of technology to automate and control the business, the company has been able to reduce operating costs. The low cost and high efficiency of the business is supported by systems such as the "cradle to grave" tracking of packages system. The IT dependency envisioned by the founders of Federal Express has been well managed and the worldwide market share that Federal Express now has is testimony to this.

The above examples show how supply chains have been managed and integrated to achieve a competitive advantage for the organisation. However, they also show the extent to which such companies now rely on information technology to do business. Take away IA, and the technology can't be trusted or stops functioning. Take away the technology or not trust it, and the company would simply stop functioning.

## 5.5   Summary

IA processes are used to assist in providing "trust" of information systems and information. The NICE model of trust incorporates need, identification, competence and evidence. Supply chains and just-in-time inventories rely on IA to succeed. If any part of the IA is weak, there is an increased risk to information and information systems, thus to the corporation.

# Chapter 6

## Basic IA Concepts and Models

Information Assurance (IA) is based on concepts and models that have migrated from the field of information systems security. This chapter will discuss these basic concepts as well as some models adapted for IA use. Although many of these models have been around for some time, they are sometimes controversial. For example: some believe they are inaccurate, others believe they are no longer useful. However, the models are valid and useful when properly implemented and integrated into an IA program. These basic IA concepts and models are of little use if applied in an isolated, stovepipe approach. None on their own is the answer to information protection and defence. They are just part of a totally integrated IA program.

## 6.1    Introduction

The various information assurance (IA) models that will subsequently be addressed may all seem different; however, there are some similarities. They all do have one common theme. They are the building blocks, the sub-systems, sub-processes of a basic information assurance system and/or program.

It is important to have a common definition and understanding of terms in order to understand the concepts and ideas behind the models. For those that believe they understand the terms, re-reading them will help reinforce that understanding or ensure a better understanding. After all, miscommunications are at the heart of many misunderstandings. If you are responsible for establishing an information assurances program, and are relying on some aspects of this book to help you, the last thing you need is to misinterpret what is being discussed because of different definitions for the same terms.

## 6.2   IA Goals and Objectives

Like information systems security and information security, the models discussed below are based on simple, yet often misunderstood basic concepts of information assurance's goals and objectives:

- *Minimise the probability of information assurance vulnerability*: in other words, you want to minimise the risks that your information systems and the information that they store, process and transmit are vulnerable to any threats, whether they are deliberate or accidental.
- *Minimise the damage if a vulnerability is exploited*: if you are attacked because of some vulnerability you were not aware of or you decided to take a chance, a risk, that the vulnerability would not be exploited, you want to be sure that the damages caused by the attacker are minimal. Also, one must be prepared to defend against human errors.
- *Provide a method to recover efficiently and effectively from the damage*: since no one can be assured that it is impossible to successfully attack them, there must always be a "back-up plan", a process in place to get back to normal operations as quickly as possible. Remember that in today's fast-paced environment, the old saying "time is money" is truer now than ever before. By the way, watch out for human errors. They will occur more often than attacks and can cause as much, if not more damage.


## 6.3   Three Basic Concepts

There are three basic concepts that should be established in order to assist in the above stated goals.  These baseline concepts are as follows:

- Access controls.
- Individual accountability.
- Audit trails.

Let's look at each of this triad in order to understand why they are so important to the protection and defence of information and information systems.

### 6.3.1   Access Controls

The basic defence to support information assurances is the concept of access control. The two basic forms of access controls are physical access controls and logical access controls.

#### 6.3.1.1   *Physical Access Controls*

In today's modern corporations, the information systems are located on almost every desktop and in every department of the corporation. Thus, access to the facility is the first line of defence in protecting the information maintained, processed and stored by those systems.

Physical access controls consist of human and mechanical access controls. Human access controls are the people who have responsibility for ensuring only authorised personnel enter a building, specific office or area. When one thinks of such human access controllers, one quickly thinks of security guards. However, access control responsibility may also rest with each employee and others such as the receptionists, and other administrative personnel who work in a specific area or office where access must be controlled due to the sensitive information and information systems contained therein.

### 6.3.1.2   *Logical Access Controls*

Once one has obtained physical access to the facility or information system, logical access controls are used to provide the next filtering system to assist in ensuring that only authorised users have access to information systems and information. Because of the need for telecommuting and mobile access to information systems and their automated information, the use of physical barriers have decreased in importance while the need for good logical access controls have increased. One cannot provide the same degree of information protection through physical access controls as before since more and more information systems' users are mobile. One must understand that information assurances are never a one hundred percent proposition. There are many trade-offs with the priority established by executive management — and that priority is, business operations have priority over assurances.

Logical access controls consist of the software programs on an information system that controls access to that system.[1] Just as physical access controls are vulnerable to penetration, so are the software programs used to control logical access to information. Generally, the access control software requires that a user enter some sort of identification. That identification may be a group identification name or number, or one specific to that user. Once entered, a password is generally required. That password may be a shared password, or one specific to that individual.

In this day and age, it is surprising that not all systems control access through a unique, individual user access control identification number or name, and password. If such a process were in place, it violates another basic concept of information assurances through access and that is individual accountability.

## 6.3.2   Individual Accountability

Individual accountability simply means that each individual who has access to an information system has a unique identification number or name and also a password known only to that individual – or some other way of determining the specific individual taking action, e.g. biometric devices. This assists in identifying systems users in the event there is a violation of information assurance policies, procedures or processes.

---

[1] The term "system" includes standalone (non-networked systems), networks to include intranets and any Internet or other global network interfaces.

It is true that such a system is vulnerable as someone's identification and password can be compromised. Thus, another individual would be in a position to "masquerade" as the authorised user. Remember that the computer through its access control software allows access to information by *assuming* that the individual entering a correct user name or other identification and a correct password, assumed to be known only by the authorised user, is in fact that authorised user.

There are numerous, and free, software programs available from various sources, e.g. Internet Web sites, that can be implemented to do a mass attack against a system to determine the identification and password used by particular users. So, this process is far from secure. However, it is not only one of the first line of defences in an IA program, it is often the mainstay and only line of defence. A true but sad commentary on the state of IA efforts in this modern, information dependent and information based world.

One must understand that each of these methods acts as a "filter" which allows the presumed authorised users access to systems and information. Thus it helps assure such things as the confidentiality, integrity and availability of information, while at the same time filtering out, and providing physical and logical barriers to the less sophisticated unauthorised users' access attempts.

## 6.3.3   Audit Trails

The last basic concept to discuss is the use of audit trails. The audit trails are nothing more than historical records of events that have already occurred. They do not help assure any information or information systems protection or defences. Their sole purpose from an IA standpoint is to provide a historical record of events that can be re-enacted or tracked to assist in identifying events that had occurred which compromised in some way sensitive information or the information systems. Audit trail records consists of such things as manual logs of individuals who entered a facility or area, video recordings from closed circuit television cameras (CCTVs), automated logs maintained by the systems themselves. In addition, there are many software products on the market that assist in maintaining audit trails of events on the systems that track both programs (e.g. batch programs implemented and running) and users' activities.

Often automated audit trail records are kept to a minimum as many information technology (IT) staffs say that it impedes efficient processing of information. It is not surprising to find that the automated audit trail records keeping have been completely turned off by some IT staffs.

As a minimum, most automated audit trail records track individual users through their identification name or number. The use of the individual and unique password by a user, as noted above, is considered the unique identifier that ties the user to the activities on the systems as noted by the audit trail records or logs. Often, the logs only identify a user as accessing a specific system at a specific time and date. Many access control programs have audit trail records that can record a users activities to different degrees of granularity, to include monitoring each key stroke made by a user.

# 6.4    The Information Value (IV) Model

Information has value and to determine that value, various models have been developed. They have not been a resounding success; however, the basic philosophy of information value as it relates to time must be discussed as a premise to information assurances. This is because information assurance is only required when information has some value. Information without value need not be protected or defended as it is of little importance to the holder of the information.

## 6.4.1    Valuing Information

The basic premise is that certain information and information systems have value. The value of information systems varies over time and is depreciated on the accounting books of the corporation. However, from an information assurance viewpoint, the value of information systems does not depreciate since it is obviously vital to storing, processing and transmitting the corporation's or government agency's information. However, the main emphasis here is on the value of the information processed, stored or transmitted by the corporate information systems.

All information, regardless of its value, is time-sensitive and time-dependent. In other words, information has value for only a certain period of time. For example: information relative to a new, unique corporate widget must be highly protected, and that includes its related electronic drawings, diagrams, processes, etc.  However, once the new widget is announced to the public, complete with photographs of the widget, selling price, etc., much of the protected information no longer needs protection.

That information which once required protection to maintain the secrecy of the corporation's new widget can now be eliminated. This will obviously save money for the corporation because information protection is expensive when correctly done. Those costs must be reduced or eliminated as soon as possible. It is the constant task of those responsible for the corporation's IA program to continuously look for methods to accomplish this objective.

## 6.4.2    How to Determine the Value of Corporate Information

Determining the value of a corporation's information is a very important task, but one that is very seldom done with any systematic, logical approach by any corporation. However, in order to provide a cost-effective IA program, this task should be undertaken. The sophistication of such a process must be weighed against the costs and benefits to the corporation.

The consequences of not properly establishing a value and then classifying the information accordingly could lead to over-protection which is costly, or under-protection, which could lead to the loss of that information, thus profits and/or the competitive edge.

To determine the value of information, the IA professionals must first understand what is meant by information; what is meant by value. The IA professionals must also know how to properly categorise and classify the information; and what guidelines are set forth by the corporation for determining the value and subsequently the protection requirements for that information. In addition, how the corporation perceives the information and its value is crucial to classifying it.[2]

Remember that if the information has value, it must be protected; protection is expensive. One should only protect that information which:

- Requires protection.
- Only in the manner necessary based on the value of that information.
- Only for the period required.

## 6.4.3   The Value of Information

One might ask, "Does all the information of a corporation or government agency have value?" If you were asked that question, what would be your response? The follow-on question would be "What information does *not* have value?" Is it that information which the receiver of the information determines has no value? When the originator of the information says so? Who determines if information has value?

These are questions that the IA professionals must ask – and answer – before trying to establish a process to set a value to any information. As you read through this material, think about the information where you work, how it's protected, why it is protected in the manner it is being protected, etc.

The originator of the information should determine its value based on a standard corporate criterion. People who rely on access to specific information place a value on that information. That value may be different from that stated by the originator of that information. That is understandable since not only is the value of information time-dependent, but it is also dependent upon the perceptions and needs of its holder. The following example is provided:

- It may be the task of an engineer to design a specific part. After the part is designed for a highly advanced widget, it is given a high protection value due to the need to keep it away from the corporate competitors. However, once that part is designed, classified as "corporate proprietary" and transmitted to a corporate database, it is no longer of importance to the engineer who then goes on to the next assigned task. However, that part design now being accessed by a person responsible for making the mould for that part is of utmost importance. For without that information, that person could not accomplish the task of making the mould. In addition, its protection from an overall corporate viewpoint is still required at the highest level to assist in protecting it from the corporation's competitors. However, once the widget is produced, marketed

---

[2] In the context used here, the term "classify" has nothing to do with classification as it relates to national security information such as Confidential, Secret, and Top Secret, but only as a way of categorising information based on its value.

and sold, the part design is not important, as reverse engineering the product is a very simple process. So the drawing for that part is no longer information worth protecting. Furthermore, those involved in the initial development of the part also no longer consider that information worthy of protection. However, the corporation may still provide some level of protection so that the corporation's competitors must expend at least some effort in making the same part for their competitive product.

Ordinarily, the originator should determine the value of the information, and that person categorises or classifies that information, usually in accordance with the established corporate guidelines. This may be a function of an IA organisation or a function of the corporation's executive management who, based on legal guidance, may establish that guideline since any compromise of that information may result in legal action by the corporation.

Generally, the types of information which has value to the corporation and which requires protection include all forms and types of:

- financial;
- scientific;
- technical;
- economic; and
- engineering.

The information includes, but is not limited to data, plans, tools, mechanisms, compounds, formulas, designs, prototypes, processes, procedures, programs, codes, or commercial strategies, whether tangible or intangible, and whether stored, compiled or memorialised physically, electronically, graphically, photographically, or in writing.

## 6.5   Three Basic Categories of Information

Although there are no global or national business standards that are used to categorise the sensitivity and value of information, information can logically be categorised into three categories:

- personal, private information;
- national security (both classified and unclassified) information;[3] and
- business information.

### 6.5.1   Personal, Private Information

Personal, private information is an individual matter, but also a matter for the government agencies and corporations. A person may want to keep private such information about themselves as their age, weight, address, cellular phone number, salary, and their likes and dislikes.

---

[3] National security classified information will be addressed in Chapter 9.

While at the same time, many countries have laws that protect information under some type of "privacy act", in businesses and government agencies it is a matter of policy to safeguard certain information about an employee such as their age, address, salary, etc. Failure to do so may have serious consequences since the corporation may be liable for failing to safeguard that private, personal information. Such liabilities can result in a poor public relations image for the corporation as well as significant monetary losses as established by the fines directed against the corporation by the courts.

Although the information is personal to the individual, others may require that information, but at the same time, they have an obligation to protect that information because it is considered to have value. As more and more information is being stored in massive databases and accessed from every part of the globe, this issue will take on increased significance and will play a major role in the arena of IA.

## 6.5.2   Business Information

Business information also requires protection based on its value. This information is sometimes identified in one or more of the following categories:

- company confidential;
- company internal use only;
- company private;
- company sensitive;
- company proprietary; and
- company trade secret.

The number of categories used will vary within each corporation; however, the less categories, the less problems in classifying information, and also, possibly, less problems in the granularity of protection required. Again, something that must always be considered – the cost versus the benefits of protection. The corporation's information must be protected because it has value to the corporation.

The key point to remember is that *the degree of protection required is dependent on the value of the information to the holder of that information during a specific period of time.*

The following are examples of various types of valuable information:

- Types of Company Internal Use Only Information:
  - not generally known outside the corporation;
  - not generally known through product inspection;
  - possibly useful to a competitor; and
  - provide some business advantage to competitors.

  Examples are corporation telephone books; corporation policies and procedures; and corporation organisational charts.

- Types of Company Private Information:
  - technical or financial aspects of the corporation;
  - indicates corporation's future direction;

- describes portions of the corporate business not known by the public;
- provides a competitive edge; and
- identifies personal information of employees.

Examples are personnel medical records; salary information; cost data; short-term marketing plans; and dates for unannounced events.

- Types of Company Sensitive Information:
  - provides significant competitive advantage;
  - could cause serious damage to the corporation if released to the public or competitors; and
  - reveals long-term corporate direction.

Examples are critical corporate technologies; critical engineering processes; and critical cost data.


## 6.6   Determining Information Value Considerations

Based on an understanding of information, its value, and some practical and philosophical thoughts on the topic as stated above, the IA professionals must have some sense of what must be considered when determining the value of information.

When determining the value of information, the IA professionals must determine what it cost to produce that information. Also, to be considered is the cost in terms of damages caused to the corporation if it were to be released outside protected channels, e.g. to the competitors. Additional consideration must be given to the cost of maintaining and protecting that information. How these factors are combined determine the value of the information. One must also remember to factor in the time element.

There are two basic assumptions to consider in determining the value of information:

- all information costs some type of resource(s) to produce, e.g. money, hours, use of equipment; and
- not all information can cause damage if released outside protected channels.

If the information costs resources of any kind to produce (and all information does) and no damage is done if released, you must consider, "Does it still have sufficient value to require that it be protected?"

Since the time factor is a key element in determining the value of information and cannot be over-emphasised, let's look at a simple example where information is not time dependent, or is it? There is a corporate picnic to take place on 22 August 2001. What is the value of the information before, on, or after that date? Does the information have value? To whom? When?

If you're looking forward to the corporation's annual picnic, as was your family, the information as to when and where it was to take place had some value to you. Supposing you found out about it the day after it happened. Your family was disappointed, they were mad at you for not knowing, you felt bad, etc.

However, to the corporation, the information had no value, vis-à-vis competitive advantage. However, your not receiving that information caused you to be disgruntled and you blamed the corporation for your latest family fights. Based on that, you decided to slow down productivity for a week.

This is a simple illustration, but indicates the value of information depending on who has and who does not have that information, as well as the time element. It also shows that what appears to be information not worth a second thought may have repercussions costing more than the value of the information.

The following is another example: a new, secret, revolutionary widget built to compete in a very competitive marketplace is to enter the market on 1 January 2001. What is the value of that information on 2 January 2001?

Again, to stress the point, one must consider the cost to produce the information and the damage done if that information were released. If it costs to produce and can cause damage if released, it must be protected. If it costs to produce, but cannot cause damage if released, then why protect it?

*The IA professional must always be sensitive to the dissemination process. Information, to have value, to be useful, must get to the right people at the right time. An IA program can impede that process with adverse impact on the competitive edge of a corporation.*

## 6.6.1   Questions to Ask When Considering Information Value

When determining the value of corporate information, the IA professional should, as a minimum, ask the following questions:

- How much does it cost to produce?
- How much does it cost to replace?
- What would happen if I no longer had that information?
- What would happen if my closest competitor had that information?
- Is protection of the information required by law and if so, what would happen if I didn't protect it?

The value of information is one of the most important aspects of information assurance. The late United States Admiral Grace Murray Hopper once said, "*Some day on the corporate balance sheet there will be an entry which reads 'Information'; for in most cases the information is more valuable than the hardware which processes it.*" Yes, we all know that we need information, automated information stored, processed and transmitted by information systems in order to function in our information environment. Thus it stands to reason that information has value, but how much value? When is it valuable? To whom? That is what an IA program should determine when establishing information protection and defence processes.

# 6.7    Another View of Information Valuation

The following discussion centres on another's perspective of information value:[4] headlines and titles tell us we are in the Information Age, we are using the Information Highway, and we are part of a knowledge-based economy. Information must be important. The number one issue facing corporations and government agencies is how to value information beyond subjective estimates, changing it from an intangible to a tangible asset. This leads directly to an approach for protecting information because certain types of information are worth more than others. Value, or perceived value, drives resource allocation. But if information is important, why aren't there national accounting standards for it? How should a corporation value information? Can there be more than one value? What information is critical enough to require deadly force by law enforcement or the military? Articles have been published on the value of information by accountants, economists, psychologists, artificial intelligence researchers, knowledge management experts, and others. However, quantitative approaches still elude us. Until a national standard is established, information will have simultaneous multiple values.

## 6.7.1    The Information Environment (IE)

The IE is comprised of several interrelated areas. Information moves across information infrastructures to support information-based processes. Information as used here means data, information, knowledge, and wisdom – the classic hierarchy. No doubt horrific to purists, there is no one good word to describe all four concepts together. All four exist within the corporation. Rather than argue about definitions and which is more important, the issue is how to value the intangibility of information, be it data, information, knowledge, or wisdom. At any given time, one could be of greater value than the others. The tacit knowledge of employees is the most difficult resource to quantify and value.

Information infrastructure is the media within which we store, process, and transmit information. Examples are people, computers, fibre optic cable, lasers, telephones, and satellites. Examples of information-based processes are the established ways to obtain and exchange information. This includes people to people (e.g., telephone conversations and office meetings), electronic commerce/electronic data interchange (EC/EDI), data mining, batch processing, and surfing the Web.

## 6.7.2    Value of Information

The corporation must take proactive measures to protect business operations and the bottom line. The corporation could self-insure – in other words eat a loss. Such a decision needs to be made in the presence of hard facts, not a gut feeling. Does the corporation and its individual business units know how much profit they make

---

[4] The authors are grateful to Perry Luzwick, Logicon, who provided his views of IV.

per year? Per quarter? Per month? Per day? Per hour? Per minute? Is the information protected? How do you know the information has not been stolen or altered? If transactions at Citibank cannot be accomplished, tens of millions of dollars of business can be lost, and that doesn't count the ill will of customers and permanent loss of future business to competitors.

How does a corporation know what information to acquire, retain, protect, and discard? Laws and practices cover some, product line and consumer base others. What information is more valuable? It depends on the time and context sensitivities of the situation. The corporation's business units produce information elements. At any given time, it's possible to determine the importance of specific information. In the absence of national accounting standards for information as a tangible asset, qualitative approaches are necessary.

From a contextual perspective, the information is of either tactical, operational, or strategic nature. From a time perspective, the information is either routine, important, or critical. Keeping the categories to a small number is essential, otherwise subjectivity will creep in and result in a rating that is either under- or over-inflated. At any given time, selecting an information element, its contextual perspective, and its time perspective will result in the perceived value of that information element. The way to differentiate between identical ratings is to add weighting to the information elements. That unique information in time and context will then be rated relative to other information elements. Does this produce a tangible pound figure? No. Does it help to value intangibles? Absolutely. Can there be more than one perceived value at the same time? Possibly, when two or more people view the contextual and time perspectives differently. A policy can be written to achieve common understanding.

A valuation of information would help prosecutors in computer crime cases. The jury must be convinced there was a loss. What is information in a database worth? A simple approach is that it took people (their compensation) and IT assets to acquire, process, store, and maintain.

## 6.8   The Need-To-Know (NTK) Model

The NTK model has been in use long before the invention of computers, and probably as long as information itself has been around. The military establishments and governments of nation-states have used the NTK philosophy for hundreds of years in order to protect national security.

This model is based on the philosophy that no information is provided to anyone in any form unless they have a need to have that information in order to complete some assigned task. In order to determine if someone meets the criteria for access to certain NTK information, a process based on policies and procedures should be formerly established to determine who requires access to what information, and when, in order to accomplish his assigned tasks.

Let's look at an example of how this model is used in a corporation. A corporation has a policy in place that states that information designated as sensitive must be accessed and used only by those personnel who have a need-to-know for that information in order for them to do their assigned jobs. Furthermore, the corporation delegated down to its mid-level managers the task of validating that NTK for employees in their respective organisations. The managers have done so by evaluating what specific, corporate sensitive information each employee required access to in order for them to accomplish their assigned tasks. This was done by evaluating what each person did; validating their job descriptions; and then designating those positions as sensitive. Thus, anyone in a position designated as sensitive would require access to some sensitive information.

However, that was just the beginning. Once the sensitive positions were identified, the specific type of sensitive information for which they required access was identified. Obviously, no such process is foolproof; however, it is another IA filter used to assist in protecting sensitive information.

So, for example: a person in the accounts payable department required access to the sensitive information contained in a database listing all the suppliers, their charges and payments to them. Someone in the human resources department in a sensitive position would have access to personnel records showing an individual's private information such as salary, home telephone number, and the like. However, neither employee would have a NTK for the other's information.

It is then up to the IA professionals in co-operation with the IT staff to develop an IA architecture and install a system to ensure that those individuals in sensitive positions had access to that information they needed. However, they also must ensure that no other sensitive information not needed by them to perform their assigned tasks could be accessed.

The NTK model is not easy to implement by any means. It grows in complexity as the corporation, number of employees, databases and networks grow. For efficiency purposes, sensitive information of all kinds is generally kept on the same networks and on large databases. Compartmenting that information on a NTK basis is a very complex and dynamic undertaking. Once must first of course identify that information that is considered sensitive and how much of it time-dependent as was discussed earlier. Thus, although a very logical and easy model to discuss, it is a very complex model to implement and with many dependencies. However, implementing at least a broad and somewhat general application of such a model is necessary if one is to provide information assurances.

## 6.9   The Confidentiality-Integrity-Availability (CIA) Model

The CIA model was developed decades ago. No, the United States' Central Intelligence Agency did not develop it, nor did it have anything to do with its development. As to who first thought of the term that has not been determined. Suffice it to say it is an easy term to remember if you remember the acronym. It is also one of the basic models of IA. This model obviously has three components:

- confidentiality;
- integrity; and
- availability

### 6.9.1    Confidentiality

Confidential information means information that is *"private or secret carried out or revealed in the expectations that anything done or revealed will be kept private...for a select group not available to the public, e.g. because it is commercially or industrially sensitive or concerns matters of national security..."*.[5]

Confidential information is only given on a need-to-know basis. Using this model, as a subset of information assurance, means that the goal is for obtaining reasonable assurance that the information stored, processed or transmitted by an information system will not be revealed to anyone who has not been identified as authorised to receive that information.

### 6.9.2    Integrity

As it relates to information, integrity means that the information is adhering to *"professional standards... the state of being complete or undivided...sound or undamaged"*.[6] Thus there is some reasonable assurance that the information is accurate, can be relied upon to be factual and not modified or otherwise changed without going through a formal process to ensure integrity is maintained.

### 6.9.3    Availability

Availability means that one is assured, with reasonable confidence and certainty, that the information and the information systems are always available when needed.

In summary, one can see the importance of this model as it relates to information assurance. In fact, it is the baseline, the heart of any information assurance process, system or program. The model when successfully implemented, ensures that the information is accurate and can be relied on to be available only to those who need that information when it is needed.

## 6.10    The Protect-Detect-React-Deter (PDRD) Model

The PDRD model has just recently been formalised into a working model. Bits and pieces of it have been around since the inception of information systems security but not as a formal concept. However, in the past, and especially since the advent of the information assurance concept, IA professionals have begun more and more to look at the entire spectrum of information assurances as one complete system or process.

---

[5] *Encarta World English Dictionary*; St. Martin's Press: New York, 1999, p.380.
[6] Ibid. p. 933.

The PDRD is a true system, a holistic approach to the issue of information assurances. Let's dissect this model into its four basic components and see how they work and interact.

## 6.10.1   Protect

When discussing protection and defence of information, one must be sure to define exactly what is meant. For example: does protection include physical safeguards of the information systems themselves? The hardcopy output of the information stored, processed, and transmitted by those systems? The answer: yes, if you want it to. After all, you can use this model in any way that logically suits your information environment.  However, we will use it here to look only at the protection of the automated information. The logic is this: if the systems are destroyed by fire, flood, earthquakes or some other disasters and assuming adequate back-up of the files as part of a disaster recovery-contingency planning program, then the physical destruction of the hardware or even software programs is not an issue.

So in this case, protection, as stated earlier in this book, deals with the issues of ensuring the integrity, reliability, et al of information. Hardcopy is not an issue in this model as once it has been printed, it is a matter of physical security of the printed material.

## 6.10.2   Detect

Detection is an interesting and somewhat new aspect of information assurances. Yes, detecting unauthorised access – attackers – has been, generally speaking, why audit trail records of systems were to be reviewed. However, that is always after the fact. The detection aspect of information assurances now is widely not considered a lone aspect of IA but labelled as "intrusion detection", and should be viewed in real-time to be truly useful.

What is intrusion detection? Quite simply, an intruder is a person attempting to gain unauthorised access, or has gained unauthorised access, to an information system and/or information residing on the system. Intrusion detection is the ability to detect the intruder, e.g. through the unauthorised actions of the intruder. This is obviously important because:

- information may be stolen;
- information may be deleted;
- misinformation may be entered;
- systems may be compromised; and
- use of the systems may be denied.

Over the last several years, intrusion detection software has become more sophisticated in nature and in its ability to identify attacks. However, as of this date, it is not as good at the global attackers harassing our information systems. As with most information assurance-related products, it is always one step behind the attackers' latest techniques.

To understand intrusion detection as part of this model or any model, one must be able to profile the potential intruders, their methods, the software programs they use and the like. These intruders may be anyone and include:

- Computer and telecommunications fraudsters.
- Organised crime.
- White-collar workers.
- Drug dealers.
- People in debt.
- People wanting revenge.
- Greedy people.
- Hackers, crackers, phreakers.
- Economic and industrial espionage agents.
- Disgruntled and ex-employees.
- Vendors/suppliers.
- Customers.
- Business partners.
- Military infowarriors.
- Political activists.
- Animal rights activists.
- Competitors.
- Foreign government agents.
- Subcontractors.
- Terrorists.
- Contractors, e.g. maintenance personnel.
- Outside auditors.
- Consultants.
- Anyone under the right circumstances.

All that is needed is a target, motive, opportunity and the skills to be successful. The intruders have become more prevalent because of:

- more distributed computing environment;
- more standardised systems and programs;
- more networking nationally and internationally;
- blurring of computers and telecommunication systems;
- remote systems maintenance;
- Internet;
- electronic Commerce;
- general standardisation, e.g. UNIX and Windows NT;
- UNIX, NT, and other platforms have known vulnerabilities; and
- more attackers.

The basic intruder approach is to:

- research target organisation;
- gather documentation;
- systematic dial-up scanning, web site attacks and penetrations or any number of methods depending on their target;
- once inside, set up a secure foothold;
- erase evidence of intrusion in audit logs;
- attack internal systems; and
- search for target system.

The intrusion detection model does not include such non-penetration attempt techniques as "dumpster diving" or scavenging (stealing document); social engineering, e.g. intimidation, manipulation; and the "more human" techniques used to gather information. It is based on the use of software programs and methods.

## 6.10.3   Case Example – Don't Rush to Judgement

When one is concerned with what appears to be attempted or actual unauthorised access, how does one know it is some form of malicious attack that adversely impacts information assurances? One must consider the affects of human error and mis-configuration of systems may have on the issue. To illustrate the point, the following actual event is described:

*"A large international corporation called in an information systems security consultant and explained that they were under attack by their competitor who was headquartered in another country. They were ready to file a lawsuit against that competitor who appeared to be accessing their systems without authorisation and possibly also performing a denial of service attack against them. Furthermore, the attack appeared to be coming through a third party in a third country in an apparent attempt to hide the origin of the attacks. This of course is not unusual and was considered a further indication of the covert attacks by the competitor. The consultant travelled to both other countries, talked to law enforcement authorities on the best course of action. The consultant also discussed the matter with the apparently unwitting third party whose systems were being used as the conduit for the attacks. While collecting audit trail evidence and conducting detailed analysis of the third party's system configuration, it was determined that the third party had a business relationship and was networked with both parties. It was further determined that the systems were mis-configured in such a manner as to cause the problems being experienced. Thus, it was not an attack at all! Can you imagine the consequences of a lawsuit if the 'victim' corporation had hastily filed the lawsuit and the subsequent cause of the attacks were determined?"*

## 6.10.4   React

How one reacts to attacks is based primarily on the corporate culture, which is generally spelled out in the corporate policy on IA and the like. Is the corporate culture one of a "campus atmosphere" where one is more open? Is the culture a more closed environment with more emphasis on protecting the information assets of the corporation as a high priority in order to protect its competitive edge in a volatile and globally competitive marketplace? How one should react then should be determined ahead of time and integrated into the corporate culture, or at least with the corporate culture in mind.

Reaction may be based on the development of an aggressive defence. Such a defence, however, should still be based on information assurance processes as its first line of defence.

Sometimes the best defence is an aggressive offence, once the attackers have been identified "beyond the shadow of a doubt". However, this may be dangerous and in fact a violation of law. The wrong approach may lead to attacking the wrong site as was possible in the case stated above. There are serious ramifications with the philosophy that "the best defence is a good offence".

As part of reacting, the first step may be to report anomalies occurring on discrete components (sub-networks) of the private or public network to a corporate "centralised analysis centre". If the major components of this model are successfully installed, it is possible to achieve awareness of these anomalies on a grand scale. Then when processed, this data may yield a practical warning system for attacks. Such a model entails correlation of the anomalies, disturbances, outages, and penetrations.

One may react by examination of the resulting database for interdependencies (overlaps) as well as gaps in order that the IA professional can summarise what was known and inventory what was not known. The utilisation of the resulting database can then be used to determine and document baseline trends, expected behaviours, and deviations from the baseline. Then the IA professional can correlate the exception or trend data between the various sub-nets.

This approach offers the benefits of providing a holistic perspective; may be combined with similar data from others; may be used as input for an inductive process that would combine this data with knowledge of intruders as a means of investigating incidents.

## 6.10.5   Deter

Deterrence is probably one of the most difficult components of this model. If the model thus far has been properly implemented and aggressively maintained, e.g. kept current at all times, then one may deter attacks by using one or more of the following methods:

- The corporation maintains a low profile (not usually practical if one is to sell products on a national or global scale, e.g. one must aggressively advertise).
- The corporation has a publicly known policy of aggressively pursuing and supporting prosecution of attackers.
- The corporation implements an information assurance program based on the multiple models described in this chapter and thus makes it too time consuming and difficult for an attacker to penetrate the system.

### 6.10.6    Questions and Some Answers to Think About

When developing an IA program, the IA professionals should consider the following:

- *Question*: how do you know you are actually under attack and not the victim of mis-configured systems? *Answer*: you may not know until it is too late; you may never know; you may know, but can't stop it.
- *Question*: what are the warning signs of potential or actual attacks? *Answer*: there may not be any.
- *Question*: is it possible to know of pending attacks? *Answer*: yes. No. Maybe – depending on conditions.
- *Question*: what can you do to set up an "imminent" attack warning system? *Answer*: base it on history; latest techniques identified in CERTs; on target visibility; on your defences; on your countermeasures; on your use of technology; and on vendor products.
- *Question*: what is the basis for deploying intrusion detection to assist in countering the attacks? *Answer*: what is normal activity? What is abnormal? Compare activity against known attack methods; establish countermeasures; and one must have, as a minimum, an IA policy, procedures, and awareness program.
- *Question*: what must be considered when deploying the intrusion detection system and processes? *Answer*: any available tools should be adapted to your unique environment. The intrusion detection process must always be secure, operating, and "foolproof". It must detect all anomalies and misuse; must have audit-based systems for history; must have real-time monitoring and warnings; provide for immediate action based on each unique attack; and one must know what to do if attacked.
- *Question*: any other things to consider? *Answer*: audit entry ports especially to critical areas; prioritise processes, shutdown others; isolate the problem; and establish alternate routing paths. One can never have too many intrusion detection "bells and whistles".

## 6.11    IA Success Considerations

To be successful, the IA professional, as a minimum, should:

- develop and maintain a threat toolkit containing strategies, software, tactics, tools, and methodologies used to attack systems;
- continuously maintain a current IA toolkit and methodologies that can defend information systems against attacks;
- model the capabilities of the potential intruders against real-time defences;
- collect information related to the corporation's information systems' vulnerabilities; and
- establish, implement and maintain an aggressive IA program.

## 6.12  Summary

The primary purpose of IA is to: minimise the probability of an IA vulnerability; minimise the damage if an attack occurred; and provide a method to quickly recover in the event of a successful attack. There are many models that can be used to assist in that endeavour. All of them have some value and should be considered for integrating into a corporate IA program. The IA professional must also consider the cost and benefits of such implementations.

# Section 2

# IA in the World of Corporations

This section begins with a discussion of the duties and responsibilities of the Corporate Security Officer (CSO) in Chapter 7. The CSO plays a major role in information assurance since that person is responsible for the protection of the corporation's assets, which of course includes information and information systems.

This discussion continues in Chapter 8 where the functions of the Corporate Security Officer are discussed in detail and shown how they are an integral part of a corporate information assurance program. This is followed by a look at information assurance in the nation-state's national security sector in Chapter 9. In the national security sector, information protection and defence is taken much more seriously. After all, the fate of the nation-state is at stake if information assurance is not properly addressed.

In Chapters 10 and 11, the need for a corporate position as Corporate Information Assurance Officer is discussed. Although many corporations have yet to recognise the need for such a position, a few corporations, e.g. Microsoft Corporation, and government agencies are taking the initiative to appoint people to such positions. These chapters discuss the basic qualifications, duties, responsibilities and possible organisational structures and functions of an information assurance person and supporting organisation.

# Chapter 7

# The Corporate Security Officer

The Corporate Security Officer is responsible for the protection of corporate assets. Since information and information systems are some of the most vital corporate assets, the duties of the Corporate Security Officer also include some aspects of their protection. This chapter addresses the Corporate Security Officer's responsibilities for the protection of corporate assets and their relationship to information assurance.

## 7.1   Information Assurance – Whose Responsibility Is It?

Information permeates corporations at all levels. All employees in today's modern, information-dependent corporations depend on the information systems and the information that the systems store, process and transmit to successfully accomplish their assigned jobs. In addition, many professionals within a corporation are responsible for various aspects of information assurance (IA), not the least of these is the corporate security officer (CSO). There are various titles given to people in such positions, such as Director of Security, Security Manager, Business Security Manager, Director of Industrial Security, just to name a few. However, no matter their title, they have one basic responsibility and that is to protect the assets of their employer, e.g. the corporation.

Like information systems security (InfoSec) issues, there continues to be ongoing discussions centring on the issue of information assurance responsibilities. Since automated information permeates all aspects of a corporation, everyone shares some responsibility for information assurance, e.g. ensuring that the corporate sensitive information and information systems are protected and defended. There are very few arguments about that these days. However, in any bureaucracy, someone must take on the responsibility for providing the leadership and guidance for information assurance, but who? This is the crux of the issue. Should that responsibility fall on the information technology (IT) people, the corporate security people, auditors, or some guru of IA?

As for auditors assuming the IA leadership role, no, they are not qualified. Their entire profession is based on compliance and auditing for compliance. IT personnel may have InfoSec responsibility in some corporation and since IA incorporates InfoSec, maybe they should provide the IA leadership? No, even their InfoSec responsibilities are a conflict of interest. How can one set the InfoSec policy and then audit objectively to ensure they are adequate? One can see that InfoSec under IT has not worked for decades. One just has to look at the successful attacks against corporate systems, their Web pages, and the like.

In order to answer that question of IA leadership, a short history of the evolution of information systems security, which has led to information assurance, is necessary:

*IT personnel usually do not understand basic security principles, nor true InfoSec. Their concept of security and InfoSec is usually a software program that controls access to the systems. Many corporations, however, still rely on IT personnel to resolve InfoSec problems. They do not have a choice. Who else is currently up to the challenge?*

## 7.2   Is IA a Corporate Security Responsibility?

As stated earlier, the primary responsibility of the CSO is to protect the corporation's assets.[1] There is no doubt that information and the information systems are some of the corporation's most valuable assets. Yet, other than physical security, the CSOs of today's modern corporations have generally not been involved in InfoSec, let alone IA.

Although many of today's modern CSOs have some understanding of InfoSec and IA, they do not have the knowledge, the skills and, in many cases, even the desire to deal with InfoSec, and now the problems associated with IA, which is even more complex.

How did this happen? Why did this happen? Can anything be done by corporate security personnel to enhance information assurance in a more effective and efficient way than is now the case? This is a topic of many debates between and within professions. One corporate security professional put it this way:

*"When modern-day automated information systems (AIS) were first developed, they were not user friendly. They occupied large rooms with air conditioners set at extremely low temperatures so the heat of the vacuum tubes would not melt the system. To turn the machine on, one needed a 'PhD in physics, electrical engineering, and/or mathematics'. Besides, no one worried about security because the system only crunched numbers.*

*"All that was needed was a lock or a security officer at the door to the computer room with an access list noting who was authorised entrance into the*

---

[1] If the reader is interested in learning more about the corporate security profession, see the American Society for Industrial Security's (an international association of security professionals) web site at http://www.asisonline.org.

*computer room. The main security concern was someone stealing the hardware and because of its size, even that was unlikely.*

*"Gradually, over the last several decades, AIS became more powerful, cheaper, easier to use and more user friendly. Nowadays, children are using AIS before they enter kindergarten.*

*"Unfortunately, security professionals are looking at AIS security as we did in the 1950s. We are still locking the door so no one steals the hardware. In today's technological world, however, hardware is not nearly as important as the information used by those computers.*

*"After more than 40 years of security neglect, an industrial security specialist today would have a difficult time wrestling the AIS security functions away from the information technology department, or others. IT people know the systems better than anyone. After all, they interact with them on a technical level on a daily basis. So is it wrong for the IT staff to be responsible for such things as InfoSec and information assurances?*

*"Let me answer that question with two questions: Would a farmer want a fox to guard his hen house? Are IT people trained security personnel?*

*"The answer to both questions is No! IT people have taken on the responsibility for information security and information assurance because security professionals did not. The IT staff's primary function is to operate the computers and provide the necessary support to enable systems' users to perform their assigned tasks.*

*"Protecting information requires a triad approach:*

- *the primary responsibility for the protection of information and information assurance rests with the owner of that information;*
- *it is up to the IT personnel to provide the necessary technical service and support; and*
- *it is the responsibility of corporate security specialists to provide the leadership, policies, procedures, awareness training, inspections, and risk assessment for protecting the corporation's systems and information. In most corporations, the security specialist's portion is missing and they fall short of their responsibilities.*

*"Some security people say the process has worked well so far and why take on this extra and large burden? The situation has not been going along fine. IT people sometimes come to the security office and say that information in the systems are not secure, that they have problems on the systems affecting security of the information, or that they took off audit trails because it slowed down the system's performance over the weekend.*

*"It takes a security professional with that bit of paranoia and a questioning attitude to provide the overall security and information assurances required for those corporate assets.*

*"The function and responsibility of the corporation's security personnel is to protect corporate assets. AIS and the information are today's corporation's most valuable assets. It then follows that the security and information assurance is the security department's responsibility. Security personnel must take the*

*leadership role. We owe it to our corporation, our profession, and ourselves it we are to truly consider ourselves security professionals.*"

It is acknowledged that a CSO has certain responsibilities for providing the leadership for protecting corporate assets; however, they are light-years away from assuming the professional responsibility for leading a corporate-wide IA program. However, they are now sharing some of that leadership role with IT professionals. It is hoped that one day the InfoSec profession matures to an IA role that is led by one specialising in information protection and defences, regardless of the information environment, e.g. non-information systems environment.

# 7.3   Introduction to Corporate Security

As mentioned above, the duties and responsibilities of the corporate security department revolve around the protection of corporate assets. When one thinks of assets, one generally thinks of people, places and things. Although people do not "belong" to a corporation; however, a corporation employs them. Thus, the corporation considers them a valuable asset while places and things do belong to a corporation. As assets, they have value. Thus, they must be protected from those that want to take the assets for their own use, destroy them, modify them, or the like.

The corporate executive management establishes the corporate security department and charges that department with the responsibility for protecting the assets of the corporation. As was alluded to above, the primary responsibility for the protection of any of the corporate assets generally meant that some form of physical security was required so the assets could not be stolen. The guards usually accomplished this form of asset protection. When it came to the protection of information, this was also the case as even in centuries past, the guards were the ones who safeguarded and transported documents containing valuable information.

Gradually, we have seen that information has grown in importance as the corporations and nation-states entered deeper into the information age. However, what has really changed is the environment in which information flows. That, coupled with our almost complete dependency on information and information systems, and the expansion of responsibilities for their protection and defence, has made the task of protecting these valuable assets more complicated and difficult.

## 7.3.1   The Corporate Security Officer

It is the duty and responsibility of the CSO to provide the management leadership, based on the CSO's expertise, to cost-effectively safeguard the corporate assets. Therefore, the CSO has certain responsibilities vis-à-vis information assurance.

The reporting structure for the CSO varies based on the desires of the corporation's executive management. Some CSOs report directly to the corporate president or chief executive officer (CEO), others report to the head of the legal department or the head of human resources. The CSO is accountable for providing direction for the corporation and overall responsibility for ensuring that all the security functions were performed in a manner that is cost-effective, meets employee, corporate, and customers' needs/requirements and complies with corporate policies, applicable laws and regulations. Thus the CSO is vested with the authority to carry out assigned duties in accordance with the responsibilities assigned and delegated by corporate policy.

Generally speaking the CSO is therefore responsible for overseeing the development and implementation of security processes that are designed to protect the people, property and *information* of the corporation.

## 7.3.2   Corporate Security Duties and Responsibilities

Although each corporation establishes its own unique form of asset protection and information assurance processes, the responsibilities identified below provide an example of those responsibilities as they relate to the CSO:

- Develop methodologies and implement processes to evaluate current security requirements and project future requirements on new business proposals and future contracts.
- Develop and oversee the implementation of a long range, corporate-wide security plan that details the efficient and cost-effective utilisation of security resources.
- Provide overall management direction for all security activities within the corporation focusing on centralised delivery on a corporate-wide basis, maximising the development of regional and corporate-shared services.
- Interface with the directors of environmental, health, safety, medical and others as appropriate to resolve issues involving the security of assets by the business sectors.
- Act to ensure that security processes are performed in full compliance with all customers, contractual and regulatory security requirements.
- Oversee the development of a corporate-wide information security program to protect corporate and customer information.
- Oversee the development of a corporate-wide Crisis Management Program.
- Work with regional security managers to ensure the identification and implementation of common processes, shared services, and best practices.
- Work with the sector managers of environmental, safety, health, medical, and facilities to ensure an integration of functions to provide a productive and safe working environment for sector employees.
- Oversee the development and implementation of a corporate security measurement system, which permits evaluation of the effectiveness of the security program, based on the factors of cost, customer satisfaction, and compliance.
- Perform common managerial accountabilities and tasks in accordance with established corporate guidelines.
- Provide a physically secure environment for the corporate office to protect property, people and information.

- Direct the development and implementation of security processes that comply with government requirements.
- Provide guidance to corporate management regarding security policy and the interpretation, intent, or application of security-related laws and regulations.
- Provide additional support to the corporate elements as required.
- Maintain active liaison with government security agencies in order to participate in the development of security policy and represent the corporation in professional and industrial associations to influence the interpretation and implementation of that policy.
- Work with other corporate departments to develop and implement company policies and procedures that have important security implications for the company.
- Manage the development and implementation of an integrated, company-wide contingency plan.
- Ensure the corporate crisis management room is maintained in a state of constant readiness and provide the resources required to operate the room during actual emergencies and simulations.
- Develop, implement and maintain a company-wide security measurement system that permits evaluation of the effectiveness of each company element security program, the total company security programs and benchmarking with security programs of comparable companies.
- Liaisons with federal, state and local law enforcement, investigative and fire agencies.
- Chair the corporate Security Council to develop a common company-wide approach to address security processes and problems.
- Develop corporate security policy and procedures to address the following security processes:

  - Security quality and oversight.
  - Personnel security.
  - Information security (Generally taken to mean hardcopy documents).
  - Physical security.
  - Investigations.
  - Fire protection.
  - Contingency planning.

## 7.3.3  Corporate Security Support Tools and Processes

The CSO and security organisational staff relies on IT to provide the formation systems and applications that meet their needs. In that respect, the security organisation is no different than that of any other department within a corporation – they are internal customers of the IT professionals. However, the systems that they use are some of the most important, if not the most important, systems within a corporation for they have to do with the safety and security of the corporation. The following are examples:

- Today's corporations use badge readers to replace guards when controlling access to a facility, area or room. That system is computer-based and relies on specific application software to properly work. That system, including the hardware, firmware, database of information and software, must meet an IA criterion in order to assure it works as required. If not, the system may allow unauthorised physical access to the facility, or it may not allow anyone access. In either case, it could adversely impact the system and the system must continuously work as expected.

- Often the CSO's responsibilities include fire protection and other emergency services. Fire alarms are based on microprocessors to set off an alarm and report that alarm to the fire department. Such a system must also meet specific IA criterion in order to safeguard the lives of the corporate employees and property of the corporation.

- The security awareness program processes and other functional processes are often automated, thus making the CSO's job more efficient and hopefully effective. However, in doing so, the IA requirements must be strictly enforced so as not to compromise security of the corporation, thus placing its assets at risk.

The more a CSO relies on information and information systems to assist in successfully accomplishing the assigned security tasks, the more that IA is a factor. It then stands to reason this need and their assets protection role makes that profession a logical choice for the IA leadership role. However, they don't seem to be up to the challenge. Therefore, IA leadership within today's corporations is divided among the several professions of security, IT and auditors.

## 7.4 Summary

Since automated information permeates all aspects of a corporation or government agency, everyone shares some responsibility for InfoSec and IA, e.g. ensuring that concept of confidentiality, integrity and availability are maintained. There are very few arguments about that these days. However, in any bureaucracy, someone must take on the responsibility for providing the leadership and guidance for IA, but who? This is the crux of the issue. Should that responsibility fall on the IT staff, the corporate security staff, internal auditors, or others?

In today's corporate information environment, IA tasks seem to be shared between corporate security, IT and auditors. However, the leadership for IA seems to be lacking from a corporate, holistic viewpoint with several professions having some piecemeal responsibility.

The function and responsibility of the corporation's security personnel is to protect corporate assets. Information systems and the information that they store, process and transmit are some of today's most valuable assets. It then follows that IA is the security department's responsibility. Should security personnel take the IA leadership role? Yes. Will they? This is unlikely.

# Chapter 8

## Corporate Security Functions

This chapter identifies and describes the basic security functions of a corporation's security organisation that is lead by the Corporate Security Officer. It includes a description and discussion of those functions that are an integral part of any corporation's information assurance program.

## 8.1 Corporate Security IA – Related Functions

Although each corporation establishes its own unique asset protection program, to include information assurance-related functions, there is a common thread that runs through most of these corporate asset protection functions. Using the Corporate Security Officer (CSO) duties and responsibilities noted below, the functions related to IA will be identified and discussed. The assumption here is that the CSO does not have direct IA functional responsibility, only those generally known as corporate security functions, e.g. physical security, personnel security, administrative security.

### 8.1.1 Evaluate Current Security Requirements

*"Develop methodologies and implement processes to evaluate current security requirements and project future requirements on new business proposals and future contracts."*

In evaluating the current security requirements and future requirements, those of information and information systems should also be addressed. This would require the CSO to gain input from those responsible for IA so as to be able to evaluate the security requirements based on a holistic corporate assets protection requirements approach. The source of the requirements, known as requirements drivers, would have to be established and then a process developed to ensure requirements were updated based on the drivers from the requirements being changed, e.g. drivers such as changes in laws, contracts.

In order to project future requirements, a different approach would be needed, one that the CSO is generally not accustomed to dealing with. CSOs generally establish a basic corporate assets protection program and then usually maintain a reactive posture. To be able to begin to do trend analyses, see where the main drivers are headed two to five years from now, requires a different process. Since technology advances are a driving force in IA, the CSO must rely on the IA staff to provide that information. Unfortunately, most of those responsible for IA also seem to be in a reactive mode and seldom have time (at least that is a usual excuse) to look at future trends, as they are too busy fighting today's battles. If that is not bad enough, the CSO must understand business trends, especially in the industry that the corporation is in. For example: electronic commerce or business and global market information would be needed. After that is in place, the CSO must then be able to look in the "crystal ball" to determine where they are today, vis-à-vis security requirements, and where they must be tomorrow. Furthermore, the CSO must develop a process for getting there.

## 8.1.2   Corporate Security Plan

*"Develop and oversee the implementation of a long range, corporate-wide security plan that details the efficient and cost-effective utilisation of security resources."*

Incorporating the information developed in trend analyses (see paragraph 8.1.1), the CSO would be in a better position when developing a corporate-wide security plan. That plan must also look at the IA issues since the plan encompasses the entire corporation. Furthermore, it is very difficult to provide an efficient and cost-effective use of security resources without considering the security aspects of information and information systems. After all, somewhere within the corporation there are personnel responsible for IA. If one were to ignore their input and fail to integrate their requirements, concerns, functions and processes, the CSO would be ignoring some of the main assets of the corporation that require protection. In doing so, the CSO could not successfully accomplish the task.

While at the same time, it is believed most CSOs tasked with accomplishing this project only consider those tasks under their authority. Thus, if they do not have responsibility for IA, they will ignore that aspect when developing their plan. The security resources of all organisations must be considered and their input solicited.

## 8.1.3   Management Direction for Security Activities

*"Provide overall management direction for all security activities within the corporation focusing on centralised delivery on a corporate-wide basis, maximising the development of regional and corporate-shared services."*

The key is *overall management direction*. This does not mean that the IA functions are under the CSO; however, the CSO can make a case for leading the IA efforts of the corporation. While at the same time, the focus on providing a *centralised delivery* would seem to give the CSO the mandate for absorbing those IA resources and functions necessary to accomplish this function.

If politically and culturally feasible within the corporation, the CSO should establish a project to identify all the IA resources within the corporation, determine their current costs, and then determine the cost benefits of centralisation under the security organisation. If it is determined to be cost-effective, the corporate executive management should be briefed with the intent of gaining their approval to consolidate the IA functions, personnel, and other resources. If the executive management disapproves, then the CSO should request that this function be modified to exclude the IA functions.

The CSO would not be very smart to leave the function as written and then not have the authority to manage those aspects of the function. Management responsibility without authority to manage is not a position any CSO would want to be in as they can get blamed when things are not going right but have no authority to make things right.

### 8.1.4   Interface with Other Directors

*"Interface with the directors of environmental, health, safety, medical and others as appropriate to resolve issues involving the security of assets by the business sectors."*

This is not an IA type of function per se; however, these directors have information, databases and information systems that as a minimum must be protected and defended if for no other reasons than those of privacy and liability concerns.

These directors and their organisations support the entire corporation and it appears that these functions fall under the responsibility of the CSO. Therefore, the CSO must act as mediator between these directors and the business sectors of the corporation.

### 8.1.5   Comply with Contractual, Customer, and Regulatory Requirements

*"Act to ensure that security processes are performed in full compliance with all customers, contractual and regulatory security requirements."*

As with the other functions identified above, this function has some very important IA concerns. There are very serious liability issues and non-compliance with contract specification issues that may develop. One can begin to see an obvious trend and that is the CSO cannot perform those functions being identified in this chapter without having some management responsibility relative to IA. How can a CSO ensure that the customers' information and even the customers' information systems interfacing with the corporate information systems are being properly protected and defended against attacks and human errors that may damage the customers' systems and information?

The CSO can co-ordinate this function with the audit staff and request that the auditors verify and validate compliance with these requirements. The difficulty is how and when that audit is performed. Generally, the audit staff is very busy with meeting audit requirements of their own. They may not have the resources to support this activity, and if they did, then shouldn't that function then be transferred to the audit department? That is an option to be considered. The other option is for the CSO to have his staff conduct security compliance surveys or inspections. The term audit should not be used as this could be confused with the audit organisation's use of the term. Furthermore, it would be more of a security compliance process that is somewhat different from an audit. It would not only evaluate for compliance but also at the same time be considered as part of a risk assessment so that one can cost-effectively consider accomplishing one task for two different purposes with little extra effort.

The term inspection has a harsher tone to it and may not be considered, from a "public relations" or "political" viewpoint, the best way to proceed. However, the term "survey" seems less intrusive and less threatening. The choice of terms when dealing within the political and cultural reality of a corporation can make a difference. One must always approach such issues from a non-threatening standpoint as much as possible.

## 8.1.6   Corporate-Wide InfoSec Program

*"Oversee the development of a corporate-wide information security program to protect corporate and customer information."*

Here again there is a case to make for the CSO to have the authority to manage IA functions. However, the word *oversee* provides the CSO with an "out" as such functions vis-à-vis IA can be done by the CSO developing an overall corporate security policy. The CSO could then leave the procedural matters to the various organisations having IA responsibilities within the corporation. The other option is a matrix management approach where the CSO assigns security resources to assist other organisations. However, the success of a matrix management approach is always dependent on the personalities of those managers who own the resources being "loaned" to another manager's organisation as well as the budget availability of both managers. For example: who must relinquish the budget for the time and money to be expended for someone to support a given function, e.g. IA, in another's organisation?

## 8.1.7   Corporate-Wide Crisis Management Program

*"Oversee the development of a corporate-wide Crisis Management Program."*

The CSO having this responsibility would undoubtedly have representatives from the various corporate organisations as part of the crisis management team responding to a crisis. When a crisis was identified that met the crisis criteria definition established earlier by the CSO, then the parties would meet to handle the crisis. Such a crisis could include such incidents as a successful denial of service attack, the destruction of databases, theft of sensitive corporate information. Such matters as incident response teams' emergency procedures and the like would also be part of the crisis management program.

## 8.1.8    Establish Common Security Processes

*"Work with regional security managers to ensure the identification and implementation of common processes, shared services, and best practices."*

As it relates to assets protection, this responsibility would be a matter of proliferating those related processes that are used at the corporate location to the regional offices, to include IA processes, and best practices. After all, it would be cost-effective to do so. Why re-invent the wheel so to speak.

The problem that may, and often does, arise is that regional offices consider themselves autonomous and more so the further they are from the corporate headquarters. This attitude must be considered and regional input to all processes to be identified as common processes must be considered. Management support and personalities play a large role here. However, an attitude of teaming and cost-benefits must be used by all. The bottom line is this: what is best for the corporation, not individual "empires" whether they be corporate or regional, must apply.

## 8.1.9    Provide Productive and Safe Working Environment

*"Work with the sector managers of environmental, safety, health, medical, and facilities to ensure an integration of functions to provide a productive and safe working environment for sector employees."*

The employees of these organisations can not be productive if they rely on information systems, for example, and those systems are not accessible due to some virus, human error or attack.

This responsibility is not directly related to IA except that a case can be made for the CSO to assist the IA staff to ensure that the sector managers comply with the IA requirements established by the corporate staff responsible for IA.

## 8.1.10    Corporate Security Measurement System

*"Oversee the development and implementation of a corporate security measurement system, which permits evaluation of the effectiveness of the security program, based on the factors of cost, customer satisfaction, and compliance."*

Again, this would apply only to those functions under the authority of the CSO. As it relates to IA, the CSO may ask for but can not require a measurement system to be established and results provided to the security staff if those functions are not under the direct control of the CSO.

## 8.1.11    Common Managerial Accountabilities

*"Perform common managerial accountabilities and tasks in accordance with established corporate guidelines."*

This is a normal managerial responsibility and usually concerns such managerial matters as meeting goals, establishing and managing organisational budgets, career development of assigned personnel, conducting performance reviews and the like. Therefore, they are not directly related to IA. However, if a corporation was truly supportive of IA and security, the managerial responsibilities identified would include supporting and complying with IA and security policy, protecting corporate assets and the like.

## 8.1.12   Physically Secure Environment

*"Provide a physically secure environment for the corporate office to protect property, people and information."*

This is definitely one function that undoubtedly has been, is and will continue to be performed by the CSO. However, if we look at IA, as we should (but usually don't), we must consider information in every conceivable environment in which it flows. This would include on electronic media, hardcopy, video, or by whatever means. However, that aside, physical security will always be an important and basic defence against information theft.

When one thinks of physical security, one thinks of the human access controls. One thinks of the guards stationed at entrances to facilities, areas, and even some rooms or offices. However, in some corporations, the receptionists and administrative personnel at the visitors' entrances or entrance to a particular suite of offices for example are also controlling access.

When one enters a visitor's lobby, there may be a uniform guard behind the desk, or the guard may be wearing business attire with maybe a corporate logo on the breast pocket of the sport coat. If the corporation has out-sourced its guard force duties to an outside agency, the logo of the guard company may be on the breast pocket. In some corporations, the executive management has decided that a guard force was not necessary or is cost-prohibitive, thus they use administrative support personnel such as receptionists and secretaries to double as access controllers. Regardless, these individuals are required to ensure only authorised personnel have access to the facility.

Besides the human element of physical access controls, there are the mechanical access controls. Some forms of mechanical access controls include:

- *Fences and Walls*: one often sees fences surrounding a corporation. These physical barriers range from chain-link fences topped with barbed wire to concrete walls. The fences are used to control access by making it difficult for intruders to proceed beyond that barrier and also to guide personnel to the gates.
- *Gates*: the gates are established to control access by controlling physical access to an area, facility and the like. Guards may be stationed at the gates or they may require the use of a device such as a special badge to "swipe" through a badge reader in order to allow access beyond that point. Often these entrances can only accommodate one individual at a time through the portal. This prevents someone from allowing others to "piggyback" by also following them in through the gate without having a proper badge.

- **Badge readers**: badge readers have gained in popularity and are used to control physical access and eliminate the need for a guard to control access. Thus providing a more "foolproof" physical access control method at usually much less cost. The badge reader may allow the holder to just swipe it through the reader to gain access or it may also require the user to enter a group or personal identification number (PIN).
- **Facility**: the facility itself by its very design may form a physical access barrier, e.g. no windows on the first floor, bars on the windows, etc.

Physical security is always the first line of defence; however, keeping unauthorised personnel out is only one process. Another is how to keep information and information systems from leaving the facility in an unauthorised manner. With today's Internet accesses; small, removable electronic media; and the ability to make copies and print sensitive documents with little control; this is almost an impossible task.

## 8.1.13   Government Compliance Requirements

*"Direct the development and implementation of security processes that comply with government requirements."*

Since the inception of the nation-state, there have been governments who try to influence, regulate or otherwise control information and its usage. In addition, there is information that is related to the national security of a nation-state. This has always been under the purview of the CSO for government contractors or for any business that must comply with various requirements of the nation-states' government agencies. The issue of privacy is one that comes to mind as one of a government's requirements.

While the staff responsible for IA, are involved at the implementation level, the CSO has historically been in the leadership role in such instances, when security issues are involved. However, that responsibility can also be assigned to others, e.g. the corporate legal staff.

This function can be accomplished through a teaming, project plan effort to develop and establish a process for accomplishing this task. In addition, the use of security surveys can assist in assuring compliance.

## 8.1.14   Corporate Management Guidance

*"Provide guidance to corporate management regarding security policy and the interpretation, intent, or application of security-related laws and regulations; provide additional support to the corporate elements as required."*

Corporate management looks to the CSO as the in-house consultant for security matters; however, that may or may not apply to IA. On those occasions, the matter may be IA related and thus when the word "security" comes up, the CSO is usually the first one to be contacted. However, on matters that involve anything to do with information systems and IA, the CSO is generally not even considered.

The corporate management will usually turn to the IT executive for guidance, who is probably also the Corporate Information Officer (CIO). When considering the IT executive as the CIO, the corporation's executive management either considers all their information being on information systems or are missing the point. The CIO/IT executive generally has no experience in information as such but in systems. Furthermore, they usually lack experience and management authority over non-systems processed, stored and transmitted information. Therefore, they are not true CIOs as the term implies. It seems corporate management continues to miss the point – it is not about information systems but about information in any environment! Is it any wonder that we have the problems that we do?

## 8.1.15  Security Liaison Activities

*"Maintain active liaison with government security agencies in order to participate in the development of security policy and represent the corporation in professional and industrial associations to influence the interpretation and implementation of that policy."*

Within a corporation, it is better to have only one focal point when dealing with the government security agencies. That focal point is usually the CSO. In many corporations, the CSO is a retired military or government agency security officer, or law enforcement officer. Thus, that CSO usually understands how government security agencies operate, making the liaison task not only easier but also more successful. Even if an issue relative to IA is concerned, the communications link is through the CSO and not directly to those responsible for IA within a corporation.

## 8.1.16  Co-ordinate Corporate Security Policy and Procedures

*"Work with other corporate departments to develop and implement company policies and procedures that have important security implications for the company."*

It is inconceivable (but true) that today's CSOs in information-dependent corporations do not include the IA requirements and needed policy as part of the corporate security policies and procedures.

While the CSO would be more interested in the document, personnel and physical security aspects, these processes also impact how IA is conducted. Therefore, whatever direction is pursued by the CSO in order to accomplish this task, IA will be impacted.

In this case, the CSO would identify all the assets that required protection and identify those organisations responsible for those assets. A project would be established and a project team made up of representatives from all those organisations that have responsibility for those assets. The project would be led by the CSO. The project team would establish those requirements.

The goal would be to ensure that as much as possible the protection requirements would be standardised and consistent for all assets. Variations would only be allowed where the asset was unique and required different protection requirements. The requirements would be documented and that documentation would be the baseline for a corporate assets protection policy. Procedures for implementing and complying with that policy would be established within individual organisations at a more detailed level. For example: the policy may require access control, both physical and logical. It may be more cost-effective to have a security guard in some areas while others used badge readers, biometric devices, and the like.

A CSO should co-ordinate and team with those responsible for IA to develop all-inclusive security policies that also consider information and information systems. Thus provide the CSO with the opportunity to influence IA policies and procedures to ensure they are not only consistent with the total information asset protection needs of the corporation, but that they also meet the generally accepted security standards for the protection of corporate assets.

## 8.1.17   Corporate-Wide Contingency Plan

*"Manage the development and implementation of an integrated, company-wide contingency plan."*

No contingency plan in any information dependent corporation can be complete without addressing the issues of information and information systems as part of the overall corporate contingency plan. In order to do so, the CSO must integrate the IA contingency planning details into the overall plan.

To accomplish that function, the CSO must establish a project team with all organisations represented. This is because contingencies are about more than just security or IA. They are about dealing with emergencies, disasters, and other issues that require a contingency plan so that one can get back to normal business as soon as possible with the least impact on the business. The project team, led by the CSO would be responsible for establishing a contingency plan. This plan would undoubtedly consider all the information and information systems issues, e.g. IA. The IA specialists' input must be a mandatory requirement to ensure that such a plan was developed using a corporate holistic philosophy and methodology.

One also must remember that within contingency planning, there may be as many as three distinct subsystems:

- Emergency response: this is self-explanatory; however, one should remember that the security, fire, environmental, and medical processes play the biggest roles in this effort.
- Crisis management: managing a crisis is a team effort usually made up of at least the representatives of the emergency response components, human resources, facilities engineers and executive management.
- Business continuity: generally consists of the disaster recovery components, with IT and IA staffs usually playing a major role, along with business resumption elements. The business staff establishes the priorities, and leads

this effort, supported by IT, IA, user community, and the like. In this effort, security may serve as an "integrator" of processes to successfully meet the challenges imposed by an emergency or crisis.

## 0.1.18   Corporate Crisis Management Room

*"Ensure the corporate crisis management room is maintained in a state of constant readiness and provide the resources required to operate the room during actual emergencies and simulations."*

This is an extension of the crisis management function described in paragraph 8.1.7. Therefore, there is no need to further address it here, except to say that those issues related to IA that are to be addressed by the IA specialists and others, should be as team players. They should undoubtedly be authorised to use this room as needed for their response teams, etc.

## 8.1.19   Corporate-Wide Security Measurement System

*"Develop, implement and maintain a company-wide security measurement system that permits evaluation of the effectiveness of each company element security program, the total company security programs and benchmarking with security programs of comparable companies."*

In order to accomplish this function throughout the corporation, the CSO must have integrated by whatever means, e.g. matrix management, teaming, the IA processes at the CSO level. If not, it would be difficult to view the total company security functions, and accurately benchmark them.

## 8.1.20   Law Enforcement Liaison

*"Liaisons with federal, state and local law enforcement, investigative and fire agencies."*

The same process that applies for liaison with security personnel in government agencies applies (see paragraph 8.1.15).

## 8.1.21   Chair Corporate Security Council

*"Chair the corporate Security Council to develop a common company-wide approach to address security processes and problems."*

The CSO can use this opportunity to ensure that the issues of IA are addressed by ensuring that members of the Council include those responsible for IA within the corporation.  However, this may not be the case. The CSO would usually include representatives of the legal, audit, human resources, and others, but may often neglect those with some of the most important roles related to corporate assets protection – the IA staff.

## 8.1.22    Corporate Security Policy and Procedures

*"Develop corporate security policy and procedures to address the following security processes: Security quality and oversight; Personnel security; Information security; Physical security; Investigations; Fire protection; and Contingency planning."*

The corporate security policy must be based on specific requirements. Those requirements must come from somewhere. After all, the CSO, or anyone for that matter, should not just make them up as something that seems to be good to do. Such an approach would cause the establishment of requirements and subsequently policy and procedures that may not be necessary or cost-effective.

Requirements should be traced back to authoritative sources such as audit standards, security standards, contractual requirements, laws, etc. Once those were identified, their intent could be discerned and based on that information a security policy to include information protection and defence can be developed. Once developed with input from all those who have asset protection responsibility, the corporate security policy document would be one that met the requirements from the authoritative sources. Thus providing a process for establishing only the minimum security necessary for the protection of all corporate assets. From that policy, procedures would be developed by lower level organisations that would implement that policy and meet the various mandated requirements.

Taking that one step lower, the following addresses the specific functions noted above and how they relate to IA:

- *Security quality and oversight*: the corporate policy and procedures requirements for this function provides that the CSO would be responsible for leading the overall corporate security and asset protection program and ensuring that it was done in a cost-effective, quality manner.
- *Personnel security*: the policy would require that all employees undergo a minimum background check prior to employment; with those in positions identified as sensitive (such as operations staff, programmers, IA personnel) would require a more in-depth background check.
- *Information security*: this policy and subsequent procedures would undoubtedly require the input from the IA staff; however, it must cover more than that. It must cover information that is not automated nor related to information systems.
- *Physical security*: the policy must not only address the physical access to facilities, areas, and the like; but also how electronic media, videos, and documents containing sensitive information are to be physically protected.
- *Investigations*: how one would conduct investigations relating to information systems attacks, theft and destruction of information and the like must also be addressed. This policy would obviously provide the leadership under the CSO, but should include forensic support from the IA staff or those in IT. Regardless, an investigation related to information systems would undoubtedly be due to a breach in protection and therefore of serious concern to the IA staff

who must be involved in such investigations as integral members of the investigative team.

- *Fire protection*: obviously fire protection plays an important role in protecting information and information systems. No policy or procedures can be complete without IA input.
- *Contingency planning*: as stated above, contingency planning policy must also address IA issues, and input from IT and IA staffs are mandatory if it is to be done right.

## 8.1.23   The CSO as the IA Leader

One can easily see that almost all of the functions of a CSO have a direct impact and relationship to IA functions. It stands to reason that the CSO should also be the IA leader. However, this will never be possible if the CSOs continue to neglect their professional responsibilities and fail to understand information systems. Until that professional responsibility is accepted by CSOs, IA responsibility will continue to allude them and fall under the purview of the IT staff. As one can understand after reading the above, there is also too much opportunity for conflicts on how best to proceed in doing the IA functions in a manner that is best for the corporation. The way that the CSO believes IA functions should be accomplished to be cost-beneficial and best for the corporation is often different from the approaches by the IT staff. Under such conditions, teaming is difficult as office politics come into play. Furthermore, IA suffers and will continue to suffer under such conditions. Is it any wonder then that surviving in the information environment is so difficult?

# 8.2   Summary

The CSO and the corporate security functions under the CSO's purview all have some impact on how the IA functions are performed. Since the IA functions are normally not a corporate security function, but usually an IT function, there must be continuous communication and co-operation between the two professions. This is not always the case. The CSO should be in the corporate leadership position when it comes to the corporate assets protection program and that includes the IA functions.

# Chapter 9

## IA in the Interest of National Security

This chapter identifies and explains information assurance requirements, specifically those related to information systems, in the national security environment of a government-related corporation. This chapter also discusses the philosophy and processes that can be adapted to information assurance programs in the world of business. [1]

## 9.1 Introduction

One may wonder why discuss national security in the context of information assurance. There are several reasons for this as noted below:

- National security obviously impacts government agencies; however, it also impacts individuals and businesses of every size and type. This also includes other nation-states, thus foreign governments; as well as foreign businesses and citizens from other nations.
- In today's global marketplace and global information environment, what happens in one nation often impacts what happens in other nations. In this age of information warfare, one has many examples of national security affecting other nations and businesses. The defacing of government and business web sites and denial of service attacks between the Chinese in mainland China and those on Taiwan; the Israeli-Arab incidents and the Serb-NATO incidents, just to name a few.
- If national security is impacted, businesses are impacted. One can look to World War II and see the bombing of industrial plants – commercial businesses – by the other's adversaries. In any incident, police action or war

---

[1] The reader who does not work for a company or university with government contracts may want to skip this chapter. However, many of the requirements set forth by various government agencies for the protection of their (the government's) information and information assurance can cost-effectively be applied to the protection of non-government information. Also, one never knows whom they may be working for from time-to-time. Thus, the information presented in this chapter may provide some future value.

where a nation's security is adversely impacted, the businesses of that nation are also adversely impacted. Therefore, it is obvious that any conflicts between nations where at least one of the nations is information dependent, attacks will be made against telecommunications systems, web sites, Internet accesses, and the like. These are for the most part non-government systems. Furthermore, in today's global, competitive marketplace, economic power is being emphasised more than military power. Therefore, in order for an adversary to weaken a nation, the adversary would undoubtedly attack the economic might of a nation – its economic might is derived from its businesses. So, virus attacks, denial of service attacks, theft of sensitive information, placing misinformation on corporate networks, etc. are very likely to be used.

- In every modern nation and especially information-based nations of the world, corporations are under contract to research, design, develop and produce weapons that can be used for the protection of the nation-state. In today's modern, information based nations, there are literally thousands of universities and corporations under contract to government agencies. These businesses may exist solely for developing products for government agencies or may be producing various products for government agencies and also producing products for commercial use. They may be accomplishing these projects using the same information systems, application programs and even the same information. Corporations do many of the current government-sponsored research projects under contract. These not only can and will be used to assist government agencies, but also eventually can be used by businesses. The research into information-based defensive weapons is of such a nature.

- A cyber-attack on a corporation can also be viewed as an attack against national security. Nations are preparing to attack other nation's information infrastructures, which are generally private businesses.

- The modern world is rapidly becoming one integrated supply chain. Corporations for government agencies, other corporations that may be involved in the defence industry or for commercial businesses and customers, are producing products. Some of these may even be of a foreign nature. This inter-relationship means that what may happen to one corporation or nation, may adversely impact other corporations on a global scale. And since these modern corporations are information dependent and information based, information assurance plays an important role. One just has to look at the devastating earthquake in Kobe, Japan, and its affect on worldwide supply of chips, to see this global dependency.

## 9.2    National Security Classified Information

When one thinks of information valuation in the national security arena, one has just as difficult a time determining its value as is the case in the corporate world. However, there is no doubt that the value of information of national security interest is obviously much greater than that of any corporation. If a corporation's information is not adequately protected and defended, one's corporation may go out of business. However, if the same thing were to happen to a nation's national security information, the nation may cease to exist except as part of another nation. National security classified information is one of the most important categories of information which must be safeguarded by all in the interest of national security. It is mentioned here briefly because the process used to place a value on that information goes through more stringent analyses than personal, private and business information.

In the United States, as an example, national security classified information is generally divided into three basic categories:

- *confidential*: loss of this information can cause damage to national security;
- *secret:* loss of this information can cause serious damage to national security; and
- *top secret*: loss of this information can cause grave damage to national security.

There is also national security information that is not classified, as that stated above, but requires some lesser degree of controls and protection because it has value, but less value. These include:

- For Official Use Only;
- Unclassified But Sensitive Information; and
- Unclassified Information.

There is also a category of classified information that is considered "black" or "compartmented". Such information is further protected by not only requiring a security clearance and the need-to-know, but also often an additonal background investigation and special briefing. Such efforts are often called "Special Access Required information", "Special Access Program information", and "Sensitive Compartmented information". In these compartments, IA must include some of the most stringent processes as this information can truly be considered the "crown jewels" of a nation.

Using the United Kingdom as another example, security is treated in a similar fashion, as it is by most other nations. The following is quoted from referenced web site[2] to give you some idea as to the thinking surrounding national security information and its value:

*"The Prime Minister: In recent years, the nature of the threats to Government security has changed. While some of the traditional threats to national security may have somewhat reduced, others have not. The security of Government is also increasingly threatened by, for example, theft, copying and electronic surveillance, as well as by terrorism.*

*"To ensure that their approach to security reflects current threats, the Government have recently completed a review of their arrangements for the management of protective security in Departments and agencies. This has recommended a new protective marking system for documents which will help*

---

[2] http://www.parliament.the-stationery-office.co.uk/pa/cm199394/cmhansrd/1994-03-23/Writtens-4.html

*identify more precisely those which need protecting, enabling them to be protected more effectively according to their value. The new system will also be more closely related to the code of practice on Government information announced in the Government's White Paper on openness.*

*"In addition, the review has concluded that existing security measures should be examined closely to ensure they are necessary in relation to today's threats; that commercially available security equipment should be more widely used; and that personnel vetting enquiries should be streamlined particularly in routine cases. Overall, the aim is to give Departments and agencies, and management units within them, greater responsibility for assessing the nature of the risks they face and for making decisions, within a framework of common standards of protection, about the security measures they need to put in place. Substantial cost savings will result.*

*"The first stage of the implementation of the proposals of this review will be the introduction of a new protective marking system with effect from 4 April 1994 alongside the code of practice on access to Government information. The new definitions, which will allow fewer Government documents to be classified, particularly at the higher levels, are set out. The other elements of the new approach to protective security will be put in place in due course. The four categories of protective marking: Definitions. The markings to be allocated to any asset, including information, will be determined primarily by reference to the practical consequences that are likely to result from the compromise of that asset or information. The levels in the new protective marking system are defined as follows:*

- *"**Top secret**: the compromise of this information or material would be likely: to threaten directly the internal stability of the United Kingdom or friendly countries; to lead directly to widespread loss of life; to cause exceptionally grave damage to the effectiveness or security of United Kingdom or allied forces or to the continuing effectiveness of extremely valuable security or intelligence operations; to cause exceptionally grave damage to relations with friendly governments; to cause severe long-term damage to the United Kingdom economy.*

- *"**Secret**: the compromise of this information or material would be likely: to raise international tension; to damage seriously relations with friendly governments; to threaten life directly, or seriously prejudice public order, or individual security or liberty; to cause serious damage to the operational effectiveness or security of United Kingdom or allied forces or the continuing effectiveness of highly valuable security or intelligence operations; to cause substantial material damage to national finances or economic and commercial interests.*

- *"**Confidential**: the compromise of this information or material would be likely: materially to damage diplomatic relations (i.e. cause formal protest or other sanction); to prejudice individual security or liberty; to cause damage to the operational effectiveness or security of United Kingdom or allied forces or the effectiveness of valuable security or intelligence operations; to work substantially against national finances or economic and commercial interests;*

*substantially to undermine the financial viability of major organisations; to impede the investigation or facilitate the commission of serious crime; to impede seriously the development or operation of major government policies; to shut down or otherwise substantially disrupt significant national operations.*

- **"Restricted***: the compromise of this information or material would be likely: to affect diplomatic relations adversely; to cause substantial distress to individuals; to make it more difficult to maintain the operational effectiveness or security of United Kingdom or allied forces; to cause financial loss or loss of earning potential to or facilitate improper gain or advantage for individuals or companies; to prejudice the investigation or facilitate the commission of crime; to breach proper undertakings to maintain the confidence of information provided by third parties ; to impede the effective development or operation of government policies; to breach statutory restrictions on disclosure of information; to disadvantage government in commercial or policy negotiations with others; to undermine the proper management of the public sector and its operation."*

## 9.2.1 An Example of National Security Information Impact

When looking at the impact of information assurance failure in the national security arena, there are more serious consequences than just losing the corporate competitive advantage. The following example by Mr. Perry Luzwick, an information assurance expert at Logicon Corporation in the United States, put it this way:

*"What is the cost to replace the information, and the cost of lost business/profits or national security? Here's an example of perceived value. The Department of Defense sends a roll-on/roll-off (RORO) ship with 100 M1A1 Abrams main battle tanks to South Korea. The ship encounters bad weather in the North Pacific, suffers damage from mechanical problems and cargo which became unsecured, takes on water, and sinks. The nation bemoans the loss of life, Military Sea Lift Command calculates sealift shortfall workarounds, and Material Command orders more tanks. The value of the tanks, ship, and loss of life can be accurately calculated by traditional accounting methods.*

*"Change the scenario. North Korean actions indicate probable conflict. The United States wishes to show its resolve and support for an ally, so it sends a RORO with 100 M1A1s to meet activated Army and Marine Corps Reservists airlifted to South Korea. The ship sinks. What is the value of the tanks? The perceived value is definitely higher than the accounting value. What is the value of the information the ship sunk to the North Koreans?"*

There are many more examples that can be given; however, the point is made: national security information impacts nation-states and corporations.

## 9.3 Information Assurance Requirements in the National Security Arena

There are many similarities between the IA requirements in the corporate world and the world of national security as practised by government agencies and defence industry-related corporations. Of course, such things as initial and recurring background investigations of employees are more stringent; as well as physical security requirements and the implementation of the need-to-know principle. This section will concentrate on those related directly to information and information systems protection and defence requirements. The information systems are sometimes called automated information systems (AIS).

In the case of a defence industry-related corporation, the IA requirements are incorporated into the contract between the government agency and the contractor. A defence industry-related corporation would then include such IA requirements into contracts with subcontractors, associated contractors, team members, etc. where those businesses will also be handling government information. This is logical as it does no good to provide IA in one corporation while another uses the same information and is not required to do likewise.

The main emphasis of information assurance deals with compromise of national security information. Unless there is a state of war, information that is destroyed or inappropriately modified may be reconstructed, albeit possibly taking a great deal of time. However, the compromise of national security information may make the product being developed of little use since the adversary has the information and can build like products or products of a defensive nature. The worst-case scenario is when a compromise occurs and no one knows that it has occurred. Thus, time, money and other resources are expended that will be of little use if they are needed since, as noted earlier, using the compromised information the adversary has developed defensive systems that make the other nation's products useless. So, the IA requirements are implemented so that:

- National security information is to be protected from compromise that would allow an adversary to compete in building like systems, developing countermeasures, or delaying operational use of the systems.
- The compromise or delays in product development would be accomplished through manmade, hostile acts of:
  - Espionage through authorised or unauthorised accesses to information, e.g. theft.
  - Sabotage through fire (destruction), water (destruction), or software (e.g. destruction, theft, manipulation) using such malicious codes as Trojan horses, viruses, logic bombs.
- IA in a national security environment must also protect and defend against natural acts such as fire, water, earthquakes, windstorms, and the like.

It is the responsibility of the IA specialist to understand the national security requirements, especially those specified in the contract. The IA specialist must be able to provide an IA program for the defence industry-related corporation that includes increasing awareness of the need for an effective IA program in the government environment and also provide basic guidance and understanding necessary for the development of the IA program in that environment.

The fundamental national IA requirements are that there be:

- *IA policy*: the set of laws, rules, and practices that regulate how a defence industry-related corporation manages, protects, defends and distributes national security information.
- *Accountability*: individual and information accountability is the key to protecting, defending and controlling any system that processes, stores, and transmits national security information on behalf of the individuals or groups of individuals.
- *Assurance*: guarantees or provides confidence that the IA policy has been implemented correctly and the IA elements of the system accurately mediate and enforce that policy.
- *Documentation*: development documentation records how a system is structured and what it is supposed to do and gives the background information upon which the design is founded. Control documentation records the resources used in developing and implementing a system that will process, store and transmit national security information.

## 9.3.1    IA Objective in the National Security Environment

The overall objective of IA in the national security environment is to prevent unauthorised access to classified information during or resulting from information processing and prevent unauthorised manipulation that could result in national security information being compromised. This is done by:

- protecting and defending information stored, processed and transmitted by an automated information system (AIS);
- preventing unauthorised access, modification, damage, destruction or denial of service; and
- providing assurances of:
  - compliance with government and contractual obligations and agreements;
  - confidentiality of private, sensitive and classified information;
  - integrity of information and related processes;
  - availability, when required, of information;
  - use for authorised business and by authorised personnel only of information and AIS; and
  - identification and elimination of fraud, waste, and abuse.

## 9.3.2    Responsibilities

The responsibilities for compliance with the AIS security requirements in the world of national security are similar to those of the corporate world. Management is responsible for ensuring compliance with IA requirements, policies and procedures; as well as ensuring the reporting of violations. All employees are of course responsible for understanding their responsibilities; as well as complying and reporting violations to management. However, in this case, the seriousness of the information and its implications due to loss or compromise, requires that violations be immediately reported and inquiries conducted. The disciplinary action taken against violators is usually more severe.

### 9.3.3 Collective IA Controls

The IA controls that must be considered for any national security environment include:

- individual accountability;
- physical controls;
- system controls;
- system stability;
- data continuity;
- least privilege;[3]
- communications security; and
- national security information controls.

These controls are based on the contractual and non-contractual requirements and generally established national security principles. The IA program that includes the objectives and controls noted above are usually approved by the government security officer responsible for the security of the corporation's contractual efforts. In fact, each system that is considered for use to process, store and transmit national security-related information must be approved by the government's security officer (GSO) for the contract. The entire effort often has a name designated for it by the government customer and it is also called a program instead of a contract, e.g. Widget Program.

### 9.3.4 Government Customer Approval Process

In order to process national security information, the government customer must approve each AIS prior to authorising its use to process, store or transmit national security information. In order to gain that approval, the government customer usually requests:

- identification of the AIS;
- physical location;
- mode of operation;
- level of national security information to be processed;
- equipment listing:
  - size and type of internal memory and storage media;
  - components where national security information is retained;

---

[3] "Least privilege" means that the user or program can only access that information needed and no more. Furthermore, the user does not have any authority that is not absolutely necessary to perform the work assigned, e.g. add, delete, modify databases or information.

- • disconnect methods used to separate various components, e.g. printers;
- • switching devices to disable equipment; and
- • block diagram of hardware with links.
- software information to include the types of operating system(s) and firmware; application programs, vendors name, and version numbers; and
- communications devices:
  - • configuration;
  - • interfaces;
  - • identification;
  - • points of encryption;
  - • remote devices; and
  - • protection procedures.

## 9.3.5   AIS Modes of Operation

There are a number of modes of operation that can be used to process, transmit and store various types of national security information. The mode used is authorised by the government customer based on the authorised variations in the AIS IA environment. It is based on the personal security clearances of the users and national security information access needs, e.g. secret clearance held by the users and their need to use that information to accomplish the contractual tasks assigned. It is also based on the automated and manual information protection and defence controls that will be used.

The modes of operation that are used generally fall into four distinct categories:

- *Dedicated*: the users all have a personal clearance equal to the highest level of national security information being processed, stored, and transmitted by the AIS, and a need-to-know (NTK) for all the information on that AIS.
- *Systems high*: all the users have a personal clearance but not a NTK for all the information on the AIS. The users must be separately identified and controlled. This is generally done through passwords, identification devices and add-on software packages.
- *Partitioned*: all users have a personal clearance for the highest level of national security information processed, but not necessarily have they had a special briefing and NTK for all the information on the AIS. The general controls include a separate identity and password for each user, possibly a special briefing and NTK. The AIS is partitioned, to include possibly two or more CPUs in the same "box", using the same communication links.
- *Multilevel*: this mode permits concurrent processing of various, separate national security-related, multi-contractual programs' information. This is the highest level, most costly, and least flexible of the security modes and is seldom used. Users on these AIS may or may not have a personal security clearance or NTK for all the information on the AIS. Thus, someone with no national security background check or clearance can use the system containing national security information. This is possible because the system is so secure

that it prevents the user from accessing national security information or national security information of a higher level than the user is cleared to access.

## 9.3.6   The Appointment of the Defence Industry-Related Corporation's Focal Point for IA

Gaining approval to process, store and transmit national security information usually requires the approval of the government customer security officer. As with any such process, documentation is required on which to base that approval. The types, format and specific requirements will vary depending on the customer and the classification of the information, e.g. Top Secret, Secret, Confidential.

This IA-related document usually requires that the defence industry-related corporation appoint a focal point with the responsibility for ensuring the national security information is protected in accordance with the contract and applicable related laws, regulations, and other provisions as specified by the government customer.

The responsibilities of the IA leader[4] include:

- directing the IA program for the contract;
- ensuring that the personal clearance and NTK of users is in place and enforced;
- ensuring that the users receive national security briefings and training;
- ensuring audit trails are in place and audit records reviewed in a timely manner;
- ensuring the AIS is operating as approved by the government customer;
- ensuring that any IA-related problems are promptly handled; and
- designating IA custodians for each AIS who are responsible for the day-to-day IA program for the specified AIS.

## 9.3.7   Documenting and Gaining Government Customer Approval for Processing, Storing and Transmitting National Security Information

As mentioned earlier, many government customers require that they approve individual AIS or groups of similar AISs that will be used to process, store and transmit national security information. However, this approval may be delegated to the corporate IA leader. The approval is considered after reviewing the AIS IA-related documentation in a format that they specify and which is usually stated in the contract. The documentation requirement can be very detailed or it can be

---

[4] The individual appointed may have a different title than IA depending on the government customer, nation-state, or defence industry-related corporation. That person may be known as the Corporate IA Officer, the Corporate Information Security Officer, the Widget Program IA Officer, etc. Furthermore, the need for documentation, type, etc. will vary not only by nation but also by government agencies within a nation.

general in nature, depending on the AIS and the government customer's requirements. The government customers using the government-approved document for that AIS written by the defence industry-related corporation may then periodically inspect the AIS. Regardless of the format, what is of primary importance is that the IA-related issues be addressed and documented. The following is an example describing the various IA-related issues that may be addressed in documentation:

- *Identification*: identify the specific AIS or AISs (if they are all identical, e.g. desktop computers, local area networks with workstations). This would include their make, model, serial numbers, physical location, and mode of operation.
- *Summary of System Usage*: this section would include the level of national security information to be processed, any local and remote capabilities; hours of national security information processing; and the percentage of information on the AIS that is considered national security, classified information.
- *AIS Hardware*: the specific hardware must be identified and include a floor plan, schematic, disconnect methods if networked, and any switching devices for disabling the AIS.
- *AIS Software*: the name, type, versions of the software and how they are safeguarded to ensure that they were not replaced with another version; this includes protection and defence software such as those used for access control, intrusion detection etc.
- *Communications*: this section would include the identification of the equipment and transmission lines, disconnect methods, configurations and interfaces, remote devices, protection procedures, and physical controls on the lines.
- *Personnel*: their IA responsibilities, controls to restrict access, visitor and maintenance personnel controls.
- *Physical Controls*: this section would include a description of the physical safeguards and characteristics to include any computer facilities and remote areas.
- *General Access Controls*: described herein would be how passwords were used, logon and logoff procedures, and how users with various national security clearances and NTK were segregated.
- *AIS Operations*: this section would describe how systems were started, used, and shutdown, to include how they were reconfigured if used at different times for different government programs.
- *Information Storage, Protection Controls*: this section would be used to describe how information was controlled, handled, marked, stored (using what type of accountability system), declassifying the information (e.g. process used to downgrade information, e.g. from Secret to Restricted), and how the information will be destroyed when required. This section not only deals with the hardcopies coming off the systems but also the electronic media used as storage devices.
- *Audit Trails and Records*: this section would be used to describe the various types of manual and automated audit trail programs and records that would be

used. Included herein would be samples of each; as well as their analyses processes.

- **Emergency Plan**: this section would describe the procedures to be used in the event of any emergency to include a security violation, system crash or other emergencies that may be possible depending on the information environment.

Remember, the level of description and details documented would be based on the national security requirements as specified in the contract.

# 9.4 Summary

Thousands of universities, as well as large and small corporations have government contracts. These contracts vary from research and development contracts to production contracts. Most of them rely heavily on information systems and the use of national security information. These corporations are targets of attacks by other corporations, as well as a nation's adversaries. This includes some of its "allies" (who are allies in a military sense but adversaries in a economic sense) who also want to gain that competitive edge in economic and military development. Furthermore, they want to do so without paying the high costs of research and development. It is cheaper to steal the information than to develop it on one's own.

A defence industry-related corporation whose systems will process, store and transmit national security information has a responsibility not only to the corporation but to the nation and its citizens. How well the corporation implements an IA program that will be used to safeguard the national security information has a direct bearing on the security of the nation.

The IA-related requirements and the processes implemented to meet those requirements, although having more serious consequences than that of corporate sensitive information, really is not that much different than those of a corporation's IA program.

Establishing an IA focal point; establishing IA controls; documenting how systems will operate; and how information and systems will be protected is always a good practice – regardless of the type of sensitive information processed, stored and transmitted.

# Chapter 10

## The Corporate IA Officer

The need for a Corporate Information Assurance Officer is discussed in this chapter. The topics discussed include the required basic qualifications for a person in that position; as well as the duties and responsibilities needed to lead an information assurance program for a 21$^{st}$ century corporation.

## 10.1 The Corporate Information Assurance Officer (CIAO)[1]

The position of the CIAO is a relatively new, but necessary position. It is more than that of the Corporate Security Officer (CSO) or the Corporate Information Systems Security Officer (CISSO) because the information assurance (IA) functions are much more than that of the "old" information systems security or corporate security professions.

The discussion of the position of a CIAO will be based on what it should be as there are only a few such positions today, and they are relatively new positions, e.g. at Microsoft. However, it is felt that when one looks at the totality of the IA and information systems security administration and management functions, one can see the need for such a position. In addition, this position in today's information dependent environment includes issues related to privacy and liability issues. This is a logical progression of the professional CSO and CISSO to a CIAO. This is because the issue of privacy and liability have a direct bearing on why a formal IA program is necessary and the ability of the CIAO to provide adequate IA.

---

[1] Some of the information provided are excerpts from Dr. Kovacich's book, *Information Systems Security Officer's Guide: Establishing and Managing an Information Protection Program*, published by Butterworth-Heinemann, May 1998 and reprinted with permission.

## 10.1.1 CIAO Position

The CIAO's position requires someone with education and experience that is so much more than that of "just a computer techie". In fact, it is believed that the CIAO's duties are somewhere between 75% management and 25% of actual IA work. Therefore, whoever assumes that position should generally have the following education and experience:

- *Education*: a combination of undergraduate and graduate degrees in computer science/information systems, criminal justice/criminology, information systems security/business security, social science, investigations, psychology, business management and related fields. An MBA in international business or related graduate degree would be a plus. One may ask, why an MBA? The rationale for this is that at the corporate level, the individual in the position of the CIAO must have a good understanding of business, especially global business these days, because each IA-related decision made by the CIAO will have an impact on resource allocations, budgets, productivity, and the like. One can have the best IA program in the world but if it stifles productivity and dramatically increases business costs, then the corporation may not be able to compete as effectively, thus losing their market share. This may even lead to a business going out of business. Maybe such a statement is a little overly dramatic but the point is made. For those in government agencies, the same would apply since there is little difference these days in managing a government agency and a business organisation from the standpoint of information dependencies, resource allocations, budget, and the like.
- *Certifications*: the CIAO should be, as a minimum, a Certified Information Systems Security Professional (CISSP). Additional certifications such as a Certified Information Systems Auditor, Certified Fraud Examiner, Certified Protection Professional, all help ensure that the individual filling the position of a CIAO understands the issue of IA from a holistic perspective.
- *Experience*: the CIAO should have a minimum of 10 years of experience managing an IA, information systems security, or corporate security organisation, to include experience in: formal project management; budgeting; people-skills; teambuilding; total quality management/continuous process improvement; matrix-management; time management; problem-solving, and other related management experience.

## 10.1.2 CIAO Duties and Responsibilities

In concert with the executive management of the corporation, the CIAO should develop and receive approval for formally establishing a charter of the CIAO duties and responsibilities. The following charter example is provided:

Summary of the purpose of the corporation's CIAO position: *develop, implement, maintain, manage and administer a corporate-wide IA program to include all plans, policies, procedures, processes, assessments, and authorisations necessary to protect and defend the corporation's information and information systems. This includes ensuring their availability, integrity, authentication, confidentiality, non-repudiation, as well as also providing for restoration of information and information systems by incorporating protection, detection and reaction.*[2]

Since the CIAO is also assumed to be a manager and manage an IA organisation, the CIAO's duties and responsibilities should include those noted below:

### 10.1.2.1   *Managing people which includes:*

- building a reputation of professional integrity;
- maintaining excellent business relationships;
- dealing with changes;
- communicating;
- developing people;
- influencing people in a positive way;
- building a teamwork environment; and
- developing people through performance management, e.g. help IA staff to be results-oriented.

### 10.1.2.2   *Managing the business of IA which consists of:*

- a commitment to results;
- being customer/supplier focused;
- taking responsibility for making decisions;
- developing and managing resource allocations;
- planning and organising;
- being a problem-solver;
- thinking strategically;
- using sound business judgement; and
- accepting personal accountability and ownership.

---

[2] The CIAO position summary is taken from United States directive NSTISSI 4009 which defines IA. The definition is used because it not only defines IA but also describes what the CIAO is directed to do.

### 10.1.2.3  *Managing IA processes which includes:*

- project planning and implementation;
- persistence of quality in everything;
- maintaining a systems perspective; and
- maintaining current job knowledge.

## 10.1.3  Goals & Objectives

The CIAO must have goals and objectives. These must directly support the goals and objectives of the corporation. Since any IA program for a corporation is centred on providing service and support to meeting the corporation's goals and objective, this is quite logical.

### 10.1.3.1  *The CIAO's Goal*

The CIAO's primary goal should be to *administer an innovative IA program which minimises risks to information and liability risks at least impact to costs and schedules, while meeting all of the corporation's and customers' (internal and external) reasonable expectations.* This goal sounds very bureaucratic, "managerial", and possibly even a little "academic". Well, all that may or may not be true. However, as a goal, it sets the direction of an IA program for the corporation and assists the CIAO in focusing on doing what must be done to attain that goal. Let's dissect that goal and see why that is so.

*Administer an innovative program* means that the CIAO manages a program that must be flexible and have the ability to rapidly change to meet the needs of the corporation. The idea of innovation means that just because it has not been done a certain way before does not mean that it should not be tried. Such ideas as brainstorming with others and "thinking outside the box" are integrated into solving problems and implementing processes to meet the corporate needs.

*Minimises risks to information and liability risks at least impact to costs and schedules* means that all processes integrated into the IA program, and all decisions made must be considered on the basis of ensuring that the minimal amount of risks are taken. In addition, what must also be considered and decided is how to do that, how to obtain that "perfect balance" between minimal risks; while at the same time of having the least impact. By least impact we mean impact on people's productivity, additional costs to projects and the business, and also without adversely impacting the project and business schedules of the corporation. It is extremely important that such decisions incorporate this thought process, whether or not this is a formally established goal. The CIAO may even want to use a checklist identifying such items when making a decision. As a minimum, when such decisions are implemented or submitted to management for approval, such information will greatly assist the decision makers in supporting a CIAO's decision.

*While meeting all of the corporation's and customers' (internal and external) reasonable expectations* means that the IA processes, IA program and IA-related decisions accomplish what is expected of the CIAO and the IA program in terms of IA. Internal customers means that the management and employees of a corporation that the CIAO provides IA services and support to are considered customers and should be treated as such. Additionally, external customers are those identified as customers by the corporation, to possibly include suppliers, associates, subcontractors and the like.

Sometimes the CIAO is placed in a difficult position by trying to meet this goal. Management may disapprove of a particular IA approach but then the CIAO is held responsible for any adverse impact to information, even though the proposal by the CIAO, if it had been implemented, would have mitigated the problem. Such is the life of a CIAO!

### 10.1.3.2  The CIAO's Objective

It is assumed that the CIAO will be responsible for managing an IA organisation in order to meet the needs of the corporation. The CIAO's objectives should include the following:

- Enhance the quality, efficiency, and effectiveness of the IA organisation.
- Identify potential problem areas and strive to mitigate them before the corporate management and/or customers identify them.
- Enhance the corporation's ability to attract customers because of the ability to efficiently and effectively protect information.
- Establish the IA organisation as the IA leader in its industry.

## 10.1.4  Leadership Position

The CIAO must be in a leadership position. In that position, it is extremely important that the CIAO understands what a leader is, and how a leader is to act. According to the definition of *Leadership* found in numerous dictionaries and management books, it is basically about the position or guidance of a leader, the ability to lead, the leader of a group; a person that leads; directing, commanding, or guiding head, as of a group or activity. As a *leader*, the corporation's CIAO must set the example; create and foster an information protection "consciousness" within the corporation.

As a *corporate leader,* the CIAO must communicate the corporation's community involvement; eliminate unnecessary expenses; inspire corporate pride; and find ways to increase profitability.

As a *team leader,* the CIAO must encourage teamwork; communicate clear direction; create an IA environment conducive to teaming; treat others as peers and team members not as competitors; and recognise their needs also.

As a *personal leader,* the CIAO must improve personal leadership skills; accept and learn from constructive criticism; take ownership and responsibility for decisions; make decisions in a timely manner; and demonstrate self-confidence.

### 10.1.4.1   Providing IA Service and Support

As the CIAO and leader of an IA service and support organisation, the CIAO must be especially tuned to the needs, wants and desires of the corporation's customers.

To provide service and support to the corporation's external customers, the CIAO must:

- identify their information protection needs;
- meet their reasonable expectations;
- show by example that the IA program can meet their protection expectations;
- treat customer satisfaction as top priority;
- encourage feedback and listen;
- understand their needs and expectations;
- treat customer requirements as an important part of the job;
- establish measures to assure customer satisfaction; and
- provide honest feedback to customers.

To provide service and support to the corporation's internal customers, the CIAO must:

- support their business needs;
- add value to their services;
- minimise IA impact on current processes; and
- follow the same guidelines as for external customers.

The CIAO will also be dealing with suppliers of IA products. These suppliers are a valuable ally because they can explain to the CIAO the many new IA problems being discovered, how their products mitigate those problems, and generally they can keep the CIAO up-to-date on the latest news within the CIAO/IA profession.

In dealing with suppliers of IA-related products, the CIAO should:

- Advise them of the corporation's needs and what types of products that can help.
- Assist them in understanding the corporation's requirements and products that the corporations may want from them, to include what modifications they must make to their products before the corporation is willing to purchase them.
- Direct them in the support and assistance they are to provide the corporation.
- Respect them as team members.
- Value their contributions.
- Require quality products and high standards of performance from them.

### *10.1.4.2   Use Team Concepts*

It is important that the CIAO understand that the IA Program is a corporate program. To be successful, the CIAO cannot operate independently, but as a team leader, with a team of others who also have a vested interest in the protection of the company's information and information systems.

It is important to remember that if the IA functions are divided among two or more organisations, there will naturally be a tendency for less communication and co-ordination. If that occurs, the CIAO must be sensitive to this division of functions and must ensure that even more communication and co-ordination occurs between all the departments concerned.

The IA program must be "sold" to the management and staff of the corporation. If it is presented as a law that must be followed or else, then it will be doomed to failure. The CIAO will never have enough staff to monitor everyone all the time, and that's what will be needed. For as soon as the CIAO's back is turned, the employees will go back to doing it the way they want to do it. Everyone must do it the right IA way because they know it is the best way and in their own interests, as well as in the interest of the corporation.

In the corporation, as in many companies today, success can only be achieved through continuous inter-departmental communication, co-operation, and specialists from various organisations formed into integrated project teams to solve company problems. The CIAO should keep that in mind – teaming and success go together in today's modern corporation.

## 10.1.5   Vision, Mission, and Quality Statements

Many of today's modern corporations have developed vision, mission, and quality statements using a hierarchical process. In other words, they flow up and down the management chain. The statements should link all levels in the management and organisational chain. The statements of the lower levels should be written and used to support the upper levels and vice versa.

The following examples can be used by the CIAO to develop such statements, if they are necessary.

### *10.1.5.1   Vision Statements*

In many of today's businesses, management develops a vision statement. The vision statement is usually a short paragraph that attempts to set the strategic goal, objective or direction of the company. It is:

- clear, concise and understandable by the employees;
- connected to ethics, values and behaviours;
- states where the corporation wants to be (long term);
- sets the tone; and

- sets the direction for the corporation.

An IA vision statement may be to: provide the most efficient and effective IA program for the corporation, which adds value to the corporation's products and services, as a recognised leader in the financial industry.

### 10.1.5.2   Mission Statements

Mission statements are declarations as to the purpose of a business or government agency.

An IA mission statement may be to: Administer an innovative IA program which minimises security risks at least impact to cost and schedule, while meeting all of the corporation's and customers' IA requirements.

### 10.1.5.3   Quality Statements

Quality is what adds value to the corporation's products and services. It is what the corporation's internal and external customers should also expect from the CIAO.

An IA quality statement may be to: Consistently provide quality IA professional services and support that meet the customers' requirements and reasonable expectations, in concert with good business practices and company guidelines.

### 10.1.5.4   Project and Risk Management Processes

Two basic processes that are an integral part of an IA program are project management and risk management concepts.

- *Project Management Concepts*: as the CIAO and IA program leader, the CIAO will also provide oversight of IA-related projects which are being worked by members of the CIAO staff.  The criteria for a project should be as follows: formal projects, along with project management charts, will be initiated where improvements or other changes will be accomplished and where that effort has an objective, beginning and ending dates, and will take longer than 30 days to complete.  If the project will be accomplished in less than 30 days, a formal project management process is not needed. The rationale for this is that projects of short duration are not worth the effort (costs in terms of hours to complete the project plan, charts, etc.) of such a formal process.
- *Risk Management Concepts*: to be cost-effective, the CIAO must apply risk management concepts (see Chapter 3 for risk management concepts) and identify:
  - threats to the information and information systems;
  - vulnerabilities (information systems' weaknesses);
  - risks; and
  - countermeasures to mitigate those risks in a cost-effective way.

## 10.2 Summary

The Corporate Information Assurance Officer (CIAO) position is needed in today's information-driven and information-dependent corporation. The position requires someone who has the education and experience to lead a corporation's IA efforts. The position calls for someone who understands systems, security, and business, as well as the risks to information and how to cost-effectively mitigate those risks. The CIAO must be focused on the goals and objectives of the corporation and integrate an IA program into the corporation's processes that will assist (or at least not deter the corporation) in meeting those goals and objectives. The CIAO must be results-oriented, use team concepts, and project management techniques to be successful.

# Chapter 11

## IA Organisational Functions

This chapter describes and discusses the establishment of a corporate information assurance organisation and its major functions. The Corporate Information Assurance Officer would manage the organisation.

## 11.1 Determining Major IA Functions

There are many IA functions and these functions can be grouped and assigned to various organisations within the corporation. For example: the physical security function would undoubtedly remain within the corporate security organisation. The function of auditing for compliance to corporate policies would also undoubtedly remain within the audit department. To integrate those functions into an IA organisation would dilute the main tasks of the corporate information assurance officer (CIAO), as well as being almost impossible politically. In addition, there should be some basic separations of functions, e.g. the organisation establishing IA policy should not also be auditing that policy to ensure that it is adequate.

The CIAO's duties and responsibilities within any medium or large corporation cannot be successfully accomplished by the CIAO alone. Therefore, it is logical that specialists be assigned as staff to the CIAO. The size of that staff is driven by several factors. These factors include what is known as IA drivers. In other words, those factors that cause the CIAO's workload to increase and decrease. The following three drivers are offered as examples:

- *Number of systems*: the more systems and their various configurations, type of hardware and software and the like all have a bearing on the amount of information and systems activity going on within the corporation. Thus, the more information systems the greater the task of protection and defence.

- *Number of system's users*: the number of system users has a direct bearing on the workload of the CIAO. The more users, the more IA infractions that will occur, and the more information on those systems that require protection.
- *Importance of information being stored, processed and transmitted*: the CIAO's workload is also driven by the sensitivity of the information being stored, processed and transmitted by the systems. For example, IA is not an issue if the information is not important and it is an important issue if the information is deemed sensitive and important to the corporation.

The CIAO and the IA organisations should have at least the following basic IA-related functions and processes under their authority:

- requirements;
- policy;
- systems IA architecture;
- awareness and training;
- access control;
- security tests and evaluations;
- non-compliance inquiries;
- risk management; and
- disaster recovery/contingency planning program.

One must consider the office politics and related aspects of these functions. Each corporate culture is unique and the functions that should be performed by the IA organization in lieu of another organization within the corporation is generally solely based on the amount of support that is given to the CIAO by the corporation's executive management. Thus, the need for the CIAO to manage an IA program using teambuilding concepts and other management techniques as stated in Chapter 10, will determine whether or not the CIAO will be successful. What is essential is for the CIAO to make a case to the corporation's executive management as to why certain functions belong within the IA organziation. However, if that support is not forthcoming, the CIAO should concentrate on being successful in accomplishing the job assigned and not worry about obtaining the other functions, regardless of their importance to the IA program. The next step would then be to co-ordinate IA-related interests with the managers assigned to the IA-related functions and try to integrate the IA interests into those functions.

An example is the awareness program. If that function is given to the corporate security officer's organisation, the CIAO should work with that manager to ensure that the AI interests are integrated into the overall corporate security awareness program. This has several advantages such as the IA staff not having to develop an entirely new awareness program; not require additional budget and also not require the allocation of at least one dedicated individual to that function. It also eliminates the perception that the CIAO is neither a "team-player" nor an "empire builder".

## 11.2   IA Functions and Process Development

Let us assume that the CIAO has been authorised and given an approved budget (a very key and necessary aspect of corporate life) by executive management to establish an IA organisation to meet the IA program needs of the corporation. Let us further assume that the basic IA functions noted above have been approved to be under the authority and responsibility of the CIAO. With that in mind, the CIAO can proceed to establish an IA organisation so that a corporate IA program can be established. It is not the intent of this book to delve into how to recruit and hire IA staff, but only to address the functional aspects of an IA organisation.

Such functions should be established using an orderly and systematic method. In fact, this is the first IA project that should be formalised into a project plan, complete with objectives, tasks, dates for accomplishment; identify who will do each task, and an estimated time for accomplishing the tasks. It is also important from a management aspect to formalise this project so the project plan can be used to periodically brief executive management on the status of the project as well as to track the costs of the project. Remember the old saying "time is money". Well, that is certainly truer today than ever before. By costing out such projects, it will assist the CIAO in establishing the cost-factors associated with developing, implementing and maintaining a cost-effective IA program. This in turn will provide a history on which to base future costs of functions and portions of the IA program; as well as to justify budget requirements.

This all supports and relates back to the goals and objectives stated through the vision, mission, and quality statements noted in Chapter 10. By using those goals and objective statements, one can begin to see how a CIAO can focus on "doing it right the first time". In other words, the CIAO is beginning this effort from ground zero and thus can integrate good management practices as the IA program is developed. This is much easier than trying to integrate such methods and philosophies into an IA program after that program has matured.

In order to effectively and efficiently identify and establish the IA functions to be accomplished by the CIAO's IA organisation, a standard process should be developed. By establishing a process for each function as the first task, it will assist in ensuring that the functions will begin in a logical, systematic way that will lead to a cost-effective IA program. By identifying and using IA work drivers as noted above, the CIAO can begin to develop such a process. In addition, an experienced CIAO will pretty much know what needs to be done usually in what order and how to accomplish those tasks. More than likely, the CIAO brings to this position the methods that have been successful in the past – at least one hopes that is the case.

## 11.2.1   IA Requirements Function

The CIAO has determined that one of the main drivers for any IA program is obviously the requirements for IA. The requirements are the reason for the IA program. After all, if it was not required, it would not exist as the corporation has no intention of spending precious resources, e.g. money, on programs that are not needed. This is obvious but sometimes it is necessary to state the obvious. This *need* is further identified and defined, and subsequently met by the establishment of the IA functions.

So, to begin the functions' process identification, it is important to understand where the requirements, where the need, comes from. For most corporations, it includes:

- a need for an IA program as stated by the corporation's executive management to protect the corporation's competitive edge which is based on information systems and the information that they store, process and transmit;
- a requirement as specified in contracts with corporate customers, e.g. protect and defend their information;
- a requirement as specified in contracts with corporate subcontractors, e.g. protect and defend their information;
- a requirement as specified in contracts with corporate vendors, e.g. protect and defend their information;
- the desire of the corporation to protect its information and systems from unauthorised access by customers and subcontractors, vendors, and others; and
- national and international laws that are applicable to the corporation, e.g. requirements to protect the privacy rights of individuals and corporations as they relate to the information stored, processed and transmitted by the corporation's systems.

## 11.2.2   IA Policy Function

Based on the requirements and IA drivers as stated above, the CIAO must take the next step which is to develop an overall corporate IA policy; co-ordinate that policy with applicable department managers; and gain executive management approval for that IA policy. That policy should be clear, concise and written at somewhat of a high level. It must conform to the corporate policy format of course. The IA policy should not get bogged down in details at a system identification level but set the IA guideline for the corporation.

The IA policy should be distributed to all department managers and that distribution should be done through a cover letter, signed by the CEO, President, and/or Chairman of the Board. That letter should basically state the information is important to the corporation's well being and competitive edge; the IA policy document provides the overall policy for protecting that competitive edge and obligates all of the corporate employees to support that policy.

The policy establishes the baseline for the corporation for the protection and defence of information and information systems. It must be the first function to be addressed after establishing the requirements because all other functions must flow from, or derive their guidance from the policy function. If there is not a logical and cost-effective policy in place, a logical and cost-effective IA program can not be established.

The IA policy should be set forth in a corporate IA Requirements and Policy Directive. The directive should generally include the following:

- introduction section, which includes some history as to the need for IA;
- purpose section which describes why the document exists;
- scope section which defines the breadth of the Directive;
- responsibilities section, which defines and identifies IA responsibilities at all levels to include executive management, organisational managers, systems custodians, IT personnel, and users. The Directive should also include the requirements for customers', subcontractors', vendors', and others access to the corporate systems and information;
- requirements section, which includes the requirements for:
    - identifying the value of the information;
    - access to the information and to the systems;
    - access to specific applications, databases and files;
    - audit trails and their review;
    - reporting responsibilities and action to be taken in the event of an indication of a possible violation;
    - minimum protection requirements for the information, hardware, firmware and software; and
    - a requirement for developing, implementing and maintaining current IA procedures at all levels of the corporation.

## 11.2.3   IA Procedures Function

Based on the corporate IA policy, each organisation must establish procedures, based on its unique environment, number of systems, types of configurations, hardware, software, types of information and the value of the information under its responsibility. These organisational IA procedures provide detailed direction as to how each organisation is to comply with and support the corporate IA policy.

This has several advantages including:

- the individual organisational managers are in a better position to write the document and develop cost-effective procedures which work for their organisation;

- it makes the department, especially managers, responsible for compliance with the IA policy. In other words they have a shared investment in the IA program;
- it negates the managers' complaints that their situation was unique and thus they could not comply with all aspects of an IA procedure as written (if one had been written by the CIAO staff); and
- it also relieves the CIAO of dealing with this large a magnitude of procedures throughout the corporation; and places it squarely where it belongs: on the individual organisational managers and employees.

## 11.2.4   Systems IA Architecture Function

One of the primary functions of any IA program should be the systems IA architecture function. This function ensures that IA requirements are met through integration of IA architecture into the systems architecture of each corporate IT project. Furthermore, it is imperative that this function be integrated into the total corporate systems architecture. When the IA architecture requirements are met, it will automatically comply with IA policy. Therefore, IA systems architecture specialist(s), assigned to the IA organization should be involved as a team member of each new systems development project. The philosophy is this:

- design it to protect and defend information and information systems;
- build it to protect and defend information and information systems;
- test it to protect and defend information and information systems;
- implement it to protect and defend information and information systems; and
- maintain it to protect and defend information and information systems.

## 11.2.5   IA Awareness and Training Function

It naturally follows that once the IA policy has published there must be some process to make the corporate employees aware of the IA requirements. There must be a process to:

- advise new employees of the IA policy;
- advise non-employees who use the systems and information of the IA policy;
- advise all users of the information and systems of changes in that policy;
- provide reminders to users as to that policy; and
- gain the support of everyone by explaining the need for such a policy and requirements.

   The Awareness Program process can be broken into four major parts:

- awareness briefings for new employees;

- awareness briefings for non-employees but users of the corporate information and systems;
- recurring, e.g. annual, awareness briefings; and
- IA training for IA staff members and those employees with some IA responsibilities.

### 11.2.5.1   Awareness Briefings

The IA awareness briefings in some corporations are integrated into new-hire orientation briefings and they are also integrated into security-related briefings. As mentioned earlier, it may be required to integrate the IA awareness material to be used for an IA briefing into the other corporate briefings. If that is the case, there is a concern that the personnel giving the briefings do not understand IA concepts in sufficient detail to give the briefings and answer questions relative to IA – or worse yet, provide erroneous information. Another concern is that the IA portion of any of the other briefings does not allow sufficient time to adequately inform the attendees of all the pertinent IA information that they should know. If an IA awareness briefing must be integrated into other briefings, it may be possible for an IA specialist to provide that portion of the briefing.

Ideally, the IA awareness briefings should be tailored, based on the unique jobs of the specific audiences as follows:

- all new hires, whether or not they used a system. The rationale is that they all handle information and come in contact with computer and telecommunication systems in one form or another;
- managers;
- system users;
- information technology department personnel;
- engineers;
- manufacturers;
- accounting and finance personnel;
- procurement personnel;
- human resources personnel;
- security and audit personnel; and
- the system IA custodians (those that would be given day-to-day responsibility to ensure that the systems and information were protected in accordance with the IA policy and procedures, e.g. access control administrators; firewall administrators, audit trail records reviewers.

A process should be established to identify these personnel, input their profile information into a database, and using a standard format, track their awareness briefings attendance, both their initial briefings and any annual re-briefings, etc. That information could also be used to provide them, through the corporate e-mail system, with additional awareness material.

As part of the IA awareness process, those attending such a briefing should acknowledge in writing that they understand their responsibilities and agree to comply with the requirements and policy.

It is well understood that all users and others must understand the IA requirements and policy in order to support the protection and defence of information and information systems. However, another key element supporting the need for the IA awareness briefings is to hold the users accountable for their actions if they are subsequently identified as violating the IA policy. Such violations may be cause for not only disciplinary action but civil or criminal action as well. In any case, a basic requirement that must be presented as evidence in any proceedings is as follows:

- a current IA policy exists;
- the IA policy was violated;
- the person was made aware of that policy;
- the person acknowledged in writing that the IA policy was understood and would be followed; and
- the person acted with intent to violate that IA policy.

Most of the violations will probably be due to human error. Even if human error and no malicious intent is identified, it still has an impact on the protection and defence of the corporation's sensitive information and information systems.

### 11.2.5.2   IA Awareness Material

One of the other means used to make systems users and others aware of IA requirements, policy and their responsibilities is to provide reminders through various media. This should be done in a cost-effective manner. It is often difficult to quantify the costs-benefits of awareness material. However, it is still recommended as a good procedure to keep users aware of IA matters, and includes such material as:

- annual calendars;
- posters;
- labels for systems and diskettes;
- articles published in the corporate news publications; and
- logon notices and system broadcast messages, especially of IA changes.

## 11.2.6   Access Control and Audit Records Analyses Functions

Once the IA requirements are identified, the IA policy published and everyone made aware of that policy, the next logical step would be to look at the processes used to control access to systems, applications and information. Access controls must be maintained on all systems and to all information that are considered sensitive. In other words, if the systems or information can be destroyed without adversely impacting the corporation's business, then access controls are not considered necessary – it may be prudent to still control access, but it is not an IA requirement. Access controls are expensive and require intensive amount of resources to adequately maintain them. Therefore, their use should always be based on IA requirements and IA policy. The requirements and policy are based on the value of the information and the information systems to the corporation.

### 11.2.6.1   Access Control

Access control is based on the need-to-know principle. That means that access to information and to information systems is only provided to those personnel with the need for access to information and systems. The criteria is that access is required in order for them to successfully function in their position within the corporation, or as non-employees to support the corporation as part of their contracts or other legal agreements. A basic principle of IA is that access is only provided to that information and systems required for the individual to complete their tasks – no more and no less. Thus, there is a need for access control processes.

As part of any access control function and process, there must be personnel in positions of authority who are the designated owners of the information and/or systems. These owners must authorise the identified personnel access to the information and/or systems. It is not the responsibility of an IA organisation to authorise access to information and/or systems but to either directly control access as an IA function or indirectly through various organisational personnel designated as access controllers and assigned to other organisations. For example: as part of the IA program, the CIAO, in co-ordination with other departments' managers, can establish a process for all corporate employees and others who require access to the systems. The employees would obtain system access approval from the manager or designated representative who owned that system.   The information owners' approval is based on a justified need-for-access as stated by the employee's manager. If the systems' owners and information owners agreed, access is granted. Thus, the access control process included a justification by an employee's manager stated not only what systems and why they needed access to them, but also what information they required access to in order to perform their jobs.

An audit trail is then maintained of who approved access to whom, and for what purposes. It also helps provide a separation of functions, which is a vital component of any IA program, e.g. accounts payable personnel should not also have access to all the accounts receivable files.

### 11.2.6.2   Access Control Systems

Access control systems may be integrated hardware, firmware and/or software applications. They also may be an integrated manual and automated process; or even an administrative and technical process. However it is established, the process must be safeguarded at the highest levels because a compromise or successful attack against the access control systems means the heart of the IA goals of protection and defence have been violated. After all, these are the front-line defences of a corporation's systems and information. Access control systems must be thoroughly and often tested to validate and verify that they are operating as expected.

### 11.2.6.3   Audit Records Analyses

Having access control systems in place, no matter how good, does nothing to identify that an attack or probe of the access control systems was being conducted. It is bad enough to be under attack but much worse not to even know that an attack is occurring until that fateful moment when it is successful, e.g. the systems are not available such as in a denial of service attack (DOS). What if the objective of the attack was to probe the system for weaknesses and when found steal sensitive information? There would be no DOS, no missing or modified information. No one would even know that the probe had taken place and that it was successful and that now the competitor of the corporation had the proprietary information that it had long sought.

It is amazing how many corporations do not require audit trail records or if so, place them in storage in either hardcopy or on electronic storage devices – without being reviewed. The rationale is that there is no time to review and analyse the records for indications of attacks and probes. In today's information environment this is unconscionable.

When an attack is discovered, often after the damage has been done, the audit records may be analysed to determine what happened. However, these are historical documents and cannot replace real-time monitoring where an attack may be identified and stopped before it can be successful. So, it would fall into the "too little, too late" category.

It is true that in major corporations there are massive amounts of data that can and are being collected that would give indications of attacks and probes. However, the problem is more complicated than just the vast amount of audit trail records available from systems. There are also other problems:

- audit records are unique to each system;
- audit records for each system provide different levels of information granularity in different ways and formats;
- reviewers of audit trail records are not trained on what to look for and what actions to take in the event certain, specific events were noted; and
- audit records are not integrated into a database for analyses across the entire corporation to present an "IA picture" from a holistic point of view.

It is often a misconception that the reviewer only should look for unauthorised access attempts. That is only part of the issue. The unauthorised access attempts can and often do indicate attacks and probes against the systems, but what is often more important is a look at the authorised accesses. These indicate that someone using a valid userid and password entered the system, but how is one to know that the person was not using a stolen userid and password?

What is needed if this basic concept of access control and audit records analyses is to work is to develop an automated process to collect all the corporate systems' audit records. Then using artificial intelligence and neural networks one can begin to truly conduct the analyses required. Integrated into this automated process would be the profile of what each user requires access to under the need-to-know concept, what they had been approved to access and profiles of all the users' activities, what they access, when, etc. Such an automated audit records analyses would compare the normal activity of the users and alert IA personnel or access administrators to deviations from the norm. Such a system is urgently required in order to begin to establish a true IA program.

## 11.2.7  Evaluation of all Hardware, Firmware, and Software Function

After IA requirements have been identified, incorporated into an IA policy document, and the CIAO's staff of IA requirements and IA system architecture specialists are working with systems development project teams, it is imperative that the hardware, software, and firmware be evaluated. These evaluations are needed to ensure that their vulnerabilities are identified and processes established to mitigate those vulnerabilities using such processes as the risk management methodologies noted in Chapter 3.

The evaluations can be done by various methods. The key is to know what the vulnerabilities are for each system. Some of the evaluation methods are as follows: '

- Contact the supplier of the product and identify the vulnerabilities and seek their advice on how to mitigate them. It should be noted that they may not be completely honest; however, that is why a rapport and trust must be developed with the suppliers as noted in Chapter 10 concerning the CIAO and suppliers/vendors.
- Establish an in-house team of specialists that are intimately familiar with the product and determine the product vulnerabilities and how to mitigate them.
- Contact other professionals in the field to get their opinions and advice on the product's vulnerabilities and how to mitigate them.
- Review magazines, web sites, CERT announcements related to the products and their vulnerabilities and how to mitigate them.
- Outsource vulnerability testing to a company with the expertise to identify product vulnerabilities and how to mitigate them.

The objective is to build systems that meet at least the minimal protection and defence requirements as established by the corporation's IA program. One must also remember that the systems currently in place must also be evaluated in a similar fashion. This process is not limited to systems in development.

An additional process that may be helpful is to establish an IA baseline checklist that would be completed by the prospective suppliers of the product, in concert with the IA staff. The process would include a technical evaluation by IA personnel in concert with IT personnel. If the product was considered *risk-acceptable*, it can be approved for purchase. If not risk-acceptable, the risk management process would be used to identify countermeasures. If the risks were unacceptable and weighed using a cost-benefit-risk methodology, and the products were still to be purchased, executive management should be called upon to make the final decision of acceptable and unacceptable risks.

Some items may have an unacceptable level of risk, but would still be accepted due to its value to the corporation and its competitive edge. In those instances, special audit trails should be considered to monitor the use of the product with the goal of identifying threat agents that could take advantage of the products' vulnerabilities. In any case, it is better to at least know that a system is vulnerable, than to not know the vulnerability existed until it was too late.

## 11.2.8  Applying Risk Management Principles and Establishing a Risk Management Function

Although Chapter 3 discussed the risk management principles and methodologies, it is a process that permeates the entire IA program and should be the basis for all decisions made to protect and defend information and information systems. Thus, its application and summary information is stated here.

Remember the objective of an IA program's risk management process is to *maximise information protection and defences, and minimise cost through risk management.*

*What Is Risk Management?* In order to understand the risk management methodology, one must first understand what risk management means. Risk management is defined as the total process of identifying, controlling, and eliminating or minimising uncertain events that may affect corporate information and information system resources. It includes risk assessments; risk analyses including cost-benefit analyses; target selection; implementation and test; security evaluation of safeguards; and overall IA review.

### 11.2.8.1  Risk Management Process Goals
The goal of the risk management process is to provide the best protection and defence of systems and the information they store, process and/or transmit at least cost consistent with the value of the systems and the information.

### 11.2.8.2    Risk Management Process

Remember that the IA program is a corporate program made up of IA professionals and others who provide service and support to their corporation. Therefore, the risk management process must be based on the needs of the corporation, its customers, et al, and not on the needs of the CIAO, staff or IA program. It is also important that one be sure that the risk management concepts, program and processes are informally and formally used in all aspects of the IA program to include when and how to do awareness briefings, the impact of information systems security policies and procedures on the employees, etc.

The following steps should be considered above and beyond the "normal" risk management approach in the risk management process:

- *Management Interest*: identify IA areas which are of major interest to executive management and customers; approach from a business point of view. So, the process should begin with interviews of your internal customers to determine what areas of IA are adversely affecting their operations the most. Then, target those areas first as the starting point for the risk management program.
- *Identify Specific Targets*: software applications, hardware, telecommunications, electronic media storage, etc.
- *Input sources*: users, system administrators, auditors, security officers, technical journals, technical bulletins, CERT alerts (Internet), risk assessment application programs, etc.
- *Identify Potential Threats*: internal and external, natural or man-made.
- *Identify Vulnerabilities*: through interviews, experience, history, testing.
- *Risk Identification*: match threats to vulnerabilities with existing countermeasures, verify, and validate.
- *Assess Risks*: acceptable or not acceptable, identify residual risk, then certify the process and gain approval. If the risks are not acceptable, then:

  - identify countermeasures;
  - identify each countermeasures' costs; and
  - compare countermeasures, risks and costs to mitigated risks.

### 11.2.8.3    Recommendations to Management

When the risk assessment is completed, the CIAO must make recommendations to management. Remember in making recommendations to think from a business point of view: cost, benefits, profits, public relations, etc.

### 11.2.8.4    Risk Management Reports

A briefing that includes a formal, written report is the vehicle to bring the risks to management's attention. The report should include identifying areas that need improvement; areas that are performing well; and recommended actions for improvement, to include costs and benefits.

Remember that it is management's decision to either accept or mitigate the risks, and how much to spend to do so. The CIAO and IA staff are the specialists, the in-house consultants. It is management's responsibility to decide what to do. They may follow the CIAO's recommendations, ignore them, or take some other action. In any case, the CIAO has provided the service and support required.

If the decision is made that no action will be taken, there is still a benefit to conducting the analyses. The CIAO at least now has a better understanding of the environment, as well as an understanding of some of the vulnerabilities. This information will still help in managing an IA program.

## 11.2.9    IA Tests and Evaluations Function

The IA tests and evaluations function (T&E) is a required function to be used in the testing phases of new system development as part of the normal system development lifecycle. It is also an integral part of the product evaluation process, and risk management function.

T&Es should be done using formal project management techniques and a formal testing and evaluation approach. A minimum criterion for testing should be established as a baseline. This criterion should be based on the IA requirements and IA policy. For example: the T&E would include obtaining a userid on a system with various access privileges. The IA staff member, using that identification would violate that system and attempt to gain unauthorised access to various files, databases, and systems. That information would be analysed in conjunction with a comparison of the systems' audit trails. Thus, profiling the IA of an information system. Also, the T&E would include a review of records and prior audit trail documents to help establish the "IA environment" being tested and evaluated.

## 11.2.10    IA Non-Compliance Inquiries (NCI) Process

When users or other employees do not follow established IA policy and procedures, there must be a process in place to determine the who, where, when, why, and how of the incident. An auditor, a corporate security investigator or a member of the IA staff can be designated to complete that function. There are advantages and disadvantages of each. For example:

- The auditor may know how to audit for compliance and some knowledge of audit-related interview techniques; however, they are not investigative specialists familiar with collection of evidence techniques, interrogation techniques and related laws.

- The corporate security investigator may have a good understanding of evidence collection, laws and interrogation techniques, but limited knowledge in computer forensics and systems in general.
- The IA specialist may know information protection and defences, systems in general and computer forensics, but is limited in knowledge of relative laws, interrogations, and evidence collection.

In order to conduct NCIs in a professional manner, the CIAO should be responsible for a preliminary review of the incident and a decision made to refer it to corporate security investigators based on a predetermined criteria.

The corporate security investigator with an IA staff member identified to assist should conduct the inquiries into matters referred to them by the CIAO. The IA staff member would conduct the computer forensics (e.g. electronic media searches for evidence) portions of the investigation, under the guidance of the investigator. NCIs are at least 75% accomplished using the normal investigative techniques. What is different is the "scene of the crime". Thus, the need for an IA staff specialist assistance. In addition, the IA staff specialist, while working with the investigator, can obtain information that will assist in determining the impact of the incident on the IA program. For example: new vulnerabilities may be identified, new threat agent techniques may also be identified, and the IA policy may need to be updated. Such information must also feed back into the other IA processes and considered when conducting T&Es, awareness briefings, access control system configurations and the like. It is imperative that each IA process supplements and supports the other IA processes.

Regardless of who takes the lead in conducting NCIs, there must be a process to at least conduct them in a professional and expeditious manner. In addition, they should be done in a confidential manner in order to protect the privacy of those involved. Remember not everyone accused of a violation is guilty of that violation.

To call such incidents inquiries instead of investigations is done for a specific purpose. The term "investigation" generally is considered more serious. Law enforcement agents with badges and guns who investigate violations of laws normally conduct them. This is considerably different to an "investigation" into whether or not someone shares his or her password with another. Thus, when an investigation is being conducted within a corporation, one can differentiate between the two. Furthermore, when someone outside the corporation hears the world "investigation" they are more inclined to think of it as a serious incident and not one where passwords were shared. Such matters when heard by the news media and stockholders provide for very bad public relations.

## 11.2.11    IA Contingency Planning and Disaster Recovery Function (CP-DR)

Establishing an IA contingency planning and disaster recovery function is one of the least difficult programs to establish, and yet, always seems to be a difficult task to accomplish. With the change in information systems' environments and configurations, e.g. client-server, LAN, distributed processing, etc., this problem may be getting worse.

Prior to discussing CP-DR, it is important to understand why it is needed. It is really a very important aspect of an IA program, and is its most vital function if the protection and defences fail. The CIAO must remember that the purpose of IA is to:

- minimise the probability of an information and systems protection vulnerability;
- minimise the damage if a vulnerability is exploited; and
- provide a method to quickly recover efficiently and effectively from the damage.

### 11.2.11.1    What is it?
Contingency planning is a plan for responding to emergencies, back-up operations, and recovering after a disaster; it addresses what action will be taken to return to normal operations. Emergencies requiring action would include such natural acts as floods, earthquakes, human-caused acts of fires, hacker attacks causing denial of services, etc.

Disaster Recovery is the restoration of the information and/or information systems, facility, or other related assets following a significant disruption of services.

### 11.2.11.2    Why Do It?
The question of why do it is a question often asked, primarily by users, e.g. why should I back-up my information? Why is a CP-DR program necessary? Everyone associated with using, protecting, maintaining information systems and the information that they store, process, and/or transmit must understand the need for such a program. It is:

- to assist in protecting vital and sensitive information;
- to minimise adverse impact on productivity; and
- to stay in business!

### 11.2.11.3 How Do You Do It?

Each CP-DR program is unique to the environment, culture and philosophy of each business or government agency. However, the basic program, regardless of business or agency, requires the development and maintenance of a CP-DR plan. It must be periodically tested, problems identified, corrected, processes changed to minimise the chances of adverse events happening again.

### 11.2.11.4 The CP-DR Plan

The CP-DR plan should be written based on the standard format for writing plans used by the corporation. The following generic format is offered for consideration:

- *Purpose*: state the reason for the plan and its objective. This should be specific enough so that it is clear to all who read it why it has been written.
- *Scope*: state the scope and applicability of the plan. Does it include all systems, all locations, subcontractors?
- *Assumptions*: state the priorities, the support promised, and the incidents to be included and excluded. For example: if the area does not have typhoons, will you assume that typhoons, as a potential disaster threat, will not be considered?
- *Responsibilities*: state who is to be responsible for taking what actions. This should be stated clearly so everyone knows who is responsible for what. Consider a generic breakdown such as managers, systems administrators, users, etc. Also, specific authority and responsibility should be listed by a person's title and not necessarily their name. This approach will save time in updating the plan due to people changes.
- *Strategy*: discuss back-up requirements; how often they should be accomplished based on the sensitivity of the information; state how it will be recovered, etc.
- *Personnel*: maintain an accurate, complete and current list of key CP-DR personnel, to include addresses, phone numbers, pager numbers, cellular phone numbers, etc. Be sure to establish an emergency prioritised, notification listing, and a listing of response teams members and how to contact them in an emergency.
- *Information*: maintain on-site inventory listing and an off-site inventory listing; identify the rotation process to ensure a history and current inventory of files. Identify vital information. This information must come from the owners of that information and must be classified according to its importance, based on approved guidelines.
- *Hardware*: maintain an inventory listing, to include suppliers, name, serial number, property identification number, etc.; ensure emergency replacement contracts are in place; maintain hardcopies of applicable documents on-and-off site.

- *Software*: identify and maintain back-up operating systems and application systems software. This should include original software and at least one back-up copy of each. Be sure to identify the version numbers, etc. In this way, you can compare what is listed in the plan and what is actually installed. It would not be the first time that software back-ups were not kept current and compatible with the hardware. Thus, the systems may not able to work together to process, store and transmit much-needed information.

- *Documentation*: all important documentation should be identified, listed, inventoried and maintained current in both on-and-off site locations.

- *Telecommunications*: the identification and maintenance of telecommunications hardware and software listings are vital if the corporation is operating in any type of network environment. Many systems today can not operate in a standalone configuration. Thus, the telecommunications lines, back-ups, schematics, etc. are of vital importance to getting back in operation within the time period required. As with other documentation, their identification, listing, etc. should be maintained at multiple on-and-off site locations. The CIAO should be sure to identify all emergency requirements and all alternate communication methods.

- *Supplies*: supplies are often forgotten when establishing a CP-DR plan as they often take a "back-seat" to hardware and software. However, a listing and maintenance of vital supplies are required, to include the name, address, telephone numbers, contracts information concerning the suppliers of those supplies. The CIAO should also be sure to store sufficient quantities at appropriate locations on-and-off site. If the CIAO doesn't think this is an important matter, try using a printer when its toner cartridge has dried out or is empty and no others are available. Physical supplies for consideration should include plastic tarpaulins to cover systems from water damage in the event of a fire where sprinkler systems are activated.

- *Transportation and Equipment*: the CIAO should also determine if a back-up facility is needed or whether or not to obtain back-up copies of software for storage at that facility, etc. The CIAO obviously must have transportation and the applicable equipment (e.g. a dolly for hauling heavy items) to do the job. Therefore, the CIAO must plan for such things to include: listing emergency transportation needs and sources; stating how emergency transportation and equipment will be obtained; and which routes and alternate routes to take to off-site location(s). The CIAO must also be sure to include maps in the vehicles and also in the plan; and there are fully-charged, hand-held fire extinguishers available which will work on various types of fires, e.g. electrical, paper, chemicals.

- *Processing Locations*: many businesses and agencies sign contractual agreements to ensure that they have an appropriate off-site location to be used in the event their facility is not capable of supporting their activities. Also one must ensure that emergency processing agreements are in place which will provide you with priority service and support in the event of an emergency or disaster. Even then, you may have a difficult time using the facility if it is a massive disaster and others have also contracted for the facility. The facility should also be periodically used to ensure that one can process, store and/or transmit information at that location. Also it is a good idea to identify on-site locations which can be used or converted for use in the event of other than a total, major disaster.

- *Utilities*: identify on-site and off-site emergency power needs and locations. Don't forget that these requirements change as facilities, equipment, and hardware changes. Battery power and un-interruptable power might not be able to carry the load or are too old to even work. They must be periodically tested. For as with the printer cartridge supplies, systems without power are useless. Besides power, one should not forget the air conditioning requirements. It would be important to know how long a system can process without air conditioning based on certain temperature and humidity readings.
- *Documentation*: identify all related documentation; store it in multiple on-and-off site locations; and be sure to include the CP-DR plan!
- *Other*: miscellaneous items not covered above.

### *11.2.11.5   Test the Plan*

There is no use in having a plan that has not been tested, for only through testing can the CIAO determine that the plan has any chance of working when required. Therefore, it must be periodically tested. It needs not be tested all at once because that would probably cause a loss of productivity by the employees that would not be cost-effective.

It is best to test the plan in increments, relying on all the pieces to fit together when all parts have been tested. Regardless of when and how one would test the plan, which is a management decision, it must be tested. Probably the best way to determine how and what to test, and in what order, is to prioritise testing based on prioritised assets.

When testing, the scenarios used should be as realistic as possible. This should include: emergency response; testing back-up applications; systems; and recovery operations. Thorough testing, documenting the problems and vulnerabilities identified must be done. Also, why problems occurred must be determined and formal projects established to fix each problem. Additionally, the CIAO and other team members should make whatever cost-effective process changes are necessary to ensure that the same problem would not happen again, or the chance of it happening is minimised.

# 11.3   Summary

The CIAO and the IA organisational functions and processes will vary depending on the culture, management commitment, and business of the corporation. However, a summary of these functions is provided as an example of what should be done as part of an IA program and thus by the CIAO and IA staff.

- Identify all government, customers, and corporate IA requirements necessary for the protection and defence of all information processed, stored and/or transmitted by the corporation's information systems; interpret those requirements; and develop, implement and administer plans, policies and procedures necessary to ensure compliance.
- Evaluate all hardware, firmware, and software for impact on the protection and defence of the information and the information systems; direct and ensure their modification if requirements are not met; and authorise their purchase and use within the corporation and applicable customers, subcontractors, associates, and other locations.
- If needed, establish and administer a technical security countermeasures program to support IA requirements. (Example: this program would mitigate emanations across communications links that would cause "data leaks" across cables)
- Establish and administer an IA tests and evaluations program to ensure that all the corporation's and applicable subcontractors', suppliers', and customers' information systems are operating in accordance with their contracts.
- Direct the use of, and co-ordinate: monitoring of the corporation's information systems access control software systems; analyses of all systems' protection and defence infractions/violations; and reporting of the results to the CIAO for review and appropriate action.
- Identify information systems business practices and IA violations/infractions; support the conducting of inquiries; assess potential damage; and implement/recommend corrective/preventive action.
- Develop, implement and administer a risk management program; provide analyses to management; modify IA requirements accordingly to ensure a least-cost IA program.
- Establish and administer an IA awareness program for all corporate employees and other users of the information systems to ensure they are cognisant of information systems threats; and IA policies and procedures necessary for the protection and defence of information and information systems.
- Direct and co-ordinate a corporate-wide information systems disaster recovery/contingency planning program to mitigate the possibility of loss of systems and information, and to assure the rapid recovery of information systems in the event of an emergency or disaster. This function should be co-

ordinated and integrated into the Corporate Security's corporate CP-DR program.

- Support the Corporate Security organisation in conducting high-technology crime and abuse inquiries where there are indications of intent to damage, destroy, modify, or release to unauthorised people, information of value to the corporation. (Note: the main task is to provide computer forensics and computer-related technical service and support)
- Direct the development, acquisition, implementation and administration of IA software systems.
- Direct and establish a process to mitigate the potential for the corporation's systems' protection to cause liability and privacy issues that would adversely affect the corporation.
- Represent the corporation on all IA matters with customers, government agencies, suppliers and other outside entities.
- Provide advice, guidance, and assistance to corporate management and employees relative to IA matters.

# Section 3

# Technical Aspects of IA

This section will discuss the technical aspects of information assurance as it relates to information and information systems storing, processing and transmitting of information. No book, even one providing an introduction to information assurance, can be complete without some discussion of operating systems, application software and their relationship to, and integral part of, an information assurance program. Chapter 12 provides that overview.

Since no information assurance program can provide any sort of protection without encryption, Chapter 13 discusses the use of cryptography, e.g. PKI, as a means of information protection in a corporate information-dependent environment. This section concludes with Chapter 14 looking at technical equipment that can be used to protect or attack an information system, e.g. TEMPEST, HERF guns, EMP weapons.

# Chapter 12

## IA and Software

No discussion of information assurance is complete without at least an overview of IA as it relates to operating systems and application software. This chapter will discuss information assurance problems and possible solutions as they relate to operating systems and application software. The discussion will include views on malicious codes such as viruses, logic bombs and Trojan horses.

## 12.1 Operating Systems and Trusted Systems

### 12.1.1 Security Policies

Mandatory access control (MAC) means that access control policy decisions are made beyond the control of the individual owner of an object. A central authority determines what information is to be accessible and by whom. With a mandatory access control policy, a user cannot change their, or another's, access rights. By contrast discretionary access control (DAC) leaves a certain amount of control to the discretion of the owner of an object. With DAC the owner of an object has the ability to define the access rights that are granted to a user. Commercial operating systems such as NT and Unix use discretionary access controls to facilitate the accounting and auditing functions.

As stated earlier, a policy is a statement of the security that we expect the system to enforce. An operating system can only be trusted in relation to its security policy. The military policy of security is based on a need-to-know. Each asset is given a protective marking. The higher the protective marking the greater the need for security. In general, the military model of information security defines information security in terms of confidentiality. A person wishing to access an information asset must have been given the necessary clearances to access the information. A clearance is an indication that a person is trusted to access information up to a certain level of sensitivity. The most commonly used security model to analyse military security policy is the Bell-La Padula model.

The commercial world is less rigid and hierarchically structured than the military one. This has led to a set of alternative security policies being developed and utilised. Clark and Wilson proposed a security policy based upon *well-formed transactions*, which they assert are as important in the commercial domain as confidentiality is in the military domain. In terms of a business process, performing the actions in order, performing exactly the actions listed, and authenticating the individuals who perform the actions, constitutes *a well-formed transaction*. Clark and Wilson present their policy in terms of *transformation procedures* which process *constrained data items*. A transformation procedure is a function that only operates on specific kinds of data items, and these data items are manipulated only by transformation procedures.

The *Chinese Wall Security Policy* is a security policy that reflects certain commercial needs for information access protection. In order for this security policy to function we need to define three levels of abstraction:

- *Objects*: at the lowest level are elementary objects, such as files. Each file contains information concerning only one corporation.
- *Corporation Groups*: at the next level, all objects concerning each corporation are grouped together.
- *Conflict Classes*: at the highest level, all groups of objects for competing companies are clustered.

Each object belongs to a unique corporation group and each corporation group is contained in a unique conflict class. The access control policy is rather simple. A person can access any information as long as the person has never accessed information from a different corporation in the same conflict class. That is, access is allowed if either the object requested is in the same corporation group as the object that has been previously accessed, or the object requested belongs to a conflict class that has never been accessed before.

## 12.1.2   Models of Security

The Bell-La Padula model is a formal description of the allowable paths of information flow in a secure system. The objective of the model is to identify allowable communication where it is important to maintain security. This model uses the following definitions:

- The *subject* refers to the entity that can access the information. A subject could be a computer, a program or a person.
- The *object* refers to the information that the subject is attempting to access.

The Bell-La Padula security model only allows a subject to access an object in two ways: *read* and *write*. The security class of an object "*o*" is denoted by the function $C(o)$. Typical security classes are Top-Secret, Secret, Confidential, and Unclassified. This security model makes use of two axioms to characterise a secure information flow.

- Simple Security Property. subject $s$ may have *read* access to an object $o$ only if $C(o) \leq C(s)$

This says that the security class (clearance) of someone receiving a piece of information must be at least as high as the class (classification) of the information.
- *-Property.  subject $s$ who has *read* access to an object $o$ may have *write* access to an object $p$ only if $C(o) \geq C(p)$

This says that a person obtaining information at one level may pass that information along only to people at levels no lower than the information. This property is to prevent Write-Down of information, which occurs when a subject with write access to high-level data transfers that data by writing it to a low-level object. The implications of these two axioms are illustrated in Figure 12.1

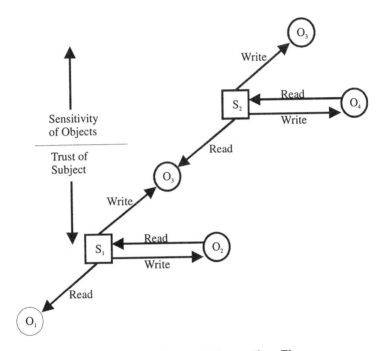

**Figure 12.1   Secure Information Flow**

The flow of information is generally horizontal, with information flowing to and from the same level.  The security classification of subjects (represented as squares) and objects (represented as circles) is indicated by their position. As the classification of an item increases so its height on the diagram increases.

In 1978 the Take-Grant model for the analysis of security was published.  In this model there are only four primitive operations: *create, revoke, take* and *grant*. Let $R$ be a set of rights and $S$ be a set of subjects and $O$ be a set of objects. It is important to note that objects can be either active (subjects) or passive (non-subject objects). Each subject or object is denoted by a node on a graph; the rights of a particular subject to a particular object denoted by a label direct from the subject to the object. This security model is the security model most often used when designing and implementing modern operating system security.

Figure 12.2 depicts a simple take-grant model, the subject is depicted as a square and denoted using the letter $S$, while the object is depicted as a circle and denoted using the letter $O$. Finally, an access right that exists between $S$ and $O$ is depicted as an arc and denoted by the letter $R$.

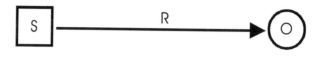

**Figure 12.2    A Take-Grant Model**

A description of the four primitive operations is given below.

- **Create** $(o, r)$: a new node with label $o$ is added to the graph. From $s$ to $o$ there is a directed edge with label $r$, denoting the rights of $s$ on $o$.
- **Grant** $(o, p, r)$: subject $s$ grants to $o$ access rights $r$ on $p$. A specific right is *grant*. Subject $s$ can grant to $o$ access rights $r$ on $p$ only if $s$ has grant right on $o$, and $s$ has $r$ rights on $p$. Informally, $s$ can grant (share) any of its rights with $o$, as long as $s$ has the right to grant privileges to $o$. An edge from $o$ to $p$ is added; with label $r$. $O$ is an active subject.
- **Revoke** $(o, r)$: the right $r$ is revoked from $s$ on $o$. The edge from $s$ to $o$ was labeled $q \cup r$; the label is replaced by $q$. Informally, $s$ can revoke its rights to do $r$ on $o$.
- **Take** $(o, p, r)$: subject $s$ takes from $o$ access rights $r$ on $p$. A specific right is *take*. Subject $s$ can take from $o$ access rights $r$ on $p$ only if $s$ has take right on $o$, and $o$ has $r$ rights on $p$. Informally, $s$ can take any rights $o$ has, as long as $s$ has the right to take privileges from $o$. An edge from $s$ to $p$ is added with label $r$.

## 12.1.3   Security Methods of Operating Systems

The basis of protection is separation, keeping one user's objects from another user. It should be noted that separation in an operating system could occur in several ways.

- *Physical separations*: in which processes use separate physical resources to store and access objects.
- *Temporal separation*: in which processes having different security requirements are executed at different times.
- *Logical separation*: in which users operate under the illusion that no other processes exist, as when an operating system controls and limits the access of a program executing on behaviour of a user. The operating system functions to ensure that the user is not allowed to access objects outside its permitted domain.
- *Cryptographic separation*: in which processes conceal their data and processes through the system of symmetric and asymmetric cryptographic algorithms.

## 12.1.4 Typical Operating System Flaws

Typical security flaws that have been encountered in operating systems include:

- *Authentication of User*: the operating system must identify each user who requests access and ascertain that the user is actually who they purport to be. The most common authentication mechanism is password comparison.
- *Protection of Memory*: each user's program must run in a portion of memory protected against unauthorised accesses. The protection will certainly prevent outsiders' access, and it may also control a user's own access to restricted parts of the program space. Differential security access controls such as read, write, and execute can be applied to the control of the user's memory space.
- *File and I/O device Access Control*: the operating system must protect user's and operating system's files from access and modification by unauthorised users.
- *Allocation and Access to General Objects*: general objects, such as constructs to permit concurrency and allow synchronisation, must be provided to users. However access and user of these objects must be strictly controlled so that no one user is able to adversely affect the behaviour of another.
- *Enforcement of Sharing*: resources on most common operating systems need to be shared among users. Sharing of resources brings about the need to guarantee integrity and consistency. Integrity controls such as monitors and transactions processors are often used to support sharing controls.
- *Guarantee of Fair Service*: all users expect a fair share of the services offered and support by the operating system. No one user should indefinably be starved from using and accessing a service. Hardware clocks and scheduling combine to ensure fairness.
- *Inter-process Communication and Synchronisation*: executing processes sometimes need to communicate with each other. Operating system provides this service by acting as a bridge between communicating processes. Access control tables mediate interprocess communication.
- *Protection of Operating System Protection Data*: the operating system must maintain data by which it can enforce security. This data must itself be protected from unauthorised access and modification. The operating system itself cannot provide enforcement of protection of this data, thus we must make use of other techniques such as encryption, hardware control and physical access controls.

## 12.2 Databases and Database Security

A database is a collection of data and a set of rules that organise the data by specifying certain relationships among the data. Within most organisations certain databases have become mission critical information systems. This means that without access to these databases and trust in the information contained in them, then the organisation would cease to function. Consequently, the security and effective use and management of the organisational assets have become vital to the success and viability of the organisation.

The security requirements for a database are very similar to the security requirements for an operating system or any other organisational mission critical information system. The basic problems are as follows:

- *Physical Database Integrity*: physical database integrity is concerned with the protection of data contained in a database from the effects of physical problems such as power failure.
- *Logical Database Integrity*: logical database integrity is concerned with the protection of data at the logical level. For example: the modification of a piece of data in the database should not affect other pieces of data in the database.
- *Element Integrity*: element integrity is concerned with the protection of integrity of each element of data in the database.
- *Access Control*: this is concerned with the policy that a user is allowed to access only authorised data, and that different users can be restricted to different modes of access, such as read and/or write.
- *Auditability*: this is concerned with the tracking of who has accessed the database and/or modified elements in the database.
- *User Authentication*: this is concerned with ensuring that every user is positively and uniquely identified, both for the audit trail and for permission to access certain data.
- *Availability*: this is concerned with the availability of the database to be utilised by the users of the database in a useful and meaningful manner to the business process.

## 12.2.1   Physical Database Integrity

Physical database integrity is concerned with the protection of data contained in a database from the effects of physical problems such as power failure.

- *Non-Natural Vulnerabilities*: intruders can break into your computing facilities. Once in they can sabotage and vandalise your computers, and they can steal hardware, diskettes, printouts etc. For example:
  - A former cost estimator for Southeastern Color Lithographers in Athens, Georgia, was convicted of destroying billing and accounting data on a XENIX system. The lost data had the effect of disrupting the supply chain for the organisation. The conviction was based on an audit trail linking the delete commands to his terminal (but not necessarily to him). The employer claimed damages of $400,000 in lost business and downtime.
  - An AT&T crew removing an old cable in Newark, New Jersey, accidentally severed a fiber-optic cable carrying more than 100,000 calls. Starting at 9.30a.m. on 4 January 1991, and continuing for much of the next day, the effects included:
    - downtime of the New York Mercantile Exchange and several commodities exchanges;

- disruption of Federal Aviation Administration (FAA) air-control communication in the New York metropolitan area;
- lengthy flight delays into, and out of, the New York area; and
- blockage of 60% of the long-distance telephone calls into, and out of, New York City.

- *Natural Vulnerabilities*: computers are very vulnerable to natural disasters and to environmental threats. Disasters such as fire, flood, earthquakes and power loss can wreck your computer and destroy data. For example: a squirrel caused a short circuit in a transformer, causing a power surge in Providence, Rhode Island, in October 1986. The surge affected numerous computers.

General tactics for the management of physical database integrity include:

- Risk transfer through the outsourcing or facilities management of the organisation's critical business information infrastructure. Thus the identification and response to the IA problem should be included in any service level agreement (SLA).
- A comprehensive disaster recovery play that covers both natural and non-natural disasters such as fires, floods and theft. This type of plan only functions if it is adequately funded, tested and maintained.

For non-natural vulnerabilities one can adopt the following countermeasures:

- Physical security on buildings and equipment. This can be achieved using technologies such as biometrics. In addition, educating users and adopting clear desk policies also aids in minimising the risk of a security breach. The goal is to uniquely identify a user so that a complete audit trail exists for all security related actions of a user, so that when a breach in physical database integrity occurs you can identify how it happened, who made it happen and recover from the resulting loss.
- Logical security on key information assets. This can be achieved through the use of technologies such as cryptography key management and certification authorities. If, when data is stolen, it is encrypted using algorithms such as triple DES, Blow-Fish and/or RSA, then it is unlikely that that unencrypted data can be accessed with a valid cryptographic key. In addition, the use of digital signatures or certification purposes strengthens logical security as signatures can be revoked and new signatures issued.

For natural vulnerabilities one can adopt the following counter measures:

- The use of online back-up devices and other devices in hot-stand-by mode. This can be achieved using various technologies that introduce redundancy into the system and consequently increase reliability. The goal is to run the systems in parallel so that when one system fails another system automatically compensates for the failure. Thus, availability is maintained.

- The use of a separate physical location and the duplication of all information storage and information processing capabilities. This option is extensive both in terms of physical cost and manpower costs.
- The use of off-line and off-site back-ups of key information assets.

## 12.2.2  Logical Database Integrity

Logical database integrity is concerned with the protection of data at the logical level. For example: the modification of a piece of data in the database should not affect other pieces of data in the database. This is achieved through the normalisation of the data in the database. For example: if a database is normalised into Boyce-Codd normal form (BCNF), then every element in every relation is only dependent upon the primary key. In formal database terms, this is expressed as a relation as in Boyce-Codd Normal Form (BCNF) if and only if every determinant is a candidate key. The term "determinant" refers to an attribute that is on the left-hand side of a functional dependency. If we have a relation, R, then the attribute R.B is functionally dependent on attribute R, if and only if each value of R.A is associated with exactly one value of R.B at any time.

```
Relation Dep: Product (Product ID, Price, Description)
Functional Dep: Product ID → (Price, Description)
```

The above also tells us that the attribute ProductID is the primary key and that the attributes Price and Description are functionally dependent upon it.

## 12.2.3  Element Integrity

The term "element integrity" is used to refer to the correctness and accuracy of an element in a database. In principle only authorised users should insert data into a database. When adding a database to a database, some database management systems (DBMS) also make it simple to ensure that the data is of the correct type to be inserted into that element. For example: a database management system would not allow one to insert a string into a element that is of type number.

In an attempt to minimise the effect of a loss of element integrity, a database should have the data in it placed into relations and then the relationships should be normalised. In its simplest terms, a database is simply a set of relations. Relations (often referred to as tables) have a set of properties that attempt to ensure element integrity, and these are:

- Every relation in a database must have a distinct name. That name must be unique in the database.
- Every column in a relation must have a distinct name within the relation. Each column of a relation is also a set and hence should also be unambiguously named.
- All entries in a column must be of the same kind, i.e. from the same domain.

- The order of columns in a relation is not significant. The head of a relation – its list of column names, is also a mathematical set. Sets in mathematics are not ordered.
- The order of rows is not significant. There should be no implied order in the storage of rows in a relation. The body of a relation is a set.
- The row in a relation must be distinct. Duplicate rows are not allowed in a relation. In other words, a relation must have a primary key.
- Each cell or column/row intersection in a relation should contain only an atomic value. In other words, multi-values in a cell are not allowed.

The primary key of a relation is an attribute or composite attribute that has the properties of uniqueness and minimality. In a relation, we define which attribute is the primary key by underlining it. When manipulating a relation, there are three types of entity integrity that concern us:

- The first is that when we are inserting some data into a relation we must ensure that the components that we are inserting have a primary key associated with them.
- The second type is that when we removed the last element from a relation the relation should not disappear from the database.
- The third and final type is that when we update a database, we should ensure that all the elements that need to be updated are updated.

When entering data into a database, there are various checks that the organisation can perform to ensure element integrity. Even if the data entered into an element of a database is of the correct type (a DBMS will ensure this), there is no guarantee that the value of the data is correct. So an organisation may either enter the data twice and check to make sure that the two pieces of data entered are the same or if some property between data elements in a database can be identified, then a check can be executed to ensure that this property holds for all instances of the elements in the database.

## 12.2.4   Access Control

Databases are often logically separated by user access privileges. For example: within an organisation, users may not have access to the salary information associated with employees on the database. Access to that information may be restricted to the personnel department. When a database is being created, the database administrator should specify the areas of the database that the different users can see. In database design terms, this is called a user schema or view. In SQL-92 a view is conceptually a relation, but its records are taken from another relation. So for example: suppose we had a relation defined as follows:

```
Employee-Data(Emp ID, Name, Job-Description, Salary)
```

Where EmpID is the primary key of the relation Employee-Details. For security reasons we may only want the personnel department to have access to the entity Salary. So we would define a view of the relation that excludes this attribute. In SQL-92 this would be expressed as follows:

```
CREATE VIEW Current-Employee-Details(EmpID, Name, Job)
AS SELECT E.EmpID, E.Name, E.Job FROM Employee-Data
```

Most database management systems use the Take-Grant model of security to implement access controls. SQL-92 supports discretionary access control through the GRANT and REVOKE commands.

```
GRANT privileges ON object TO users
```

For our purposes an object is either a relation or a view of a relation. Several privileges can be specified:

- *Select*: the right to access (read) all columns of the table specified as object.
- *Insert*: the right to insert rows with values in the named column of the table named as object.
- *Delete*: the right to delete rows from the table named as object.
- *References*: the right to define foreign keys (in other tables) that refer to the specified column of the table named as object.

Suppose that Andrew has created a relation called Incident and that there are two other users called Alison and Francesca. Some examples of the GRANT command that Andrew can execute are:

```
GRANT SELECT ON Incident TO Alison, Francesca
GRANT INSERT, DELETE ON Incident TO Francesca
```

## 12.2.5  Auditability

In some applications, it may be desirable to generate an audit record of all access (read or write) to a database. Such a record can help maintain the integrity of a database or at least to help discover, after the fact, who affected what values and when. The second advantage is that a user can make use of inferences to deduce information that they are not security cleared to know (this is called the Inference problem). An audit log of what actions a user has performed can allow an administrator to create a picture of what a user really knows. In database terms, this type of audit log is called a transaction log and it records all the transactions that have been executed over a database since the database was last backed-up. The transaction log allows a database administrator to recover a database when, for whatever the reason, the database crashes and all information in the database is lost.

The level of recording that is performed to create an audit log for a database is defined in the security policy for the database. Just as with most operating systems, a database can record every statement that every user executes in the database. For the purposes of a transaction log for a database, we are only concerned with those actions that create, modify or delete data from the database and those actions that create, modify or delete the access rights for a user of the database.

## 12.2.6   User Authentication

This is concerned with ensuring that every user is positively and uniquely identified both for the audit trail and for permission to access certain data. Most typical databases make use of a user name and password for every use, and when a user connects to the database, they are authenticated with reference to the user name and password. Typically, the user name and passwords are sorted in a special table in the database, and the database management system makes use of a one-way hashing function to sort the passwords. Consequently, when a user is authenticated, the password that they entered is encrypted using the hashing function and that is compared with the stored hash of the password. If the two match, then the password is the same and the user is allowed access to the database.

From a security perspective the biggest headache that the database administrator will have is with users not adequately managing their passwords. In addition, some database management systems install default username and passwords on their systems for diagnostic purposes. Such usernames and passwords should be disabled as they form a backdoor for an intruder to enter the system.

## 12.2.7   Availability

This is concerned with the availability of the database to be utilised by the users of the database in a useful and meaningful manner relative to the business process. A database can only be used if the information contained within the database is available, so the requirement of availability is high on the list of requirements relating to the implementation of a database management system.

## 12.2.8   Database Case Study

Today's databases contain millions of pieces of information, and corporate databases themselves are probably extremely sensitive when viewed as a whole. However, individual elements of it may not be considered sensitive. Information classification management plays a large role in determining the sensitivity of information and then classifying it accordingly. However, in today's massive database environment the task is almost impossible.

From an IA standpoint, it is "easy" to protect the entire database; however, what about its individual elements? What if some elements were combined? The result is that some non-sensitive pieces of information not requiring protection may require protection when combined.

Due to the massive amounts of information contained in today's databases, it is almost impossible to establish and maintain the protection of such pieces of information when combined. It would require that each piece of information be integrated with all the other pieces of information in the database in an infinite number of combinations, then checked against some rule-based system to determine its sensitivity. To establish and maintain a current and cost-effective system for such a process is not within the capabilities of any IA professional nor are systems currently available to accomplish such tasks. The result is that database information accessed piecemeal can provide extremely sensitive information. For example: a major US aerospace corporation was building missile warheads for the military. The number of warheads on each missile was classified Secret. An unclassified database was used to maintain information relative to warhead parts, etc. The information in the database included the total number of bolts used to hold all the warheads in place – unclassified information. Also, included in the database was the total number of bolts used to hold down an individual warhead – unclassified information. However, one can take the total number of warhead bolts for each missile, e.g. 12 and divide it by the number of individual warhead bolts, e.g. three, and one discovers that there four warheads per missile – Secret information.  This simple, but true, example indicates some of the difficulty in protecting individual pieces of information to the level of granularity required to be effective.

# 12.3   Application Software

Application software is second only to operating systems in its importance to information protection and IA. Application software must be protected to ensure it is maintained as originally intended without being contaminated by malicious code or in any way modified in such a manner as to allow additional vulnerabilities and/or minimise its secure integration with other applications software, e.g. intrusion detection software.

Some of the most important application software that requires protection at the highest levels is the software that is used to protect information, e.g. intrusion detection, access control, audit trails recording. If this software is compromised, then no information on the information systems will be protected. Ironically, security software is often given no more protection than an accounting software package.

Over the years, there have been more and more examples of malicious codes, e.g. viruses, logic bombs, Trojan horses being written and executed globally through the Internet and other networks.

## 12.3.1   Malicious Code

The following are definitions used to identify and categorise malicious software:

- **Back Doors**: sometimes called *trapdoors*, which allow unauthorised access to one's systems.
- **Logic Bombs**: or hidden features in programs that are executed after certain conditions are met.
- **Trojan Horses**: are programs that say they are doing one thing while they are doing another, e.g. a program hidden in a program.

- *Viruses*: or programs that modify other programs on a computer, inserting copies of themselves.
- *Worms*: programs that propagate from computer to computer on a network, without necessarily modifying other programs on the target machine.
- *Bacteria*: or *rabbit programs*, make copies of themselves to overwhelm a computer system's resources.

The following are all examples of Logic Bombs:

- *General Dynamics Logic Bomb*: a programmer, Michael John Lauffenberger, was convicted of logic bombing General Dynamics' Atlas Rocket Database. He quit his job and hoped to be rehired at a premium when the logic bomb went off. However, another programmer discovered it.
- *Pandair Logic Bomb*: a contractor programmer, James McMahon, was accused of planting logic bombs in a Pandair Freight system in the United Kingdom. One bomb locked up terminals, and another bomb was set to wipe out memory. He was cleared of all charges due to insufficient evidence.
- *Logic Bomb Deletes Brokerage Records*: Donald Gene Burleson was prosecuted on felony charges for planting a time bomb that, shortly after he was fired, deleted more than 168,000 brokerage records from the USPA in Fort Worth, Texas. He was convicted and jailed.

### 12.3.1.1  Trojan Horse Software

There has been a literal plague of what have been described as "Trojan horse" programs. These software tools are named in honour of the famous beast of history that allowed the mighty walls of the city of Troy to be breached by cunning Greek warriors. Today's "Trojan" software is more likely to appear in the guise of a cute little attachment sent by what appears to be a friendly e-mail account. These programs represent a fundamental change in the threat matrix, they are particularly dangerous in the small and medium sized businesses where there may not be any formal IA program.

All the various Trojan software provides a common core of functions which typically includes the following:

- Operate concealed, in "stealth mode" without any indication to the user of their presence. Nothing will be visible in the WINDOWS system tray or will appear if the user activates the "close program" dialog box.
- Open and close the CD-ROM drive.
- Run programs already resident on the "target" system remotely without the user's intervention.
- Capture (log) user keystrokes without alerting the user.
- Capture screen shots.
- Reboot the computer.
- Upload (and execute) programs to the "target" computer without the user's knowledge.

- Operate microphones, web cameras, modems and other peripherals to gain information, to include remotely turning on computers, downloading their contents and turning them back off.

### 12.3.1.2    BackOrifice2000

The program which probably best exemplifies the large number of new software tools that are magnifying the IA risks is called "BackOrifice"(abbreviated as BO) which in its most current form is known as "BackOrifice2000" (which is often abbreviated as BO2K). Named in a mocking double entendre to deride Microsoft's "BackOffice" with a teenager's sense of potty humour (the logo shows what one might infer to be human buttocks), the software itself is no laughing matter. The original software was developed by a hacker who goes by the name "Sir Dystic" in what he has claimed is an effort to get Microsoft to improve the security features of the widely used Windows operating systems. The original version was released by the hacker group the Cult of the Dead Cow at the annual DefCon hacker conference in Las Vegas in July 1998 and only operated under Windows 95. The BO2K version operates under Windows 95, 98 and NT 4.0 (sometimes). This most current version was released in July 1999 again at the DefCon conference.

The software is shareware, and is available for free to anyone, anywhere in the world with an Internet connection. By some estimates, several hundred thousand copies of this tool were downloaded in 1998 alone and it continues to be very popular among hobbyists and hackers and others with interest in computer and network security.

The program has a number of features that set the standard for other tools to follow and also has several unique features that distinguish it from the many "copy cat" utilities. Some of the features included in the software itself and described in the documentation that are of greatest interest for the application of the product to Netspionage (network-enabled espionage) include the following:

- Session and keystroke logging.
- HTTP file system browsing and transfer.
- Direct file browsing, transfer, and management.
- Multimedia support for audio/video capture, and audio playback.
- NT registry passwords and Win9x screensaver password dumping.

A computer user must be running either Windows 95 or 98 to allow the Trojan to automatically infect a target machine. The software will not install itself automatically on an NT system. The software comes in two parts: the client and the server. The server is installed on a target computer system. The client is used from another computer to gain access to the server and control it. The client connects to the server via a network.[1]

Once connectivity is established it is possible to exercise considerable control over the server/ target system. For example: the server (target) can be made to send an email message to a designated address with key information about the system included in the message. It is also possible to connect to an Internet Relay

---

[1] This information is derived from the BO documentation.

Chat (IRC) server to inform all the users of a particular IRC channel that a specific computer is now available for remote operation and control.

*What Does This Mean?* If someone successfully installs BO or one of the many imitators on a target system they have at least as much control as the assigned owner/user. Anything the user could do while sitting at their keyboard can probably be done by the techno-spy sitting at their own computer which may be located in the same building as the target, or could possibly be located on the other side of the world. The techno-spy running the client software is able to search through the file listings of the target system, find any that are of interest and copy, modify or delete them as desired, or transmit them to another computer for future use. Cached passwords (passwords stored on the computer for example to login to a remote system or Internet service provider, can likewise be copied and transmitted. The keystroke logging allows the client to capture any passwords entered by the user (for instance, those that have not been cached) and use them later, perhaps to impersonate the authorised user and gain access to an important database system.

The fact that the BackOrifice product accommodates "plug-ins" provides more reasons to be aware of this tool. As if the basic functionality was not dangerous enough, there are extensions that allow even unsophisticated users to package BO *into* another program. What this does is allow BO to infect a target when the "doctored" program is executed. The plug-in called *"SilkRope"* also modifies BO so it can't be found with a common file scan. These tools are one reason why the various holiday executables can be a source of real danger. Although the "dancing Santas" or "happy Halloween ghosts" executable may be cute, it's a very simple matter to load BO into the file and send them out via e-mail to the desired target. When the target executes them, they enjoy the display, unaware of the infection and subsequent control over their system enjoyed by the operator of the client code.

These are features that are nearly ideal for the purposes of theft of sensitive information from computer and network systems. These tools are optimised for theft of passwords, documents and other materials right out from under the noses of the often unsophisticated users (such as senior executives, managers and other less technical staff), which means they are ideal tools for attackers.

Although BO and it's variants and imitators are potentially very dangerous, the makers of security and anti-virus software have largely neutralised the threat from unsophisticated use of these tools. Common anti-virus tools often detect them in their normal state and can even "disinfect" systems that have been attacked. However, in the hands of experts, one should not assume that "off the shelf" anti-virus tools alone are sufficient. It is possible for BO to be compiled in a manner that will change its file signature and thus defeat file comparison anti-virus software. The network operations group of the corporation should monitor network traffic for unusual transmissions using the UDP protocol that BackOrifice uses to communicate between the client and server.

Regardless of the current effectiveness of specific protective measures, there is a running arms race between the developers of such attack tools as BO and those who develop protective tools. The mere fact that the capability now exists ensures that some Netspionage agents and techno-spies will exploit the vulnerability.

Potentially, any one of the many Trojan software programs could be used by a techno-spy to steal sensitive files or modify or delete data, from any computer running Windows 95 or Windows 98 and many systems running Windows NT. However, there are a few factors limiting their effectiveness at present:

- First, every one of these programs requires some sort of server application to first be installed on the target machine that the techno-spy is seeking to plunder. Achieving this installation requires either physical access to the computer system or some way of convincing the authorised user to install it. Where physical access is not feasible, it is often possible to trick an unsuspecting user into installing the code by inserting it into some pretty executable then sending it to the target via electronic mail. Alternatively, the operator of a targeted system may be invited to a web site/URL to download a copy of the modified executable onto the target system. Once the unsuspecting user double clicks on the downloaded file they will unknowingly install a copy of the Trojan onto their system.
- Once a copy is installed, the attackers must then find the IP address of the target machine before the software can be activated and controlled remotely. The attacker can often use their client application to search through a range of possible IP addresses. However, this is a serious challenge if they do not have enough information about the network to limit the range of addresses to be searched because there are four billion possible IP addresses.

The installation of a properly configured firewall between the target machine and the attacker will probably make it impossible for the attacker to communicate with the target machine. Since many corporations install firewalls between their internal networks and computers and the Internet this means that, if the firewall operates correctly, there should not be any Trojan remotes controlling internal systems via the Internet. More likely the use of a Trojan utility will occur inside the corporation since internal compartmentalisation of networks using internal firewalls is not common.

Although a leading anti-virus vendor advises that corporations can defend themselves from Trojan software problems by "following safe computing practices, for example: not downloading or running applications from unknown sources..."[2] this advice is too simplistic. Users are increasingly likely to do just that, download software from new and unknown sources and will therefore remain vulnerable to these tools. And of course if the operator of the Trojan is a trained attacker who has infiltrated the corporation in the guise of a lowly temporary employee holding a position as a secretary, they won't be downloading anything, except possibly the crown jewels of the company via a Trojan utility.

### 12.3.1.3  *Other Trojan Software*

BO is not the only sophisticated tool available. There are many others. An excellent listing of many additional "network Trojan" software programs can be found at http://xforce.iss.net/alerts/. The X-Force service, sponsored by ISS has documented more than 120 of them for the various versions of Windows. This site

---

[2] http://www.sarc.com/avcenter/venc/data/backorifice.html

also provides a full technical description of how the software operates as well as techniques for detecting and removing them from computers.

The following is a short list of some of the most common additional tools and the special features associated with each one. Please note that the feature described is not the only function the software performs, most of them have the full complement of basic features similar to BO but also other unique features:

- *NetBus Pro*: presents itself as a remote administration and spy tool.
- *NetSphere*: will operate the ICQ real time messaging utility.
- *SubSeven*: uses Internet Relay Chat or ICQ to inform the attacker when a target is infected.

The following are all examples of Trojan Horses:

- **Password-Catching Trojan Horses**: beginning in Autumn 1993, Trojan horses appeared in the network software of numerous Internet computers. In particular, Telnet, a program that permits people to connect from one machine to another, was altered so that all user names and user passwords were logged for later illegal use.
- **Emergency System Trojan Horse**: a former employee maliciously modified the software of the Community Alert Network installed in New York and San Jose, California. The software did not fail until it was needed in response to a chemical leak at Chevron's refinery in Richmond, California. The emergency system was then down for 10 hours.
- **Beware of Smart Telephones**: a scam was detected involving third-party pay phones that could capture and record credit card numbers for later illegal use. This type of Trojan horse attack is also seen in automated teller machine frauds.

The best example of what can happen when malicious code escapes onto the Internet happened in November 1988. In that month, the Internet Worm was released onto the Internet. This worm was a program that invaded Sun 3 and VAX Computers running versions of the Berkeley 4.3 Unix Operating Systems, and containing the TCP/IP Internet protocols. Robert T. Morris created this program. The worm used the following security vulnerabilities to replicate itself:

- Finder demon stack overflow to gain root access.
- Sendmail debug option to gain root access.
- Password cracking to gain access to a user and then replicating using its rhosts table.

The net effect of the Internet Worm was that the Internet stopped functioning as people and organisations removed themselves from the Internet to stop the spread of the infection – a self, denial-of-service.

## 12.3.2   Viruses

A virus is a program that can pass on malicious code to other non-malicious programs by modifying them. In modifying the other programs, the virus is said to infect them. Some viruses have little to no effect on the machine that they have infected, while other viruses can have devastating consequences, e.g. reformatting the hard drive.

The ILOVEYOU virus was released from a source in the Philippines in year 2000. Within hours of its release, many information systems and networks were overwhelmed and ceased to function. It is estimated that this virus alone caused damages in the order of millions of US dollars to the global economy.

The only way to prevent infection by a virus is not to share executable code. Techniques for keeping you and your organisation free from viruses include:

- Use only commercial software acquired from reliable and trusted sources. Most large commercial organisations will go to great lengths to ensure that software that is supplied to a customer is fit for its purpose and is virus free.
- Test all new software in an isolated environment. If you must use software from non-trusted sources, then make sure that the software is well tested before it is released into your network.
- Make and retain back-up copies of the operating system and any applications installed. This way, in the event of an infection you can remove infected files and reinstall them from clean and trusted back-up copies.
- Regularly use virus detection software and make sure that they are supplied from a reputable and trusted source. Also, be sure to protect them from modification and destruction.

# 12.4   Digital Tradecraft

Digital tradecraft combined with the global Internet accesses, offer the IA professionals some of their greatest challenges. The following is a real-world look at some of those challenges.[3]

The Internet and specifically the Web, has now made available to increasing numbers of people with widely varying legal, ethical and personal motivations and constraints the tools and technologies that are nearly ideal for the theft of the increasingly valuable digital assets of the typical corporation. The global reach now afforded to prospective attackers by the expanding connectivity provided by the Internet, has created a situation of unparalleled opportunity for anyone who is willing to go after a corporation's assets.

The pages that follow describe software programs and utilities that allow even unsophisticated attackers to steal the prime assets of their own or other corporations, then safely transfer those assets to others.

The focus in this section differs somewhat from a description of traditional hacker tools and how they have been used. Whereas a hacker may chose to engage in stealing sensitive information, e.g. Netspionage, it is also possible for a Netspionage agent to commit Netspionage without being an accomplished hacker.

---

[3] This section was excerpted from Dr. Kovacich's co-authored book, *Netspionage: The Global Threat to Information* published in September 2000 by and reprinted with permission of Butterworth-Heinemann, Woburn, Massachusetts, USA

In fact successful techno-spies may never need to engage some of the sophisticated technical tools, such as port scanners and attack simulators. Such powerful software requires a great deal of technical knowledge and tends to be the hacker's weapons of choice for neutralising traditional information security technologies. Instead we will discuss a new application of software and technical tools which we describe as "digital tradecraft".

## 12.4.1   Digital Tradecraft Defined

Tradecraft is defined as "the technical skills used in espionage"[4] and typically might include knowledge of lock picking, clandestine photography, secret writing, surveillance and dead drops.[5] As one can deduce from such examples, a great deal of the traditional spy's life revolved around the means of acquiring information and then communicating it to the sponsoring agency for processing and analysis. Of course it is obvious that such means are intended to allow the spy to operate in stealth and with anonymity, largely in hopes that they might continue to survive and perhaps even someday return safely to their homeland.

In many ways the objectives of Netspionage are exactly the same as they have been for traditional espionage. The new tools are intended to allow the "virtual agents" operating against on-line business corporations to penetrate the internal systems of the target. Once successfully "inside" they may obtain information without detection, then communicate it so the sponsoring corporation may operate with the advantage of superior information while the attacked corporation remains blissfully unaware of the nature and extent of their losses.

## 12.4.2   Digital Dead Drop

Imagine you are a techno spy and you need to set up a secure place where you can "stash" copies of the critical information you have obtained from the penetrated corporation. As you read this, identify techniques that you can use to stop the theft of sensitive information by this method.

As good as you are there is always the chance, no matter how small, that the authorities may raid your computer someday. If they find the copies of the stolen crown jewels on your company computer system you are going to be in big trouble. One way to avoid such professional embarrassment is to load a "digital dead drop" with the copies of the stolen valuables and get them out of your system as quickly as possible.

There is no need to purchase a server and set up an Internet connection as there are already many services offering 10, 20, 30 or more megabytes of online storage for free. The most generous provide 300MB of personal "Free Disk Space" on "secure servers".[6] All they require is some personal information about the subscriber, which of course could be completely fabricated, since the service apparently makes no effort to verify anything. The advantages to the techno-spy

---

[4] H. Keith Melton, *The Ultimate Spy Book*, p. 159, DK Publishing 1996
[5] Ibid, p. 161
[6] http://www.freediskspace.com

are obvious. They get a free online storage place that is accessible from anywhere on the Internet at any time of the day or night. Of course if they are especially careful they will protect the valuable stolen contents by using one or more methods of cryptography, perhaps even steganography (see below) to ensure that even an examination of the files deposited in the dead drop will be fruitless for investigators. Those that use such services should also be aware that the sites might be excellent targets for the Netspionage agents.

Even if the process is detected and investigated by the security group they face an uphill battle. If the techno-spy uses digital dead drops properly the "control agent" from their team or customer contact will be unloading the contents soon after the agent loads them. This downloading operation will be done using another expendable account, probably a new web mail or front company address for every transmission. This will be done from a safe location, probably outside the country. The contents will then be transferred to a safe location inside the sponsor's home corporation, probably outside the target's homeland. Using a number of foreign locations for the transfer and processing of the stolen contents will make recovery more complicated and reduce the ability of the security officials to gain search warrants and execute them on a timely basis against multiple foreign locations and operations.

## 12.5   Steganography

Hiding information by embedding a file inside another, seemingly innocent, file is a technique known as "steganography". It is most often used with graphics, sound, text, HTML and PDF files. Steganography with digital files works by replacing the unused bytes of data in a computer file with bytes that contain concealed information.

Steganography (which translated from Greek means *covered writing*) has been in use since ancient times. One technique was to carve secret messages into wooden objects and then cover the etched words with coloured wax to make them undetectable to an uninitiated observer. Another method was to tattoo a message onto the shaved messenger's head. Once the hair grew back they were sent on their mission. Upon arrival the head was shaved revealing the message. The microdot, which reduced a page of text to the size of a typewriter's full point so that it could be glued onto a postcard or letter and sent through the mail, is another example.[7]

*Usually, two types of files are used when embedding data into an image. The innocent image that holds the hidden information is a "container". A "message" is the information to be hidden. A message may be plain text, cipher text, other images or anything that can be embedded in the least significant bits (LSB) of an image.*[8]

Steganographic software has some unique advantages as a tool for Netspionage agents, but also for protecting and defending information:

---

[7] http://webopedia.internet.com/TERM/s/steganography.html
[8] http://www.jjtc.com/stegdoc/

- First, if an agent uses regular cryptographic software on their computer systems the files may not be *accessible* to investigators but they *will* be visible and it will be obvious that the agent is hiding something. Steganographic software allows the agent to "hide in plain sight" any valuable digital assets they may have obtained until they can transmit or transfer the files to a safe location or to their customer.
- As a second advantage steganography may be used to conceal and transfer an encrypted document containing the acquired information to a digital dead drop. The agent could then provide the handler or customer with the password to unload the dead drop but not divulge the steganographic extraction phrase until payment is received or the agent is safely outside the target corporation.
- This technique can be used to transmit sensitive information and even incorporated into an encryption scheme before transmitting.
- It can also be used to hide sensitive information in databases, on desktop systems, etc.
- As a final note, even when a file is known or suspected to contain information protected with steganographic software, it has been almost impossible to extract the information unless the pass phrase has been obtained.

## 12.6  Summary

Operating systems and applications software must be used and integrated as part of an overall IA program. Therefore, their use must not violate IA protection and defence policies and procedures, e.g. don't use an application that does not provide some sort of audit trail records and access control integration. There are various models of secure systems, one of which is the Bell-La Padula model which formally describes the allowable paths of information flow. Secure methods of operating systems include physical separation, temporal separation, logical separation and cryptographic separation. Databases must have integrity at all times, control access to itself or in conjunction with other software, and must be auditable. Malicious codes such as BackOrifice and Netspionage activities using digital tradecraft offer new and greater challenges to the IA professional now and even more so in the future.

# Chapter 13

## Applying Cryptography to IA

Cryptography is one of the key ingredients in a successful information assurance program. In this chapter, cryptography as it relates to information assurance in the modern commercial age will be discussed. Included will be a discussion of the role of cryptography in e-commerce, algorithms; public and private key; key management; digital signatures; and the world of PKI.

## 13.1  Principles of Encryption

In 1949 Claude Shannon proposed the following principles describing the characteristics of a good cipher:

- *Principle 1*: the amount of secrecy needed should determine the amount of labour appropriate for encryption and decryption.
- *Principle 2*: the set of keys and the enciphering algorithm should be free from complexity.
- *Principle 3*: the implementation of the process should be as simple as possible.
- *Principle 4*: errors in ciphering should not propagate and cause corruption of further information in the message.
- *Principle 5*: the size of the enciphered text should be no longer than the text of the original message.

Cryptography is used to fulfill the following functions:

- *Confidentiality*: the information contained in a message is only accessible by those people authorised to access it.
- *Authentication*: it should be possible for the receiver of a message to ascertain its origins; an intruder should not be able to masquerade as someone else.
- *Integrity*: it should be possible for the receiver of a message to verify that it has not been modified in transit; an intruder should not be able to substitute a false message for a legitimate one.
- *Non-repudiation*: a sender should not be able to falsely deny later that he/she sent a message.

At its simplest, there are two types of encryption: symmetric and asymmetric. A symmetric algorithm is a cryptographic algorithm that uses the same key to decrypt as it uses to encrypt.

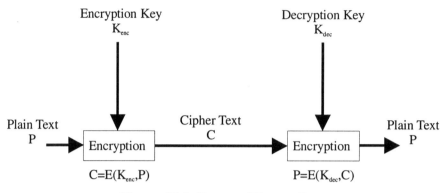

**Figure 13.1  Types of Encryption**

The whole point of cryptography is to keep the plain text secret from eavesdroppers. Eavesdroppers are assumed to have complete access to the communication between the sender and receiver. There are seven types of attacks that a cryptanalysis can make against a cipher, and these are:

- *Cipher text-only attack*. The cryptanalyst has the cipher text of several messages, all of which have been encrypted using the same encryption algorithm.
- *Known-plain text attack*. The cryptanalyst has access not only to the cipher text of several messages, but also the plain text of those messages.
- **Chosen-plain text attack**. The cryptanalyst not only has access to the cipher text and associated plain text for several messages, but he/she also chooses the plain text that gets encrypted. This attack is more powerful than a known-plain text attack as the cryptanalyst gets to choose the plain text that is encrypted.
- *Adaptive-chosen-plain text attack*. This is a special case of a chosen plain text attack. Not only can the cryptanalyst choose the plain text that is to be encrypted, but can also modify his/her choice based on the results of previous encryption.
- *Chosen-cipher text attack*. The cryptanalyst can choose different cipher texts to be decrypted and has access to the decrypted plain text. This is the type of attack that is primarily applicable to public-private key algorithms.
- *Chosen-key attack*. This attack means that the cryptanalyst has some knowledge about the relationship between different keys.
- *Rubber-hose cryptanalysis*. The cryptanalyst threatens, blackmails, or tortures someone until the key is given. Bribery is sometimes referred to as a purchase-key attack. These are all very powerful attacks and are often the best way to break an algorithm with a minimum amount of time and effort.

## 13.2   Symmetric Ciphers

With a symmetric cipher the same key that is used to encrypt a message is used to decrypt the message. These ciphers require both the sender and receiver to have exchanged keys.  Symmetric algorithms can be divided into two categories. Some operate on the plain text a single bit at a time; these are called stream algorithms or stream ciphers.  Others operate on the plain text in groups of bits. These groups are called blocks, and the algorithms are called block algorithms or block ciphers.  The most commonly used block cipher is the Data Encryption Standard (DES).

## 13.3   Asymmetric Ciphers

Public-Private key encryption is an asymmetric cryptographic method. That means that two keys are used: one key to encrypt a message and the other to decrypt the message. With a Public Key Cipher each user has two keys: a public key and a private key. The user may publish their public key freely. The keys operate as inverses. Let $K_{PRIV}$ be a user's private key, and let $K_{PUB}$ be the corresponding public key. Then,

$$P = D(K_{PRIV}, E(K_{PUB}, P) )$$

That is, a user can decode with a private key what someone else has encrypted with the corresponding public key.

$$P = D(K_{PUB}, E(K_{PRIV}, P) )$$

That is, a user can decode with a public key what someone else has encrypted with the corresponding private key. This is used for Digital Signatures.

The simplest example of an asymmetric cryptographic algorithm is a 24-hour clock. The algorithm that we use is that we add the key to the input to produce the output. So if one wishes to encrypt the time 12:56 with a key of 3 hours 17 minutes (3:17), then the output is 16:13. However one cannot use the same key to decrypt as was used to encrypt as adding 3:17 to 16:13 would give 19:30. So a separate key is needed to decrypt. In this example, the key used to decrypt is 20:43. In effect, the 24-hour clock is implementing modulo arithmetic.

Within the world of electronic commerce it is the creation of asymmetric cryptographic algorithms that has facilitated the creation of an infrastructure that allows businesses to communicate with each other in a trusted manner, and to be able to depend on the systems to provide a commercially acceptable level of confidentiality and non-repudiation.  Examples of products that are used in commerce to provide information assurance include:

- Pretty Good Privacy (PGP) is a cryptophytic package that implements public-private keys and key management via various certification authorities.
- The Secure Socket Layer (SSL) is an add-on to the HTTP standard that makes use of both symmetric and asymmetric cryptographic algorithms to achieve secure communications across an insecure network.

## 13.4   Digital Signatures and Certificates

Signatures have for a long time been used as a method of authentication and proof of ownership. So the properties of a signature are:

- *The signature is authentic*: the signature convinces the recipient that the signer deliberately signed the document.
- *The signature is unforgeable*: the signature is proof that the signer and no one else signed the document.
- *The signature is not reusable*: the signature is an integral part of the document and cannot be moved to another document without damaging the original document.
- *The signature is unalterable*: after the document has been signed, the signature cannot be altered.
- *The signature cannot be repudiated*: the signers of the document cannot deny at a later stage that they signed the document.

In reality, none of the above statements about a signature is completely true. A digital signature is a way of marking a document so that the above five principles hold. A digital signature should produce the same effect as a real signature: it is a mark that only the sender can make, that other people can easily recognize as belonging to the sender. Just like real signatures, a digital signature is used to confirm agreement to a message. Digital signatures must meet two primary conditions:

- *Unforgetable*: if person P signs a message M with a signature S(P,M) it is impossible for anyone else to produce the pair [M, S(P, M)].
- *Authentic*: if person R receives the pair [M, S(P, M)] purportedly from P, R can check that the signature is really from P. Only P could have created this signature, and the signature is firmly attached to M.

Two additional requirements are also desirable:

- *Not Alterable*: after being transmitted, M cannot be changed by R or an interceptor.
- *Not Reusable*: R will instantly detect a previous message presented.

While it is impossible to achieve perfection with regard to the five principles, digital signatures when combined with public-private key cryptography certainly makes a very good start. In particular, a digital signature provides proof of ownership, and provides an element of privacy:

- For a given document *M*, Alice signs the message with her private key $S_A$.
  $S_A [M]$
- Alice encrypts the signed message with Bob's public key $E_B$ and sends it to Bob.
  $E_B[S_A[M]]$
- Bob decrypts the message with his private key $D_B$.
  $D_B[E_B[S_A[M]]] = S_A [M]$

- Bob verifies with Alice's public key $V_A$, and recovers the message $M$.
  $$V_A [S_A [M]] = M$$

The above example works as the whole document is encrypted with a private key and the act of encryption functions as the act of signing a document. There are many Digital Signature Algorithms that have been developed, and they all make use of large prime numbers and modular arithmetic on the plain text to be signed.

- The *Digital Signature Algorithm (DSA)* has been proposed by the US National Institute for Standards and Technology (NIST) for use in their Digital Signature Standard (DSS). The standard was proposed in August 1991. Digital Signature Algorithm was developed by the US National Security Agency (NSA).
- *RSA* is a general public-key/private-key encryption system.
- *Schnorr and ElGamal Algorithm* is a specific digital signature algorithm.
- *GOST Digital Signature Algorithm* is the Russian digital signature standard and is officially called GOST R 43.10-94.
- *ENSIGN* is a digital signature scheme from NTT Japan.

A public-private key certificate is someone's public key signed by a trustworthy person. Within the world of electronic commerce certificates are used to thwart attempts to substitute one key for another. Certificates will become the vehicle for electronic commerce as laws are slowly introduced that give the same legal standing to digital signatures that is currently given to paper-based signatures. In some digital payment systems such as SET, certificates and certification authorities are already being used.

There are a number of advantages and disadvantages associated with the use of certificates and the protocols by which they are generated and used:

- what operational restrictions are there? For example: does the protocol for the use of certificates require a continuously available facility such as a key distribution centre?
- what trust requirements are there? Who and what entities must be trusted to act properly?
- what is the protection against failure? For example:
  - can an outsider impersonate any of the entities in the protocol and subvert security? or
  - can any party of the key distribution cheat without detection?
- how efficient is the algorithm? An algorithm requiring several steps to establish an encryption key that will be used many times is one thing; it is quite another to go through several time-consuming steps for a one-time use.
- how easy is the algorithm to implement?

This person that is trusted and used to authenticate the key is called a certification authority (CA). Certification authorities can award certificates, and certificate authorities can themselves have certificates. When using certification authorities, the central question becomes "what structure do the certification authorities have with each other?" Figure 13.2 depicts a tree structure for the certification authorities for a group of universities. The root of the tree functions to accredit all certification authorities under it. Each university accredits its own certification authorities. For example: the CA for the University of Glamorgan has three authorities underneath it called COMP, HASS and ISD respectively. Each of these CA would function as a CA for a University Department; so the COMP certification authority would function as the CA for the school of computing. A digital signature would be certified by the COMP CA, which in turn is certified by the Glamorgan CA.

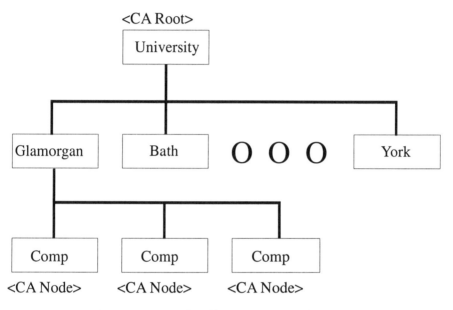

**Figure 13.2   A Certification Authority Tree**

There are four base structures that certification authorities can adopt. They are:

- *A single root*: the single root model has a single agency functioning to acredit every other's certification authority. This root authority would have the power to revoke any other certificate or certification authority in the system. The problem with the single root model is that it introduces a single point of failure into the system and gives a single authority power over all other certification authorities.

- *Multiple roots*: in the multiple roots model, there are many root certification authorities. This model has the advantage over the single root model in that no one single root has absolute control over all of the other certification authorities. For example: with the multiple root model, you could have a single certification tree for all universities in the UK, and a single certification tree for all the banks in the UK. These two certification trees would then co-operate with each other and the root certification authority of each tree would trust the other root certification authority.

- *Peers*: in this model, each organisation has its own CA and each organisation defines the set of CA that their CA will trust and accept certificates from. Consequently, the effect of the peer models of CA is to create domains and for certificates to flow across domains via trusted relationships from one CA to another. The problem with this model is that one incorrect trusting relationship can allow an intruder to introduce a false signature into the system and to get that signature certified by a valid authority. Having had a signature certified, an intruder can engage in fraudulent or other unauthorised acts.
- *Bridge*: this is where each organisation has many certification authorities. The certification authorities are used to bridge relationships between organisations. Thus, if an organisation has a commercial relationship with five other organisations, then it would require five certification authorities. The main problem with this model is its complexity.

## 13.5   Key Management and Key Distribution

The fundamental security requirement of every key management system is the control of keying material through the entire lifetime of the keys in order to prevent unauthorised disclosure, modification, substitution, replay and improper use.

- *Data Confidentiality*: secret keys and possibly other data are to be kept confidential while transmitted or stored.
- *Modification Detection*: is to counter the active threat of unauthorised modification of data items.
- *Replay Detection/Timeliness*: reply detection is to counter unauthorised duplication of data items. Timeliness is required that the response to a challenged message is prompt and does not allow for playback of some authentic response message by an impersonator.
- *Entity Authentication*: is to corroborate that an entity is the one claimed.
- *Data Origin Authentication (Proof/Nonrepudiation of Origin)*: is to corroborate that the source of a message is the one claimed.
- *Proof/Nonrepudiation of Reception*: shows the sender of a message that the message has been correctly received by its legitimate receiver.
- *Notarisation*: is the registration of messages to attest at a later stage their content origin.

Every management system must support and provide a set of management services, and these include:

- *Entity Registration*: any secure system ultimately requires a procedure by which an individual or device is authenticated to the system. A key management system has to provide some link between an entity and its uniquely defined keys. In any system, an entity is represented by some public data (called its public credentials) such as a User-ID or an Address, and some private credentials such as testimonials or passwords. When an entity is registered, a certificate based upon its credentials is issued as a proof of registration.

- **Key Generation**: this refers to the procedure by which keys or pairs of keys of good cryptographic quality are securely and unpredictably generated. This requires the use of a good method for generating random numbers.
- **Certification (OnLine/Off-Line)**: certificates are issued for authentication purposes. A credential containing identifying data together with other information (e.g. public keys) is rendered unforgeable by some certifying information (e.g. digital signatures provided by the key certification centre). Certification may be:
  - an online service where some certification authority provides interactive support and is actively involved in the key distribution processes; or
  - it may be an off-line service so that certificates are issued to each entity only at some initial stage.
- **Authentication/Verification**: the three main types of authentication are 1) entity authentication, 2) message content authentication, and 3) message origin authentication. The term verification refers to checking the appropriate claims, i.e. the correct identity of an entity. The validity of a certificate may then be verified using some public information (e.g. a public key), and can be carried out without the need for assistance from the certification authority.
- **Key Distribution**: key distribution refers to the procedures by which keys are securely provided to parties legitimately asking for them. The basic elements of a key distribution are:
  - **Encipherment**: enciphering the data item with an appropriate key can ensure the confidentiality of a data item.
  - **Modification Detection Codes**: to detect the modification of a data item, one can add some redundancy that has to be calculated using a collision free function (e.g. a CRC check).
  - **Replay Detection Codes**: to detect the replay of a message and to check its timeliness, some explicit or implicit challenge and response mechanism has to be used, since the recipient has to be able to decide on acceptance.
  - **Proof of Knowledge of a Key**: authentication can be implemented by showing knowledge of a secret (e.g. a secret key), or by responding to a challenge in a defined manner. This response will typically involve the use of the key to encrypt and decrypt messages.
- **Key Maintenance**:
  - **Storage of Keying Material**: refers to a key storage facility which provides secure storage of keys for future use, e.g. confidentiality and integrity for secret keying material, or integrity for public keys. For all keying materials, unauthorised modification must be detectable by suitable authentication mechanisms.
  - **Key Archival**: refers to procedures by which keys for notarisation or non-repudiation services can be securely archived. Archived keys may need to be retrieved at a much later date.

- *Key Replacement*: enables parties to securely update their keying material. A replaced key shall not be reused. A key shall be replaced when its compromise is known or suspected.
- *Key Recovery*: refers to cryptographic keys which may become lost due to human error, software bugs, or hardware malfunction.
- *Key Deletion*: refers to procedures by which parties are assured of the secure destruction of keys that are no longer needed.

## 13.6   Summary

Encryption is one of the best ways to protect information, whether it is being transmitted or stored in a database. It is used to fulfil the functions of confidentiality, authorisation, integrity and non-repudiation. There are at least seven types of attacks that can be made against a cipher. Ciphers are symmetric and asymmetric. Digital signatures and certificates are some of the latest techniques relating to practical applications of cryptography. Key management is one of the most crucial aspects of using cryptography to support IA.

# Chapter 14

# IA Technology Security

This chapter addresses technology security, specifically the technical equipment available and in use to protect or attack the information assurance processes including Biometrics, EMP weapons, HERF guns, CCTV and TEMPEST.

## 14.1 Biometrics

### 14.1.1 The Role and Function of Biometrics

One of the most dangerous security threats that organisations face is the physical impersonation of a trusted employee. The security services that counter this threat are identification and authentication. Identification is the service where an identity is assigned to a specific individual, and authentication is the service designed to verify a user's identity. The verifier can be identified and authenticated by what one knows (e.g. password), by what one owns (e.g. smart card) or by human characteristics (biometrics).

Specifically, identification is defined as a process whereby a real-world entity is recognised, and its "identity" is established. Identity in the abstract world of information systems is a set of information about an entity that differentiates it from another. The set of information may be as small as a single code, specifically designed as an identifier, or may be a mixture of data such as a family name, date-of-birth and postcode. An organisation's identification process comprises the acquisition of the relevant identifying information. Therefore, there is a variety of means for identifying a person's identity:

- Appearance (how the person looks, e.g. height, gender, weight).
- Social behaviour (how a person interacts with others, e.g. voice characteristics, style of speech).
- Name (what a person is called).
- Codes (what a person is called by an organisation).
- Knowledge (what the person knows).
- Possession (what the person owns).

- Bio-dynamics (what the person does, e.g. the manner in which one's signature is written, statistically-analysed voice characteristics, keystroke dynamics, particularly in relation to login-id and password).
- Natural physiology (e.g. skull measurements, teeth and skeletal injuries, thumbprint, fingerprint sets and handprints, retinal scans, earlobe capillary patterns, hand geometry, DNA patterns).
- Imposed physical characteristics (what the person wears, e.g. tags, collars, bracelets).

On the other hand, authentication is defined as a process designed to verify a user's identity. The goal of authentication is to protect a system against unauthorised use. This element enables the authentication to be based on some basic approaches:

- In the first case, the verifier knows information regarding the claimed identity as this can only be known or produced by an assignor of that identity (e.g. passport, password, personal identification number (PIN)). This case is defined as proof by knowledge.
- In the second case, the claimant will be authorised by the possession of an object (e.g. magnetic card, smart card). This case is defined as proof by possession.
- In the third case, the claimant directly measures certain claimant properties using human characteristics (e.g. biometrics). This case is defined as proof by property.

Generally, members of big organisations use ID cards or passwords to identify themselves. This is a security risk, because IDs can be stolen, passwords can be forgotten or cracked. Therefore, what is needed is a more secure approach to protect the information systems. This approach is the concept of biometrics.

Biometrics refers to the automatic identification of a person based on his/her physical or behavioural characteristics. Specifically biometric systems verify a person's identity by analysing his physical features or behaviours (e.g. face, fingerprint, voice, signature, keystroke rhythms). The systems record data from the user and compare it each time the user is using it. Therefore in this section we will:

- Define and analyse the basic models of biometrics in the security of information systems.
- Compare biometrics with password techniques.
- Discuss biometrics according to risks and threats.
- Present the law implications when a biometric is hacked.

## 14.1.2   Analysis of Basic Biometric Models

The biometric models can be separated into two main categories:

- The first category is *physiological based techniques,* which include facial analysis, fingerprint, hand geometry, retinal analysis, and DNA and measure the physiological characteristics of a person.

- The second category is *behaviour based techniques*, which include signature, keystroke, voice, smell analysis and measure behavioural characteristics.

Additionally for biometric systems, "templates" are required. By template, we mean the recorded biometric measurement of a user. A template is associated with an identifier (e.g. PIN, password) in order to be called up when it is requested. The templates can be stored in:

- *Memory of Biometric Device*: in this case, the templates can be stored in the memory of the biometric device. The memory capacity of the various biometric devices varies. Storing the templates in the memory of the device enhances security since the templates are not transmitted. It is also economic since no additional cost is required for issuing cards to the users. However, this is not the best choice if the application requires many users or if the users need to be verified at different locations.
- *Central Database*: the templates can be stored in a central database if the number of users required by the application is large or remote verification is needed. The security aspect of storing templates in a central database should be carefully considered.
- *Plastic Cards or Tokens*: this method of storage enables users to carry with them their templates in identification devices. This method is most appropriate when the number of enrolled users is too large to be stored in a central database.

## 14.1.3    Fingerprint Verification

The patterns and geometry of fingerprints are different for each individual and they do not change when the body grows. The classification of fingerprints is based on certain characteristics (arch, loop, whorl). The fingerprint systems available for recognising these characteristics are complex. Some systems are not capable of differentiating a fingerprint from a live user or a copied fingerprint. Finger surgery, injury, or condition of hands might affect the performance of the systems. The method has also the problem of public acceptance.

Fingerprint systems can be used in law enforcement and in other applications. These two types of systems are different. In law enforcement, applications of fingerprints are compared (usually manually) with a large store of fingerprints, where as in other applications the fingerprint is stored once and it only checks that fingerprint. This technology is mostly used in welfare, immigration, law and banking applications.

Such networks have also been developed in the US with children's fingerprints in order to identify a child (whose identity might have been changed) by comparing the fingerprints against a national database of children's fingerprints.

Fingerprint verification is associated with criminality and in many sections (e.g. medical) fingerprint technology would not be acceptable. In order to avoid the association with crime, fingerprints should be stored in a card and not in a large central database. It should also be emphasised that fingerprints cannot be reproduced in any law enforcement applications. So the fingerprint is therefore preferred as very secure, fast, reliable and easy to use.

People with missing fingers cannot use fingerprint systems. People with injured or swollen fingers might have a problem being verified by these systems. In working environments where workers need to wear gloves (e.g. power plants, medical or chemistry laboratories), this method of identification will not be appropriate. Age, gender, occupation, race and environmental factors influence the validity of the fingerprint systems.

Fingerprints and palm prints are extremely accurate since they rely on physical attributes, but their use for access security requires special input devices. These devices are not always compatible with standard telecommunications and computing equipment. Thus they are undesirable for remote access by travelling users. Some finger recognition systems concentrate only on the location and identification of small areas of detail whether or not such areas are identical. Neural approaches allow automation of the fingerprint encoding process which allows higher matching performance. This is particularly useful in searching for a crime image in the files of prints of other convicts. A fingerprint verifier can work with card systems such as smart cards and optical cards, to perform identity verification.

Some major credit card companies are testing fingerprint readers that are linked to the cash registers. The credit card holder gives the credit card to the store clerk who inserts it in the cash register while the customer inserts a finger into a reader. The cash register monitor displays the credit card information showing a digital photograph of the holder while comparing the fingerprint on the smart credit card with that of the alleged holder, as read by the reader.

The primary issue is one of cost as each machine is estimated to cost approximately $3-500. So, to implement such a system on a national or global basis is not considered cost-effective by many of the merchants. This is especially true in such nations as the US where the cardholder is not liable for more than $50 of unauthorised purchases – usually they don't pay anything if the purchases in fact appear fraudulent. The cost of this process is picked up by cardholders that do not pay their credit card bills in full each month – note the monthly interest charges by credit card companies. Much of this cost is due to fraudulent use of credit cards.

## 14.1.4   Iris Analysis

Ophthalmologists originally proposed that the iris of the eye might be used as a kind of optical fingerprint for personal identification. Their proposal was based on clinical results that every iris is unique and remains unchanged in clinical photographs.

The iris consists of trabecula meshwork of connective tissue, collagen stroma of fibres, ciliary processes, contraction furrows, rings, and colourations. All these constitute a distinctive fingerprint that can be seen at a distance from the person. The iris trabecula meshwork ensures that statistical tests of independence in two different eyes always pass. This test becomes a rapid visual recognition method. The properties of the iris that enhance its suitability for use in automatic identification include:

- Protected from the external environment.
- Impossibility of surgically modifying without the risk of loss of vision.
- Physiological response to light which provides a natural test.
- Ease of registering its image at some distance from the subject without a physical contact.

The retinal blood vessels highly characterise an individual so accuracy is one of the advantages of this method of identification. Duplicate artificial eyes are useless since they do not respond to light. However, medical research has shown recently that retinal patterns are not as stable as it was once thought. They show critical variations when there is an organ dysfunction or disease.

## 14.1.5  Facial Analysis

The premise of this approach is that face characteristics (e.g. size of nose, shape of eyes, chin, eyebrows, mouth) are unique, revealing an individual's identity. This increasingly developed method is expensive since it uses neural network methodologies. These use cameras to extract unique facial feature data that is stored on a chip card or a magnetic stripe card. The person swipes his card to a small camera to take an image. The software application on site compares the data with the person's stored data.

In the existing facial recognition systems, certain restrictions are imposed by the user e.g. he/she should be looking straight in the camera with a certain light in order for the system to analyse and identify the person. However, various new graph-matching techniques will enhance the quality of picture decreasing the constraints.

The system will not be able to analyse people with imposed physical characteristics such as beard, hairstyle or with certain facial expressions. Users find it very natural to be identified by their face since this is the most traditional way of identification. It is highly acceptable.

## 14.1.6  Hand Geometry

This biometric method is based on the distinct characteristics of the hands. These include external contour, internal lines, geometry of hand, length and size of fingers, palm and fingerprints, blood vessel pattern in the back of the hand. They work by comparing the image of the hand with the previously enrolled sample. The user enters his identification number on a keypad and places his/her hand on a platter. A camera captures the image of the hand and then the software analyses it.

Hand geometry systems are reasonably fast. They require little data storage space and the smallest template. They have short verification time. A technical problem that needs enhancement is caused by the rotation of the hand where it is placed on the plate.

The performance of these systems might be influenced if people wear big rings, have swollen fingers or no fingers. Dirt may also obscure the details of the hand. The reconstruction of the bone structure of an authorized user's hand may be a reason for circumvention. In those systems that are based on three-dimensional hand geometry where the three dimensions i.e. length, width, and thickness are measured, although they are more secure there is still a chance of defeat. Additionally, bone structure models of the authorised users may deceive the hand systems. Paralysed people or people with Parkinson's disease will not be able to use this biometric method.

## 14.1.7    Speech Analysis

An individual can be identified by various characteristics of the sounds, phonetics, and vocals that they produce. Vocal characteristics such as mouth, nasal cavities, and vocal tract make the production of speech different for each individual. Although humans can use these characteristics naturally for identifying someone, it is hard for a computer system to analyse the voice characteristics.

A person speaks over the telephone or into a microphone-attached system, then the system analyses the voice characteristics of that sample. Usually these methods are applied to extract a set of biometric features associated with the voice. These are coded into a data set or template. Finally, the system compares it to the voice characteristics of a pre-recorded sample.

Speech verification is not as accurate as biometric verification based on physical characteristics such as fingerprint, palm print, or retina scans. It is a suitable technology for environments where "hands free" is a requirement. System developers combine speaker verification with other forms of security.

Computers find it hard to filter out background noise. Duplication of voice using a tape recorder is a major threat to these systems. Another danger is in anti-theft biometric systems. In these systems, physical damage (or removal) can occur to the devices if they are located. Additionally, women have more complex voice frequencies, which makes them harder to be identified. People with sore throats who are unable to speak will not be able to use such systems. People affected by alcohol, by dental anaesthesia, or by oral obstruction, might face a difficulty in being verified by speech verification systems.

## 14.1.8    Hand-written Signature Verification

This biometric method is based on the fact that signing is a reflex action, not influenced by deliberate muscular control, with certain characteristics (rhythms, successive touches of the writing surface, number of contacts, velocity, acceleration). The systems developed based on this biometric method fall into two categories:

- Pen based systems use special pens to capture the information.
- Tablet based systems use special surfaces to collect the data.

In the first category, the pen is the measuring device, which captures the information whereas in the second class, the tablet contains the measuring device. Some of the above systems use statistics in verifying a signature and some use event sequential methods. The items used in a statistical analysis include:

- total time of writing a signature,
- measurements of spacing number of horizontal turning points,
- number of times, and
- duration the pen touches the tablet.

In the sequential methods, the system divides the signature into independent events, and examines each piece separately. A number of signatures (depending on the system) are required for the enrolment process. At the time of verification the user is asked to sign. The system compares various aspects of its signature in a hierarchical manner. If a good match is not found between the signature characteristics (shape, sequence of events, local characteristics) and the template, then the template is rejected.

## 14.1.9  Threats and Risks to Biometrics

Threats and risks can be seen as potential violations of security with expected or unexpected harmful results, and exist because of vulnerabilities in a system. If an unauthorised user invades a system he/she can destroy information, operating systems and programs. They can disclose information or they can cause disruptions or interruptions (damage to systems, networks, organisations or institutions).

In biometric technologies where communication networks might be used for transferring templates; when a LAN can be used in identifying users in an organisation; where the storage and transmission of templates from a database is essential; or when the biometric devices are installed in insecure organisations; then the system might be abused by abusing its components (e.g. networks, computers, algorithms/protocols, database, organisations). Thus, threats and risks arising in these areas (telecommunication systems, networks, computers and organisations) become the threats that the biometric technologies face as well. How biometric technologies face these threats and risks is critical in evaluating their effectiveness. The following are some of the threats and risks:

- *Physical*: which includes natural disasters (fire, storm, water damage) and environmental conditions (dust, moisture, humidity).
- *Technical*: is the equipment of a system (or software), which might fail to carry out its functions (failure), or it might carry them out in an inappropriate way (malfunction).
- *Human*: which is the main source of communication breaches. It includes unauthorised users who wish to damage a biometric system, and authorised users who misuse the system either deliberately or accidentally. The human threats can be further categorised into internal and external. Internal human threats are disgruntled employees, hackers, former employees, system administrators, LAN, database administrators, and the like. External human threats arise from commercial espionage, government-sanctioned espionage, vendors, manufacturers, kids looking for kicks , nosy reporters, etc.

- *Theoretical*: which includes the vulnerability of the algorithms, protocols, and mathematical tools used in the methods that are implemented in the systems.
- *Accidental*: which includes risk and threats, including accident or injury to the user.

## 14.2   EMP Weapons and HERF Guns

Electromagnetic pulse (EMP) weapons are devices that when detonated create an electromagnetic pulse. The goal of the electromagnetic pulse is to induce an electrical current in the target device that is capable of destroying that device. This EMP device produces a pulse that radiates in all directions and is indiscriminate in the computers that it destroys. EMP weapons may only produce a pulse once, as the act of producing the pulse destroys the device. The act of producing the pulse also has the side effect of producing a physical explosion. These physical explosions can have the effect of causing more damage than the electromagnetic pulse itself. Currently, EMP weapons (or E-Bombs as they are known to the military) do exist and form an integrated part of a form of warfare called Electronic Warfare. For example: in the Gulf War E-Bombs were used to neutralise Iraqi radar systems.

A High Energy Radio Frequency (HERF) Gun is a device that produces a directed radio frequency that is capable of being targeted at an area/object. The objective of the radio frequency is to induce an electrical current in the target device that is capable of destroying that device. One of the differences between HERF and EMP weapons is that a HERF gun can be used multiple times. It has been alleged that HERF guns have been used to extort millions of dollars from various organisations. Currently there are no documented cases in the public domain of organisations being attacked via HERF weapons. The major problem with HERF guns at the moment is the amount of power that they require in order to operate. While the gun itself may be hand held and operated by a single user, the power pack required is large; however, as with other technologies, miniaturisation may soon make this a mute point.

However, there can be little doubt that as technology develops so the level of threat posed by EMP and HERF weapons to computer based systems will only increase. The best defence that currently exists against EMP and HERF weapons is the use of TEMPEST.

## 14.3   TEMPEST

The previous sections have demonstrated that there is much in common between the national security and private sector IA needs and information environment. However, there is one topic that is little understood or even discussed and that is TEMPEST. The word TEMPEST is an acronym for Transient Electromagnetic Pulse Emanation Standard, Transient Electromagnetic Pulse Surveillance Technology, or both. Some also consider it a short "name" when referring to the topic of compromising emanations from information processing equipment. Compromising emanations can be defined as those emanations that are emitted by systems that are unintentional and which disclose information being transmitted, received and processed.

Years ago, TEMPEST was a major factor to consider in the use of computers and telecommunications equipment in the classified environment. Several years ago in the United States, the National Security Agency decided that there was little risk of systems' emanations compromising National Security in the United States. Thus, with a few exceptions, TEMPEST considerations were made less stringent or eliminated from government contracts saving sometimes millions of US dollars in the process. That aside, a little information on TEMPEST may be of value to the IA professional.

When an adversary wanted to take advantage of TEMPEST vulnerabilities, they were usually a government agency as the equipment to pick up system emanations was somewhat unique and also very expensive. In addition, picking up specific emanations was often made difficult just by the sheer number of emanations from the hundreds or thousands of systems in the facility being targeted. Another reason that it is not often talked about is that no spy agency of any country wants anyone to know that they have the capability to sit out in a van and pick up every piece of information being processed by targeted information systems.

With the cheaper, smaller and more sophisticated equipment available, the use of such equipment and methods to spy on one's competitors is more likely than ever. Besides, because global economic warfare seems to be replacing or supplementing military warfare, nation-states' spy agencies are more and more targeting foreign corporations in order to support their nation's corporations in gaining the competitive advantage in the global marketplace. What easier way to do massive collections of information than to take it from information systems of the adversaries without even being within physical reach of their systems? Also, by now, the chances are pretty good that the emanations may even be available from satellites targeting specific government agencies, government contractors and commercial enterprises.

All systems emanate; however, not all at the same distance. So, such things as a physical "zone of control" can be considered as a possible defence. This method is just what the name implies. If one can physically control an area to such an extent that noone nor any equipment can be used within that zone without being subject to security review, evaluation and control, then much of the TEMPEST risk can be eliminated or at least mitigated to a great extent. Thus, if one knows how far a system emanates and can control the physical area to at least that length, then one can be pretty well assured that the emanating signals won't be compromised – at least by that "broadcast" method.

It is possible to take more elaborate and expensive measures. These include special shielding walls that won't allow the emanations out of the walled area. Also there are filters that are used on telecommunications lines, to protect telephone communications. There are also specific distances a networked, unclassified system must be separated from systems processing classified information. There is also the use of "red-black" engineering specifications for separating telecommunications lines transmitting at least some classified information from those transmitting absolutely no classified information. Then of course, all classified information leaving a classified area is encrypted using the latest government-supplied encryption equipment.

From a corporate viewpoint, an IA professional would do well to look into this phenomena and when conducting a risk assessment, determine if the threat agents' capabilities are such that TEMPEST should be in some way considered for implementation when processing and transmitting the corporate "crown jewels". If "TEMPESTING" certain portions of your facility or systems is deemed appropriate, one will find that it may be quite expensive; however, there are companies that may assist by making TEMPEST-shielded systems that will meet your needs.

We hope that the Information Security professional in the corporate world will not be too quick to discount the requirements, policies, procedures, and processes now being used in the national security environment. One can learn from them and adapt them to the business world where today there are serious threats from global competitors and their nation-states who have the means to collect sensitive corporate information – and are doing it right now.

## 14.4   CCTV

Closed circuit television (CCTV) is currently being used as a tool for the implementation of physical security. A closed circuit television (CCTV) system uses a hand-held or stand-mounted video camera to project a magnified image onto a video monitor or a television (TV) screen. There is considerable versatility in the types of CCTV systems available today. Cameras with zoom lenses provide variable magnification and are used in the more expensive CCTVs. In most of these systems, magnification level and focus are set after choosing a comfortable and functional working distance between the camera and the material to be viewed. Lower cost closed circuit television systems often use cameras that have a fixed focus and cannot vary magnification or camera-to-target distance. Most cameras also need their own light source.

Cameras that are mounted on a fixed stand require the reading material to be placed under the camera and moved across and down the page. Stand-mounted cameras are particularly effective for handwriting because a hand can fit under the camera. To make the process of viewing easier, a table that is movable from the top of the page to the bottom and side-to-side is used with most stand-mounted cameras.

In contrast to stand-mounted cameras, hand-held cameras are portable systems designed for bringing the camera to the material to be viewed. They can magnify almost anything within reach, including labels on packages of food and medicine. Hand-held cameras are often on rollers, which make them easier to move across a flat working surface. When used in conjunction with a small (5" screen) video monitor or TV, hand-held cameras can be highly portable. Some manufacturers of CCTV systems that use hand-held cameras offer a writing stand as an accessory.

Currently, there are many specially designed CCTV systems that incorporate cutting edge technology. There is a portable system which combines the camera and the display screen in a hand-held housing. A vacuum-fluorescent display provides a magnified image as the camera is moved across the reading material. A radical departure in design from conventional CCTV systems is the use of head-mounted displays (HMD). They offer portability and new ways of viewing the display. All monochrome CCTV systems offer the option of viewing black letters on a white background or white letters on a black background. Controls for contrast and brightness are also standard. Video monitors provide a sharper image than do TVs and many CCTVs that use video monitors also provide other special features such as underlining/overlining text, masking, etc. Some systems offer the option of simultaneous viewing of the computer screen and the CCTV using either a video monitor or a computer monitor. Colour CCTVs are useful for reading materials in which colour is crucial, such as maps and colour photographs.

In some areas, CCTV cameras have been linked into Web sites to provide pictures of a given area that are updated at regular intervals. A typical example of this is CCTV cameras that are mounted over roads, and an example of a site that provides access to such images in the UK is the Nottingham Travel Wise Web Site (http://utc.nottscc.gov.uk/roadeye.htm). This site provides comprehensive traffic and travel information for the Nottinghamshire area, catering for car users, public transport users, pedestrians, cyclists and disabled travellers.

Within Europe, Human Rights legislation is currently being brought into force. These laws give individuals the right to privacy within their private lives. Within the UK the *Human Rights Act 1998* was recently enacted, and this act under Article 8 gives the following rights:

- Everyone has the right to respect for his/her private and family life, home and correspondence.
- There shall be no interference by a public authority with the exercise of this right except such as is in accordance with the law and is necessary in a democratic society in the interests of national security, public safety or the economic well-being of the country, for the prevention of disorder or crime, for the protection of health or morals, or for the protection of the rights and freedoms of others.

Thus the *Human Rights Act* has implications for how and why organisations use CCTV. For example: it can be argued that a commercial organisation does not have the right to use CCTV to capture pictures of individuals in a public place, such as a road, without the express consent of an individual. The accepted practice currently within the UK is for signs to be placed informing the public that they are being monitored. Then by proceeding it can be argued that the person is giving consent to the monitoring.

## 14.5   Summary

Biometrics is becoming a more accepted and reliable form of controlling access to physical areas and logical access to information systems and information. Such biometric systems as facial, fingerprints, iris, hand geometry and speech analyses are just some of the methods being used or under development. However, such devices have some risks: physical, technical, human, theoretical and accidental.

Weapons such as EMP-based and HERF guns are being developed to attack information systems; while TEMPEST-based activities are available to steal sensitive information from adversaries and competitors.

# Section 4

# The Future and Final Comments

This section will summarise the main points of the book in Chapter 15, draw some conclusions, and look into the future and its impact on information assurance as we enter the 21$^{st}$ century.

# Chapter 15

# The Future, Conclusions and Comments

This is the concluding chapter of this book and as such, it is only fitting that we provide a combination summary, some history and a look at the future and its impact on information assurance. This chapter provides that perspective as well as some concluding comments.

## 15.1  Information Assurance: Getting There

So, now we come to the end of this book on information assurance. In doing so, we reflect back on writing this book and want to draw the readers to also reflect back on what they read and form their own conclusions on the entire topic of information protection, assurance and defences.

Information assurance is a step in the process of how we manage the protection of information and information systems. When we look back from whence we came, we see that we began by first protecting, not so much information, as standalone computers and their associated programs. This was accomplished through some personnel security, e.g. background checks on personnel using the computers and physical security.

We gradually moved to the field of computer security and expanded some of its functions such as logical access controls, and audit trail recording. Yet, the protection of information was not a major factor in computer security since we always had hardcopy back-up. If the computers went down, as they often did, people reverted back to the old paper forms and typewriters.

Then we began to rely more on computers and the information that they stored, processed and sometimes transmitted. Networks developed, and we began to think of these computers as more than physical, electrical calculating machines. They were information systems and the information that they processed, stored and almost always transmitted somewhere, were the *"crown jewels"* of modern, information-based, and information-dependent corporations. The professions of computer security, information systems security, and now information assurance, were (and are) being developed as systems develop. Hardcopy forms are hard to find and by the way, no more carbon paper although we continue to use "cc" on e-mails and the like to indicate "carbon copy".

Information assurance is the next step in the on-going process and encompasses much more than computer security. However, this is not the end, but a step in the process and development of both the protection and defence processes of information and systems. As systems become more sophisticated, so do the attacks on them and so do our tools and techniques for protecting and defending these vital assets. We have so much further to go and so much more to learn. However, even corporate executive management, who once did not recognise the need for information protection, is now allocating resources we only dreamed of as little as ten years ago. So, although we have a very long way to go to get one step ahead of the attackers, we are slowly making progress.

## 15.2    Welcome to the World of Constant Change

Professional information assurance specialists must find time to get out of the reactive mode and into a proactive one. The trends that impact the protection of information and information systems must be studied and plans, techniques, processes, tools, and the like must be developed now. If not, they will not be ready five years from now when adverse changes occur that will affect the protection and defence of information and information systems.

The trends that impact information assurance are based on many, and often subtle, changes. They can be categorised in many ways that include the following:

- societies, those of nation-states and the global society;
- economic, global competition;
- threat agents and their techniques; and of course
- technology.

### 15.2.1    Changes in Societies

As we enter the $21^{st}$ century, we are faced with many challenges brought on not only by technology, but other changes – human changes. Nations will be torn apart with ever-increasing chaos and rapid disintegration into factions. These factions will use the Internet to communicate their grievances, desires, and try to build a "world consensus" in their favour to force governments to allow more freedom to these factions, as well as dissolving portions of these nations into smaller nations. The nations will use the Internet to justify their controls, government policies, etc. The break-up of the Soviet Union, and the old Yugoslavia, are just two examples of what other nations may have to look forward to in the $21^{st}$ century. Such break-ups have made some nations such as China left in a quandary. How can they compete in the global economic market with technology and the information it brings, and yet, control the information that their citizens can access? Make no mistake about it, more than ever before, information is power. Power in the hands of the citizens; knowledge of the real world they live in, is not what a communist or dictator wants to happen. They must maintain control of information or perish. Is it any wonder that many nations are doing what they can to control access to information through Internet, radio, faxes, cellular phones, and the like in the societies who lack even the basic freedoms?

The people of all the nations who have Internet, global radio, satellite communications connections will become more sophisticated in the use of these information devices. They will have ever-increasing, massive amounts of information at their disposal; thus allowing them to become more knowledgeable on global matters. They also will become more aware of those throughout the world who have similar and different views.

With the Internet as the base for a massive, personal communications pipeline, technology will provide the means for people to communicate globally as never before. Such massive one-on-one communications will be the driving force that will affect governments, businesses, and societies to such an extent that the governments and businesses will develop extremely sophisticated techniques to influence these Internet communicators on a global scale.

For the IA professionals, they may have to decide which side of the *"freedom of information"* line they will stand. Will they help assure that information is accurate and available to members of society and the world? Will they instead be involved in supporting nation-states in controlling information – not from competitors or other nation-states, but their fellow citizens? Will they help a nation-state perpetuate propaganda as factual information? There are some interesting choices that some IA professionals will have to make – and maybe are even making as you read this book.

The Internet and other global networks will also become some of the primary education vehicles replacing many of today's Industrial Age school systems. Already, colleges and universities are offering courses and degrees through the Internet accesses. This will allow individuals to obtain degrees from universities and colleges located in different nations of the world. Thus, external forces will influence the societies of nation-states as never before.

## 15.2.2 Economic, Global Competition

We are now in the beginning stages of global economic warfare, not only among corporations but among nation-states. The Cold War is over and there is no great global military power in the world. Yes, some nations such as Russia and the United States can still pretty much destroy civilisation, as we know it. However, each is also controlled by world influence on when and how they can use that power. The United States cannot act alone as its military has been "downsized" as has been the case with other nations. The recent need to obtain allied support in Iraq and Serbia are but two examples. So, the power once gained from the barrel of a gun is now second to the power of world economics – world trade.

The influence one nation has over another is now often measured in terms of imports and exports – balance of trade concepts. Trade wars can devastate the global and regional power of a nation today just as surely as any nuclear bombs, excluding physical damage of course.

Nation-states derive their economic power from their government businesses, e.g. Chinese People's Liberation Army's global businesses, as well as private corporate businesses. Large, international corporations now have more money, influence and power within some nations than the government of that nation.

Many of the changes in the world environment are the basis for the rapid changes in how we do business, both nationally and internationally. Businesses can, and do, adapt to these changes quite rapidly. However, in government agencies these changes come more slowly, and sometimes threaten the very existence of some government agencies.

If we look at current trends in technology, Internet crime, attackers and security, we can project with some degree of certainty what the Internet electronic business environment will be like as we enter the 21st century. The following is a look into that future:

- Internet will continue to rapidly expand.
- The number of attacks on Internet that impact electronic business will increase.
- The attackers will increasingly be the techno-criminals (not hackers without malicious intent), a nation's adversary, and terrorists who see electronic business as a means to damage a country and bring down its government.
- Economic and industrial espionage on the Internet (Netspionage) will increase.
- Security products will continue to improve and thwart the less sophisticated attackers.
- Attacks will be more sophisticated, harder to detect and more difficult to identify the criminals, and once identified, prosecution of these international criminals will continue to be inhibited by the lack of treaties and agreements between nations relative to international co-operation and subsequent prosecution.
- Businesses and government agencies will continue to be slow to react and continue to treat security as a low priority.
- Attackers will continue to network internationally and share attacking techniques and systems' vulnerabilities.
- As electronic contracts are relied on for business deals, there will be more challenges to the legality of the contracts: agreed to as written by all parties involved, proving provisions changed or not changed after "signing", proving contracts are "originals", and "electronic signatures" will be tested in court.

## 15.2.3  Technology

The saying, *"the world wants to talk to the world"* is closer to reality than ever before. These global communications phenomenon with all its hopes, promises and problems is based primarily on the Internet and its associated and connected nation-states, and businesses' networks. However, it is not all Internet-connected – yet. This massive global communications network includes cellular phones, private branch exchanges, fax machines, and various other communications tools. These non-Internet networks are quickly being integrated and becoming part of one massive, global communications system. This massive system is developing into the global information infrastructure (GII) that is made up of the information infrastructures of nation-states. It is very important for the IA professionals to understand this new and growing global information age environment because it is the environment in which the IA professional will work.

The current trend in technological advancements will continue and probably increase in speed. The power of the computer will continue to increase as its price declines; as well as its size. It is expected that communication devices such as televisions, computers, cellular phones, and even watches will combine to provide miniaturised, wireless, global communication tools for information-dependent users. Advancements in robotics will allow for them to accomplish more human tasks; as well as tasks that are beyond our comprehension today. The use of nano-bots may be used not only in the medical field, but also as techno-spies who steal, compromise or corrupt information and information systems. The day may come when it will be impossible to protect sensitive information except by going full-circle. That is, store, process but not transmit the most sensitive information on a standalone information system in a secure room with alarms, robotic guards, and closed circuit television monitors.

The development of more sophisticated systems that are able to understand and react to normal human speech will become commonplace. This technology will be a major break-through that will allow previously computer illiterate individuals to use the power of the computers, networks, and the Internet to work, play, and communicate. This will allow poor people and minorities who could neither afford a computer, nor learn how to use one, to become better educated and valuable members of societies with less effort.

The future will also bring us biological computers. For example: it is rumoured that some are even looking at using electrically charged amoebas or other methods that can allow a direct interface with the human brain! Such incredibly advanced computers could perhaps store the entire history of the human race on a single chip. Who will determine what is contained in that history? What are the social ramifications of such dramatic extensions to personal information access? What happens if a criminal or a terrorist embeds a virus, logic bomb or other malicious software in a computer extension attached to your brain? The IA professionals may require a degree in some field of medicine in order to successfully perform their duties vis-à-vis tele-medicine IA.

The *"wireless age"* is already upon us and with it the increased use of technology allowing mobile electronic communications from any place on earth to anywhere. As the growth of networks continues worldwide, it will bring with it more threats from sophisticated, international criminals. Such threats will include an increased use of jamming techniques as a denial of service, to commit electronic extortion or to adversely impact a competitor's ability to perform electronic commerce on the Internet. As more forms of public communication come to rely on the Internet, we expect more sophisticated eavesdropping techniques will arise, which will allow Internet robbers, businesses and government agencies to invade personal privacy to their respective ends. The increasing use of the many Internet telephone and video teleconference systems which are vulnerable to eavesdropping will make this more common.

Software robots have already bombarded us and soon nanobots will be everywhere being used for a multitude of purposes: from spies to "artery cleaners". Software robots or "bots" are already constantly being sent out to roam the

Internet. Some belong to corporations while some are personal. However, they can cause accidental denial of service attacks, destroy information, violate copyright laws, and test the limits of information systems resources. As pointed out in a CNN.com article,[1] "...early bots crawled the Net for information. Archie looked for software available through the Net's file-transfer protocol. The World Wide Web Wanderer and its successors scoured the Web or site to list search engines...bots have already been developed for corporate information-gathering and espionage...bots raise privacy issues..." As the Internet and other global networks are integrated and the use of today's bots and more sophisticated bots are developed in the future and let loose on the networks, the IA professionals will have a more difficult time in protecting and defending their information systems and sensitive information.

## 15.2.4    The IA Professional

The IA professional who does not look ahead at the trends in society, technology, business, global competition, and any associated rapid changes, will have a stagnant IA program that does not meet the needs of the corporation or government agency. After all, an IA program must be a service and support organisation. Therefore, it must be responsive to the needs of its customers.

Remember the saying, "Time is money"? Well, in our world of international global competition and global communication, that saying is truer now than ever before.    The IA professional must understand this better than ever before. Information assurance processes cannot be a roadblock to business. Yet, they must provide the protective and defensive framework required by the corporation or government agency.

Another area for the IA professional to consider is that the people in other countries are becoming more educated and they have a better understanding of the world and technology. There are more world travellers. People in the Information Age seem to demand more from their government and society while demanding less of themselves. They expect and demand professionalism at all times. This too will have a major impact on the IA programs. More computer-literate people in the world, with increased global communications, means more access through world-wide networks, and also more potential threat agents taking advantage of the global communications to attack the IA defences of a corporation or government agency. The protection and defence of information systems and the information that they process, store and/or transmit is of vital concern in this information world.

Many people look at the use of technology as an excellent tool that can be used now and into the new century. It is ushering in a new beginning, the beginning of an age when, with the help of technology, we can make life better for all of us. However, our journey of leaving the old century and starting into the new one will not be without hardships and with some chaos. This too will have an impact on how successful the IA program will be.

---

[1] CNN.com/Sci-tech, 10 February 2001. Software robots roam the net, for better and for worse (http://www.cnn.com/2001/TECH/02/10/robots.net.ap/index.html)

It is important for the IA professional to think about trends and changes and reflect on its meaning for the IA program and its relationship and responsibilities in the global communications environment of the 21st century. As society changes, so must many of the old processes that include how the IA functions are performed.

## 15.3   Summary and Final Comments

The IA professionals' world of the 21$^{st}$ century will continue to change rapidly. IA will play a major role in how nations, societies, businesses, and technology, will change. By looking at current trends, one can see many indications of the changes yet to come; while at the same time, the IA professionals can only be sure of one thing: they and their profession must also change rapidly. However, one should be cautious. It is great to be on the cutting edge, but not on the bleeding edge. Good luck and be sure to carry a few bandages with you, just in case!

# Appendix A

## References and Recommended Reading

Aburdene P, Naisbitt J (1990) Megatrends 2000. Avon Books, New York

Akdeniz Y, Walker C, et al. (eds) (2000) The Internet. Law and Society, Longman

Alberts DS (1996) Defensive Information Warfare. National Defence University

Alderson K (1995) Nurse is Sacked For Altering Records. The Times: 10

Allen HE, Simonsen CE (1986) Corrections in America: An Introduction. Fourth Edition. Macmillan Publishing Company, New York

Anonymous (1997) A Hacker's Guide to Protecting Your Internet Site and Network, Maximum Security. Sams.net Publishing, Indianapolis, IN

Association of Certified Fraud Examiners (ACFE) (1995) High-Tech Fraud Seminar, San Francisco, CA

Applegate LM, Holsapple CW, et al. (1996) Electronic Commerce: Building Blocks of New Business Opportunity. Journal of Organisational Computing and Electronic Commerce 6(1): 1-10

Aron JD (1969) Information Systems in Perspective. Computing Surveys 1(4): 213 - 236

Auger P, Gallaugher JM (1997) Factors affecting the adoption of an Internet-based sales presence for small businesses. The Information Society 13(1): 55-74

Bainbridge, D (1996) Introduction to Computer Law. Pitman Publishing

Baran F, Kaye H, et al. (1990) Security Breaches: Five Recent Incidents at Columbia University. Second Security Workshop Program, USENIX

Barrett N (1996) The State of the CyberNation: Cultural, Political and Economic Implications of the Internet. Kogan Page

Barrett N (1997) Digital Crime: Policing the Cybernation. Kogan Press

Banks MA (1997) How to Protect Yourself in Cyberspace, Web Psychos, Stalkers and Pranksters. The Coriolis Group, Inc., Scottsdale, AZ

Bellovin SM, Cheswick WR (1994) Firewalls and Internet Security. Addison-Wesley Publishing Company, New York

Benjamin R, Gladman B, et al. (1998) Protecting IT Systems from Cyber Crime. The Computer Journal 41(7)

Benynon-Davies P (1995) Information Systems 'Failures': The Case of the London Ambulance Service's Computer Aided Despatch Project. European Journal of Information Systems 4: 171-184

Benynon-Davies P, Tudhope D, et al. (1995) Prototyping, Risk and Information Systems Failure. The Third British Computer Society Conference on Information Systems Methodologies, Wrexham, Wales, Warwick University

Bogner MS (ed) (1994) Human Errors in Medicine. Lawrence Erlbaum Associates

Boni WC, Kovacich GL (1999) I-Way Robbery: Crime on the Internet. Butterworth-Heinemann, Boston

Boni WC, Kovacich GL (2000) Netspionage: The Global Threat to Information. Butterworth-Heinemann, Boston

Brelis M (1995) Hospital Worker Charged under New Massachusetts Password Law. The Boston Globe, Boston, MA

Brooks FP (1987) No Silver Bullet: Essence and Accidents of Software Engineering. IEEE Computer 20(4): 10-19

Cameron D (1998) E-Commerce Security Strategies: Protecting the Enterprise. Computer Technology Research Corp.

Campen AD (ed) (1998) Cyberwar 2.0: Myths, Mysteries and Reality. AFCEA

Canazos EA (1996) The Legal Risks of Setting Up Shop in Cyberspace. Journal of Organisational Computing and Electronic Commerce 6(1): 51-60

Casey E (2000) Digital Evidence and Computer Crime: Forensic Science, Computers and the Internet. Academic Press

Charette RN (1991) The Risks with Risk Analysis. Communications of the ACM 34(6): 106

Chernow R (1990) The House of Morgan. Atlantic Monthly Press

Commission A (1998) Ghost in the Machine: An Analysis of IT Fraud and Abuse. HMSO

Copaacion WC (1997) Supply Chain Management: The Basics and Beyond. Saint Lucie Press

Defence, Ministry of (1991) Defence Standard 00-55: The Procurement of Safety Critical Software in Defence Equipment. Ministry of Defence

Denning DE, Denning PJ (1998) Internet Besieged: Countering Cyberspace Scofflaws. Addison Wesley

Dhillon G, Backhouse J (1996) Risks in the Use of Information Technology Within Organisations. International Journal of Information Management 16(1): 65-74

Disckson G (1995) Principles of Risk Management. Quality in Health Care 4(2): 75-79

Dobson J, McDermid J (1988) Security Models and Enterprise Models. Database Security, Kingston, Ontario, Canada, IFIP North-Holland

Dobson JE (1988) Security and Databases: A Methodological Approach. The University of Newcastle Upon Tyne

Dunlap CJ (1996) How We Lost the High-Tech War of 2007. The Weekly Standard: 22-28

Fox R (1995) No Laughing Matter. Communications of the ACM 38(5): 10

GAO (1992) Mission Critical Systems: Defence Attempting to Address Major Software Challenges. Washington, D.C.

Garfinkel S, Spafford G (1996) Practical Unix and Internet Security. O'Reilly and Associates Inc.

Glasser J (1981) Organisational Aspects of System Failures: A Case Study at the LAPD. 2nd International Conference on Information Systems

Goldman S, Nagal R, et al. (1995) Agile Competitors and Virtual Organisations. Van Nostrand Rienhold, New York

Goodman SE (1996) War, Information Technology, and International Asymmetries. Communications of the ACM 39(12): 11-15

Greening T (1996) Ask and Ye Shall Receive: A Study in Social Engineering. ACM SIG Security Audit and Control Review 14(2): 8-14

Griethuysen JJ, Jardine DA (1988) Introduction to Infomod. Philips Applications and Software Services. Philips International

Grossman WM (1997) Net Wars. New York University Press, New York

Group, J. S. I. (1998) U.S. Information Warfare: Jane's Special Report 1997-1998. Jane's, London

Guisnel J (1997) Cyberwars: Espionage on the Internet. Plenum Press, New York

Harknett RJ (1996) Information Warfare and Deterrence. Parameters 26(Autumn): 93-107

Harper M (1992) I.S. Cover-up charged in System Kill. Computer World. 26

Hinde S (1998) Cyber Wars and Other Threats. Computers and Security 17: 115-118

Hoffman DL, Novak TP, et al. (1999) Information Privacy in the Marketspace: Implications for the Commercial Uses of Anonymity on the Web. The Information Society 15(2)

Hood CC, Jones DKC, et al. (1992) Risk Management. Risk: Analysis, Perception and Management. The Royal Society, London

Howard JD (1997) An Analysis of Security Incidents on the Internet 1989-1995. Engineering and Public Policy. Carnegie Mellon University, Pittsburgh, PA

Kabay ME (1996) Enterprise Security: Protecting Information Assets. McGraw-Hill

Kovacich GL (1998) Information Warfare and the Information Systems Security Professional. Computers and Security 17: 12-24

Kovacich GL (1994) Hackers: From Curiosity to Criminal. The White Paper, ACFE

Kovacich GL (1998) The Information Systems Security Officer's Guide: Establishing and Managing an Information Protection Program. Butterworth-Heinemann, Boston

Kovacich GL, Boni WC (1999) The High-Technology Crime Investigator's Handbook: Working in the Global Information Environment. Butterworth-Heinemann, Boston

Kramer RM, Tyler TR (1996) Trust in Organisations: Frontiers of Theory and Research, Sage Publications

Leveson N (1991) Software Safety in Embedded Systems. Communications of the ACM 34(2): 34-46

Leveson NG (1995) Safeware: System Safety and Computers. Addison Wesley

Leveson NG, Turner CS (1993) An Investigation of the Therac-25 Accidents. IEEE Computer 12(7): 18-41

Lucas HC (1975) Why Information Systems Fail. Columbia University Press, New York

Markoff J, Hafner K (1991) Cyberpunk: Outlaws and Hackers on the Computer Frontier. Simon and Schuster, New York

McLean J (1990) Security Models and Information Flow. IEEE Symposium on Security and Privacy, IEEE Computer Society Press

Mellor P (1994) CAD: Computer Aided Disaster. High Integrity Systems 1(2): 101 -156

Melton HK (1996) The Ultimate Spy Book. DK Publishing

Miller E (1987) The Therac-25 Experience. Conference of State Radiation Control Program Directors

Morris R, Thompson K (1979) UNIX Password Security: A Case History. Communications of the ACM 22(11): 594-597

Mulhall T (1998) Where Have All The Hackers Gone? A Study in Motivation, Deterrence and Crime Displacement. Computers and Security 17: 277-315

Neumann PG (1991) The Human Element. Communications of the ACM 34(11): 150

Neumann PG (1992) Bugs. ACM Software Engineering Notes 17(4)

Neumann PG (1995) Computer Related Risks. ACM Press

Neumann PG (1996) Risks to the Public in Computer and Related Systems. Software Engineering Notes 21(2): 16-22

Neumann PG, Parker DB (1989) A Summary of Computer Misuse Techniques. Twelfth National Computer Security Conference, Baltimore

Overill RE (1997) Computer Crime - A Historical Survey. Third International Symposium on Command and Control Research and Technology

Parker DB (1976) Crime by Computer. Charles Scribner's Sons, New York

Parker DB (1989) Criminal Justice Resource Manual on Computer Crime. National Institute for Justice, U.S. Government Printing Office. Washington DC

Parker MM, Benson RJ, et al. (1988) Information Economics: Linking Business Performance To Information Technology. Prentice-Hall International

Pfleeger CP (1997) Security in Computing. Prentice-Hall

Poirier CC, Reiter SE (1996) Supply Chain Optimization: Building the Strongest Total Business Network. Berrett-Koehler Pub

Porter ME (1985) Competitive Advantage. Free Press

Rathmell A, Overill R, et al. (1997) The Information Warfare Threat from Sub-State Groups: An Interdisciplinary Approach. Third International Symposium on Command and Control Research and Technology

Reason J (1995) Understanding Adverse Events: Human Factors. Quality in Health Care 4(2): 80-89

Riggins FJ, Rhee HS (1998) Towards a Unified View of Electronic Commerce. Communications of the ACM 41(10): 88-95

Rindfleisch TC (1997) Privacy, Information Technology and Health Care. Communications of the ACM 40(8): 93-100

Rochlis, JA, Mark E (1989) With Microscope and Tweezers: The Worm from MIT's Perspective. Communications of the ACM 32(6): 689-698

Russell D, and Gangemi GT (1992) Computer Security Basics. O'Reilly and Associates Inc.

Sasse MA, Adams A (1999) Users Are Not The Enemy. ACM Communications 42(12): 41-46

Sauer C (1993) Why Information Systems Fail: A Case Study Approach. McGraw Hill

Schneider FB (1998) Towards Trustworthy Networked Information Systems. Communications of the ACM 40(11): 144

Schwartau W (1994) Information Warfare. Thunder Mouth Press

Segev A, Porra J, et al. (1998) Internet Security and the Case of the Bank of America. Communications of the ACM 41(10): 81-87

Shimomura T, Markoff J (1996) Takedown. Martin Secker and Warburg Ltd.

Smuckler RH (1991) Ontario's Health Number: A Threat to Privacy and a Solution. Canadian Medical Association Journal 145(12): 1567-1569

Snijders C, Keren G (1996) Determinants of Trust. Journal of Mathematical Psychology 40(4)

Spafford EH (1989) Crisis and Aftermath. Communications of the ACM 32(6)

Spafford SG (1997) Web Security and Commerce. O'Reilly and Associates, Inc.

Stoll C (1989) The Cuckoo's Egg. Doubleday

Summers RC (1997) Secure Computing: Threats and Safeguards. McGraw-Hill

Vaughan D (1996) The Challenger Launch Decision: Risky Technology, Culture and Deviance at NASA. The University of Chicago Press

Vincent C, Ennis M, et al. (eds) (1993) Medical Accidents, Oxford University Press

Waltz E (1998) Information Warfare: Principles and Operations. Artech House Publishers

Wiener LR (1993) Digital Woes: Why We Should Not Depend on Software. Addison-Wesley

Winkler JR, Landry JC (1992) Intrusion and Anomaly Detection: ISOA Update. 15th National Computer Security Conference, Baltimore

Wise JA, and Debons A (eds) (1987) Information Systems: Failure Analysis. Springer-Verlag, Berlin.

# Appendix B

## The Computer Misuse Act 1990

This was clearly an area where new and appropriate legislation was required. A Royal Commission was set up to look at the whole area of computer misuse. As a result of the findings and recommendations of the Commission, the UK *Computer Misuse Act 1990* was enacted.

### So, What is Hacking?

Computer hacking is the accessing of a computer system without the express or implied permission of the owner of that computer system. A person who engages in this activity is known as a computer hacker. A hacker may gain access remotely, using a computer in his own home or office connected to a telecommunications network.

### The Basic Hacking Offence

Section 1 of the *Computer Misuse Act 1990* says that a person is guilty of an offence if:

1. he/she causes a computer to perform any function with the intent to secure access to any program or data held in any computer,
2. the access he/she intends to secure is unauthorised,
3. he/she knows at the time when he/she causes the computer to perform the function that this is the case.

The terms used in the Act for Section 1 are as follows:

*1 (1) A person is guilty of an offence if*
*(a) he causes a computer to perform any function with intent to secure access to any program or data held in a computer, and*
*(b) the access he intends to secure is unauthorised*
*or*
*(c) he knows at the time when he causes the computer to perform the function that this is the case.*

*1(2) The intent a person has to commit an offence under this section need not be directed at*
  *(a) any particular program or data*
  *(b) a program or data of any particular kind*
*or*
  *(c) a program or data held in any particular computer.*
*1(3) A person guilty of an offence under this section shall be liable on summary conviction to imprisonment for a term not exceeding six months or to a fine not exceeding level 5 on the standard scale or both.*

The intent does not have to be directed at any particular program or data or at programs or data of a particular kind. The offence is triable only in a Magistrates' Court, and the maximum penalty is imprisonment for a term not exceeding six months or a fine not exceeding £5,000 or both. Over the years since the Computer Misuse Act was introduced there have been many prosecutions.

In 1993 Paul Bedworth was acquitted of conspiracy to commit offences under Section 1 and Section 3 of the *Computer Misuse Act 1990*. Paul Bedworth's defence counsel argued that Bedworth was addicted to computer hacking and, as a result; he was not capable of forming the necessary intent to commit the offences charged. Although addiction is not a defence to a criminal charge, the jury acquitted him.

It is certainly possible for the employees of a company to commit the basic hacking offence when using their own computer terminals at work if they intend to gain access to any program or data in respect of which they know they do not have authority to access. In the case of *Denco Ltd* v *Joinson (1991)* it was held that an employee who used an unauthorised password to gain access to information stored on a computer which he was not entitled to see, and which he knew he was not entitled to see, was guilty of gross misconduct and could be summarily dismissed from his employment.

In December 1993 a male nurse was convicted of hacking into a hospital's computer system and modifying entries, including prescriptions. The hacker gained access to the computer system after learning the password through observing a locum doctor having trouble logging in. The hacker:

1. prescribed drugs normally used to treat heart disease to a 9-year-old patient with meningitis;
2. prescribed antibiotics to a patient in a geriatric ward;
3. "scheduled" an unnecessary X-ray for a patient; and
4. "recommended" a discharge for another patient.

The hacker was sacked for unprofessional behaviour and jailed for 12 months.

## The Ulterior Intent Offence

Section 2 of the *Computer Misuse Act 1990* describes the offence of unauthorised access with the intent to commit or facilitate the commission of further offences.
The terms used in the Act for Section 1 are as follows:

*2(1) A person is guilty of an offence under this section if he commits an offence under section 1 above ("the unauthorised access offence") with intent*

*(a) to commit an offence to which this section applies*

*or*

*(b) to facilitate the commission of such an offence (whether by himself or by any other person) and the offence he intends to commit or facilitate is referred to below in this section as the further offence.*

*2(2) This section applies to offences*

*(a) for which the sentence is fixed by law*

*or*

*(b) for which a person of twenty one years of age or over (not previously convicted) may be sentenced to imprisonment for a term of five years (or in England and Wales might be so sentenced but for the restrictions imposed by Section 33 of the Magistrates Courts Act 1980).*

*2(3) A person guilty of an offence under this section shall be liable*

*(a) on summary conviction, to imprisonment for a term not exceeding six months or to a fine not exceeding the statutory maximum or both*

*and*

*(b) on conviction on indictment, to imprisonment for a term not exceeding five years, or to a fine, or both.*

Another way of looking at Section 2 of the Act is to say that it is an aggravated form of the basic hacking offence. The further offence must be one for which the sentence is fixed in law - such as murder, or one for which the maximum sentence is not less than five years. Thus Section 2 of the Act applies to blackmail, or obtaining property or services by deception.

So, for example: if a hacker breaks into a computer system and uses the compromised system as a springboard to break into other systems, and does not alter any files or access any information on the original system, then the hacker can be charged under Section 2 of the *Computer Misuse Act 1990.*

A final requirement is that of double criminality; that is, if the person operates within the UK intending to commit a further offence under Section 2 in a different country, that offence must be a criminal offence in the other country as well as in the home country. An example is where a hacker gains access to a computer with the intention of blackmailing a person. In order to gain a conviction under Section 2 of the *Computer Misuse Act 1990* the following intentions and knowledge must be proved:

- the intention to secure access;
- the knowledge that the access is unauthorised; and
- the intention to commit blackmail.

## Criminal Damage and the Computer Misuse Act 1990

Section 3 of the *Computer Misuse Act 1990*. The terms used in the Act for Section 1 are as follows:

*3(1) A person is guilty of an offence if*

*(a) he does any act which causes the unauthorised modification of the contents of any computer*

*and*

*(b) at the time when he does the act he has the requisite intent and the requisite knowledge.*

*3(2) For the purposes of subsection 3(1)b above the requisite intent is an intent to cause a modification of the contents of any computer and by so doing*

*(a) to impair the operation of any computer*

*(b) to prevent or hinder access to any program or data held in any computer*

*or*

*(c) to impair the operation of any such program or the reliability of any such data.*

*3(3) The intent need not be directed at*

*(a) any particular computer*

*(b) any particular program or data or a program or data of any particular kind*

*or*

*(c) any particular modification or a modification of any particular kind.*

*3(4) For the purpose of subsection 1b above, the requisite knowledge is knowledge that any modification he intends to cause is unauthorised.*

*3(5) It is immaterial for the purposes of this section whether an unauthorised modification or any intended effect of it of a kind mentioned in subsection (2) above is, or is intended to be, permanent or merely temporary.*

*3(6) For the purposes of the Criminal Damage Act 1971 a modification of the contents of a computer shall not be regarded as damaging any computer or computer storage medium unless its effect on that computer or computer storage medium impairs its physical condition.*

The word *"modification"* is defined in Section 17 as the alteration or erasure of any program or data or the addition of any program or data to the contents of a computer. This covers the computer viruses, worms, Trojan horses, logic and time bombs[1].

The first example of the use of a "Trojan horse" was seen in the UK before the enactment of the *Computer Misuse Act 1990*. At the end of 1989, the FBI arrested a 39-year-old man, who had been involved in an ambitious attempt to blackmail thousands of personal computer users throughout the world. The FBI worked closely with New Scotland Yard's Computer Crime Unit to apprehend Dr Popp, of Ohio, who sent free bogus computer diskettes to 20,000 people in London and around the world containing a program which, Popp claimed, assessed the user's risk of contracting the AIDS/HIV virus. In fact, the diskettes were merely a means of introducing a Trojan horse into the user's computer. This device was designed to go into action after the computer had been used approximately 100 times. Recipients were warned that their computers would stop functioning unless they paid the licence fees of £225 to a bank account in Panama. This case is thought to be the world's most ambitious computer crime. Dr Popp was extradited to the UK but his case never came to trial. His counsel presented evidence that Dr Popp's mental state had deteriorated. The Crown Prosecution Service accepted that

---

[1] PG Neumann, *Computer-Related Risks.* ACM Press

Popp was mentally unfit to stand trial (Clough & Mungo 1993, p 146). Today, if found fit for trial, it is likely that Popp would have been liable under the Section 3 offence.

Section 3(2) states that:

*For the purposes of ss.1(b) above the requisite intent is an intent to cause a modification of the contents of any computer and by so doing -*

*(a) to impair the operation of any computer;*
*(b) to prevent or hinder access to any program or data held in any computer; or*
*(c) to impair the operation of any such program or the reliability of any such data.*

Section 3(3) shows that it is immaterial whether the intent is directed at any particular computer, program or data or programs or data of a particular kind or at any particular modification or any modification of any particular kind. The requisite knowledge is knowledge that the intended modification is unauthorised. Section 3(6) provides:

*For the purposes of the Criminal Damage Act 1971 a modification of the contents of a computer shall not be regarded as damaging any computer or computer storage medium unless its effect on that computer or computer storage medium impairs its physical condition.*

The 1971 Act will, therefore, still be relevant to cases where modification results in impairment of the physical condition of a computer or computer storage medium, and further, although Section 3(6) reverses the effect of Cox and Whiteley in so far as they relate to computers, they should remain relevant authorities in other situations involving the alteration and erasure of information stored in electro- magnetic form such as, on a video or audio tape (Cowley 1992, p 37-38).

The Section 3 offence is triable either way and a person found guilty of an offence under Section 3 is liable to a maximum sentence of five years imprisonment and/or an unlimited fine in the Crown Court. The accused will be tried summarily if the value of the damaged property does not exceed the relevant sum of £2,000 (Criminal Justice Act 1988, Section 38). In this case the maximum penalty that can be imposed is three months imprisonment or a fine of £2,500.

## Other UK Legislation

The following is a list of UK legislation that relates to information security and computer crime:

The Data Protection Act 1998
The Computer Misuse Act 1990
The Telecommunications Act 1984
Copyright, Design and Patients Act 1988
Copyright (Computer Software) Amendment Act 1985
Police and Criminal Evidence Act 1984
Criminal Justice Act 1988
Electronic Communications Act 2000

Freedom of Information Act 2000
Protection of Children Act 1999
Human Rights Act 1998
Wireless Telegraphy Act 1998
Regulation of Investigatory Powers Act 2000

# Appendix C

## The Computer Misuse Act 1990 - Loopholes and Anomalies by Keith Lawrence Buzzard, B.Sc, M.Sc.[1]

### Preface

*"Hacking is a recreational and educational pastime; it consists of attempting to make an unofficial entry into computers and explore what is there".* [Cor 88]

*"The media depiction of a hacker tends to be that of a male teenager in a greasy t-shirt and torn jeans who spends 27 hours slumped over a terminal, eyes gazing fixedly at the green glow of the VDU monitor. Before his very eyes, banks, military installations, universities, companies and financial institutions fall before his relentless onslaught. Nowhere is safe, no one can keep him out, no one knows the scale of the threat, the silent deadly menace stalks the networks".* [LS 96]

*"Our conclusion on the evidence that we have received is that hacking by unauthorised entry .. is sufficiently widespread to be a matter of major and legitimate concern ............ Although the computer enthusiast at home is the stereotypical hacker, most of the hacking cases reported involved employees obtaining unauthorised access to information stored on their employer's computers".* [LC 89]

Vast amounts of digital data are stored and processed in large computer systems and transmitted between computers linked together in complex communication networks. Without appropriate safeguards this data is susceptible to interception during transmission, or may be subject to various forms of attack whilst in storage or during processing; resulting in unauthorised access, deletion, and modification. Computer misuse is a growth industry and a serious threat which is frequently undetected and under reported. The aim of this dissertation is to highlight problems with the legislation used to combat so called "computer hacking".

---

[1] © K. L. Buzzard. Reprinted with the permission of the author.

## Introduction

Until the introduction of the *Computer Misuse Act 1990* there was no separate class of criminal mischief known as "computer misuse". Existing legislation could deal with some of the problems but there were gaps. Prosecutions relied upon the interpretation of statutory provisions such as the *Theft Act 1968* and the *Criminal Damage Act 1971*, and academic interest focused on the extent to which computer misuse exposed loopholes in the existing law, when attempts were made to bend this legislation to fit new circumstances. Computer technology had opened up opportunities for mischief makers to inflict considerable inconvenience and economic loss on computer users, without fear of any criminal sanction.

Public attention was first drawn to the issue of computer misuse in the case of *R* v *Gold & Schifreen*. The defendants (computer games magazine journalists) were arrested in March 1985 for hacking into the BT Prestel Gold viewdata service using customer identification information[2] which had been posted on a Bulletin Board system. Having entered the Prestel system they obtained information without payment and without authority.

*"The system consisted of a central computer system which provided a variety of computer related services to its subscribers[3] including electronic mail. Subscribers would be issued with a password and user identification code. This would allow the system to monitor the extent of usage & charge them accordingly. Special passwords were issued to BT employees who required access to the system for the purposes of their employment. The attraction of these passwords for a would be hacker was that they did not cause any bills to be generated".* [LS 96]

Upon the discovery of their activities, consideration was given as to what offence had actually been committed.

*"There seems no doubt that the hackers were seeking to masquerade as authorised users for the purpose of obtaining free access to services. In England & Wales, the Theft Act 1968 had replaced the concept of obtaining services by means of a false pretence [still part of Scottish criminal law] with that of obtaining services by deception ... the difficulty with this approach in the computer context is the question whether a machine can be deceived".* [LS 96]

There appeared to be no clear ruling[4] on this point, and faced with uncertainty on this crucial issue, the defendants were charged with, and initially convicted of forgery under Section 1 *Forgery and Counterfeiting Act 1981*; which provides that an offence is committed by a party who presents a false instrument with the

---

[2] Mr G.Reynolds - Prestel ID: 2222222222  Password: 1234 a member of BT staff, who was entitled to access privileged areas of the Prestel database.

[3] Among the mailboxes accessed by Gold & Schifreen was one belonging to the Duke of Edinburgh, from where the following mail message was sent to the Prestel system manager: *"I do so enjoy puzzles and games. Ta Ta. Pip! Pip! HRH Hacker"*

[4] In *DPP* v *Ray*, Lord Morris said that for the purposes of the Theft Act 1968 *"for a deception to take place there must be some person or persons who will have been deceived".*

intention that it should be taken as genuine, and that attempts to deceive a machine should be equated with those affecting a human. The prosecution had to prove that the defendants had made a false instrument":[5]

*"... namely a device on or in which information is recorded or stored by electronic means with the intention of using it to induce the Prestel computer to accept it as genuine and by reason of so accepting it to do an act to the prejudice of British Telecommunications plc".*

In other words, the forgery of an area of RAM, using a modem over a telephone line, which existed for a fraction of a second before being wiped clean. The prosecution could not provide the instrument (the area of RAM) in court, since it was ethereal. On appeal it was held that the brief period taken for the authenticity of the password to be verified by the system was too short a period to constitute a recording as required by the Act. Their Lordships suggested that "recorded" or "stored" connoted a process of a lasting and continuous nature from which the instrument could be retrieved in the future. Therefore *Gold & Schifreen* had not made an instrument and could not be guilty of the offence with which they were charged. The convictions were overturned by unanimous judgements both by the Court of Appeal and House of Lords, Lord Chief Justice Lane stating that if hacking was to be considered a crime, then a change in the law was required.

*"The appellant's conduct amounted in essence ... to dishonestly obtaining access to the relevant Prestel data bank by a trick. That is not a criminal offence. If it is thought desirable to make it so, that is a matter for the legislature rather than the courts. We express no view on the matter."*

The main question raised by this case was whether the unauthorised access into a computer system where no damage is done should be a criminal offence (other forms of trespass are a civil not a criminal wrong). This case in particular, plus the issues raised in two other cases, *Cox v Riley* and *R v Whiteley*, which highlighted the problems in using the Criminal Damage Act where there was damage to intangible rather than tangible property,[6] attracted a great deal of media attention and led to pressure for legislation to bring the criminal law up-to-date with new technology. Failure to successfully prosecute [*Gold & Schifreen*] was widely regarded as *"leaving corporate computer systems exposed to the predatory activities of hackers"* [LS 96]. In a world that is increasingly dependent on the confidentiality, integrity and availability of computer systems, it is right and proper that criminal sanctions be imposed upon those who deliberately seek to impair the operations of a computer system. This pressure resulted in a referral to the Law Commission which produced a report.[7] Emma Nicholson MP introduced a private member's bill to address computer hacking in 1989, but withdrew it after a

---

[5] The Act defines "instrument" as including any disk, tape, sound track or other device in or on which information was recorded or stored.

[6] That is, damage to or the destruction of, software or data held on a computer or on storage media in electronic form rather than damage to the computer or storage media itself.

[7] Report No 186 "Computer Misuse", October 1989.

government promise to legislate in this area. That promise was broken and so in 1990 Michael Colvin MP introduced another private member's bill. This bill was put before parliament to implement the Law Commission's recommendations and became the *Computer Misuse Act 1990*, which came into effect on 29 August 1990.

## Chapter I  Computer crime

*"The criminal may be considered as the individual most responsive to the changes taking place in society. Protect society with guns, then the criminal will attack with guns. Store valuable assets in robust safes, then the criminal will use dynamite. Control society through information held in computers, then the criminal will turn to information technology itself to perpetrate the crime".* [Bla 87]

The impact of information technology on society has been immense. Historically, paper money and confidential documents were locked away in safes and vaults. Today, money and information is stored in electronic form inside computer systems, which are the new vaults. All major financial institutions throughout the world use computers to carry out their business and vast sums of money are transferred by computer. As far as the criminal is concerned, the creation of a bank account, followed by instructions to the bank mainframe to transfer large sums into that account, is much more attractive than robbing the bank with a shotgun. Computer crime provides newsworthy headlines with a number of attention grabbing ingredients; the glamorous world of high technology, young whizz-kid hackers, associations with organised crime and espionage, and large sums of money or very sensitive information disclosure. While the press may over sensationalise and over estimate the problem, there has clearly been an increase in computer related crime. This is due to a number of factors, the main ones being the increase in computerisation and networking in the workplace, and the ease with which the home computer may connect into national and international computer networks (such as the Internet).

The term computer crime covers traditional crimes, such as theft, fraud and forgery, where the computer is incidental to the commission of the crime, and new crimes where the computer is the object of attack (computer misuse), such as conduct which deprives the owner of a computer system of an opportunity to use it in the manner desired, and conduct whereby an unauthorised person seeks to obtain access to, and information held in a computer system. Under Section 1 of the *Theft Act 1968*:

A PERSON IS GUILTY OF THEFT IF HE DISHONESTLY APPROPRIATES PROPERTY BELONGING TO ANOTHER WITH THE INTENTION OF PERMANENTLY DEPRIVING THE OTHER OF IT.

Under Section 4(1) of the *Theft Act 1968*:

PROPERTY INCLUDES MONEY AND ALL OTHER PROPERTY REAL OR PERSONAL, INCLUDING THINGS IN ACTION AND OTHER INTANGIBLE PROPERTY.

What of the situation where information is copied but remains in the possession of the owner. The hacker who, having gained access to a computer and reads or prints out information from it, cannot be prosecuted for the theft of that information, because the owner has not been permanently deprived of it.

*"While the English law of theft does extend to a number of items of intangible property, such as bank balances,*[8] *and the category of intangibles does not appear to be closed for these purposes, information as such, whether confidential, valuable or otherwise, cannot be stolen".* [Was 92]

In the leading case of *Oxford v Moss*, a civil engineering undergraduate from Liverpool University removed a forthcoming examination paper. After he had had a good look at the questions he returned the paper but was caught in the process. It was held that although the defendant's conduct was to be condemned and would be described by a layman as cheating, the confidential information so obtained did not fall within the definition of "intangible property" as defined by Section 4(1) *Theft Act 1968*, and was therefore incapable of being stolen. What if a hacker copies say, a computer data file, and then immediately afterwards goes on to erase the original file from the computer system. *Lloyd & Simpson* [LS 96] argue that the difficulty here will be if the hacker believes the owner has another copy of that information (it is reasonable for a hacker to assume that back-up files exist) then there is no intention to permanently deprive. Therefore the unauthorised copying of computer data coupled with the subsequent destruction of the original is also unlikely to be theft. Prior to the CMA, damage or erasure of computer programs or data was an offence under Section 1(1) *Criminal Damage Act 1971* which provides that:

A PERSON WHO WITHOUT LAWFUL EXCUSE DESTROYS OR DAMAGES ANY PROPERTY BELONGING TO ANOTHER INTENDING TO DESTROY OR DAMAGE ANY SUCH PROPERTY ... SHALL BE GUILTY OF AN OFFENCE.

The definition of this offence requires that the person intended such consequences to occur or was reckless as to whether property would be so destroyed or damaged. In *MPC v Caldwell*, it was held that whether a person has been reckless was an objective test, that is, whether the course of action undertaken by the accused created what would be an obvious risk of damage in the eyes of an ordinary prudent individual. However, Section 10(1) *Criminal Damage Act 1971* defines property as being "OF A TANGIBLE NATURE WHETHER REAL OR PERSONAL" which does not seem applicable where data is erased or damaged. In *Cox v Riley*, the accused, who acted without authority and for no valid reason, deliberately erased a number of programs from a printed circuit card used to control his employer's computerised saw (for cutting out window frame timber sections). He was charged under Section 1(1) CDA and found guilty on the basis that the printed circuit card had been damaged and was now useless. The defendant, having been convicted before magistrates, appealed on the point that no damage had been caused to physical property.

---

[8] *R v Kohn*; *R v Chan Man-Sin*.

*"Although the contents of the printed circuit card had been erased, it remained a viable storage device. Upholding the conviction, the Divisional court held that the requirement of damage to property had been satisfied, in that the owner of the saw ... had been required to expend time and effort of a more than minimal amount in order to restore it to its original condition."* [LS 96]

*"It seems to me to be quite untenable to argue that what this defendant did on this occasion did not amount to causing damage to property."* Stephen-Brown LJ.

The fact that the damage could be undone by reprogramming and need not be permanent was held by the court not to matter. In *R v Whiteley*, the Court of Appeal held that the offence of criminal damage did apply where damage was done to computer data. Nicholas Whiteley (aka the "Mad Hacker") was charged with intending or recklessly damaging property by hacking into various university computers via JANET[9] during 1988.

*"Computer disks contain millions of magnetic particles which provide a medium for the recording of information. The effect of writing [data] to a disk is to produce particular combinations of magnetic polarity. These correspond to the binary symbols which form the basis of all digital computer operations. Whiteley's activities, it was argued, altered the makeup of magnetic particles causing impairment to the operation of computer systems and thereby committing the offence of criminal damage."* [LS 96]

Whiteley was a skilled hacker who acquired system manager status. This gave him freedom to do what he wanted with the systems he gained access to. He was malicious and vindictive and taunted system managers, and when shut out of a system he took it as a challenge to break back in. His conduct caused considerable inconvenience and expense.

*"As a result of his actions, computers failed, were unable to operate properly, or had to be shut down for periods of time."* [Akd 96]

Two charges were brought under the provisions of the CDA; damage to computers by virtue of their operations being disrupted or stopped for periods of time, and damage to the disks which held the computer programs and data.

*"The first charge was dismissed by the jury, a verdict with which the Court of Appeal indicated their approval. A conviction on the second count for which Whiteley was sentenced to a term of 12 months imprisonment was the subject of the appeal, it being argued that the Criminal Damage Act required that damage be tangible."* [LS 96]

This reasoning was rejected by the Court of Appeal, Lord Chief Justice Lane stating:

---

[9] Joint Academic NETwork - which links the computing facilities of most UK universities.

*"What the Act requires to be proved is that tangible property has been damaged, not necessarily that the damage itself should be tangible. There can be no doubt that particles upon magnetic disks were a part of the disk and if the appellant was proved to have intentionally and without lawful excuse altered the particles in such a way as to cause impairment of the value or usefulness of the disk to the owner, there would be damage within the meaning of section 1(1) CDA. The fact that the damage could only be perceived by operating the computer did not make the damage any less within the ambit of the Act."*

Lord Lane referred to a judgement by Auld J in *Morphitis* v *Salmon*, where the accused had removed a scaffolding clip and bar from a barrier. Although there was no damage to either, the barrier itself was dismantled and therefore arguably damaged.

*"If the hacker's actions do not go beyond, for example, mere tinkering with an otherwise empty disk, no damage would be established. Where, on the other hand, the interference with the disk amounts to an impairment of the value or usefulness of the disk to the owner, then the necessary damage is established."*

*"Damage should be interpreted so as to include not only permanent or temporary physical harm, but also permanent or temporary, impairment of value or usefulness."*

Thus the decision in *Whiteley* represented authority that an act causing damage to data held on a computer storage device can constitute the offence of criminal damage. However, if the facts of *Cox* or *Whiteley* were to happen today the accused would not be guilty of criminal damage but of an offence under the Computer Misuse Act. The Law Commission took the view that the problem of computer misuse needed to be tackled head on.

## Chapter II  Computer Misuse Act

The *Computer Misuse Act 1990* is:

*"An Act to make provision for securing computer material against unauthorised access or modification; and for connected purposes"*.

The primary aim of this legislation is to deter computer misuse and convey the message that hacking is socially unacceptable. The Act created a hierarchy of three new criminal offences to deal with those situations where the computer itself is the object of attack. It also introduced new rules governing the jurisdiction of UK courts to deal with the international nature of computer misuse.

SECTION 1 - UNAUTHORISED ACCESS (BASIC) OFFENCE. [TECHNO-TRESPASS]
A PERSON IS GUILTY OF AN OFFENCE UNDER SECTION 1 IF:
A.  HE CAUSES A COMPUTER TO PERFORM ANY FUNCTION WITH INTENT TO SECURE ACCESS TO ANY PROGRAM OR DATA HELD IN ANY COMPUTER;
B.  THE ACCESS HE INTENDS TO SECURE IS UNAUTHORISED; AND
C.  HE KNOWS AT THE TIME THAT IT IS UNAUTHORISED.
THE INTENT NEED NOT BE DIRECTED AT:

A. ANY PARTICULAR PROGRAM OR DATA, OR
B. ANY PARTICULAR KIND OF PROGRAM OR DATA, OR
C. PROGRAMS OR DATA HELD IN ANY PARTICULAR COMPUTER.

This is the most far reaching offence under the Act, and is analogous to the tort of trespass. The deterrence factor is at the forefront of this offence and criminalises the activities of so-called innocent hackers (nosy parkers) who seek access to computer systems *"purely out of idle curiosity or for the challenge and excitement of breaking down security barriers designed to restrict access"* [Dum 89]. In English law, burglary may be committed where a person enters premises as a trespasser with intent to commit one of a range of ulterior offences (most importantly theft and criminal damage). However, trespass is not a criminal offence. The Section 1 offence thus criminalises electronic access to a person's computer where physical access to that person's home would not amount to a crime.

Criminal liability starts at an early stage. The offence applies not only to the person who evades the security measures and intrudes into a system, but also to the person who is denied access by a computer security device, because that person has caused a computer to perform a function.

*"No particular computer needs to be targeted [by the accused] and it is enough that he is out fishing without a licence. Indeed it is enough that he sets out to fish without a licence."* [Bai 96]

Effectively, any action which causes a computer to function in any way will come within the scope of Section 1 (including the act of simply switching on a computer). The *actus reus* of the offence requires that a person caused the computer to perform any function. The *mens rea* of the offence has two limbs: firstly, the prosecution must prove that the accused intended to secure access to any program or data held in any computer. Secondly, it must be proved that the defendant knew at the time that the access was unauthorised.

SECTION 17(2)
A PERSON SECURES ACCESS TO ANY PROGRAM OR DATA IN A COMPUTER IF BY CAUSING A COMPUTER TO PERFORM ANY FUNCTION HE:
A. ALTERS OR ERASES THE PROGRAM OR DATA;
B. COPIES OR MOVES IT TO ANY STORAGE MEDIUM OTHER THAN THAT IN WHICH IT IS HELD OR TO A DIFFERENT LOCATION IN THE STORAGE MEDIUM IN WHICH IT IS HELD;
C. USES IT; OR
D. HAS IT OUTPUT FROM THE COMPUTER IN WHICH IT WAS HELD.
SECTION 17(3)
A PERSON USES A PROGRAM IF THE FUNCTION HE CAUSES THE COMPUTER TO PERFORM:
A. CAUSES THE PROGRAM TO BE EXECUTED; OR
B. IS ITSELF A FUNCTION OF THE PROGRAM.
SECTION 17(5)
ACCESS IS UNAUTHORISED IF:
A. HE IS NOT ENTITLED TO CONTROL ACCESS OF THE KIND IN QUESTION TO THE PROGRAM OR DATA; AND

B. HE DOES NOT HAVE THE CONSENT TO ACCESS BY HIM OF THE KIND IN QUESTION TO THE PROGRAM OR DATA FROM ANY PERSON WHO IS SO ENTITLED.

The definition of access is very broad and may be summed up as causing a computer to perform any function to alter, erase, copy, move, use or output any program or data held in a computer. The question of whether access is unauthorised will be determined by reference to the state of mind of the computer owner, or of the person entitled to control access. Reckless, careless or inattentive behaviour is insufficient. If the accused believes, however unreasonably, that he is entitled to access or that his access is authorised by someone entitled to control access, he cannot know that his access is unauthorised. If the accused believes his access is unauthorised when it is in fact authorised he does not commit the offence, eg. if in the given circumstances the owner of the data would have authorised such access. Nor is he guilty of an attempt since the offence is summary only. Access is thus a definite action. Watching over someone's shoulder, electronic eavesdropping[10] and other passive behaviour does not constitute access.

In *R* v *Cropp* (the first person charged under the CMA), Sean Cropp, a former employee of a wholesale locksmith, visited his former workplace in order to purchase some key cutting equipment and, while the staff were otherwise engaged, entered instructions into a computer without authority, thereby obtaining for himself a 70% discount on goods purchased. He was charged with securing unauthorised access to a computer contrary to Section 1 CMA, with intent to commit a further offence (namely false accounting) contrary to Section 2. Judge Aglionby, on a submission of no case to answer, held that in order to prove a contravention of Section 1, the Crown had to establish that the accused had used one computer with intent to secure unauthorised access to another computer (ie. two computers must be involved), and accordingly upheld the submission.

*"It seems to me, doing the best that I can in elucidating the meaning of S.1(1)a, that a second computer must be involved."*

The Attorney General referred this case to the Court of Appeal - Attorney General's Reference (No 1 of 1991) on a point of law.

*"The point of law referred for consideration by the court is; in order for a person to commit an offence under S.1(1) CMA 1990 does the computer which the person causes to perform any function with the required intent have to be a different computer to the one into which he intends to secure unauthorised access to any program or data held there ?"*

---

[10] All electronic devices emit electromagnetic radiation, and it is possible to intercept and reconstruct electronic information emitted from computer screens and circuitry using TEMPEST (Transient ElectroMagnetic Pulse Emanation Standard) technology. The use of TEMPEST is not illegal under UK law. The reason for this is that the *Interception of Communications Act 1985* states that transmission should be intended. Radiated transmissions are unintended. The Law Commission argued that this conduct did not pose a threat to the operational integrity of system in the way hacking does, but is aimed more specifically at the confidentiality of the information which it contains.

It was held that the words of the statute in their plain and natural meaning did not require that two computers be used in order for an offence to have been committed. An offence contrary to Section 1 would be committed even if the data was accessed directly from the computer used. It was not incumbent upon the prosecution to prove that the computer used to secure such access was in some way "separate" from the computer containing the data or program sought to be accessed. Parliament had been very clear that Section 1 was intended to protect all computer systems from all forms of unauthorised access.

It must be established that an accused knew that access was unauthorised, and the evidential burden of establishing such knowledge is a heavy one. The question of authority is one of fundamental importance. In the case of a library system with terminals located throughout the library "it is likely to be the case that access is authorised to the world at large, or at least that portion entitled to enter the library". [LS 96]

Where a hacker has details of a telephone number or an Internet address corresponding to a computer system and attempts to connect to that system from home via a modem, then at this moment in time it is unlikely that a Section 1 offence has been committed. First contact with a remote computer system is normally via a log-in screen which identifies the system. The hacker may suspect that he is not authorised to use the system, but suspicion may fall short of knowledge since many systems allow guest users access using a username such as "anonymous" with no password. However, if the log-in screen makes specific reference to the provisions of the CMA[11] and states that unauthorised access amounts to a criminal offence, then such a warning should be enough to establish the guilt of a person who moves on from the log-in screen to the contents of the system itself.

"The difficulty of establishing knowledge [that the accused knew that access was unauthorised] will be even greater when a user possesses limited access rights and the allegation is that these rights have been exceeded." [LS 96]

"In the case of employees the offence will only be committed if the employer has clearly defined the limits of authorisation applicable to each employee and that employee knowingly and intentionally exceeds that level of authority." [Dum 89]

In *Denco Ltd* v *Joinson*, the accused had limited access to a computer system in connection with his employment, and was dismissed when he allegedly sought access to sensitive information from a subsidiary company (who shared the

---

[11]A suggested banner is:

"The programs and data held on this system are the property of [Company Name] and are lawfully available for authorized users for company purposes only. Access to any data or program must be authorized by the company. It is a criminal offence to secure unauthorized access to any program or data held in, or make any unauthorized modification on the contents of this computer system. Offenders are liable to criminal prosecution. If you are not an authorized user, disconnect immediately." [Nig 92]

computer facilities) using a username/password allocated to another employee[12]. He complained to an industrial tribunal that he had been unfairly dismissed. The tribunal upheld his complaint on the ground that the employer had not shown that the employee had gained access to the computer for an illegitimate purpose rather than idle curiosity, and therefore the allegation of gross misconduct had not been made out. The employer appealed to the Employment Appeal Tribunal, where it was held that if an employee deliberately used an unauthorised password to enter or attempt to enter a computer system which he knew contained information to which he was not entitled to have access, then that itself amounted to gross misconduct which *prima facie* justified summary dismissal. Accordingly the tribunal had misdirected themselves in law as to what constituted gross misconduct. However, it was established that the culture existing within the workplace was such that *"management encouraged employees to make use of the computer even though this was not required for the performance of their duties. In such a climate it might be difficult to establish the requisite knowledge"* [LS 96].

*"It must surely be common sense that where a system such as the present has been instituted that the unauthorised use of a password is a very serious matter indeed. If it is not so realised by industry generally then perhaps this case will make it so. Unauthorised use of or tampering with computers is an extremely serious industrial offence. However it is clearly desirable to reduce into writing the rules concerning the access to and use of computers and not only to post them but to leave them near the computers for reference."* Wood J.

In *British Telecommunications plc* v *Rodrigues*, the accused (a BT employee) was observed gaining unauthorised access to customer databases. He admitted using other user identities and produced a notebook containing over 90 username/password combinations. He was summarily dismissed but appealed on the basis that the penalty was too harsh. The decision to dismiss was upheld and Rodrigues initiated a claim for unfair dismissal. He conceded that he had committed an act of misconduct which had contributed to his dismissal. However, he argued that dismissal was unreasonable for a first offence by an employee who had been employed for ten years with a good record, and his employer had not made it clear to him that conduct of this kind constituted gross misconduct which would lead to dismissal. BT submitted that summary dismissal was appropriate in this case because Rodrigues had demonstrated that he was not trustworthy, and therefore it was not practical to re-instate or re-engage him. However, the Employment Appeal Tribunal unanimously decided that Rodrigues had been unfairly dismissed, and made several findings in relation to the use of the computer system. It found that neither the disciplinary rules nor the available literature made clear or specifically drew attention to any rule that summary dismissal would be automatic for computer misuse. It was therefore unreasonable for the employer to treat conduct in relation to computer misuse as an automatic reason for dismissal in the absence of a specific rule to that effect made known to employees.

---

[12] Username "TEG", Password "TAFF" - a Mrs Tegwin Morse who worked in the wages department.

In *R* v *Mahomet*, another BT employee was alleged to have gained unauthorised access to the Customer Services system, which contained sensitive ex-directory numbers. He was authorised to access the system during working hours, but accessed it outside these hours in order to demonstrate system security weaknesses to an investigative journalist. Both the employee and the journalist were charged with gaining unauthorised access. The prosecution argued that because Mahomet was not authorised to give demonstrations to journalists, his access to that computer on that particular occasion was unauthorised. However, defence counsel successfully argued that although BT may have regarded his actions as unauthorised, Mahomet remained authorised within the CMA, and he was acquitted on a Section 1 charge (the charge against the *Independent* journalist was withdrawn).

The time and purpose of access to a computer system is not specified by the CMA. Case law clearly demonstrates that employees must have clear instructions from their employer/manager/supervisor of their duties and responsibilities towards the system. Otherwise, the accused may argue that they thought they were authorised to use the system as they pleased. The Law Commission thought it highly desirable for employers to put their house in order in terms of clearly defining the limits of authorisation applicable to each employee. Ideally, a written statement as to access entitlement should be issued. Vicarious liability may also be incurred unless the employer makes it clear that the employee should not be doing the thing which causes damage (where the employee engages in a frolic of their own). The net result would appear to be that there is a difference between what is authorised for the purposes of employment law and criminal law, and employers will have to bring to their employees' attention in clear and unambiguous terms the consequences of computer misuse.

SECTION 2 - ULTERIOR OFFENCE.
A PERSON IS GUILTY OF AN OFFENCE UNDER SECTION 2 IF HE COMMITS OR INTENDS TO COMMIT A SECTION 1 OFFENCE WITH INTENT TO COMMIT A FURTHER OFFENCE FOR WHICH:
A. THE SENTENCE IS FIXED BY LAW, OR
B. A PERSON AGED 21 YEARS OR OVER (NOT PREVIOUSLY CONVICTED) MAY BE SENTENCED TO IMPRISONMENT FOR A TERM OF FIVE YEARS;

Section 2(3) provides that:

WHERE THE JURY FINDS THAT THERE IS INSUFFICIENT EVIDENCE TO CONVICT AN ACCUSED UNDER SECTION 2, THAT PERSON MAY BE CONVICTED UNDER SECTION 1.

This is an aggravated form of the basic offence accompanied by an ulterior motive. The goal of this offence is to bring forward in time the moment at which a serious criminal offence is considered to have been committed. The Law Commission felt that the law relating to criminal attempts[13] could not be used

---

[13] Section 1 *Criminal Attempts Act 1981* provides that:

IF, WITH INTENT TO COMMIT AN OFFENCE .. A PERSON DOES AN ACT WHICH IS MORE THAN MERELY PREPARATORY TO THE COMMISSION OF AN OFFENCE HE IS GUILTY OF ATTEMPTING TO COMMIT THE OFFENCE.

satisfactorily in certain circumstances relating to computer misuse and that a substantive new offence was required.

*"No attempt is made to give a finite list of the further serious offences in contemplation though in practice they will generally involve criminal dishonesty."* [Dum 89]

For example: in the case of a hacker attempting to discover a password to a banking system in order to transfer money, this would probably be seen as merely preparatory to the crime (of theft) rather than part of its perpetration and therefore would not constitute an attempt under the criminal law.

*"Under the normal law of criminal attempts, a person can only be charged with an attempted offence when they move beyond the stage of preparing to commit an offence to that of attempting to put the plans into practice. The dividing line between preparation and perpetration has always proved difficult to draw, but the argument was accepted by the Law Commission that the speed with which operations might be accomplished using a computer was such as to justify bringing forward the moment in time at which a serious criminal offence is committed."* [LS 96]

Thus a person may be guilty of an offence under Section 2 where, for example: the accused has gained unauthorised access to sensitive information held on a computer with a view to blackmailing the person to whom that information related. It is immaterial whether the further offence is committed at the same time or later than the basic offence and it is no defence that the commission of the further offence was impossible.

*"An example might concern a person attempting to obtain access to codes or passwords used by a bank to authenticate electronic fund transfers without realising that further security measures would mean that possession of this information would not be sufficient to cause a transfer to be made."* [LS 96]

SECTION 3 - UNAUTHORISED MODIFICATION OFFENCE. [TECHNO-VANDALISM]
A PERSON IS GUILTY OF AN OFFENCE UNDER SECTION 3 IF HE DOES AN ACT WHICH CAUSES AN UNAUTHORISED MODIFICATION OF THE CONTENTS OF ANY COMPUTER, AND AT THE TIME THAT HE DOES SO HE KNOWS THAT THE MODIFICATION IS UNAUTHORISED AND HE HAS THE REQUISITE INTENT; INTENT TO CAUSE A MODIFICATION AND BY SO DOING:
A. IMPAIR THE OPERATION OF ANY COMPUTER;
B. PREVENT OR HINDER ACCESS TO ANY PROGRAM OR DATA; OR
C. IMPAIR THE OPERATION OF ANY PROGRAM OR RELIABILITY OF ANY DATA.

Section 3(6) provides an amendment to the *Criminal Damage Act 1971*. There would have otherwise been confusion if the same mischief could be prosecuted under two separate Acts carrying different penalties.

FOR THE PURPOSES OF THE CRIMINAL DAMAGE ACT 1971, A MODIFICATION OF THE CONTENTS OF A COMPUTER SHALL NOT BE REGARDED AS DAMAGING ANY COMPUTER OR COMPUTER STORAGE MEDIUM UNLESS ITS EFFECT ON THAT COMPUTER OR COMPUTER STORAGE MEDIUM IMPAIRS ITS PHYSICAL CONDITION.

It is, and remains, an offence under the CDA to destroy or damage a computer and the data it contains by taking a hammer to them. Difficulties arise where there is no perceptible physical damage, ie. where computer software is interfered with which renders that software incapable or less capable, to carry out the functions that that software was designed to perform.

The Section 3 offence may only be committed by a party who acts intentionally; negligent or reckless conduct will not suffice. The requirement of intent to make unauthorised modification was seen as a useful safeguard to ensure that people would not be prosecuted for merely inadvertent acts. However, the effect (insofar as the Section 3 offence replaces the offence of criminal damage for acts of intangible modification) is that it is *"actually a weakening of the previously existing law under which a person could have been liable for reckless acts causing damage"*. [Bat 95]

*"Although section 3(6) reverses the effect of Cox and Whiteley in so far as they relate to computer programs and data, they remain relevant authorities in other situations involving the alteration and erasure of information stored in electro-magnetic form such as video and audio tape."* [Akd 96]

Modification may be to the contents of computer memory (such as ROM and RAM) or any computer storage media (such as disks and tapes) which, when loaded, are regarded as part of the contents of the computer. The use of the phrase *"the contents of"* was deemed by the Law Commission to be appropriate to cover all cases without the need for difficult technical explanations. Modification can be merely temporary, thus dealing with the *Gold & Schifreen* type problem. The *mens rea* must be to impair the operation of any computer or computer program, or destroy or impair the reliability or accessibility of any data stored or held in the computer's memory. This reference to reliability and accessibility of data was included so as to ensure that the offence included activities which might arguably be said not to impair the operation of the computer, eg. reformatting a disk so as to remove all data that it previously held. Even though this may not involve an intent to impair the operation of the computer, the Law Commission was satisfied that it involved serious interference with the running of the system and should be captured by the offence.

*"In order to commit the [Section 3] offence it is not necessary that a party makes any form of contact with a computer. A person who creates a computer virus and puts it into circulation will, assuming the necessary intention can be established, commit the unauthorised modification offence in respect to each computer system affected."* [LS 96]

An interesting omission from the CMA is the exclusion from protection of external computer storage devices. When a disk is inserted into a computer disk drive, it is treated as being part of the computer, and any unauthorised access to or modification of it will therefore be an offence. However, when the disk is outside the computer (such as the off-line storage of back-up copies), the CMA does not apply.

*"In the event that an unauthorised person placed a magnet in close proximity to a disk thereby causing the loss of any data on it, no offence would have been committed under the Act as the disk could not be regarded as forming a part of a computer at the relevant time. Any prosecution would have to have recourse to the maligned Criminal Damage Act."* [LS 96]

Section 2 and Section 3 offences qualify as "arrestable offences" and the police therefore have powers of search under Section 18 *Police and Criminal Evidence Act 1984*. An extension of the powers of search for Section 1 offences (which as summary offences do not normally attract such powers) was introduced in order for some realistic means of enforcement to be provided.

SECTION 14
WHERE A CIRCUIT JUDGE IS SATISFIED THAT THERE ARE REASONABLE GROUNDS FOR BELIEVING
A. THAT AN OFFENCE UNDER SECTION 1 HAS BEEN COMMITTED OR IS ABOUT TO BE COMMITTED IN ANY PREMISES; AND
B. THAT EVIDENCE THAT SUCH AN OFFENCE HAS BEEN OR IS ABOUT TO BE COMMITTED IS IN THOSE PREMISES
A WARRANT MAY BE ISSUED AUTHORISING A CONSTABLE TO ENTER AND SEARCH THE PREMISES, USING SUCH REASONABLE FORCE AS IS NECESSARY.

The Section 1 offence is punishable on summary conviction by up to six months imprisonment and/or a fine not exceeding £5,000. Section 2 and 3 offences are considerably more severe and conviction can lead to unlimited fines and up to five years imprisonment. Under Section 38 *Criminal Justice Act 1988* the accused will be tried summarily if the value of the damaged property does not exceed £2,000 (here, the maximum penalty that can be imposed is three months imprisonment or a fine of up to £2,500). It is interesting to note that the hacker who causes electronic vandalism may be liable to five years imprisonment under the CMA, whereas if he had used a hammer to cause the same loss he could be liable to 10 years under the CDA. Under Section 12 CMA, any person who is tried and found not guilty of a Section 2 or Section 3 offence in a Crown Court can be found guilty by the jury of the Section 1 offence and be sentenced accordingly. Some attempts were made to include defences when the CMA was being debated in Parliament. However, problems arose in defining them satisfactorily. For example: when is a computer used merely for domestic or recreational purposes, or when is unauthorised access in the public interest.

Cyberspace has no respect for national boundaries (*crimes sans frontiers*). To prevent making the UK attractive for computer criminals to operate here, the CMA contains extra provisions relating to jurisdiction and extradition. Basically, an offence will be committed if either the offender or the computer is in the UK at the time the offence is committed. Jurisdiction is subject to the principle of "double criminality" which ensures that a state with custody is not forced to extradite that person unless the conduct corresponds to an offence under both systems (in other words if the same facts were described in each country they would both amount to a criminal offence). This principle raises the important issue of the harmonisation of international computer misuse laws. Since Section 2 and Section 3 offences are punishable with a maximum sentence in excess of 12 months, they are extraditable under general provisions contained in Section 2 *Extradition Act 1989*. The CMA extends to Northern Ireland and Scotland, meaning that they are regarded as separate countries from England & Wales. Therefore if a hacker in England gained unauthorised access to a computer in Scotland, that person could be tried in either country. Although the legislation applies to Scotland, the CMA does not make any amendment to Scottish criminal law.

*"There would appear no reason why a charge of malicious mischief or vandalism could not continue to be brought in respect of computer related conduct."* [LS 96]

## Chapter III    Case Law

The CMA is only six years old and has still not been significantly tested in the higher courts. Most cases have not been reported in recognised Law Reports, because they have been resolved in the lower courts. The most notorious prosecution under the Act so far is that of Paul Daniel Bedworth, at the time a 19-year-old Edinburgh University artificial intelligence undergraduate. In June 1991, police arrested three members of a UK hacking group called "Eight Legged Groove Machine" (8LGM). Bedworth, Strickland and Woods (all students) were charged with conspiracy to commit offences contrary to Section 3 CMA. It was accepted that none of the defendants hacked for gain or for any other criminal purpose. The three had never actually met, they had communicated via hacker bulletin boards. It was alleged that the group had gained unauthorised access to government, academic and corporate computer systems,[14] and the activities of the hackers had cost the victims hundreds of thousands of pounds. At trial - *R v Bedworth, Strickland & Woods*, Bedworth's co-accused pleaded guilty. Bedworth himself pleaded not guilty and asserted as his defence that he was addicted to hacking and could not therefore have formed the necessary intention. Medical evidence was submitted to the jury and Bedworth was unanimously acquitted after a 16 day trial, despite the fact that in his summing up the judge had made it clear to the jury that addiction[15] was not a defence to criminal charges. The jury probably felt some sympathy towards the accused who was portrayed by his defence as:

*"a sad and lonely white middle-class boy whose only contact with the world was via computers who, through mischievous, but not malicious, behaviour, caused damage to others without really being aware of the consequences of his actions"*.

The Crown Prosecution Service were criticised for proceeding on conspiracy charges and not directly under Section 1 or Section 3. *Strickland & Woods* were sentenced to six months imprisonment, Judge Harris in describing the group as "intellectual joyriders" remarked that hackers needed to be given a clear signal by the courts that their activities will not and cannot be tolerated.

---

[14] Notably, the Financial Times, NASA, European Economic Community, and the European Organisation for the Research and Treatment of Cancer (EORTC).

[15] Although addiction, per se, is not a defence to a criminal charge, it could be a mitigating factor when it comes to sentencing - *R v Lawrence*.

*"There may be people out there who consider hacking to be harmless, but hacking is not harmless. Computers now form a central role in our lives, containing personal details, financial details, confidential matters .. It is essential that the integrity of those systems should be protected and hacking puts that integrity into jeopardy."*

In *R* v *Pile*, a computer virus writer Christopher Pile (aka the "Black Baron") was sentenced to eighteen months after pleading guilty to five charges of unauthorised access, five charges of unauthorised modification and one of inciting others to spread computer viruses he had written.[16] Pile spread his viruses all around the world through computer bulletin boards and Judge Griggs said that:

*"Those who seek to wreak mindless havoc on one of the vital tools of our age cannot expect lenient treatment."*

It is widely acknowledged that the Section 3 CMA offence deals with unauthorised modification with precision as it covers indirect modification through viruses, time-bombs, logic-bombs and other forms of malicious code, as well as dealing with direct modification. However, the need for the prosecution to prove that the accused possessed two states of mind (the requisite intent and the requisite knowledge) may make convictions uncertain, and even where convictions have been obtained, sentences have been light. In *R* v *Whitaker*, a software developer was prosecuted under Section 3 for including an undisclosed logic-bomb in bespoke software (which activated when the client defaulted with his payments thus disabling the software concerned). The court found him guilty. However, the magistrates who dealt with the case did not feel that his actions merited a fine, and gave him a conditional discharge.

What is notable from the available case law is the use of the charge of conspiracy by the police, whenever they have arrested a group of hackers. Under Section 1 *Criminal Law Act 1977*:

IF A PERSON AGREES WITH ANY OTHER PERSON OR PERSONS THAT A COURSE OF CONDUCT SHALL BE PURSUED WHICH, IF THE AGREEMENT IS CARRIED OUT IN ACCORDANCE WITH THEIR INTENTIONS, EITHER:

A. WILL NECESSARILY AMOUNT TO OR INVOLVE THE COMMISSION OF ANY OFFENCE OR OFFENCES BY ONE OR MORE PARTIES TO THE AGREEMENT, OR
B. WOULD DO SO BUT FOR THE EXISTENCE OF FACTS WHICH RENDER THE COMMISSION OF THE OFFENCE OR ANY OFFENCES IMPOSSIBLE, HE IS GUILTY OF CONSPIRACY TO COMMIT THE OFFENCE OR OFFENCES IN QUESTION.

*"The actus reus in a conspiracy is the agreement to execute the illegal conduct, and not the execution of it. The crime is complete when the agreement is made."* Lord Hailsham LC - *Kamara* v *DPP*.

---

[16] Named *pathogen* and *queeg* after the BBC2 comedy series *Red Dwarf*. He also produced *smeg*, a guide on how to create a computer virus. *Pathogen* caused the following to appear on computer screens:
*"Smoke me a kipper. I'll be back for breakfast. Unfortunately some of your data won't".*

This charge is particularly attractive because of its wide ranging adaptability (some would say abuse). If an accused goes into the witness box and gives evidence implicating a co-accused, then what he has to say becomes evidence and accordingly may be used by the jury as evidence against the co-accused - *R v Rudd*. On the other hand, a confession which is given in evidence and which implicates both its maker and a co-accused, is no evidence against the co-accused because a confession is admissible only against its maker. Exceptionally, however, under the common law, the statements (or acts) of a party to a conspiracy are admissible against co-conspirators provided the act conspired to has not occurred or has not yet finished - *R v Blake & Tye* and *R v Donat*. This applies even if the statements are from conspirators who have not actually been charged. Thus the prosecution may be able to adduce evidence in a conspiracy trial which would not be admissible in separate trials. *R v Governor of Pentonville Prison ex parte Osman* held that there must also be independent (non-hearsay) evidence additional to the statements (or acts) which implicate the accused was party to a conspiracy. The maximum sentence for conspiracy to commit an offence is (now) the same as that prescribed for the completed offence.

## Chapter IV    Evidence

*"The law of evidence must be adapted to the realities of contemporary business practice. Mainframe computers, mini-computers and microcomputers play a pervasive role in our society. Often the only record of a transaction, which nobody can be expected to remember, will be in the memory of the computer. The versatility, power and frequency of use of computers will increase, and if computer output cannot relatively be used as evidence in criminal cases, much crime (and notably offences involving dishonesty) will in practice be immune from prosecution. On the other hand, computers are not infallible. They do occasionally malfunction. Software systems often have bugs. Unauthorised alteration of information stored on a computer is possible. The phenomenon of a virus attacking computer systems is also well established. Realistically, therefore, computers must be regarded as imperfect devices."* Steyn J - *R v Minors*; *R v Harper*.

The legal system has problems accepting computer generated statements as evidence. The law of evidence is concerned with the means of proving the facts in issue and this involves the adduction of evidence which is presented to the court. The law admits evidence only if it complies with the rules governing admissibility. In criminal proceedings documents are treated as hearsay evidence, which are not admissible, on the basis that a document cannot vouch for the truth of its contents; only the person who produced the document could do that. The application of the hearsay rule in criminal law has always been particularly strict because of the danger of depriving a person of his liberty on evidence the truth of which cannot be tested in cross-examination. This problem with documentary evidence was first highlighted in *Myers v DPP*, where the defendant was accused of *ringing* motor vehicles. The prosecution wished to show that the cars he sold and the registration documents he produced did not match up by reference to engine block numbers, and introduced microfilm evidence kept by the manufacturer (prepared from cards which were themselves prepared by workers on the assembly line).

*"The House of Lords decided that these records were inadmissible because they were hearsay and the only admissible evidence would have been that of the assembly workers who had recorded the numbers. The workers could not be identified and even if they could it was unlikely that they could truthfully swear they could recall the serial numbers."* [Col 94]

The House recognised the folly of their position but felt strongly that it was for Parliament to reform the law and create exceptions to the hearsay rule. Following this decision, legislation was introduced in the form of the *Criminal Evidence Act 1965*. The current statutory provisions relating to computer generated evidence are Section 24 *Criminal Justice Act 1988* and Section 69 *Police and Criminal Evidence Act 1984*, which set out the circumstances in which computer evidence will be admitted as an exception to the hearsay rule in criminal proceedings and make provision to ensure that such documents when stored on computers are sufficiently accurate to be used in evidence.

It is well established from cases such as *R* v *Wood* and *R* v *Spiby* that a printout from a computer which automatically records information without the intervention of any human agency, involves no question of hearsay and is admissible as real evidence, since it does not purport to reproduce any human assertion which has been entered into it.

*"Where real evidence is tendered it is always open to challenge on the basis of malfunction, unreliability or improper use of the computer equipment and evidence that the computer was not working properly would entitle the court to attach little or no weight to that evidence. There is a presumption that mechanical instruments have been working properly unless evidence to the contrary is introduced and this should be applicable to computers."* [Col 94]

Therefore, whenever a computer record is a direct recording of external facts (for example: barcode readings from a supermarket checkout) there will be no need to bring the results it produces within the exception to the hearsay rule as it will be admissible. However, evidence that is not real evidence will be subject to hearsay rules, and Section 24 CJA provides that a statement in a document is admissible in criminal proceedings as evidence of any fact (nothing else) of which direct oral evidence is admissible, only when two conditions are satisfied, namely:

1. THE DOCUMENT WAS CREATED OR RECEIVED BY A PERSON IN THE COURSE OF A TRADE, BUSINESS, PROFESSION OR OTHER OCCUPATION, OR AS THE HOLDER OF A PAID OR UNPAID OFFICE; AND
2. THE INFORMATION CONTAINED IN THE DOCUMENT WAS SUPPLIED BY A PERSON (WHETHER OR NOT THE MAKER OF THE STATEMENT) WHO HAD, OR MAY REASONABLY BE SUPPOSED TO HAVE HAD, PERSONAL KNOWLEDGE OF THE MATTERS DEALT WITH.

Thus any document created or received by a "jobholder" is admissible in criminal proceedings provided that someone had personal knowledge of the matters in the document, and that the person who would otherwise give oral evidence is dead or unfit to testify, or is abroad and it is not practicable for that person to testify, or if that person cannot be found and reasonable steps have been taken to find him. Section 24(4) also permits documents to be given in evidence if the maker of the statement cannot reasonably be expected to remember the matters contained in the record. However, Section 25 CJA gives the courts powers to exclude evidence admissible under Section 24 where it ought not be admitted in the interests of justice.

Section 69 PACE sets a hurdle which any computer evidence must overcome before it will be deemed admissible in proceedings. A statement in a document produced by a computer will not be admissible in evidence as to any fact contained in it unless it is shown:

A.   THERE ARE NO REASONABLE GROUNDS FOR BELIEVING IT IS INACCURATE BECAUSE OF IMPROPER USE OF THE COMPUTER; AND

B.   IT IS SHOWN THAT AT ALL MATERIAL TIMES THE COMPUTER WAS OPERATING PROPERLY, OR IF IT WAS NOT, THAT THIS DID NOT AFFECT THE ACCURACY OF THE EVIDENCE.

Section 69 is applicable irrespective of whether the computer produces hearsay evidence. Affirmative evidence is required that it is safe to rely on a document produced by a computer, and it is not sufficient to rely on the presumption of regularity expressed in the maxim *"omnia praesumuntur rite esse acta"*. The onus is on the prosecution if they are introducing such evidence, to satisfy the requirements. Normally defence counsel will insist on proof that the computer was working properly; however this may be difficult in cases where hackers have damaged the system by deleting files or where it has been infected by viruses.

*"Section 69 is couched in negative terms making it clear that evidence which does not satisfy its requirements is inadmissible. The object of Section 69 is to impose a duty on anyone who wishes to introduce a document produced by a computer to show that it is safe to rely on that document and it makes no difference whether the computer document has been produced with or without the input of information by the human mind and thus may or may not be hearsay."* [Hoe 96]

In *R* v *Minors*; *R* v *Harper* it was established that where the admissibility of computer generated evidence is disputed, the judge should hold a *"voir dire"* and in deciding whether the statutory requirements have been satisfied by the prosecution the criminal standard of proof (beyond reasonable doubt) should be applied. Computer generated records would have to satisfy the requirements of both Acts as the mere fact that a record satisfies the accuracy requirements of Section 69 PACE does not exempt it from the admissibility requirements of Section 24 CJA.

The provisions of Section 69 PACE were reviewed by the House of Lords in *R* v *Shephard* where it was concluded that Section 69 could be satisfied by a person familiar with the operation of the computer system who could give evidence as to its reliability and that such a person need not be a computer expert. The evidence necessary in different cases would vary but generally, someone familiar with the operation of the computer in the sense of knowing what the computer was required to do and that it was doing it properly at the relevant time would suffice. This case arose out of rather mundane facts. The accused was arrested for shoplifting and in her car were found items of clothing and food (including a joint of beef) from Marks & Spencer, with no till receipt. The evidence was that the till rolls from the computerised checkouts showed no trace of the unique combination of items found in her possession. A claim that the till rolls were inadmissible because there was no evidence that the computer was working properly was rejected and the accused was convicted. On appeal the House of Lords confirmed that the till rolls were admissible, providing those seeking to rely on this evidence had shown that the computer concerned was operating properly.

*"The store detective gave evidence that she had never known the computer to break down and having spent many hours examining the till rolls would have undoubtedly noticed if there had been evidence of malfunction. On that evidence it was legitimate for the court to infer that the computer was working properly and therefore the till rolls were admissible."* [Col 94]

Much of the information recorded on the till rolls was keyed-in by cashiers, and so far as that information was concerned, it was clearly hearsay and would only be admissible if it could be brought within the exception. The significance of *Shephard* is to remove the burden and expense of calling a computer expert, where there is an individual available to give oral evidence in court who is familiar with the computer system concerned. It should, however, be noted that where the system is unusual and/or complex, a computer expert may still be required. The issue of what calibre of person is needed to give evidence in any particular case will *"inevitably vary from case to case"* (Lord Griffiths). However, all five Law Lords agreed that only rarely would it be necessary to call an expert and that in the vast majority of cases someone familiar with the operation of the computer will be able to give the necessary evidence.

In *Darby* v *DPP* a police officer operating a speed trap device concluded that a driver had exceeded the 30 mph speed limit by 13 mph. It was held that on the basis of the evidence of the police officer, who was a trained and experienced operator of the device, the machine was working correctly. However, in *East West Transport* v *DPP* the computer printout in dispute was that of a weighbridge test of an allegedly overloaded lorry. The offence was committed on 12 May. The only evidence as to the satisfactory operation of the weighbridge equipment was that of a trading standards officer who said that it was working satisfactorily on 23 March. The court was of the opinion that owing to the lapse of time between the test and the alleged offence, an inference as to the correct operation of the weighbridge on the relevant day was not justified without further evidence, and a police officer who witnessed the test was judged not to be in a position to give evidence on the machine's correct functioning. A similar conclusion was reached in the almost identical case of *Connolly* v *Lancashire County Council*.

In *R* v *Cochrane* a building society mistakenly credited the defendant's account with a large sum of money. The prosecution wished to prove that certain cash withdrawals were made from a particular cashpoint machine. Two computers were involved, a branch computer which was networked to a mainframe computer at head office, but none of the prosecution witnesses were able to explain how the computers operated, or supply affirmative evidence that they were operating correctly at the relevant time. This case concentrated on the question of whether it was proper for the court to admit computer printouts of the alleged transactions, and the Court of Appeal took the view that authoritative evidence was required to describe the function of the mainframe (primarily how it validated transactions) before considering the application of Section 69 PACE.

*"The machine would only dispense money if the correct PIN was entered. The matching was carried out by a mainframe computer and evidence of its proper functioning was thus required by the court. The prosecution did not adduce this evidence and the conviction was set aside on appeal."* [Hoe 96]

*"This was the first occasion in which a court had pressed the issue this far and advised that evidence should have been produced explaining the nature and function of the computer system even before the court could move on to determine whether Section 69 PACE need apply. Moreover the court said that the Crown Prosecution Service should have produced standard forms of evidence such cashpoint transactions were properly recorded and that the till was working well at the relevant time. Only then could the court decide whether the relevant parts of the till rolls were real evidence."* [Col 94]

## Chapter V   Loopholes and anomalies

The terms "computer",[17] "data" and "program" are not defined in the CMA. The Law Commission took the view that it would be better not to attempt to define them. Instead the word *computer* should be given its ordinary meaning in order to avoid obsolescence (a computer is easy to recognise but hard to define). Because *computer* is not defined, it may be given a liberal meaning by the courts and may include equipment with computer technology built into it, not normally described as a computer. Given the extent of microprocessors in everyday electrical goods, the latitude of the CMA legislation is potentially very broad, and may embrace forms of activity which would not normally be considered criminal. For example, Section 3 may make "unauthorised use" an offence; ie. the person who types a personal letter using a word processor belonging to his or her employer.

*"By adding data to the contents of the system, a modification is undoubtedly being performed, and the user must have intended to make such a modification. It is immaterial for the purposes of the Act whether the modification is permanent or temporary. All that remains is the question whether the modification has impaired the operation of the computer system. The Act does not require that impairment be significant and so, in principle, there would appear to be no reason why a charge should not be brought in such an instance."* [LS 96]

---

[17] Section 5 *Civil Evidence Act 1968* defines a computer as "any device storing or processing information".

However, no one so far has been prosecuted for illegal use of a washing machine[18] or for writing personal letters on their employer's word processor.

*"To prove that an offence has been committed [under the CMA] the following must be demonstrated:*

*the computer performed a function as a consequence of access being attempted or actual access (s.1, s.2);*
*the access was unauthorised (s.1, s.2);*
*the person attempting access knew that it was unauthorised (s.1, s.2);*
*the access was a preliminary to the committing of a serious offence (s.2);*
*the modification to computer material was or would have been caused (s.3);*
*the modification was unauthorised (s.3);*
*the person attempting the modification knew it was unauthorised (s.3);*
*the intention of the modification was to impair the computer's operation (s.3)."*
[CS 96]

Unless the accused is caught red-handed, it is not easy proving (beyond reasonable doubt) the above points. There must necessarily be some kind of access control system in place with a secure audit log which records all transactions, and in a multi-user multi-process computing environment it is necessary to link the perpetrator of the offence to the process performing the function.

*"Undoubtedly one of the major difficulties for all concerned in Computer Misuse cases .. is the amount and complexity of evidence which may be involved. There may be considerable difficulties for the prosecution in establishing a lack of authorisation, in showing that systems have indeed been accessed, and in proving who it was who accessed them. Without computers having tamper proof security systems it is very difficult to establish beyond reasonable doubt, that intrusions or modifications occurred when it is alleged that they did, or that they were committed by the person suspected."* [Bat 95]

Computer generated evidence has many possible sources of error: unauthorised modification, deliberate/unintentional interference by authorised users, viruses and other forms of malicious code, and hardware and software bugs. Most computer systems do not record and securely preserve sufficient information to be able to establish that it was functioning correctly at any particular time. Therefore it may still be necessary to have highly qualified expert opinion as to the state of security of a system. If the reliability of computer evidence is questionable due to hacking, then this may prevent its consideration in court, and the size and complexity of modern computer systems may make it relatively easy to establish a reasonable doubt in a jury's mind as to the proper functioning of the computer.

*"The ambiguities and illogicality arising from the complex conditions for admissibility of computer evidence can be seen in the recent case of McKeown v*

---

[18] The appropriate charge for the unauthorised use of a washing machine [laundering] would still appear to be the dishonest abstraction of electricity contrary to Section 13 *Theft Act 1968*. The offence is committed regardless of the amount of electricity so used.

*DPP, where the divisional court held that if it cannot be proved that the computer was operating properly, the computer evidence will be inadmissible."* [Hoe 96]

In *McKeown* v *DPP*, a conviction for drink driving was quashed on the basis that, despite expert witness evidence from the manufacturer of a breath testing machine Lion Intoximeter 3000, the prosecution could not prove that the machine was working properly (the computer clock was displaying a time which was an hour and a quarter slow at the police station). Although the precise time was not a matter of any importance, the Divisional Court accepted that the inaccuracy of the clock reading tainted the conviction. However, on appeal – *DPP* v *McKeown*; *DPP* v *Jones*, the House of Lords held that the malfunctioning of the clock did not affect the proper functioning of the breath testing device in processing the information and therefore that information was admissible in evidence. Lord Hoffman assumed that the inaccuracy in the time display meant that the computer was not operating properly. The question was therefore whether this was *"such as to affect the production of the document or the accuracy of it's contents"*. If the words were read literally it did. However, in his Lordship's view, the relevant paragraph was not intended to be read in such a literal fashion. The language of Section 69 recognised that a computer might be malfunctioning in a way which was not relevant to the purpose of the exclusionary rule. It could not therefore be argued that any malfunction was sufficient to cast doubt upon the capacity of the computer to process information correctly.

*"What if there was a software fault which caused the document to be printed in lower case when it meant to be in upper case? The fault has certainly affected the production of the document. But a rule which excluded an otherwise accurate document on this ground would be quite irrational."*

*"What, then, was contemplated as the distinction between a relevant and irrelevant malfunction? There was only one possible answer. A malfunction was relevant if it affected the way in which the computer processed, stored or retrieved information used to generate the statement tendered as evidence. Other malfunctions do not matter."*

In *R* v *Governor of Brixton Prison ex parte Levin*, the accused (Vladimir Levin, a Russian citizen who is currently awaiting extradition to the United States to stand trial for the theft of $400,000 from Citibank following unauthorised access to the bank's computer systems), submitted that a magistrate should not have admitted Citibank computer records as evidence because, as it is alleged the computer had been improperly used by the accused, the requirements of Section 69 could not be complied with. However, the Divisional Court held that the fact that there had been unauthorised use of the computer was not itself grounds for believing that the statements recorded by it were inaccurate. It would have been absurd to hold that a computer printout could not be given in evidence to prove that an accused had obtained unauthorised access to the computer for the purposes of the crime. Merely because there had been unauthorised use of the computer was not of itself a ground for believing that the statements recorded by it were inaccurate.

It is clear that computer generated evidence is regarded with suspicion, as is shown by the following case. John Munden, a Cambridgeshire policeman with 19 years exemplorary service, returned from a holiday abroad in September 1992 and found six fraudulent ATM withdrawals on his Halifax Building Society statement. He reported them but was told that since the Halifax had complete confidence in the security of their computer system, he must be mistaken or lying. When he persisted, the Halifax reported him to the Police Complaints Authority for fraud, and he was convicted in February 1994 of attempting to obtain money by deception. On appeal, Turner J said:

*"when a case turns on computers or similar equipment then, as a matter of common justice, the defence must have access and see whether there is anything making the computers fallible".*

In the absence of such access, the court would not allow any evidence emanating from computers, and if the bank was not prepared to let their computer systems be examined by a hostile expert witness, then they could not present bank statements as evidence.

Lack of security in computer systems is a real problem. Computers have a multiplicity of security weaknesses that are compounded by interconnection. Operating systems are designed for functionality in the constraint of performance, and are not generally designed with security in mind. Maximum security and easy accessibility are mutually exclusive concepts. An operating system is a very large and complicated piece of software, and not even computer security experts are able to determine what every single line of code is intended to do. It is impossible to exhaustively test for every conceivable set of conditions that might arise, or predict how a system will perform under all configurations of data and logic states. UNIX, a multi-user multi-process operating system (which contains approximately 2.8 million lines of computer code) is currently the most popular and widespread operating system in the world. Perhaps the greatest security weakness of UNIX is the power of the superuser (root). Whilst logged on as root, every security protection mechanism in the system may be legitimately bypassed. Clearly the intruder who achieves superuser status constitutes the worst possible breach of security. The Computer Emergency Response Team[19] (CERT) operated by Carnegie Mellon University issues security alerts relating to known computer vulnerabilities and weaknesses. Since 1988, CERT have consistently reported 10-15 alerts per year describing ways in which a UNIX hacker may obtain root privilege. Information collated from the Internet and bulletin boards on hacker tools and exploitation techniques, show that it is possible to manipulate system security audit log files so as to remove or fabricate evidence that a UNIX system has been penetrated. Given such a wealth of exploitable vulnerability information (most of which is available in the public domain) it is submitted that current commercial-off-the-shelf computer systems are inherently and (more importantly) demonstrably insecure, that the accuracy requirements of Section 69 PACE cannot in all cases be satisfied [beyond reasonable doubt] by the laws of computer science, and that the courts have woken up to this fact.

---

[19] ftp://info.cert.org/pub/cert_advisories

The Law Commission in a consultation paper[20] has suggested that Section 69 PACE be repealed and this whole matter should be left to the common law, because it may be more effective to admit computer produced documents as evidence and leave authentication problems to the courts when assessing the weight to be attached to such a document (similar to the logic behind the *Civil Evidence Act 1995*, where the rule against the admission of hearsay has been abolished in Civil proceedings).

# Chapter VI   Conclusions

*"The Act has simplified the prosecution of persons responsible for attempting to or actually penetrating computer systems, and those introducing viruses or other rogue code."* [CS 96]

The CMA does not attempt to directly protect information. The purpose of the legislation is to protect computer systems. Only by protecting the computer system is the data held within it protected. UK legislation fails to take adequate account of the fact that intangible property is as valuable an asset as tangible property. It is submitted in conclusion that a change in UK law recognising that data is property or the creation of a specific offence such as "obtaining data without the permission of the owner" is highly desirable to combat computer misuse. By analogy to Section 12 *Theft Act 1968* (offence of joyriding):

A PERSON SHALL BE GUILTY OF AN OFFENCE IF, WITHOUT HAVING THE CONSENT OF THE OWNER OR OTHER LAWFUL AUTHORITY, HE TAKES ANY CONVEYANCE FOR HIS OWN OR ANOTHER'S USE OR KNOWING THAT ANY CONVEYANCE HAS BEEN TAKEN WITHOUT SUCH AUTHORITY, DRIVES IT OR ALLOWS HIMSELF TO BE CARRIED IN IT OR ON IT.

It was necessary to define this offence precisely because of the difficulty of proving the element of permanently depriving the owner in the prosecution of joyriders, for many would say that they only wanted the car in order to get home. A specific offence of "handling stolen data" analogous to handling stolen goods (Section 22 *Theft Act 1968*) is also desirable to combat the activities of industrial espionage and information brokers who engage hackers to break into targeted computer systems. Handling is a complex offence, but the logic behind the legislation is that without "fences", there would be little theft. Handling is therefore viewed more seriously and punished more harshly than theft.

On 27 February 1997, a bill introduced in Parliament by Ian Bruce MP received Royal Assent and became the *Telecommunications (Fraud) Act 1997*. This Act amends Section 42 *Telecommunications Act 1984* and makes it an offence to possess or supply anything for a fraudulent purpose in connection with the use of a telecommunication system. Thus if a person has in his custody or under his control anything which may be used for the purpose of obtaining a "telecommunications service" to which Section 42 applies, with the intent to use

---

[20] Law CP No 138

the thing to obtain such a service dishonestly, he is guilty of an offence. The legislation covers all forms of telecommunications fraud; for example, the use of radio frequency scanners to obtain mobile phone electronic serial (ESN) numbers for the purpose of "cloning". Much depends upon how "telecommunications service" is interpreted by the courts, but it may be the case that this new legislation could be interpreted to include the possession of hacker tools such as packet sniffer programs; eg. where a hacker covertly plants such a program on a computer network with the objective of capturing data traffic yielding username/password information, with intent to use such information to then fraudulently obtain a "service".

## Terminology

1. *Back-door:* A hole in the security of a system [deliberately] left in place by designers or maintainers. The motivation for such holes is not always sinister.
2. *Bug:* An unwanted and unintended property of a computer program or piece of hardware, especially one that causes it to malfunction.
3. *Cyberspace:* First used by the science fiction writer William Gibson in his novel *Nuromancer* published in 1982 to describe the environment within which computer hackers operate.
4. *Hacker:* 1. A person who enjoys exploring the details of programmable systems and how to stretch their capabilities, as opposed to most users, who prefer to learn only the minimum necessary. 2. A computer enthusiast who attempts to make unauthorised entry into computer systems and networks and explore what is there.
5. *Hacking:* 1. The accessing of a computer system without the express or implied permission of the owner of that computer system. 2. The art of breaking into a computer system. Contrary to widespread myth, this does not usually involve some mysterious brilliance, but rather persistence and dogged repetition of a handful of well known tricks that exploit common weaknesses in the security of target systems.
6. *Handle:* An electronic pseudonym intended to conceal a hacker's true identity.
7. *Internet:* 1. Information super-highway. 2. Worldwide network of computer networks. 3. A complex web of interconnected sites whose communications is made possible by adherence to a shared protocol.
8. *Logic-bomb:* Code surreptitiously inserted into an application program or operating system that causes it to perform some destructive or security compromising activity whenever specified conditions are met.
9. *Modem:* Modulator/DEModulator - a device which converts digital signals to analogue signals (and vice versa).
10. *RAM/ROM:* Random Access Memory/Read Only Memory.
11. *Operating System:* A program that controls the resources of a computer and allocates them among its users.
12. *Time-bomb:* A subspecies of logic-bomb that is triggered by reaching some preset time, either once or periodically.
13. *Trojan horse:* A malicious, security breaking program that is disguised as something benign.

14. *Virus:* A program that searches out other programs and infects them by embedding a copy of itself in them, so that they become trojan horses. When these programs are executed, the embedded virus is executed too, thus propagating the infection. This normally happens invisibly to the user.

15. *Worm:*   A program that propagates itself over a network, reproducing itself as it goes.

## Bibliography

[Akd 96] *Akdeniz,* Y. "Section 3 of the Computer Misuse Act 1990: an antidote for computer viruses" University of Leeds 1996
Web Journal of Current Legal Issues
HTTP://WWW.NCL.AC.UK:80/~NLAWWWW/1996/ISSUE3/AKDENIZ3.HTML

[Bai 96]*Bainbridge, D.* "Introduction to computer law" Third Edition 1996 Pitman Publishing ISBN 0-273-61940-3

[Bat 95]*Battcock, R.* "The Computer Misuse Act 1990: 5 years on" Strathclyde Law School HTTP://LAW-WWW-SERVER.STRATH.AC.UK/DEPARTMENTS/LAW/STUDENT/PERSONAL/R_BATTOCK

[Bla 87]*Blatchford, C.W.* "Security in distributed information systems: needs, problems and solutions" ICL Technical Journal, pp 680-698, November 1987

[Cas 93] *Castell, S.* "Technology and the challenge for law: computers trusted and found wanting" The Computer Law and Security Report Vol 9, 155 (1993)

[Cha 93] *Charlesworth, A.* "Addiction and hacking" New Law Journal pp 540-541, April 16, 1993

[CS 96] *Collier, P.A. & Spaul, B.J.* "Problems with policing computer crime" Woolwich centre for computer crime research University of Exeter HTTP://CEN.EX.AC.UK/ECONOMICS/BIM/POLSOC.HTML

[Col 94]*Collins, V.* "Computerised evidence: finding the right approach" Nottingham Law Journal, pp 11-33, Volume 3 1994

[Cor 88] *Cornwall, H.* "Hacker's Handbook III" Century 1988 ISBN 0-7126-1147-9

[Ded 90] *Dedman, R.* "The Computer Misuse bill 1990" The Computer Law and Security Report pp 13-19 May-Jun 1990-91 1 CLSR

[Ded 91] *Dedman, R.* "Regina v Sean Cropp" The Computer Law and Security Report Nov-Dec 1990-91 7 CLSR 168

[Dum 89] *Dumbill, E.A.* "Anti-hacking proposals" New Law Journal pp 1447-1448 October 27, 1989

[Dum 90] *Dumbill, E.A.* "Computer Misuse Act 1990 - Part 1 / 2" New Law Journal pp 1117-1118, pp 1156 August 3, 1990; August 10, 1990

[Hoe 96] *Hoey, A.* "Analysis of the Police and Criminal Evidence Act, S.69" University of Ulster Web Journal of Current Legal Issues 1996 HTTP://WWW.NCL.AC.UK:80/~NLAWWWW/1996

[Kea 96] *Keane, A.* "The modern law of evidence" Fourth Edition Butterworths 1996 ISBN 0-406-08185-9

[LC 89] "The Law Commission working paper No.110 on Computer Misuse the CBI submission part II" The Computer Law and Security Report pp 23-27 Jul-Aug 1989 2 CLSR

[LS 96] *Lloyd, I.J. & Simpson, M.* "Law on the electronic frontier" Home Papers on Public Policy: Vol 2 No 4.
    HTTP://LAW-WWW-SERVER.STRATH.AC.UK/DEPARTMENTS/LAW/DIGLIB/BOOK/
[Mal 96] *Malik, I.* "Computer hacking, detection and prevention" Sigma Press 1996 ISBN: 1-85058-538-5
[Mea 95] *Meade, R.* "British Telecommunications plc v Rodrigues"
    HTTP://LAW-WWW-SERVER.STRATH.AC.UK/DIGLIB/MLR/BRITISH.HTM
[Nig 92] *Nigri, D.F.* "Investigating computer crime in the UK" The Computer Law and Security Report pp 132-135 May-Jun 1992 8 CLSR
[Nig 93] *Nigri, D.F.* "Computer crime: why should we still care?" The Computer Law and Security Report pp 274-279 Nov-Dec 1993 9 CLSR
[SH 95] *Smith, J.C. & Hogan, B.* "Criminal Law" 7th Edition 1995 Butterworths ISBN 0-406-00313-0
[Was 92] *Wasik, M.* "The role of the criminal law in the control of misuse of information technology" The Computer Law and Security Report pp 25-29 Jan-Feb 1992 8 CLSR

## Case Law

*R v Blake & Tye* (1844) 6 QB 126
*R v Rudd* (1948) 32 Cr App Rep 138
*Myers v DPP* (1964) 2 All ER 881, (1965) AC 1001
*Kamara v DPP* (1973) 2 All ER 1242
*DPP v Ray* (1973) 3 All ER 131, (1974) AC 370
*Oxford v Moss* (1978) 68 Cr App Rep 183
*R v Kohn* (1979) 69 Cr App Rep 395
*MPC v Caldwell* (1981) 1 All ER 961, (1982) AC 341
*R v Wood* (1982) Crim LR 667, (1982) 76 Cr App Rep 23
*Cox v Riley* (1986) The Times 18 March, (1986) 83 Cr App Rep 54
*R v Donat* (1986) 82 Cr App Rep 173
*R v Gold & Schifreen* (1987) 3 WLR 803, (1988) AC 1063, (1988) 2 All ER 186
*R v Chan Man-Sin* (1988) 1 All ER 1
*R v Governor of Pentonville Prison ex parte Osman* (1989) 3 All ER 701
*R v Lawrence* (1989) Crim LR 309
*R v Minors; R v Harper* (1989) 2 All ER 208, (1989) 1 WLR 441
*Morphitis v Salmon* (1990) Crim LR 48
*R v Spiby* (1990) 91 Cr App Rep 186
*R v Whiteley* (1990) The Times 8 June, (1991) 93 Cr App Rep 381
*R v Cropp* (1991) Snaresbrook Crown Court July 1991
*Attorney General's Reference (No 1 of 1991)* (1992) 3 WLR 432
*Denco Ltd v Joinson* (1992) 1 All ER 463
*R v Shephard* (1993) Crim LR 295, (1993) AC 380
*R v Cochrane* (1993) Crim LR 49
*R v Bedworth, Strickland & Woods* (1993) Southwark Crown Court March 1993
*R v Whitaker* (1993) Scunthorpe Magistrates' Court 1993
*Connolly v Lancashire County Council* (1994) Unreported
*Darby v DPP* (1994) The Times 4 November

## Table of British statutes:

# Appendix D

## US Computer Security Act of 1987

The United States Computer Security Act of 1987 provided the first major United States Government effort to legislate a form of information and information systems protection and defence for government-related computer systems. It is quoted below:[1]

COMPUTER SECURITY ACT OF 1987
Public Law 100-235 (H.R. 145)
January 8, 1988

SECTION 1  SHORT TITLE
    The Act may be cited as the "Computer Security Act of 1987".

SEC. 2  PURPOSE
    (a)  IN GENERAL.-The Congress declares that improving the security and privacy of sensitive information in Federal computer systems is in the public interest, and hereby creates a means for establishing minimum acceptable security practices for such systems, without limiting the scope of security measures already planned or in use.
    (b)  SPECIFIC PURPOSES -The purposes of this Act are—
        (1) by amending the Act of March 3, 1901, to assign to the National Bureau of Standards responsibility for developing standards and guidelines for Federal computer systems, including responsibility for developing standards and guidelines needed to assure the cost-effective security and privacy of sensitive information in Federal computer systems, drawing on the technical advice and assistance (including work products) of the National Security Agency, where appropriate;
        (2) to provide for promulgation of such standards and guidelines by amending section 111(d) of the Federal Property and Administrative Services Act of 1949;
        (3) to require establishment of security plans by all operators of Federal computer systems that contain sensitive information; and

---

[1] Quoted from US Government Chief Information Officers Council Web Site:
http://www.cio.gov/docs/csa.htm

(4) to require mandatory periodic training for all persons involved in management, use, or operation of Federal computer systems that contain sensitive information.

## SEC. 3 ESTABLISHMENT OF COMPUTER STANDARDS PROGRAM
The Act of March 3, 1901, (15 U.S.C. 271-278h), is amended--

(1) in section 2(f), by striking out "and" at the end of paragraph (18), by striking out the period at the end of paragraph (19) and inserting in lieu thereof: "; and", and by inserting after such paragraph the following:
"(20) the study of computer systems (as that term is defined in section 20(d) of this Act) and their use to control machinery and processes.";

(2) by redesignating section 20 as section 22, and by inserting after section 19 the following new sections:
"SEC. 20.

(a) The National Bureau of Standards shall--

"(1) have the mission of developing standards, guidelines, and associated methods and techniques for computer systems;

"(2) except as described in paragraph (3) of this subsection (relating to security standards), develop uniform standards and guidelines for Federal computer systems, except those systems excluded by section 2315 of title 10, United States Code, or section 3502(2) of title 44, United States Code.

"(3) have responsibility within the Federal Government for developing technical, management, physical, and administrative standards and guidelines for the cost-effective security and privacy of sensitive information in Federal computer systems except--

"(A) those systems excluded by section 2315 of title 10, United States Code, or section 3502(2) of title 44, United States Code; and

"(B) those systems which are protected at all times by procedures established for information which has been specifically authorized under criteria established by an Executive Order or an Act of Congress to be kept secret in the interest of national defense or foreign policy,

The primary purpose of which standards and guidelines shall be to control loss and unauthorized modification or disclosure of sensitive information in such systems and to prevent computer-related fraud and misuse;

"(4) submit standards and guidelines developed pursuant to paragraphs (2) and (3) of this subsection, along with recommendations as to the extent to which these should be made compulsory and binding, to the Secretary of Commerce for promulgation under section 111(d) of the Federal Property and Administrative Services Act of 1949;

"(5) develop guidelines for use by operators of Federal computer systems that contain sensitive information in training their employees in security awareness and accepted security practice, as required by section 5 of the Computer Security Act of 1987; and

"(6) develop validation procedures for, and evaluate the effectiveness of, standards and guidelines developed pursuant to paragraphs (1), (2), and (3) of this subsection through research and liaison with other government and private agencies.

"(b) In fulfilling subsection (a) of this section, the National Bureau of Standards is authorized--

"(1) to assist the private sector, upon request, in using and applying the results of the programs and activities under this section;

"(2) to make recommendations, as appropriate, to the Administrator of General Services on policies and regulations proposed pursuant to section 111(d) of the Federal Property and Administrative Services Act of 1949;

"(3) as requested, to provide to operators of Federal computer systems technical assistance in implementing the standards and guidelines promulgated pursuant to section 111(d) of the Federal Property and Administrative Services Act of 1949;

"(4) to assist, as appropriate, the Office of Personnel Management in developing regulations pertaining to training, as required by section 5 of the Computer Security Act of 1987;

"(5) to perform research and to conduct studies, as needed, to determine the nature and extent of the vulnerabilities of, and to devise techniques for the cost effective security and privacy of sensitive information in Federal computer systems; and

"(6) to coordinate closely with other agencies and offices (including, but not limited to, the Departments of Defense and Energy, the National Security Agency, the General Accounting Office, the Office of Technology Assessment, and the Office of Management and Budget)--

"(A) to assure maximum use of all existing and planned programs, materials, studies, and reports relating to computer systems security and privacy, in order to avoid unnecessary and costly duplication of effort; and

"(B) to assure, to the maximum extent feasible, that standards developed pursuant to subsection (a) (3) and (5) are consistent and compatible with standards and procedures developed for the protection of information in Federal computer systems which is authorized under criteria established by Executive order or an Act of Congress to be kept secret in the interest of national defense or foreign policy.

"(c) For the purposes of--

"(1) developing standards and guidelines for the protection of sensitive information in Federal computer systems under subsections (a)(1) and (a)(3), and

"(2) performing research and conducting studies under subsection (b)(5), the National Bureau of Standards shall draw upon computer system technical security guidelines developed by the National Security Agency to the extent that the National Bureau of Standards determines that such guidelines are consistent with the requirements for protecting sensitive information in Federal computer systems.

"(d) As used in this section--

"(1) the term computer system'--

"A) means any equipment or interconnected system or subsystems of equipment that is used in the  automatic acquisition, storage, manipulation, management, movement, control, display, switching, interchange, transmission, or reception, of data or information; and

"(B) includes--

"(i) computers;

"(ii) ancillary equipment;

"(iii) software, firmware, and similar procedures;

"(iv) services, including support services; and

"(v) related resources as defined by regulations issued by the Administrator for General Services pursuant to section 111 of the Federal Property and Administrative Services Act of 1949;

"(2) the term 'Federal computer system'--

"(A) means a computer system operated by a Federal agency or by a contractor of a Federal agency or other organization that processes information (using a computer system) on behalf of the Federal Government to accomplish a Federal function; and

"(B) includes automatic data processing equipment as that term is defined in section 111(a)(2) of the Federal Property and Administrative Services Act of 1949;

"(3) the term 'operator of a Federal computer system' means a Federal agency, contractor of a Federal agency, or other organization that processes information using a computer system on behalf of the Federal Government to accomplish a Federal function;

"(4) the term 'sensitive information' means any information, the loss, misuse, or unauthorized access to or modification of which could adversely affect the national interest or the conduct of Federal programs, or the privacy to which individuals are entitled under section 552a of title 5, United     States     Code (the Privacy Act), but which has not been specifically authorized under criteria established by an Executive order or an Act of Congress to be kept secret in the interest of national defense or foreign policy; and

"(5) the term 'Federal agency' has the meaning given such term by section 3(b) of the Federal Property and Administrative Services Act of 1949.

"SEC. 21.

(a) There is hereby established a Computer System Security and Privacy Advisory Board within the Department of Commerce. The Secretary of Commerce shall appoint the chairman of the Board. The Board shall be composed of twelve additional members appointed by the Secretary of Commerce as follows:

"(1) four members from outside the Federal Government who are eminent in the computer or telecommunications industry, at lease one of whom is representative of small or medium sized companies in such industries;

"(2) four members from outside the Federal Government who are eminent in the fields of computer or telecommunications technology, or related disciplines, but who are not employed by or representative of a producer of computer or telecommunications equipment; and

"(3) four members from the Federal Government who have computer systems management experience, including experience in computer systems security and privacy, at least one of whom shall be from the National Security Agency.

"(b) The duties of the Board shall be--

"(1) to identify emerging managerial, technical, administrative, and physical safeguard issues relative to computer systems security and privacy;

"(2) to advise the Bureau of Standards and the Secretary of Commerce on security and privacy issues pertaining to Federal computer systems; and

"(3) to report its findings to the Secretary of Commerce, the Director of the Office of Management and Budget, the Director of the National Security Agency, and the appropriate Committees of the Congress.

"(c) The term of office of each member of the Board shall be four years, except that--

"(1) of the initial members, three shall be appointed for terms of one year, three shall be appointed for terms of two years, three shall be appointed for terms of three years, and three shall be appointed for terms of four years; and

"(2) any member appointed to fill a vacancy in the Board shall serve for the remainder of the term for which his predecessor was appointed.

"(d) The Board shall not act in the absence of a quorum, which shall consist of seven members.

"(e) Members of the Board, other than full-time employees of the Federal Government while attending meetings of such committees or while otherwise performing duties at the request of the Board Chairman while away from their homes or a regular place of business, may be allowed travel expenses in accordance with subchapter I of chapter 57 of title 5, United States Code.

"(f) To provide the staff services necessary to assist the Board in carrying out its functions, the Board may utilize personnel from the National Bureau of Standards or any other agency of the Federal Government with the consent of the head of the agency.

"(g) As used in this section, the terms 'computer system' and 'Federal computer system' have the meanings given in section 20(d) of this Act."; and

"(3) by adding at the end thereof the following new section: "SEC. 23. This Act may be cited as the National Bureau of Standards Act."

## SEC. 4  AMENDMENT TO BROOKS ACT

Section 111(d) of the Federal Property and Administrative Services Act of 1949 (40 U.S.C. 759(d)) is amended to read as follows:

"(d) (1) The Secretary of Commerce shall, on the basis of standards and guidelines developed by the National Bureau of Standards pursuant to section 20(a) (2) and (3) of the National Bureau of Standards Act, promulgate standards and guidelines pertaining to Federal computer systems, making such standards compulsory and binding to the extent to which the Secretary determines necessary to improve the efficiency of operation or security and privacy of Federal computer systems. The President may disapprove or modify such standards and guidelines if he determines such action to be in the public interest. The President's authority to disapprove or modify such standards and guidelines may not be delegated. Notice of such disapproval or modification shall be submitted promptly to the Committee on Government Operations of the House of Representatives and the Committee on Governmental Affairs of the Senate and shall be published promptly in the Federal Register. Upon receiving notice of such disapproval or modification, the Secretary of Commerce shall immediately rescind or modify such standards or guidelines as directed by the President.

"(2) The head of a Federal agency may employ standards for the cost effective security and privacy of sensitive information in a Federal computer system within or under the supervision of that agency that are more stringent than the standards promulgated by the Secretary of Commerce, if such standards contain, at a minimum, the provisions of those applicable standards made compulsory and binding by the Secretary of Commerce.

"(3) The standards determined to be compulsory and binding may be waived by the Secretary of Commerce in writing upon a determination that compliance would adversely affect the accomplishment of the mission of an operator of a Federal computer system, or cause a major adverse financial impact on the operator which is not offset by government-wide savings. The Secretary may delegate to the head of one or more Federal agencies authority to waive such standards to the extent to which the Secretary determines such action to be necessary and desirable to allow for timely and effect implementation of Federal computer systems standards. The head of such agency may redelegate such authority only to a senior official designated pursuant to section 3506(b) of title 44, United States Code. Notice of each such waiver and delegation shall be transmitted promptly to the Committee on Government Operations of the House of Representatives and the Committee on Governmental Affairs of the Senate and shall be published promptly in the Federal Register.

"(4) The Administrator shall revise the Federal information resources management regulations (41 CFR ch. 201) to be consistent with the standards and guidelines promulgated by the Secretary of Commerce under this subsection.

"(5) As used in this subsection, the terms 'Federal computer system' and 'operator of a Federal computer system' have the meanings given in section 20(d) of the National Bureau of Standards Act."

## SEC. 5 FEDERAL COMPUTER SYSTEM SECURITY TRAINING

(a) In General -Each Federal agency shall provide for the mandatory periodic training in computer security awareness and accepted computer security practice of all employees who are involved with the management, use, or operation of each Federal computer system within or under the supervision of that agency. Such training shall be--

(1) provided in accordance with the guidelines developed pursuant to section 20(a)(5) of the National Bureau of Standards Act (as added by section 3 of this Act), and in accordance with the regulations issued under subsection (c) of this section for Federal civilian employees; or

(2) provided by an alternative training program approved by the head of that agency on the basis of a determination that the alternative training program is at least as effective in accomplishing the objectives of such guidelines and regulations.

(b) TRAINING OBJECTIVES.--Training under this section shall be started within 60 days after the issuance of the regulations described in subsection (c). Such training shall be designed--

(1) to enhance employees' awareness of the threats to and vulnerability of computer systems; and

(2) to encourage the use of improved computer security practices.

(c) REGULATIONS.--Within six months after the date of the enactment of this Act, the Director of the Office of Personnel Management shall issue regulations prescribing the procedures and scope of the training to be provided Federal civilian employees under subsection (a) and the manner in which such training is to be carried out.

## SEC. 6    ADDITIONAL RESPONSIBILITIES FOR COMPUTER SYSTEMS SECURITY AND PRIVACY

(a) IDENTIFICATION OF SYSTEMS THAT CONTAIN SENSITIVE INFORMATION - Within 6 months after the date of enactment of this Act, each Federal agency shall identify each Federal computer system, and system under development, which is within or under the supervision of that agency and which contains sensitive information.

(b) SECURITY PLAN -Within one year after the date of enactment of this Act, each such agency shall, consistent with the standards, guidelines, policies, and regulations prescribed pursuant to section 111(d) of the Federal Property and Administrative Services Act of 1949, establish a plan for the security and privacy of each Federal computer system identified by that agency pursuant to subsection (a) that is commensurate with the risk and magnitude or the harm resulting from the loss, misuse, or unauthorized access to or modification of the information contained in such system. Copies of each such plan shall be transmitted to the National Bureau of Standards and the National Security Agency for advice and comment. A summary of such plan shall be included in the agency's five-year plan required by section 3505 of title 44, United States Code. Such plan shall be subject to disapproval by the Director of the Office of Management and Budget. Such plan shall be revised annually as necessary.

## SEC. 7 DEFINITIONS

As used in this Act, the terms "computer system", "Federal computer system", "operator of a Federal computer system", "sensitive information", and "Federal agency" have the meanings given in section 20(d) of the National Bureau of Standards Act (as added by section 3 of this Act).

## SEC. 8 RULES OF CONSTRUCTION OF ACT

Nothing in this Act, or in any amendment made by this Act, shall be construed--

(1) to constitute authority to withhold information sought pursuant to section 552 of title 5, United States Code; or

(2) to authorize any Federal agency to limit, restrict, regulate, or control the collection, maintenance, disclosure, use, transfer, or sale of any information (regardless of the medium in which the information may be maintained) that is—

(A)  privately-owned information;

(B) disclosable under section 552 of title 5, United States Code, or other law requiring or authorizing the public disclosure of information; or

(C)  public domain information.

# Appendix E

## BS7799 – Information Security Management

[1]BS7799 is intended for use as a reference document for managers and employees who are responsible for initiating, implementing and maintaining information security within their organisations. BS7799 is divided into two sections, the first section defines a set of codes of practice and the second section instructs you how to build an Information Security Management System.

## Codes of Practice

In the first section the codes of practice are divided into ten sections:

1. Information Security Policy.
2. Security Organisation.
3. Assets Classification and Control.
4. Personnel Security.
5. Physical and Environmental Security.
6. Computer and Network Management.
7. System Access Control.
8. System Development and Maintenance.
9. Business Continuity Planning.
10. Compliance.

### Information Security Policy

**Objective:** to provide management direction and support for information security.

Top management should set a clear direction and demonstrate support for security through the issue of an information security policy across the organisation.

The Information Security Policy Document should be available to all employees and reviewed at regular intervals. In addition it should contain the following:

---

[1] Excerpts from BS 7799 Parts 1 & 2 © 1999 are reproduced by kind permission of the British Standards Institution.

1. A definition of information security, its overall objectives and scope.
2. A statement of management intention supporting the goals and principles of security.
3. An explanation of specific security policies, principles, standards, and compliance requirements, including:
   a. compliance with legislative and contractual requirements,
   b. security education requirements,
   c. virus prevention and detection policy,
   d. business continuity planning policy.
4. A definition of general and specific responsibilities for all aspects of information security.
5. An explanation of the process for reporting suspected security incidents.

## Security Organisation

This section includes information security infrastructure and security of third party access.

### Information Security Infrastructure

**Objective:** to manage information security within the organisation.

1. Management information security forum to review, monitor and give approval of information security policy and overall responsibilities.
2. In large organisations it might be necessary to coordinate information security measures.
3. Allocation of information security responsibilities.
4. A management approval process for new IT facilities should be established to ensure that the installation of equipment is for a defined business purpose.
5. Specialist information security advice and co-corporation between organisations.
6. Independent review of information security.

### Security of Third Party Access

**Objective:** to maintain the security of organisational IT facilities and information assets accessed by third parties.

1. Identification of risks from third party connections.
2. Security conditions in third party contracts.

## Assets Classification and Control

This section includes Accountability for Assets and Information Classification.

### Accountability for Assets

**Objective:** to maintain appropriate protection of organisational assets.

1. Inventory of assets.

   a.   *Information assets:* for example, databases and data files.

   b.   *Software assets:* for example, the application software, system software and development tools.

   c.   *Physical assets:* for example, computing equipment and magnetic disks.

   d.   *Services:* for example, computing, communications services and other services such as air-conditioning.

## Information Classification

**Objective:** to ensure that information assets receive an appropriate level of protection.

1.  Classification guidelines.

   a.   *Confidentiality:* the business need to share or restrict access to information with regard to confidentiality and the controls required to restrict access to the information.

   b.   *Integrity:* the business need to control modifications to information and the controls required to protect the accuracy and completeness of the information.

   c.   *Availability:* the business need to have information available when required by the business and the controls required to achieve this.

2.  Classification labeling.

# Personnel Security

This section includes Security in Job Definition and Resourcing, User Training and Responding to Incidents.

## Security in Job Definition and Resourcing

**Objective:** to reduce the risks of human error, theft, fraud or misuse of facilities.

1.  Security job descriptions, including roles and responsibilities.
2.  Recruitment screening.
3.  Confidentiality agreement.

## User Training

**Objective:** to ensure that users are aware of information security threats and concerns and are equipped to support the organisational security policy in the course of their normal work.

1.  Information security education and training.

## Responding to Incidents

**Objective:** to minimise the damage from security incidents and malfunctions.

1.  Reporting of security incidents.
2.  Reporting of security weaknesses.
3.  Reporting of software malfunctions.
4.  Disciplinary process.

# Physical and Environmental Security

This section includes Secure Areas and Equipment Security.

### Secure Areas
**Objective:** to prevent access, damage and interference to IT services.

1. Physical security perimeter.
2. Physical entry controls.
3. Security of data centers and computer rooms.
4. Isolated delivery and loading areas for supplies to reduce the risk of unauthorised access.
5. Clear desk policy.
6. Data and software should not be taken off-site without documented management approval.

### Equipment Security
**Objective:** to prevent access, damage and interference to IT services.

1. Equipment should be sited and protected so as to reduce the opportunities for unauthorised access, and risks of environmental hazards.
2. Power supplies should be protected from power failures or other electrical anomalies.
3. Cabling carrying power and data should be protected from interception or damage.
4. IT equipment should be correctly maintained to ensure continued availability and integrity.
5. Security of equipment off-premises.
6. Secure disposal of equipment.

# Computer Network Management

This section includes Operational Procedures and Responsibilities, System Planning and Acceptance, Protection from Malicious Software, Housekeeping, Network Management, Media Handling and Security, and Data and Software Exchange.

### Operational Procedures and Responsibilities
**Objective:** to ensure the correct and secure operation of computer and network facilities.

1. Documented operating procedures.
2. Incident management procedures.
3. Segregation of duties.
4. Separation of development and operational responsibilities.
5. Management of risk and threats associated with the use of external contractors for computer and network management.

### System Planning and Acceptance
**Objective:** to minimise the risks of systems failure.
1. Capacity planning.
2. Establishment of system acceptance criteria.
3. Fallback planning.
4. Operational change control.

### Protection from Malicious Software
**Objective:** to safeguard the integrity of data.

1. Virus controls to ensure awareness, detection and prevention.

### Housekeeping
**Objective:** to maintain the integrity and availability of IT services.

1. Data back-up.
2. Operators should maintain a log of all work carried out.
3. Fault logging.
4. Environmental monitoring.

### Network Management
**Objective:** to ensure the safeguard of information in networks and the protection of the supporting infrastructure.

1. Network security controls and mechanisms.

### Media Handling and Security
**Objective:** to prevent damage to assets and interruptions to business activities.

1. Management of removable computer media.
2. Procedures for the handling of sensitive data should be established to prevent misuse.
3. Security of system documentation.
4. Disposal of media.

### Data and Software Exchange
**Objective:** to prevent loss, modification or misuse of data.

1. Data and software exchange agreements.
2. Security of media in transit.
3. EDI Security.
4. Security of electronic mail..
5. Security of electronic office systems.

This section includes Business Requirements for System Access, User Access Management, User Responsibilities, Network Access Control, Monitoring System Access and Use, Computer Access Control and Application Access Control.

## Business Requirements for System Access
**Objective:** to control access to business information.

1. Documented access control policy.

## User Access Management
**Objective:** to prevent unauthorised computer access.

1. User registration.
2. Privilege management.
3. User password management.
4. Review of user access rights.

## User Responsibilities
**Objective:** to prevent unauthorised user access.

1. Password Use.
2. Unattended user equipment.

## Network Access Control
**Objective:** protection of network services.

1. Network and computer services that a user can access should be consistent with the business access control policy.
2. The route from the user terminal to the computer service may need to be controlled.
3. User authentication and node authentication.
4. Access to diagnostic ports should be securely controlled.
5. Segregation of networks, network connection control, and network routeing control.
6. Security of network services.

## Monitoring System Access and Use
**Objective:** to detect unauthorised activities.

1. Event logging.
2. Monitoring system use.
3. Clock synchronisation.

## Computer Access Control
**Objective:** to prevent unauthorised computer access.

1. Automatic terminal identification.
2. Terminal logon procedures.
3. User identifiers and a password management system.

### Computer Access Control

**Objective:** to prevent unauthorised computer access.

1. Automatic terminal identification.
2. Terminal logon procedures.
3. User identifiers and a password management system.
4. Duress alarm to safeguard users.
5. Terminal time-out.
6. Limitation of connection time.

### Application Access Control

**Objective:** to prevent unauthorised access to information held in computer systems.

1. Information access restriction.
2. Use of system utilities.
3. Access control to program source library.
4. Sensitive system isolation.

## System Development and Maintenance

This section includes Security Requirements of Systems, Security in Application Systems, Security of Application System Files, and Security in Development and Support Environments.

### Security Requirements of Systems

**Objective:** to ensure that security is built into IT systems.

1. Security requirements analysis and specification.
2. Consideration of the need to safeguard the confidentiality, integrity and availability of information assets.
3. Identification of the opportunities to use different types of control to prevent, detect and recover from major failures and incidents.

### Security in Application Systems

**Objective:** to prevent loss, modification or misuse of user data in application systems.

1. Input data validation.
2. Internal processing validation.
3. Data encryption.
4. Message authentication.

### Security of Application System Files

**Objective:** to ensure that IT projects and support activities are conducted in a secure manner.

1. Controls of operational software.
2. Protection of system test data.

### Security in Development and Support Environments

**Objective:** to maintain the security of application systems software and data.

1. Change control procedures.
2. Technical review of operating system changes.
3. Restrictions on changes to software packages.
4. Business continuity planning.

# Compliance

This section includes Compliance with Legal Requirements, Security Reviews with IT Systems and System Audit Considerations.

### Compliance with Legal Requirements

**Objective:** to avoid breaches of any statutory, criminal or civil obligations and of any security requirements.

1. Control of proprietary software copying.
2. Safeguard of organisational records.
3. Data protection.
4. Prevention of misuse of IT facilities.

### Security Reviews of IT Systems

**Objectives:** to ensure compliance of systems with organisational security policies and standards.

1. Compliance with security policy.
2. Technical compliance checking.

### System Audit Considerations

**Objective:** to minimise interference to/from audit processes.

1. System audit controls.
2. Protection of system audit tools.

# Information Security Management System

Part 2 of BS7799 instructs you how to build an Information Security Management System (SMS). The standard requires you to set up an Information Security Management System (ISMS) to make this happen. You should really, of course, set this up in the first place, but standards don't tell you how to do things, merely what you should achieve. It defines a six-step process.

1. *Information Policy*: this invites you to stand back and think about all of your information assets and their value to your organisation. You ought then to devise a policy that identifies what information is important and why. From a practical point of view, it is only that information with some significant value that should be of concern.

2. *Scope:* excluding low value information allows you to define the scope of your management concerns. You may discover that your concerns pervade your organisation as a whole. In this case you will need to regard all of your information systems and their external interfaces IT and electronic forms of communication, filing cabinets, telephone conversations, public relations and so on, as being in scope. Alternatively, your concerns may focus onto a particular customer-facing system.

3. *Risk assessment:* now you know what information is in scope and what its value is, your next move should be to determine the risk of losing that value. Remember to consider everything. At one extreme you need to consider the complexities of technology; at the other you need to consider business forces in terms of advancing technology and enterprise, as well as the ugly side of industrial espionage and information warfare.

4. *Risk management:* you then need to decide how to manage that risk. Your forces certainly include technology, but don't forget people, administrative procedures and physical things like doors and locks and even CCTV. Don't forget insurance. If you can't prevent something from happening, maybe you can discover if it does happen and do something to contain it or otherwise reduce the danger. In the end, you will of course, need an effective continuity plan.

5. *Choose your safeguards:* you will then need to choose your "*safeguards*", i.e. the ways you have selected to manage the risk. BS7799 lists a wide variety of such measures, but the list is not exhaustive and you are free to identify additional measures as you please.

6. *Statement of applicability:* you are required to identify all of your chosen security controls and justify why you feel they are appropriate, and show why those BS7799 controls that have not been chosen are not relevant.

# Appendix F

## MIS Training Institute "Swiss Army Knife"[1]

## Security Architecture, Standards, & Requirements

1. BS7799: Code of Practice to Information Security Management; British Standards Institution; May 1999; http://www.bsi.org.uk
2. Can You C2? M.L.A. Lammerse; Sys Admin; September 1999
3. Canadian Trusted Computer Product Evaluation Criteria (CTCPEC); Canadian Security Establishment; April 1992
4. Commercial International Security Requirements (CISR); I-4/Ken Cutler, Fred Jones; April, 1992; contact MIS Training Institute; 508-879-7999
5. The Common Criteria for Information Technology Security (CC) – V2; http://csrc.ncsl.nist.gov/cc; November, 1998
6. Developing a Security Architecture; Handbook of Information Security Management - 1994-95 Yearbook; Ken Cutler; Warren, Gorham, & Lamont (Auerbach); 1995
7. IBM Security Architecture - Securing the Open Client/Server Distributed Enterprise; IBM; SC28-8135-01; 1995
8. Information Technology Security Evaluation Criteria (ITSEC) V1.2; CEC, Directorate XIII/F, SOG-IS Secretariat, TR61 02/28 Rue de la Loi, 200, B-1049 Brussels; June 1991
9. Minimum Security Functionality Requirements for Multi-User Operating Systems - Issue 1 (Draft); National Institute of Standards & Technology; January 1992 (also available in machine readable form on NIST Security Clearinghouse)
10. NIST Computer Security Publications; Government Printing Office;

---

[1] Courtesy of Ken Cutler, CISA, CISSP, Managing Director, Information Security Institute, MISTI (http:www.misti.com) © MIS Training Institute

(202-783-3238/Voice) - also see NIST Security Clearinghouse (http://csrc.ncsl.nist.gov); for a list of NIST security publications, look for NIST Publication List 91

11. Practices for Securing Critical Information Assets; Critical Infrastructure Assurance Office; http://www.ciao.gov

12. Security in Open Systems; NIST Special Publication 800-7; 1994; see NIST Security Clearinghouse

13. Trusted Computer System Evaluation Criteria (TCSEC - "Orange Book" & Others); National Computer Security Center (NCSC); see also NIST Security Clearinghouse

# General Security/Audit Reference & Product Selection

1. Computer Security Basics; Deborah Russell, G.T. Gangemi, Sr.; O'Reilly; 1991

2. Computer Security for Dummies; Peter Davis & Barry Lewis; IDG; 1996

3. Computer Security Handbook; Richard H. Baker; McGraw-Hill; 1991

4. Computer Security Handbook – 3rd Edition; Arthur E. Hutt, Seymour Bosworth, and Douglas B. Hoyt; John Wiley & Sons; 1996

5. Computers at Risk - Safe Computing in the Information Age; National Research Council, National Academy Press, 1991

6. Computer Security Reference Book; K.M. Jackson, J. Hruska, D.B. Parker; Butterworth Heinemann; 1992

7. COBIT: Control Objectives for Information & Related Technology - 2nd Edition; Information Systems Audit & Control Foundation; 1998

8. Datapro Reports on Information Security; Warren, Gorham, & Lamont

9. Data Security Management; Warren, Gorham, & Lamont (Auerbach)

10. Designing Controls into Computerized Systems; Jerry Fitzgerald; (Jerry Fitzgerald Associates 415-591-5676); also available through ISACA

11. EDPACS; Warren, Gorham, & Lamont (Auerbach)

12. Handbook of EDP Auditing; Warren, Gorham, & Lamont; 1985 & annual supplements)

14. Hitting the Bull's Eye; Ken Cutler; Information Security Magazine; August 2000

13. Information Security Handbook – 4th Edition; Hal Tipton, Micki Krause; Auerbach; 2000 Information Security Magazine; ICSA Publications; www.infosecuritymag.com

14. Information Systems Security Officer's Guide; Dr. Gerald Kovacich; Butterworth-Heinemann; 1998

15. IT Baseline Protection Manual (German and English translations); Bundesamt für Sicherheit in der Informationstechnik; http://www.bsi.de/gshb/english/menue.htm
16. Secure Computing Magazine (formerly Infosecurity News); West Coast Publishing

# PBX Security & Toll Fraud

1. PBX Security; David Crowell; The EDP Auditor Journal; Volume II, 1993
2. Private Branch Exchange (PBX) Security Guideline; NIST Computer Systems Laboratory; NIST/GCR-93-635; September 7, 1993
3. Protecting Your Telephone Systems; Steve Purdy; Infosecurity News; July/August 1993
4. Taking a Hard Look at Toll Fraud Protection Services; Network World; June 8, 1992
5. Voice-Mail Security; Marc Robbins; Infosecurity News; July/August 1993

# Network Management, Administration, & Security

## General

1. All About Network Directories; Kevin Kampman, Christina Kampman; Wiley; 2000
2. Are You Safe Online?; N. Randall & S.L. Roberts-Witt; PC Magazine; September 1, 1999
3. Data & Computer Communications - Fifth Edition; William Stallings; Prentice-Hall; 1997
4. Desktop Encyclopedia of Telecommunications; Nathan J. Miller; McGraw-Hill; 1998
5. Directories: The State of the Union; Michael Chacon; Network Magazine; August 1999
6. E-Mail Security; Close Holes and Discover Problems; Dan Sullivan; Internet Security Advisor; Mar/Apr 2000
7. E-Mail Security; How to Keep Your Electronic Messages Private; Bruce Schneier; Wiley; 1995
8. Extranet Design & Implementation; Peter Loshin; Network Press/SYBEX; 1997
9. Handbook of Networking & Connectivity; Gary R. McClain; AP Professional; 1994

10. Lock Up LDAP; Joel Deitch; Windows NT Systems; December 1999
11. McGraw-Hill LAN Communications Handbook; Fred Simonds; McGraw-Hill; 1994
12. MCSE Training Guide: Networking Essentials, Second Edition; Glenn Berg; New Riders; 1998
13. The Multi-Boot Configuration Handbook; Roderick W. Smith; QUE; 2000
14. Networking Complete; Sybex; 2000
15. Network & Internetwork Security; William Stallings; Prentice-Hall; 1995
16. Network Security: Data & Voice Communications; Fred Simonds; McGraw-Hill; 1996
17. Network Security Secrets; David Stang & Sylvia Moon; IDG Books Worldwide, Inc.; 1993 (includes software)
18. Norman Data Defense Systems Virus Reports; David Stang; 703-573-8802 (US); 47-32-81-34-90 (Europe)
19. Peter Norton's Network Security Fundamentals; Peter Norton & Mike Stockman; SAMS; 2000
20. PC Confidential; Michael A. Banks; Sybex; 2000
21. Smart Computing Guide to PC Privacy; Smart Computing Guide Series – Volume 8/Issue 4; Sandhills Publishing; 2000; http://www.smartcomputing.com
22. Software Publishers Association; http://www.spa.org
23. Using Networks; Frank Derfler; QUE; 1998
24. Virus Bulletin; Virus Bulletin Ltd; 21 The Quadrant, Abingdon, Oxfordshire, OX14 3YS, England; 44-01235-555139
25. Securing POP and IMAP Sessions; Dan Backman; Network Computing; September 6, 1999
26. What's the Biggest Security Threat of the Next Decade? Directory Services; Stuart McClure & Joel Scambray; InfoWorld; August 2, 1999
27. Windows Super Guide - Privacy & Security; Ed Bott; PC Computing; September 1999

## Novell NetWare

1. Building & Auditing a Trusted Network Environment with NetWare 4; Novell Application Notes - Vol. 5, Number 4; Novell, Inc.; April 1994
2. Documenting Your Network (NetWare); Steve Kalman; Network Administrator; Nov/Dec 1994
3. Internetworking with NetWare TCP/IP; Karanjit Siyan, et al.; New Riders Publishing; 1996
4. LAN Desktop Guide to Security; Ed Sawicki; SAMS; 1992
5. Managing NDS with NWADMIN; Linda Boyer; NetWare Connection; October, 1996

6.  NetWare 4.11 & IntraNetWare; Sandy Stevens; NetWare Connection; October, 1996
7.  NetWare Connection Magazine; http://www.NetWare.com/nwc/
8.  NetWare LAN Analysis; Laura Chappell; Novell Press/SYBEX; 1993
9.  NetWare Security: Configuring & Auditing a Trusted Environment; J. Lamb, S. Jarocki, A. Seijas; Novell, Inc.; 1991
10. NetWare Training Guide: NetWare 4 Administration; Karanjit Sujan; New Riders Publishing; 1994
11. NetWare Training Guide: Managing NetWare Systems - Third Edition (NetWare 3.1x); Debra Niedermiller-Chaffins, Dorothy Cady, & Drew Haywood; New Riders Publishing; 1994
12. Networking with NetWare for Dummies – 4th Edition; E. Tittel, E. Follis, & J. Gaskin; IDG; 1998
13. Novell's Guide to Integrating NetWare & TCP/IP; Drew Heywood; Novell Press/IDG; 1996
14. Novell's Guide to Integrating UNIX & NetWare Networks; Novell Press/Sybex; 1994
15. Novell's Guide to NetWare 3.12 Networks; Cheryl Currid & Company; Novell Press; 1993
16. Novell's Guide to NetWare 4.0 Networks; Cheryl Currid, Stephen Saxon; Novell Press; 1993
17. Novell's IntraNetWare Administrator's Handbook; Kelley J.P. Lindberg; Novell Press; 1996
18. Using NetWare 4.1; Bill Lawrence, et al.; Que Corporation; 1995

## OS/2 LAN Server

1.  Connecting with LAN Server 4.0; Barry Nance; Ziff-Davis Press; 1995

## Windows NT/2000/9x

1.  The Accidental Hacker; Andrey Kruchkov; Windows NT Magazine; February, 1998
2.  Essential Windows NT System Administration; Aeleen Frisch; O'Reilly; 1998
3.  Inside Windows 2000 Server; William Boswell; New Riders; 2000
4.  Internet Security with Windows NT; Mark Joseph Edwards; Duke Press; 1997
5.  Mark Minasi's Windows 2000 Resource Kit; Mark Minasi; Sybex; 2000 (includes CD-ROM)
6.  Microsoft Windows 2000 Professional Installation & Configuration Handbook; Jim Boyce; QUE; 2000
7.  Microsoft Windows NT 4.0 Security, Audit, and Control; Pricewaterhouse

Coopers; Microsoft Press; 1999

8.  MCSE Complete – Electives; Sybex; 1999
9.  MCSE Implementing and Administering a Windows 2000 Network Infrastructure Study Guide; Thomas Shinder; Osborne/McGraw-Hill; 2000
10. MCSE Training Guide: Networking Essentials, Second Edition; Glenn Berg; New Riders; 1998
11. MCSE Training Guide: TCP/IP, Second Edition; Rob Scrimger, Kelli Adam; Sybex; 1999
12. Networking Complete; Guy Hart-Davis et al; Sybex; 2000
13. NT 4 Network Security – Second Edition; Matthew Strebe, Charles Perkins, Michael G. Moncur; Sybex; 1999
14. Stop Thief; Mark Joseph Edwards; Windows NT Magazine; February 1998
15. Teach Yourself Microsoft Exchange Server 5.5 in 21 Days; Jason vanValkenburgh, Anthony Steven; SAMS; 1999
16. The Ultimate Windows 2000 System Administrator's Guide; Robert Williams, Mark Walla; Addison-Wesley; 2000
17. Trusted and Trusting Domains in NT 4.0; L.J. Locher; Windows NT Magazine; December 1999
18. Where Windows NT Stores Passwords; Mark J.Edwards, David LeBlanc; Windows NT Magazine; August 1999
19. Windows 2000 Magazine; www.win2000mag.com
20. Windows 2000 Server Administrator's Pocket Consultant; William R. Stanek; Microsoft Press; 2000
21. Windows 2000 Server Security for Dummies; Paul Sanna; IDG; 2000
22. Windows 2000; The Complete Reference; Kathy Ivens & Kenton Gardinier; Osborne/McGraw-Hill; 2000
23. Windows NT Desktop Reference; Aeleen Frisch; O'Reilly; 1998
24. Windows NT in A Nutshell; Eric Pearce; O'Reilly; 1997
25. Windows NT 4.0 Installation & Configuration Handbook; Jim Boyce, et al.; QUE; 1996
26. Windows NT Magazine: Special Security Issue; October 1999
27. Windows NT Secrets – Option Pack Edition; Harry M. Brelsford; IDG Books; 1999
28. Windows NT Server 4.0 Administrator's Pocket Consultant; William R. Stanek; Microsoft Press; 1999
29. Windows NT Server Resource Kit - Version 4.0, Supplement 4; Microsoft Press; 1999
30. Windows NT Security; Charles Rutstein (NCSA); McGraw-Hill; 1997
31. Windows NT Security Guide; Stephen A. Sutton; Addison-Wesley; 1997
32. Windows NT Security Handbook; Tom Sheldon; Osborne; 1997
33. Windows NT Security: Step by Step; The SANS Institute; 1998 (ntsec@sans.org)

34. Windows NT 4 Server Unleashed; Jason Garms, et al.; Sams Publishing; 1996

## UNIX-Windows NT Integration

1. SAMBA – Integrating Unix & Windows; John Blair; SSC; 1998 (includes CD-ROM)
2. Windows 2000 & Unix Integration Guide; Steve Burnett, David Gunter, & Lola Gunter; Osborne/McGraw-Hill; 2000
3. Windows NT & Unix Integration; Gene Henriksen; Macmillan Technical Publications; 1998

## AIX

1. AIX RS/6000 System & Administration Guide; James DeRoest; McGraw-Hill; 1995
2. AIX Survival Guide; Andreas Siegert; Addison-Wesley; 1996
3. Audit, Control, & Security Features of the AIX Operating System; Ernst & Young; 1995
4. Elements of AIX Security: R3.1; IBM; GG24-3622-01; 1991
5. Elements of Security: AIX 4.1; IBM; GG24-4433-00; 1994

## HP-UX

1. HP-UX: System & Administration Guide; Jay Shah; McGraw-Hill; 1997
2. HP-UX System Security; Hewlett-Packard; Part # B2355-90045; 1992
3. Can You Trust HP-UX?; Ben Klein; Sys Admin Magazine; June, 1997

## LINUX

1. Implementing Security on Linux; Patrick Lambert; Sys Admin; October, 1999
2. Linux Administration: A Beginner's Guide; Steve Shah; Osborne/McGraw-Hill; 2000 (includes CD-ROM)
3. Linux Administrator's Security Guide; Kurt Seifreid; www.seifried.org/lasg
4. Linux Complete; Grant Taylor; Sybex; 1999
5. Linux Configuration & Installation - Fourth Edition; Patrick Volkerding, Kevin Reichard, Eric F. Johnson; MIS:Press; 1998 (includes CD-ROM)
6. Linux Developer's Resource CD-ROM; InfoMagic; 520-526-9565; info@infomagic.com
7. Linux for Dummies - Quick Reference - 2nd Edition; Phil Hughes; IDG; 1998
8. Linux Installation & Getting Started; Matt Welsh; SSC; 1995
9. Linux Network Administrator's Guide; Olaf Kirch; O'Reilly; 1995

10. Linux Network Toolkit; Paul G. Sery; IDG; 1998 (includes CD-ROM)
11. Linux Security Toolkit; David A. Bandel; M&T Books; 2000 (includes CD-ROM)
12. Linux System Administration; Anne Carasik; MandT (IDG); 1998
13. Linux System Security; Scott Mann & Ellen L. Mitchell; Prentice-Hall; 2000
14. Linux Web Server Toolkit; Nicholas Wells; IDG; 1998
15. Master Red Hat Linux Visually; Michael Bellomo; IDG; 2000 (includes CD-ROM)
16. Maximum Linux Magazine; Imagine Media; www.imaginemedia.com
17. Maximum Security; Maximum Linux Magazine; Nov/Dec 2000 – entire issue
18. PAM – Pluggable Authentication Modules; Kurt Seifried; Sys Admin; September 2000
19. Red Hat Linux Administrator's Handbook; Mohammed J. Kabir; M&T Books; 2000
20. Red Hat Linux 6 Unleashed; David Pitts & Bill Ball et al; SAMS; 1999
21. Red Hat Linux for Dummies; Jon "maddog" Hall & Paul G. Sery; IDG; 2000
22. Red Hat Linux – Visual Quickpro Guide; Harold Davis; Peachpit Press; 1999
23. Red Hat Linux 7 Weekend Crash Course; Naba Barkakati; IDG; 2000 (includes CD-ROM)
24. Red Hat Linux Network Toolkit – 2nd Edition; Paul G. Sery; M&T (IDG); 2000 (includes CD-ROM)
25. Running Linux 3$^{rd}$ Edition; Matt Welsh & Lar Kaufman; O'Reilly; 1999
26. Securing Linux; Mike Warfield; Ramparts; linuxworld.com; 1999
27. Securing Your Linux Box; Miff; 2600 Magazine; Summer, 1999
28. Slackware Linux for Dummies; Paul Gallegos; IDG; 2000
29. Sys Admin Magazine; Miller Freeman Publications; www.sysadminmag.com
30. Using Caldera Open Linux - Special Edition; A. Smart, E. Ratcliffe, T. Bird, & D. Bandel; QUE; 1999
31. Using Linux; Bill Ball; Que; 1998

## SUN SOLARIS

1. Hardening a Host; Dave Zwieback; Sys Admin; September 1999
2. Security Diagnostic Review for Solaris 2.x; Gary Bahadur, Dan Robertson; January 1999
3. Solaris 2.x System Administrator's Guide; S. Lee Henry, John R. Graham; McGraw-Hill; 1995
4. Solaris 2.x for Managers & Administrators – Second Edition; C. Freeland, Dwight McKay, G.K. Parkinson; Onword Press; 1998
5. Solaris Administration; Supplement to Sys Admin; Sys Admin; November 2000
6. Solaris Advanced System Administrator's Guide – Second Edition; Janice

Winsor; MacMillan Technical Publishing; 1997

7. Solaris Guide for Windows NT Administrators; Tom Bialaski; Sun Microsystems Press; 1999
8. Solaris Security; Peter H. Gregory; Prentice-Hall; 2000
9. Solaris System Administrator's Guide; Janice Winsor;  MacMillan Technical Publishing; 1997

## UNIX - General

1. Audit, Control, & Security Features of the UNIX Operating System; Ernst & Young; 1994
2. Automating Unix Security Monitoring; Robert Geiger, John Schweitzer; Sys Admin; November 2000
3. Essential (UNIX) System Administration – Second Edition; AEleen Frisch; O'Reilly; 1995
4. Freeware-Based Security; Syed Ali; Sys Admin; January 1999
5. Hardening a Host; Dave Zwieback; Sys Admin; September 1999
6. How to Hack (Unix); An Introduction; Kurt Seifried; Sys Admin; November 2000
7. How to Hack Unix: Part 2; Kurt Siefried; Sys Admin; November 2000
8. Improving the Security of Your UNIX System; David Curry; SRI International; 1990
9. Managing NFS & NIS; Hal Stern; O'Reilly; April 1992
10. Managing SUID/SGID;  David Tosch; Sys Admin; September 2000
11. Open Computing's Best UNIX Tips Ever; Kenneth H. Rosen, Richard R. Rosinski, & Douglas A. Host; Osborne McGraw-Hill; 1994
12. Practical Unix & Internet Security; Simson Garfinkel & Gene Spafford; O'Reilly; 1996
13. Role-Based Access Control; Thomas Vincent; Sys Admin; December 2000
14. Safeguard Your Systems with Free UNIX Scanner Tools; Eric Maiwald; Internet Security Advisor; Mar/Apr 2000
15. Scaring Hackers Away with TCP Wrapper; Adam Olson; Sys Admin; October 2000
16. "Security"; Sys Admin Magazine (entire issue); August 1998, June 1997, November 1996
17. Sendmail – 2nd Edition; Brian Costales; O'Reilly; 1997
18. Setting Root SUIDed Programs at Work; Didier Racheneur; Sys Admin; May 2000
19. Sys Admin Magazine; Miller Freeman Publications; www.sysadminmag.com
20. Titan - A Systems Administration Approach to Security; D. Farmer, Brad Powell, & Matt Archibald; Sys Admin; September 1999
21. The UNIX & X Command Compendium - A Dictionary for High-Level

Computing; Alan Southerton, Edwin C. Perkins, Jr.; Wiley; 1994

22. UNIX in a Nutshell; D. Gilly; O'Reilly; June 1992
23. UNIX Security; RandD Books (Sys Admin Reference Series); 1997
24. UNIX Security; S. Kapilow & G. Wilson; EDPACS; December 1989
25. UNIX System Security; R. Farrow; Addison-Wesley; 1991
26. UNIX System Security - A Guide for Users & System Administrators; D. Curry; Addison-Wesley; May 1992
27. The UNIX Audit; Using UNIX to Audit UNIX; Michael G. Grottola; McGraw-Hill; 1993
28. Visual QuickStart Guide – UNIX; Deborah S. Ray, Eric J. Ray; Peachpit Press; 1998

## DEC VAX/VMS Security

1. Security Concepts for the DECnet VAX Environment; Allen Lum; Data Security Management; Auerbach Publishers; 1990
2. Security for VAX Systems; Digital Equipment Corporation; EC-G0027-31; 1989
3. VAX/VMS (Several Articles); The EDP Auditor Journal; Volume I, 1993

## Remote Access/Virtual Private Network Security

1. 15 Tips for Troubleshooting VPN Connections; Paula Sharick; Windows 2000 Magazine; April 2000
2. Beef Up Communication Privacy over the Internet (FreeS/WAN); Michael Schmidt; Internet Security Advisor; Mar/Apr 2000
3. Being There - Remote Access Servers; Les Freed; PC Magazine; February 9, 1999
4. Building & Managing Virtual Private Networks; Dave Kosiur; Wiley; 1998
5. Cable Modem Security; Fencer; 2600 Magazine; Vol 15, No.4 - Winter 1998-1999
6. Configuring VPNs; Ken Miller, Richard Brackett; Windows NT Magazine; December 1999
7. DSL: Technology and Implementation; Randy Zhang; Sys Admin; October, 1999
8. Fast Connections in Small Packages; Les Freed; PC Magazine; January 20, 1998
9. Getting Out/Getting In; David Beecher; Sys Admin; October 2000
10. Getting Personal with Firewalls; Curtis Dalton; Network Magazine; January 2001

11. Guarding the Flank with RADIUS & TACACS; Dan Backman; Network Computing; February 1, 1998
12. Installing and Configuring OpenSSH; Matt Lesko; Sys Admin; October 2000
13. Introducing FreeS/WAN and IPSEC; Duncan Napier; Sys Admin; November 2000
14. Is RAS Safe ?; Zubair Ahmad; Windows NT Magazine; December, 1997
15. MCSE Training Kit: Microsoft Windows 2000 Network Infrastructure Administration; Microsoft Press; 2000
16. MCSE Implementing and Administering a Windows 2000 Network Infrastructure Study Guide; Thomas Shinder; Osborne/McGraw-Hill; 2000
17. Microsoft's Stellar ISA Server; Sean Daily; Windows 2000 Magazine; October 2000
18. New Advancements in User Authentication; John Vacca; Internet Security Advisor; Mar/Apr 2000
19. Novell's BorderManager Authentication Service; Cheryl Wilson; NetWare Connection; December 1998
20. OpenBSD as a VPN Solution; Alex Withers; Sys Admin; September 2000
21. RADIUS; Ron McCarty; Sys Admin; February, 1999
22. Reining In Remote Access; William Dutcher; PC Week; August 11, 1997
23. Remote Access 24Seven; Paul E. Robichaux; Sybex Network Press; 1999
24. Remote Access Management with RADIUS; Tao Zhou; Windows NT Magazine; June, 1999
25. Remote Access Security; Paul Funk; NetWare Connection; November 1996
26. Remote Access; Anita Karve; Network Magazine; April 1998
27. Securing Cable Modems; Gary C. Kessler; Information Security; July 2000
28. Sweeping Changes for Modem Security; Nathan King; Information Security; June 2000
29. A Token of Our Esteem; Timothy O'Shea; Network Computing; September 6, 1999
30. TACACS, RADIUS Secure Servers; William Dutcher; PC Week; October 20, 1997
31. Understanding the IP Security Protocol; Ken Masica; Internet Security Advisor; Sep/Oct 2000
32. A Virtual Private Affair; Mike Hurwicz; Byte; July 1997
33. Virtual Private Networks; Charlie Scott, Paul Wolfe, & Mike Erwin; O'Reilly; 1998
34. Virtual Private Network: Do You Need One?; Internet Security Advisor; Winter 1998 (Vol.1 No.4)
35. VPNs and IPSec: An Introduction; Joe Freeman and Ron McCarty; SysAdmin; June 1999

## Technical TCP/IP Network and Router Administration

1. CCNA Certified Network Associate Study Guide – Second Edition; Todd Lammle et al.; Sybex; 2000
2. CCNA Exam Notes: Cisco Certified Network Associate; Todd Lammle; Sybex; 1999
3. CCNA Virtual Lab e-trainer; Todd Lammle, William Tedder; Sybex; 2000
4. Cisco: A Beginner's Guide; Tom Shaughnessy; Osborne/McGraw-Hill; 2000
5. Cisco Certified Network Associate – Exam 640-407; Sybex-Network Press; 1999
6. Cisco LAN Switch Configuration – Exam 640-404; Richard A. Deal; Corolis; 1999
7. Cisco Routers 24seven; Andrew Hamilton, John Mistichelli, Bryant G. Tow; Sybex; 2000
8. Cisco Security Architectures; Gil Held, Kent Hundley; Osborne/McGraw-Hill; 1999
9. Cisco TCP/IP Routing Professional Reference; Chris Lewis; McGraw-Hill; 1997
10. DNS & BIND – 3rd Edition; Paul Albitz & Cricket Liu; O'Reilly; 1998
11. DNS on Windows NT; Paul Albitz, Matt Larson, & Cricket Liu; O'Reilly; 1998
12. Domain Name System Security; Diane Davidowicz; 1999; http://www.geocities.com/compsec101/papers/dnssec/dnssec.html
13. The Essential Guide to TCP/IP Commands; Martin Arick; Wiley; 1996
14. Getting Connected - The Internet at 56K & Up; Kevin Dowd; O'Reilly; 1996
15. ICMP: The Good, the Bad, and the Ugly; Ron McCarty; Sys Admin; April 2000
16. Internetworking with TCP/IP - Volume I - Third Edition; Douglas Comer; Prentice-Hall; 1995
17. IPv6: The New Internet; Christian Huitema; Prentice Hall; 1995
18. Managing IP Networks with Cisco Routers; Scott M. Ballew; O'Reilly; 1997
19. MCSE Training Guide: TCP/IP, Second Edition; Rob Scrimger, Kelli Adam; Sybex; 1999
20. Networking Personal Computers with TCP/IP; Craig Hunt; O'Reilly; 1995
21. Practical Internetworking with TCP/IP & UNIX; Smoot Carl-Mitchell & John S. Quarterman; Addison-Wesley; 1994
22. Securing the Domain Name System; Diane Davidowicz & Paul Vixie; Network Magazine; January 2000
23. SNMPv3 – User Security Model; Eric Davis; Sys Admin; May 2000
24. TCP/IP for Dummies – 3rd Edition; Marshall Wilensky & Candace Leiden; IDG Books; 1999
25. TCP/IP Network Administration - Second Edition; C. Hunt; O'Reilly; 1997
26. TCP/IP: A Survival Guide for Users; Frank Derfler & Steve Rigney; MIS Press; 1998

27. Windows NT TCP/IP Administration; Craig Hunt & Robert Bruce Thompson; 1998

## PERL - Practical Extraction & Report Language

1. Discover PERL 5; Naba Barkakati; IDG Books; 1997 (included CD-ROM)
2. PERL 5 How To; Mike Glover, Aidan Humphries, Ed Weiss; Waite Group Press; 1996 (includes CD-ROM with PERL interpreter & sample applications)
3. The PERL CD Bookshelf; O'Reilly; 1999

## Network Vulnerability & Penetration Testing

1. All About Password Crackers; Guy Rosinbaum; Internet Security Advisor; Sep/Oct 2000
2. Anatomy of a Hack; Rik Farrow; Network Magazine; May 2000
3. Audit Your NT System Quickly; Erik Hjelmstad; Internet Security Advisor; Sept/Oct 2000
4. The Art of Attack and Penetration – Understanding Your Security Posture; Chris Prosise, George Kurtz; Sys Admin; March 1999
5. The Art of Attack and Penetration – Defending Your Site; Chris Prosise, George Kurtz; Sys Admin; April 1999
6. Exploits; Alan Laudicina; Sys Admin; July 1999
7. Hacker Proof: The Ultimate Guide to Network Security; Lars Klander; Jamsa Press; 1997
8. Hacking Exposed – Second Edition; Stuart McClure, Joel Scambray, George Kurtz; McGraw-Hill; 2000
9. ICMP Stands for Trouble; Rik Farrow; Network Magazine; 2000
10. Mastering Network Security; Chris Brenton; Sybex/Network Press; 1999
11. Maximum Linux Security; Anonymous; SAMS.NET; 1999
12. Maximum Security - 2nd Edition; Anonymous; Sams.net Publishing; 1998
13. Vulnerability Assessment Scanners; Jeff Forristal, Greg Shipley; Network Computing; January 8, 2001
14. Nmap-web: Prot Scanning Made Easy; Alek Komarnitsky; Sys Admin; October 2000
15. Open-Source Security Tools; Information Security; February 2000
16. Protecting Networks with SATAN; Martin Freiss; O'Reilly; 1998
17. Resource Kit Roundup; Darren Mar-Elia; Windows 2000 Magazine; May 2000
18. Sweeping Changes for Modem Security; Nathan King; Information Security; June 2000
19. System Fingerprinting with NMAP; Rik Farrow; Network Magazine; 2000
20. Tiger; Kristy Westphal; Sys Admin; June 2000

21. Tools from the Underground; Greg Shipley; Network Computing; May 29, 2000
22. Troubleshooting TCP/IP Networks; Laura Chappell; NetWare Connection; January 1999

## IBM Large Network System Security

1. IBM Security Architecture - Securing the Open Client/Server Distributed Enterprise; IBM; SC28-8135-01; 1995
2. Introduction to System & Network Security: Considerations, Options, & Techniques; IBM, 1990, GG24-3451-01
3. MVS/ESA Planning: Security; IBM, 1990, GC28-1801-0

# USE & SECURITY OF THE INTERNET

## General Internet Information & User Guides

1. Dr. Bob's Painless Guide to The Internet; Bob Rankin; No Starch Press; 1996
2. Internet Security Advisor Magazine; www.advisor.com
3. Internet Standards & Protocols; Dilip C. Naik; Microsoft Press; 1998
4. Internet World Magazine; PO Box 713, Mt. Morris, IL 61054; info@mecklermedia.com
5. Official Microsoft Internet Explorer 4 Book; Bryan Pfaffenberger; Microsoft Press; 1997
6. Official Netscape Communicator 4 Book; Phil James; Ventana; 1997
7. Official Netscape Navigator 4.0 (Windows Edition); Phil James; Netscape Press; 1997
8. The Internet for Dummies - 4th Edition; John R. Levine, Carol Baroudi, & Margaret Levine Young; IDG Books; 1997
9. The Internet for Dummies Quick Reference - 3rd Edition; John R. Levine, Margaret Levine Young, & Arnold Reinhold; IDG Books; 1997
10. The Internet Tool Kit; Nancy Cedeno; Sybex; 1995
11. The Internet Unleashed; SAM Publishing; 1994, 1995 (includes software)

## Internet Security – General

1. Actually Useful Internet Security Techniques; Larry J. Hughes, Jr.; New Riders Publishing; 1995
2. E-Mail Security; Bruce Schneier; Wiley; 1995
3. Hazards of Hooking Up; Al Berg; LAN Times; June 17, 1996

4. Implementing Internet Security; William Stallings, Peter Stephenson, & Others; New Riders Publishing; 1995
5. Internet Besieged; Dorothy Denning, Peter Denning, et al; Addison-Wesley; 1998
6. Internet Security for Business; Terry Bernstein, Anish Bhimani, Eugene Schultz, Carol Siegel; Wiley; 1996
7. Internet Security: Guide to Web Protection;  A Supplement to Infosecurity News; July/August 1996
8. Internet Security - Professional Reference; Numerous Authors; New Riders Publishing; 1996 (includes CD-ROM with security & audit software tools)
9. Internet Security Secrets; John Vacca; IDG Books; 1996
10. Internet Security with Windows NT; Mark Joseph Edwards; Duke Press; 1997
11. Network (In) Security Through IP Packet Filtering; D. Brent Chapman; Proceedings of the Third USENIX UNIX Symposium; September 1992 (also available on NIST BBS)
12. Practical Unix & Internet Security; Simson Garfinkel & Gene Spafford; O'Reilly; 1996
13. Proactive Spam Prevention; Michael Schwager; Sys Admin; March, 1999

## Internet Security – Firewalls

1. Assembly Instructions Included (Cisco Routers); Gilbert Held; Network Magazine; January 2001
2. Building A Floppy Firewall; Andreas Meyer; Sys Admin; January 2001
3. Building Internet Firewalls – 2nd Edition; D. Brent Chapman & Elizabeth D. Zwicky; O'Reilly; 2000
4. Building Linux and OpenBSD Firewalls; Wes Sonnenreich, Tom Yates; Wiley; 2000
5. Cisco IOS: It's Not Just for Routing Anymore; Greg Shipley; Network Computing; May 31, 1999
6. Cisco IOS 12 Network Security; Cisco Press/Macmillan Technical Publishing; 1999
7. Cisco Security Architectures; Gil Held & Kent Hundley; McGraw-Hill; 1999
8. Decipher Your Firewall Logs; Robert Graham; Internet Security Advisor; Mar/Apr 2000
9. Firewall Configuration Done Right; Rik Farrow; Network Magazine; December 1998
10. Firewall Vulnerabilities; Rik Farrow; Network Magazine; August 1999
11. Firewalls 24Seven; Matthew Strebe, Charles Perkins; Sybex Network Press; 1999
12. Firewalls Complete; Marcus Goncalves; McGraw-Hill; 1998 (includes CD-ROM with demo versions of major firewall products)

13. Firewalls & Internet Security - Repelling the Wiley Hacker; Bill Cheswick & Steve Bellovin; Addison-Wesley; 1998
14. FreeBSD Firewall Tools & Techniques; Michael Lucas; Sys Admin; June 2000
15. Great Walls of Fire (Firewall Security); Linda Boyer; NetWare Connection; January 1997
16. The 'Ins' and 'Outs' of Firewall Security; Mike Fratto; Network Computing; September 6, 1999
17. Internet Firewalls & Network Security - Second Edition; Karanjit Siyan; New Riders Publishing; 1996
18. Keeping Your Site Comfortably Secure: An Introduction to Internet Firewalls; NIST Special Publication 800-10
19. Kicking Firewall Tires; Char Sample; Network Magazine; March 1998
20. A Linux Internet Gateway; Marcel Gagne; Sys Admin; June 2000
21. NAT: Network Address Translator; Ron McCarty; Sys Admin; March 2000
22. Packet Filtering and Cisco's Way; Ron McCarty; Sys Admin; May 1999
23. Router-Based Network Defense; Gilbert Held; Sys Admin; March 2000
24. The Use of Routers in Firewall Setup; Matej Sustic; Sys Admin; May 2000

## Internet Security – Intrusion Detection & Incident Response

1. Can You Survive A Computer Attack?; Rik Farrow & Richard Power; Network World; May 2000
2. Deploying an Effective Intrusion Detection System; Ramon J. Hontanon; Network Magazine; 2000
3. Detecting Intrusions Within Secured Networks; Dan Sullivan; Internet Security Advisor; Fall 1999
4. FAQ: Network Intrusion Detection Systems; Robert Graham; March 2000; www.robertgraham.com
5. Fcheck: A Solution to Host-Based Intrusion Detection; Ron McCarty; Sys Admin; December 2000
6. An Introduction to Intrusion Detection and Assessment; Rebecca Bace; ICSA; 2000
7. Intrusion Detection: An Introduction to Internet Surveillance, Correlation, Trace Back, Traps & Response; Edward G. Amoroso; Intrusion Net Books; 1998
8. Intrusion Detection; Rebecca Bace; New Riders Publishing; 2000
9. Intrusion Detection: Network Security Beyond the Firewall; Terry Escamilla; Wiley; 1998
10. Intrusion Detection Primer; Benjamin J. Thomas; March 13; 2000; linuxsecurity.com

11. Intrusion Detection Strategies & Design Considerations; Ron McCarty; Sys Admin; September 1999
12. Investigating Potential Intrusions; Eric Maiwald; Internet Security Advisor; Fall 1999
13. Snort – A Lock Inside an Intrusion Detection System; Kristy Westphal; Sys Admin; September 2000
14. Watching the Watchers: Intrusion Detection; Greg Shipley; Network Computing; November 13, 2000

## E-Commerce & Worldwide Web Security

1. ActiveX Demystified; David Chappell, David S. Linthicum; Byte Magazine; September, 1997
2. Administrating Web Servers, Security, & Maintenance; Eric Larson, Brian Stephens; Prentice Hall PTR; 2000
3. Apache Server for Dummies; Ken A.L. Coar; IDG Books; 1998
4. Bots & Other Internet Beasties; Joseph Williams; SAMS.net Publishing; 1996
5. Building Web Commerce Sites; Ed Tittle, et. al; IDG Books; 1997
6. Digital Cash: Commerce on the Net; Peter Wayner; Academic Press; 1996
7. Extranet Design & Implementation; Peter Loshin; Network Press/SYBEX; 1997
8. How Secure is XML; J.C. Hassall; Internet Security Advisor; Jan/Feb 2001
9. Intranet Working; George Eckel; New Riders Publishing; 1996
10. Java & ActiveX Security; J. Stearn, Alex Ciurczak, & Corwin Yu; IS Audit & Control Journal; Vol III 1999
11. Java & Web-Executable Object Security; Michael Shoffner, Merlin Hughes; Dr. Dobb's Journal; November, 1996
12. Java Security; Gary McGraw & Ed Felten; Wiley; 1997
13. The Lotus Domino Server: Integrating Lotus Notes 4.6 With the Internet; Steve Londergran; MandT Books; 1997
14. Keeping Up with IIS Security; Randy Franklin Smith; Windows 2000 Magazine; October 2000
15. Lotus Notes & Domino Network Design; John Lamb, Peter Lew; McGraw-Hill;1997
16. Maintaining Secure Web Applications; Jeff Forristal; Network Computing; March 20, 2000
17. Microsoft FrontPage 98; Laura Lemay; SAMS.net; 1997
18. Microsoft Site Server 3 Bible; Brad Harris; IDG; 1998
19. Netscape Server Survival Guide; David Gulbransen; SAMS.net Publishing; 1996
20. Perl and CGI for the World Wide Web – Visual Quickstart Guide; Elizabeth Castro; Peachpit Press; 1999

21. Professional Site Server 3.0; Nick Apostolopoulos, et al; Wrox Press; 1999
22. Protect Your Privacy on the Internet; Bryan Pfaffenberger; Wiley; 1997
23. Running Microsoft Internet Information Server; Leonid Braginski, Matthew Powell; Microsoft Press; 1998 (includes IIS 4.0 Option Pack CD-ROM)
24. Secure Sockets Layer is Not a Magic Bullet; Rik Farrow; Network Magazine; January 2001
25. Securing Apache; Kyle Dent; Sys Admin; May 1999
26. Securing Windows NT/2000 Servers for the Internet; Stefan Norberg, Deborah Russell; O'Reilly; 2000
27. Securing Your Web Server; Ray Soriano, Gary Bahadur; Sys Admin; May 1999
28. Taming the Wide Open Web; Mandy Andress; Internet Security Advisor; Jan/Feb 2001
29. Tunneling Under (Napster); Al Berg; Information Security; November 2000
30. Using Netscape Communicator; Peter Kent; Que Corporation; 1997
31. Webmaster in A Nutshell; Stephen Spainbour & Valerie Quercia; O'Reilly; 1999
32. Webmaster's Handbook; John M. Fisher; Prima Publishing; 1996
33. Webmaster's Professional Reference; Loren Buhle, et al.; New Riders Publishing; 1996
34. Web Security; Lincoln Stein; Addison-Wesley; 1998
35. Web Security: A Matter of Trust; Word Wide Web Journal - Volume 2, Issue 3; O'Reilly; Summer 1997
36. Web Security & Commerce; Simson Garfinkel, Eugene Spafford; O'Reilly; 1997
37. Web Security Source Book; Avi Ruben, Dan Geer, Marcus J. Ranum; Wiley; 1997
38. Web Site Administrator's Survival Guide; Jerry Ablan, Scott Yanoff; SAMS.net Publishing; 1996
39. Windows NT 4 Web Development; Sanjaya Hettihewa; Sams.net; 1996
40. Your Personal Net; Michael Wolff; Wolff New Media; 1996 (free updates at http://www.ypn.com)

# Cryptography

1. A PKI Primer: E-Security for the Enterprise; Uday O. Ali Pabrai; Internet Security Advisor; Sep/Oct 2000
2. Applied Cryptography: Protocols, Algorithms, & Source Code in C; Bruce Schneier; Wiley; 1997
3. Building Trust in Digital Certificates; Robert Moskowitz; Network Computing;

April 19, 1999
4. Cache on Demand (SET, IOTP); Gary C. Kessler, N. Todd Pritsky; Information Security; October 2000
5. Compression & Encryption; Dr. Dobb's Journal; January 1996
6. Crypto 101; Kurt Seifried; Sys Admin; May 2000
7. Deciphering Cryptography; Gary C. Kessler; Windows NT Magazine; December 1999
8. IBM Cryptographic Concepts & Facilities; IBM; GC22-9063
9. Internet Cryptography; Richard E. Smith; Addison-Wesley; 1997
10. Network Security: Private Communications in a Public World; Charlie Kaufman, Redia Perlman, Mike Spenciner; Prentice-Hall; 1995
11. PKI: The Myth, The Magic and the Reality; Information Security; June 1999
12. The Official PGP User's Guide; Philip R. Zimmermann; The MIT Press; 1995
13. Picking Packets; Lenny Liebmann; Infosecurity News; September/October 1995
14. Public Key Infrastructure Basics; Rik Farrow; Network World; January 1999
15. Sec Specs (X.509); Stephen Cobb; Internet Security Advisor; Fall 1999
16. SET Standard Secures the Future of E-Commerce; Dan Blacharski; Internet Security Advisor; Fall 1999
17. Sorting Out Security: Digital Certificates; Brett Mendel; Infoworld; August 9, 1999
18. Understanding Digital Signatures; Gail Grant; CommerceNet Press; 1998
19. Understanding VPN and PKI Integration; Ken Masica; Internet Security Advisor; Jan/Feb 2001
20. Unlocking PKI – Special Report; Network Magazine; October 2000

# Open, Distributed Systems Security & Management

1. Client/Server Architecture; Alex Berson; McGraw-Hill, Inc.; 1992
2. Client/Server Computing; Dawna Travis Dewire; McGraw-Hill; 1993
3. DCE Security Programming; Wei Hu; O'Reilly, Inc.; 1995
4. DCE: Unifying Your Network Fabric; Eric Hall; Network Computing; November 1, 1996
5. Distributed CICS; Richard Schreiber, William R. Ogden; Wiley-QED; 1994
6. Distributed Computing (Byte Special Report); Byte Magazine; June 1994
7. IBM Security Architecture - Securing the Open Client/Server Distributed Enterprise; IBM; SC28-8135-01; 1995
8. Essential Client/Server Survival Guide – Third Edition; R. Orfali, D. Harkey, J. Edwards; Van Nostrand Reinhold; 1998

9. Implementing Kerberos in Distributed Systems; Handbook of Information Security Management - 1994-95 Yearbook; Ray Kaplan, Joe Kavara, Glen Zorn; Auerbach; 1995

10. Kerberos – A Network Authentication System; Brian Tung; Addison-Wesley; 1999

11. LAN Times Guide to Interoperability; Tom Sheldon; Osborne McGraw-Hill; 1994

12. LAN Times Guide to SQL; J.R. Groff & P.N. Weinberg; Osborne McGraw-Hill; 1994

13. Limitations of the Kerberos Authentication System; S. Bellovin & M. Merritt; USENIX - Winter '91 - Dallas, TX  (also printed in Computer Communications Review; Oct. '91)

14. Mastering Oracle7 & Client/Server Computing; S. Bobrowski; SYBEX; 1994

15. Multivendor Networking; Dr. Andres Fortino, Jerry Golick; McGraw-Hill; 1996 (includes CD-ROM)

16. Network & Distributed Systems Management; Morris Sloman (Principle Editor); Addison-Wesley; 1994

17. Network & Internetwork Security: Principles & Practice; William Stallings; Prentice Hall; 1995

18. Network Security Policy; Terry L. Jeffries; NetWare Connection; January 1997

19. OLTP Handbook; Gary McClain; McGraw-Hill; 1993

20. Oracle DBA Handbook - 7.3 Edition; Kevin Loney; Osborne McGraw-Hill; 1994

21. Powerbuilder for Dummies; Jason Coombs, Ted Coombs; IDG; 1995

22. Securing Client/Server Applications; Peter T. Davis; McGraw-Hill; 1996

23. Security in a Client/Server Environment; P. Teplitzy; Information Systems Security; Auerbach Publishers; Summer 1993

24. Security in Distributed Computing; Glen Bruce, Rob Dempsey; Prentice Hall; 1997

25. Security Issues in the Database Language SQL; NIST Special Publication 800-8; August 1993; Government Printing Office (also available on NIST BBS)

26. SQL Server 7 24Seven; Sawtell, Lee, Bridges, & Isakov; Sybex Network Press; 1999

27. SQL Server Administration; Andy Ruth, Anil Desai; New Riders; 1999

28. Sybase Developers Guide; Daniel J. Worden; SYBEX; 1994

29. Understanding DCE; W. Rosenberry, D. Kenney, & G. Fisher; O'Reilly; September 1992

30. Using Microsoft SQL Server 7.0; McGehee, Kraft, Shepker, et al.; QUE; 1999

# Computer Crime, Hackers, & Viruses

1. 2600 Magazine; 516-751-2600; http://www.2600.com
2. Backlisted! 411 Magazine; 310-596-4673
3. Computer Crime - A Crime Fighter's Handbook; David Icove, Karl Seger, & William VonStorch; O'Reilly; 1995
4. Computer Hacking: Detection & Protection; Imtiaz Malik; Sigma Press; 1996
5. Computer Viruses; Deloitte Haskins & Sells (Deloitte & Touche); 1989 (PC's, MVS, UNIX)
6. Computers Under Attack; Peter J. Denning; ACM Press, 1990
7. Corporate Espionage; Ira Winkler; Prima Publishing; 1997
8. The Cuckoo's Egg; Clifford Stoll; Doubleday; 1989
9. Cyberpunk; Katie Hafner & John Markoff; Simon & Schuster; 1991
10. Distributed Denial of Service Attacks; Rik Farrow; Network Magazine; May 2000
11. The Hacker Crackdown; Bruce Sterling; Bantam Books; 1992
12. Hack Proofing Your Network; Richard Kristoff, Rain Forest Puppy et al.;Syngress Publishing; 2000
13. High-Technology –Crime Investigator's Handbook; Dr. Gerald L. Kovacich, William Boni; Butterworth Heinemann; 2000
14. I-Way Robbery; William C. Boni & Dr. Gerald L. Kovacich; Butterworth-Heinemann; 1999
15. The Little Black Book of Viruses; Mark Ludwig; American Eagle Publications; 1991 (reprinted 1995)
16. Maximum Security - 2nd Edition; Anonymous; sams.net; 1998
17. Secrets of A Super Hacker by the Knightmare; Dennis Fiery; Loompanics Unlimited; 1994
18. Security Insiders Report; 11567 Grove St. N, Seminole, FL 33708; (813-393-6600)
19. Spectacular Computer Crimes; Buck Bloombecker; Dow Jones-Irwin; 1990
20. Steal This Computer Book; Wallace Wang; No Starch Press; 1998
21. Terminal Compromise; Winn Schwartau; Inter.Pact Press; 1991; (813-393-6600)
22. Terminal Delinquents; Jack Hitt & Paul Tough; Esquire December 1990
23. Virus, They Wrote; Corey Sandler; PC Computing; September 1994
24. Wire Pirates (Internet Security); Paul Wallach; Scientific American; March 1994

# Sources of Security & Audit Tools
# (Public Domain/Shareware)

AGNetTools (http://www.aggroup.com)
CIS: Cerebus Internet Scanner (http://www.cerebus-infosec.co.uk)
COPS (http://www.ciac.org)
courtney (http://www.ciac.org)
crack, cracklib (http://www.ciac.org)
dig (http://www.ciac.org)
ethload/ethdump (ftp://ftp.cc.utexas.edu)
ethereal (http://www.ethereal.com)
fremont (http://www.ciac.org)
gabriel (http://www.ciac.org)
gobbler (http://ftp.wustl.edu)
Kerberos (http://athena-dist.mit.edu)
linux (http://www.linux.org)
logsurfer (http://www.art.dfn.de/eng/team/wl/logsurf)
L0phtCrack (http://www.l0pht.com)
merlin (http://www.ciac.org )
NAT: NetBIOS Audit Tool (http://www.securenetworks.com)
npasswd, passwd+ (http://www.ciac.org )
NESSUS (http://www.nessus.org)
NetScan tools (http://www.netscantools.com)
Nmap (http://www.insecure.org)
NTFSDOS (http://www.sysinternals.com)
OPIE (http://www.ciac.org)
Pandora's Box (http://www.nmrc.org)
PERL (http://cpan.org, ftp://ftp.netlabs.com, ftp://ftp.cis.ufl.edu)
PGP (http://net-dist.mit.edu)
ptscan (http://www.blueglobe.com)
SARA (http:// www.www-arc.com/sara)
Saint (http://www.wwdsi.com/saint)
SATAN (http://www.ciac.org), Satan – Patched for Linux
   (http://www.sunsite.unc.edu/pub/Linux/system/network/admin/satan-
   1.1.1.linux.fixed2.tgz)
SHADOW Intrusion Detection (http://www.nswc.navy.mil/ISSEC/CID)
S/KEY, logdaemon (http://www.ciac.org)
Snort (http:www.snort.org)
SOCKS (http://www.ciac.org)
ssh (http://ftp.cs.hut.fi/pub/ssh)
sscan (http://packetstorm.security.com)

stel (ftp://ftp.dsi.umin.it)
strobe (http://packetstorm.security.com)
sudo (ftp://ftp.cs.colorado.edu/pub/Sys Admin/sudo)
Superscan (http://www.foundstone.com)
swatch (http://www.ciac.org)
tcpdump (http://www.ciac.org)
TCP Wrapper (http://www.ciac.org)
Texas A & M Toolkit/Tiger Scripts (http://www.ciac.org)
thief, toneloc wargames dialers (http://www.ntshop.net)
tripwire (http://www.ciac.org)
winsock & related utilities (ftp://ftp.coast.net/SimTel, www.shareware.com)
winzip (http://www.winzip.com)
WS_Ping Pro Pack (http://www.ipswitch.com)
xidle (http://www.wins.uva.nl/pub/solaris)
XScreensaver (http://138.253.42.172/hppd/hpux/X11/Desktop)

# Internet Security & Audit Resources

## Browsing Tools

LYNX: ftp://ftp2.cc.ukans.edu  (text based browser)
MICROSOFT INTERNET EXPLORER: http://www.microsoft.com/
MOSAIC: http://www.ncsa.uiuc.edu/
NETSCAPE NAVIGATOR: http://www.netscape.com/
OPERA: http://www.winplanet.com

## Web Sites - General Internet Information

http://www.ietf.cnri.reston.va.us/home.html (Internet Engineering Task Force)
http://www.w3.org (WWW3 Consortium)
http://www.commerce.net (CommerceNet)
http://info.cern.ch/hypertext/DataSources/WWW/Servers.html (list of WWW
    servers)
http://www.openmarket.com/info/internet-index/current.html (Internet Facts)
http://www.cic.ohio-state.edu/hypertext/faq/usenet/FAQ-List.html (List of FAQ)
http://www.boardwatch.com/ (Boardwatch Magazine Online)
http://www.internic.net/ (directories of Internet users & resources)
http://info.webcrawler.com/mark/projects/robots/robots.html (Internet Robots)
http://tile.net/listserv/ (searchable index of internet mailing lists)
http://www.law.vill.edu/ (list of US government WWW servers)

http://www.dejanews.com (Newsgroup Q & A - use in lieu of newsgroup
   subscription)

## Web Sites - Auditors

http://www.itaudit.org/ (IT Audit Forum)
http://www.auditnet.org/ (IIA/Jim Kaplan Web site for auditors)
http://www.auditserve.com/ (Technical Research Center for Control Professionals)
http://www.theiia.org/ (Institute of Internal Auditors)
http://www.isaca.org/ (Information Systems Audit & Control Association)
http://www.misti.com/ (MIS Training Institute)

## Web Sites - Hackers

http://www.2600.com (home of famous hacker periodical)
http://www.antionline.com (numerous hack tools and references)
http://www.hackers.com (Hacker Site with numerous links to other hacker sites)
http://www.phrack.com (Phrack Magazine)
http://www/l0pht.com (L0pht Heavy Industries Hacking magazine)
http://www.enteract.com/~lspitz/papers.html (Lance Spitzner "Know Your Enemy"
   & other papers)
http://www.nmrc.org (Nomad Mobile Research Center – Hacker Tutorials & Tools)
http://www.rootshell.com (Well Indexed Hacker Tutorials & Tools – mostly Unix)
http://www.unitedcouncil.org (Links to Hacker Newsgroups)
http://www.securityfocus.com (Vast collection of well-indexed hacker exploit tools
   & information)
http://packetstorm.security.com (Packet Storm - vast collection of well-indexed
hacker exploit tools & information)
http://www.pwcrack.com/BIOS/bios.html (BIOS password cracking resources)
http://security.nerdnet.com/ (list of default logins for network devices, OS, etc.)

## Web Sites - Assorted Security Resources

http://www.alw.nih.gov/Security/security.html (National Institutes of Health -
   Computer Security)
http://www.securiteam.com (extensive security vulnerability & tool information)
http://www.ers.ibm.com/security-links/index.html (Extensive security links)
http://www.infoworld.com/security (Security Watch)
http://www.securityserver.com (Gateway to Information Security)
http://www.Security-Online.com (Security Online)
http://www.iss.net (Unix & Windows NT information & tools - commercial)

http://www.cve.mitre.org (Common Vulnerabilities and Exposures Directory)
http://www.nipc.gov (FBI National Infrastructure Protection Center – CyberNotes)
http://www.cert.org (CERT security bulletins, checklists, security tools, VIRUS-L)
http://www.cs.purdue.edu/coast/coast.html (extensive security archives/mirror site)
http://www.ciac.org (Dept of Energy CERT – extensive security bulletins & tools)
http://www.first.org (numerous generic & government related security documents)
http://www.issa-intl.org (Information Systems Security Association)
http://www.misti.com (MIS Training Institute/Information Security Institute)
http://www.telstra.com.au/Info/security.html (security reference index)
http://www.jjtc.com/Security/os.htm (Links to assorted operating system security resources)
http://www.SecurityPortal.com (numerous security resources and links)
http://www.planetnetwork.com/sec/begin.htm (Electronic Security International - numerous security links)

## Web Sites – Surveys

http://www.cc.gatech.edu/gvu/user_surveys (Georgia Tech. Web-user surveys)
http://www.ey.com/aaba/isaas/gis (Ernst & Young International Security Survey)
http://www.gocsi.com (Computer Security Institute/FBI Annual Computer Security Survey)
http://www.informationweek.com (Annual InformationWeek Information Security Surveys)
http://www.infosecuritymag.com (Information Security Magazine Industry/Security surveys)
http://www.networkcomputing.com (Network Security Survey, numerous product comparisons/lab tests)
http://www.netcraft.co.uk (monthly survey of international WWW server installed base)
http://www.umich.edu/~sgupta/hermes/survey3 (analysis charts of Georgia Tech. GVU surveys)

## Web Sites - Security Related Legislation/Standards

http://www.bsi.org.uk (British Standards Institution - BS7799)
http://www.cyberspacelaws.com (wide array of legislative & other security-related links)
http://csrc.ncsl.nist.gov (NIST Information Security Clearing House)
http://www.lib.berkeley.edu/GSSI/eu.html (European Data Protection Act)
http://www.nsi.org (National Security Institute – security legislation, security mgmt)

http://www.radium.ncsc.mil/tpep (NSA National computer Security Center criteria & references)

http://thomas.loc.gov (Bills in Congress)

http://aspe.hhs.gov/admnsimp (HIPAA Administrative Simplification)

http://niap.nist.gov (National Information Assurance Partnership)

http://www.ecommerce.gov (E-Commerce information)

http://www.lib.berkeley.edu/GSSI/eu.html (European Union Data Protection)

http://www.ita.doc.gov/td/ecom/menu.htm (EU/US Data Exchange "Safe Harbor" Principles)

http://www.ciao.gov (US Government Critical Infrastructure Assurance Office)

## Web Sites – US/European Computer Emergency Response Teams

http://www.eurocert.net (European Security Incident Information Service)

http://www.carnet.hr/CCERT (Croatian CERT)

http://www.csirt.dk (Danish CERT)

http://www.cert.funet.fi (Finland CERT)

http://www.renater.fr (France CERT)

http://www.cert.dfn.de (German CERT)

http://security.dsi.unimi.it (Italian CERT)

http://www.ja.net/CERT (JANET Network Response Team, UK)

http://www.nic.surfnet.nl/surfnet/security/cert-nl.html (Netherlands CERT)

http://www.cert.uninett.no (Norway CERT)

http://www.fccn.pt/RCCN-CERT (Portugal CERT)

http://www.arnes.si/en/si-cert (Slovenia CERT)

http://www.rediris.es (Spain Security Services IRIS-CERT)

http://www.switch.ch/cert (Swiss Academic and Research Network CERT)

http://www.cert.org (United States CERT)

http://www.ciac.org (US Department of Energy CERT)

## Web Sites – Privacy

http://www.cdt.org  (Center for Democracy and Technology)

http://www.townonline.com/privacyjournal  (Privacy Journal)

http://www.healthprivacy.org  (Health Privacy Project)

http://www.anonymizer.com (anonymous browsing services)

http://www.privacyinternational.com (comprehensive site of international developments in privacy)

http://judiciary.senate.gov/privacy.htm (US Senate Judiciary Committee on Privacy – privacy publication)

# Web Sites - Healthcare Organizations

http://www.ahima.org  (American Health Information Mgmt Association)
http://www.mahealthdata.org  (Massachusetts Health Data Consortium)
http://www.jcaho.org (Joint Commission on Accreditation of Healthcare
    Organizations)
http://www.ncqa.org  (National Committee for Quality Assurance)
http://www.amia.org  (American Medical Informatics Association)
http://www.ehnac.org  (Electronic Healthcare Network Accreditation Commission)
http://www.afecht.org  (Healthcare EDI industry group)
http://www.hhs.gov/policy  (US Department of Health and Human Services -
    samples policies)
http://www.hcfa.gov  (US Health Care Financing Administration – for sample
    policies, search on "security")
http://www.healthcaresecurity.org (Forum for Privacy & Security in Healthcare)
http://www.hostnet.org  (HOST (Healthcare Open Systems & Trials)
http://www.himss.org  (Healthcare Information and Management Systems Society)
http://www.jhita.org (Joint Healthcare IT Alliance)
http://www.wedi.org  (Workgroup on Electronic Data Interchange)
http://www.cpri.org (Computer-based Patient Record Institute)

*Acknowledgement: ISI thanks Kate Borten, President and Founder of the Marblehead Group, for her research in contributing to the list of Healthcare web sites presented in this section.*

# Web Sites - NetWare Security

http://www.nwconnection.com/ (NetWare Connection magazine archives)
http://www.novell.com/ (NetWare software & support information)
http://www.nmrc.org (Simple Nomad NetWare Hackers Site)

# Web Sites - UNIX Security

http://www.alw.nih.gov/Security/security.html (UNIX security information)
http://www.securityfocus.com (UNIX/Bugtraq archives)
http://www.stokely.com/unix.sysadm.resources/shareware.www.html (Vast Unix
    resources)
http://ciac.llnl.gov/ciac/ (CIAC security bulletins, UNIX-TCP/IP security tools)
http://www.lat.com/ (Los Alamos security repository, Gabriel, UNIX-TCP/IP
    security resources)
http://auk.uwaterloo.ca/aixgroup/ (AIX FAQs & other information)

http://www.austin.IBM.com/ (RS/6000 AIX security & other topics)

## Web Sites - LINUX

www.linux.org (cornerstone web site for Linux users)
www.linuxworld.com (numerous Linux related papers and links)
www.linuxsecurity.com (vast resources on Linux security and related Linux topics)
    metalab.unc.edu/LDP (Linux Documentation Project)
www.ecst.csuchico.edu/~jtmurphy/ (Linux Security Home Page)
    linux-center.org/en/system/security/index.html (Linux security pointers)
    tipoftheweek.darkelf.net (Linux Tip of the Week)
www.cs.texas.edu/users/kharker/linux-laptop (Ken Harker's Linux Laptop site)
    rpmfind.net/linux/RPM/ (locate Linux RPM contributions)
    sunsite.unc.edu/pub/Linux/system/network/admin/ (extensive freeware
    repository) filewatcher.org (search engine for locating Linux software)
www.trinux.org (compact version of Linux with extensive security tool links)
www.freshmeat.net (Linux tools & news)
www.xnet.com/~blatura/linux.shtml (well-organized list of Linux/Unix links)
www.lsw.uni-heidelberg.de/~aschweit/minilinux.html (list of miniature Linux
    distributions)
www.cheapbytes.com (inexpensive Linux CDs)
www.linuxmall.com (extensive discounted Linux software and references)
sites.inka.de/sites/lina/freefire-l/tools.html (extensive collection of Linux security
    tools)

## Web Sites - Windows NT/2000 Security

http://www.ntshop.net/, www.ntsecurity.net/ (Windows NT security information &
    tools)
http://www.somarsoft.com/ (Windows NT security information & tools)
http://www.telemark.net/~randallg/ntsecure.htm (Windows NT Web server security
    issues)
http://www.ntresearch.com/ (Windows NT security checklist)
http://www.iss.net/vd/ntfaq.html (Windows NT vulnerabilities database)
http://www.trustedsystems.com/ (Windows NT security checklist, security audit
    tools & white papers)
http://www.ntbugtraq.com/ (Windows NT Bugtraq archives)
http://www.microsoft.com/security/ (Security fixes & information for Microsoft
    products)
http://www.txdirect.net/~wall/ntlinks.htm (Bill Wall's Windows NT Links)
http://www.win2000mag.com (Windows 2000/NT Magazine – back issues

available on CD-ROM)

## Apple Macintosh Security

http://www.jjtc.com/Security/os.htm#MAC (Links to Macintosh security resources)

## AS/400 Security

http://www.as400.ibm.com/products/websphere/docs/as400v202/as400sec.html
(IBM AS/400 Security Resources)

## Web Sites - Internet, WWW, & Electronic Commerce Security

http://www.isr.net (Internet Security Review - Online Edition)
http://www.epic.com (Electronic Privacy Information Center)
http://www.ecommerce.gov (E-Commerce Information)
http://www.winmag.com/flanga/bt97/bt810.htm (Web Browser Security w/Security Tests)
http://www.bsdi.com/server/doc/web-info.html (information on WWW security)
http://www.sophist.demon.co.uk/ping/index.html ("Ping of Death" Web Page)
http://www.w3.org/Security/Faq/www-security-faq.html (WWW Security FAQ)
http://www-ns.rutgers.edu/www-security/reference.html (Rutgers WWW Security Reference page)
http://www.zurich.ibm.ch/Technology/Security/sirene/outsideworld/ecommerce.html (List of sites with information about secure electronic commerce)
http://www.netcraft.co.uk (Web Server Surveys and Identification)
http://www.proper.com/www/server-chart.html (comparison of WWW servers)
http://www.webcompare.com/ (comparison of WWW servers)
http://www.nue.et-inf.uni-siegen.de/~geuer-pollmann/xml_security.html (XML Security page)

## Web Sites - Mobile Code (Active Web Page Content) Security

http://www.nat.bg/~joro/ (Georgi Gununski sample web browser exploits)
http://www.ppdonline.com/demos/changesecurity.htm
("scary" ActiveX demo)
http://www.axent.com/swat (references & examples of security vulnerabilities)
http://hoohoo.ncsa.uiuc.edu/docs/tutorials/includes.html (SSI Security)
http://www.webcom/~webcom/help/inc/include.shtml (SSI Security)

http://www.primus.com/staff/paulp/cgi-security (CGI Security)
http://hoohoo.ncsa.uiuc.edu/cgi/security.html (CGI Security)
http://www.perl.com/perl/news/latro-announce.html (PERL Interpreter
    Probe/Locator "latrodectus cyberneticus")
http://www.rstcorp.com/javasecurity/links.htm (JAVA Security)
http://www.javasoft.com/sfaq/ (JAVA Security)
http://www.cs.princeton.edu/sip/pub/secure.html (JAVA Security)
http://www.math.gatech.edu/~mladue/Hostile/HostileApplets.html (JAVA Security)
http://whenever.cs.berkeley.edu/graffiti (JAVA Security)
http://microsoft.com/intdev/security/ (ActiveX Security)
http://www1.halcyon.com/mclain/ActiveX/Exploder/FAQ.htm (ActiveX Security)
http://www.security.org.il/security/iebugs.html (ActiveX Security)
http://web.mit.edu/crioux/www/ie/index.html (ActiveX Security)
http://www.osf.org/~loverso/javascript (Javascript Security)
http://www.netscape.com/newsref/std/cookies_spec.html (Cookies Security)
http://www.currents.net/cookies.html (Cookies Security)
http://www.illuminatus.com/cookie/ (Cookies Security)
http://www.research.digital.com/nsl/formtest/stats-by-test/Netscape/Cookie.html
    (Cookies Security)
http://info.webcrawler.com/mak/projects/robots/robots.html (Web robots security)

## Web Sites - Firewall Security

http://www.clark.net/pub/mjr/pubs/fwfaq (Marcus Ranum Firewall FAQ)
http://www.firewall.com (numerous links to firewall references and software
    resources)
http://www.nfr.com/forum/firewall-wizards.html (Firewall Wizards mailing list and
    archives)
http://www.zeuros.co.uk (Rotherwick Firewall Resources)
http://lists.gnac.net (GreatCircle Firewalls Digest mailing list and archives)
http://www.cert.dfn.de/eng/fwl/ (German CERT firewall laboratory)
http://www.nwconnection.com/ (Jan '97 issue - excellent technical tutorial on
    firewalls)
http://www.robertgraham.com/pubs/ (several detailed white papers on firewalls and
    intrusion detection)
http://www.cisco.com (Cisco Web Site – numerous how-to's FAQ on router
    security)
http://www.phoneboy.com/fw1/ (Unofficial CheckPoint Firewall-1 FAQ &
    freeware site)
http://www.icsa.net/ (International Computer Security Association – firewall
    certification)

## Web Sites – PERL Resources

http://www.perl.com (Mark-Jason Dominus PERL resource site)
http://cpan.rog (Comprehensive PERL Archive Network)
http://perlarchive.com (vast collection of PERL CGI programs and other PERL
    resources)

## Web Sites - Software Repositories

http://www.shareware.com (shareware/freeware software repository - Windows &
    non-Windows systems)
http://www.download.com (shareware/freeware software repository - Windows
    systems)
http://www.tucows.com (international shareware/freeware software repository -
    Windows systems)
http:www.davecentral.com (shareware/freeware Windows & Linux tools –
    extensive network diagnostic/audit tools)

## Web Sites – Information Warfare

http://www.infowar.com (Winn Schwartau Information Warfare Site)
http://www.au.af.mil/own/sandt/iw-hmpg.html (Information Warfare Links)
http://www.psycom.net/iwar.1.html (Institute for the Advanced Study of
    Information Warfare)
http://www.fas.org/irp/wwwinfo.html#infowar (Federation of American Scientists
    (FAS) Intelligence Resource Program)
http://www.rand.org/publications/RRR/RRR.fall95.cyber/ (Rand Research Review)
http://www.aia.af.mil/aialink/homepages/afiwc/index.htm (Air Force Information
    Warfare Center)
http://www.leglnet.com/libr-inwa.htm (Information Warfare Law Library)

## Web Sites - Remote Access/Authentication

http://www.nwfusion.com (Remote Access Servers Buyers Guide; Network World)
http://www.livingston.com/tech/technotes/500/index.html#RADIUS (RADIUS
    Home Page)
http://easynet.de/tacacs-faq/tacacs-faq.html#toc2 (TACACS FAQ)
http://www.biometrics.com (Biometrics Consortium)
http://www.afb.org.uk (Association for Biometrics)
http://www.biometricgroup.com (International Biometrics Group)

## Web Sites - Cryptography

http://world.std.com/~franl/crypto.html (vast links to cryptography resources)

http://csrc.nist.gov (NIST Security Clearinghouse links to encryption & PKI resources)

http://dir.yahoo.com/Computers_&_Internet/Security_&_Encryption (numerous links to encryption sites)

http://www.ietf.org/html.charters/pkix-charter.html (Public Key Infrastructure Working Group - X.509)

http://www.rsa.com/rsalabs/faq (RSA Cryptography FAQ)

http://www.counterpane.com/biblio (Bruce Schneier's extensive links to on-line cryptography papers)

http://www.cdt.org/crypto (Center for Democracy & Technology links to US encryption policy & legislation)

http://www.ssh.com (SSH Communications extensive links to cryptographic resources)

http://home.netscape.com/security/techbriefs/ssl.html (SSL Security technical references)

http://www.setco.org (Secure Electronic Transaction LLC links to SET cryptography resources & products)

http://www.pgpi.org (International PGP home page including International version of Pretty Good Privacy software)

http://members.aol.com/netnavig/pgp.htm (Benjamin's Pretty Good Privacy - PGP page)

http://www.eff.org/pub/Privacy (EFF "Privacy, Security, Crypto, & Surveillance" Archive)

## Web Sites - Residential Broadband (Cable Modems, Digital Subscriber Line)

http://rpcp.mit.edu/~gingold/cable (Cable Resources on the Web)

http://www.cablemodems.com (Cable Modem Links (products, service providers)

http://www.cablemodemclub.com (Cable Modem Information, Graphic Ping Tool)

http://cabledatacomnews.com (On-Line Cable Modem Newsletter with Links)

http://www.aspergantis.com/adsl (ADSL Resource Guide)

http:// www.dslreports.com (DSL links, including security)

http:// www.easystreet.com (EasyDSL Support)

http:// www.uawg.com (Universal ADSL Working Group)

http://www.sushisoft.com/adsl (The ADSL HOWTO for Linux - also useful for non-Linux)

http://www.uq.net.au/~zzdmacka/the-nat-page (The NAT Page - firewalls) http:// www.getspeed.com (Locate Local High-speed Network Access)

## Web Sites - Virtual Private Networks

http://kubarb.phsx.ukans.edu/~tbird/vpn.html (Tina Bird VPN Web site)
http://www.software.ibm.com/network/technology/vpn (Numerous VPN Case
    Studies & References)
http//: www.ip-sec.com (IPSec Developers Forum)
http://www.microsoft.com/communications/morepptp.htm (Point-to-Point
    Tunneling Protocol - PPTP)
http://www.cisco.com (Layer 2 Forwarding - L2F )
http://www.masinter/~l2tp (Layer Two Tunneling Protocol - L2TP)
http://www.employees.org/~satch/ssh/faq (SSH FAQ)
http://socks.nec.com (SOCKS Home Page)

## FTP Sites - Miscellaneous

ftp://athena-dist.mit.edu (Kerberos software & references)
ftp://ciac.llnl.gov (CIAC security bulletins, UNIX-TCP/IP security tools)
ftp://coast.cs.purdue.edu (security tools & references)
ftp://crvax.sri.com (RISKS Digest)
ftp://csrc.ncsl.nist.gov (NIST security FTP server)
ftp://decuac.dec.com (routers, firewalls, & UNIX tools)
ftp://ds.internic.net (primary Internet RFC repository)
ftp://ftp.auscert.org.au (Australian CERT - UNIX/Internet security)
ftp://ftp.bellcore.com (numerous UNIX & TCP/IP security resources)
ftp://ftp.cisco.com (routers & firewalls)
ftp://ftp.coast.net (vast archive of PC software including Internet/Winsock tools)
ftp://ftp.eff.org (Computer Underground Digest)
ftp://ftp.informatik.uni-hamburg.de (virus information - UNIX & other)
ftp://ftp.nisc.sri.com (Internet usage statistics, DNS registry list)
ftp://ftp.ripe.net (regional InterNIC for Europe)
ftp://ftp.sunet.se (numerous UNIX & TCP/IP security resources)
ftp://ftp.sura.net (numerous UNIX & TCP/IP security resources)
ftp://ftp.uu.net (numerous UNIX & TCP/IP security resources; USENIX)
ftp://info.cert.org (security bulletins, checklists, security tools, VIRUS-L)
ftp://nasirc.nasa.gov (NASA security bulletins)
ftp://net.tamu.edu (firewalls & UNIX security tools)
ftp://nisca.acs.ohio-state.edu (firewalls)
ftp://nist.ncsl.nist.gov (NIST BBS - security bulletins & numerous security/audit
    references)

ftp://research.att.com (firewalls)
ftp://rs.internic.net (Internet registration services - 703-742-4777)
ftp://theta.iis.utokyo.ac.jp:/pub1/security (security tools & information)
ftp://tis.com (firewalls, crypto product list, other security tools & information)
ftp://ftp.win.tue.nl (numerous UNIX & TCP/IP security tools & references,
    including SATAN)

## Security Mailing Lists/E-Mail Servers

aixserv@austin.ibm.com (AIX bulletins including security)
bugtraq-request@crimelab.com (UNIX security exposures)
cert-advisory-request@cert.org (security bulletins)
docserver@csrc.ncsl.nist.gov (NIST document mail server)
majordomo@8lgm.org (subscribe 8lgm-list: "Eight Little Green Men" -
    Unix security exposures, hacker exploit scripts)
majordomo@alive.ampr.ab.ca (HACK-L: hacker alerts)
majordomo@lists.gnac.com (subscribe firewalls-digest: Brent Chapman's firewalls
    digest)
majordomo@iss.net (subscribe ntsecurity-digest: Windows NT Security digest)
mailserv@ds.internic.net (primary Internet RFC repository)
risks-request@CSL.SRI.COM (RISKS digest)
listserv@lehigh.edu (SUB valert-L: urgent virus warnings)

## Security/Audit Related Usenet Groups

alt.2600
alt.business.internal-audit
alt.crackers
alt.hackers
alt.security
alt.security.pgp
alt.security.ripem
comp.protocols.kerberos
comp.risks
comp.security.announce
comp.security.misc
comp.security.unix
comp.unix.admin
comp.unix.wizards
comp.virus
info.pem.dev

misc.security
sci.crypt

For a full list of USENET newsgroups & FAQS:
ftp://rtfm.mit.edu/pub/ or e-mail to: mailserv@rtfm.mit/edu

# Useful Internet RFCs

## General
RFC1118   Hitchhiker's Guide to the Internet
RFC1147   FYI on Network Management Tools
RFC1359   Connecting to the Internet
RFC1392   Internet User's Glossary
RFC1402   There's gold in them thar networks!...
RFC1700   Well Known Ports (TCP/IP Applications7)
RFC1883   Internet Protocol, Version 6 (IPv6)
RFC1855   Netiquette Guidelines

## Security
RFC1038   Draft Revised IP security option
RFC1108   U.S. Department of Defense Security Options for the Internet Protocol
RFC1244   Site Security Handbook (replaced by RCF 2196)
RFC1281   Guidelines for the Secure Operation of the Internet
RFC1319   The MD2 Message-Digest Algorithm
RFC1320   The MD4 Message-Digest Algorithm
RFC1321   The MD5 Message-Digest Algorithm
RFC1334   PPP Authentication Protocols
RFC1352   SNMP Security Protocols
RFC1355   Privacy & Accuracy Issues in Network Information Center
RFC1411   Telnet Authentication: Kerberos Version 4
RFC1412   Telnet Authentication: SPX
RFC1416   Telnet Authentication Option
RFC1422   Privacy Enhancement for Internet Electronic Mail - Part I
RFC1423   Privacy Enhancement for Internet Electronic Mail - Part II
RFC1424   Privacy Enhancement for Internet Electronic Mail - Part III
RFC1446   Security Protocols for Version 2 of the Simple Network Management Protocol (SNMPv2)
RFC1455   Physical Link Security Type of Service
RFC1457   Security Label Framework for the Internet
RFC1472   The Definitions of Managed Objects for the Security Protocols of the Point-to-Point Protocol
RFC1492   An Access Control Protocol, Sometimes Called TACACS

RFC1507  DASS - Distributed Authentication Security Service
RFC1508  Generic Security Service Application Program Interface
RFC1509  Generic Security Service API : C-bindings
RFC1510  The Kerberos Network Authentication Service (V5)
RFC1511  Common Authentication Technology Overview
RFC1535  A Security Problem & Proposed Correction With Widely Deployed DNS Software
RFC1579  Firewall-Friendly FTP
RFC1636  Report of IAB Workshop on Security in the Internet Architecture
RFC1675  Security Concerns for IPng
RFC1704  On Internet Authentication
RFC1710  Simple Internet Protocol Plus White Paper
RFC1731  IMAP4 Authentication Mechanisms
RFC1734  POP3 Authentication Command
RFC1750  Randomness Recommendations for Security
RFC1751  A Convention for Human-Readable 128-bit Keys
RFC1760  The S/KEY One-Time Password System
RFC1805  Location-Independent Data/Software Integrity Protocol
RFC1810  Report on MD5 Performance
RFC1824 The Exponential Security System (TESS): An Identity-Based Cryptographic Protocol for Authenticated Key-Exchange
RFC1825  Security Architecture for the Internet Protocol
RFC1826  IP Authentication Header
RFC1827  IP Encapsulating Security Payload
RFC1828  IP Authentication Using Keyed MD5
RFC1829  The ESP DES-CBC Transform
RFC1847  Security Multiparts for MIME
RFC1848  MIME Object Security Services
RFC1851  The ESP Triple DES Transform
RFC1852  IP Authentication Using Keyed SHA
RFC1853  IP in IP Tunneling
RFC1858  Security Considerations for IP Fragment Filtering
RFC1864  The Content-MD5 Header Field
RFC1875  UNINETT PCA Policy Statements
RFC1898  CyberCash Credit Card Protocol Version 0.8
RFC1910  User-based Security Model for SNMPv2
RFC1928  SOCKS Protocol Version 5
RFC1929  Username/Password Authentication for SOCKS V5
RFC1938  A One-Time Password System
RFC1948  Defending Against Sequence Number Attacks
RFC1949  Scalable Multicast Key Distribution
RFC1961  GSS-API Authentication Method for SOCKS Version 5

RFC1968   The PPP Encryption Control Protocol (ECP)
RFC1969   The PPP DES Encryption Protocol (DESE)
RFC2196   Site Security Handbook (replaces RFC 1244)

**HOW TO GET RFCs:**
Go to the following web site: http://www.rfc-editor.org/rfcsearch.html

# COMMERCIAL INTERNET PROVIDERS

### *United States*
1. America Online; 800-827-6364
2. AT&T WorldNet; 800-400-1447
3. Compuserve; 800-336-6823, 614-529-1340
4. Holonet; 510-704-0160
5. Microsoft Network; 800-426-9400
6. Netcom; 800-501-8649
7. Pipeline; 717-770-1700, 703-904-9115
8. Prodigy; 800-PRODIGY
9. PSI; 800-827-7482
10. UUNET Technologies; 800-488-6384
NOTE: US Providers listed above may also offer international POP's.

### *United Kingdom*
1. Compuserve; 0800-289378
2. Delphi; 01223-566950
3. Demon; 0181-349-0063
4. Direct Connection; 0181-3170100
5. Eunet; 01227-266466
6. GreenNet; 0171-7131941
7. Pipex; 01223-250120

### *Canada*
1. Hookup Communications; 905-847-8000 (voice)
2. UUNET Canada; 416-368-6621 (voice)
3. UUNorth; 416-225-8649

1. Via E-mail:
     info-deli-server@netcom.com  ("Send PDIAL" in subject)
2. Via Web Page Browsing:

http://dixie.tagsys.com/Provider/ListOfLists.html
http://www.internic.net/infoguide.html
http://www.isoc.org/~bgreene/nsp-index.html
http://www.teleport.com/~cci/directories/pocia.html
http://www.thelist.com

# PROFESSIONAL & TRADE ORGANISATIONS

## Contingency Planning

1. ASSOCIATION OF CONTINGENCY PLANNERS (ACP); ACP National Headquarters, PO Box 341, Brigham City, UT 84302-0341; Phone: 800-445-4ACP; http://www.acp-international.com
2. DISASTER RECOVERY INSTITUTE; 1810 Craig Road #213; St. Louis, MO 63146; Phone: 314-434-2272; http://www.dr.org
3. INTERNATIONAL DISASTER RECOVERY ASSOCIATION (IDRA); c/o BWT Associates; PO Box 515, Turnpike Station; Shrewsbury, MA 01545; Phone: 508-845-2585; http://www.idra.com
4. MID-ATLANTIC DISASTER RECOVERY ASSOCIATION (Eastern PA, Southern NJ, DE, MD, DC, & VA); c/o Sunny Bolander (410-528-2541), Walt Helgerman (301-657-5034); http://www.madra.org
5. SURVIVE!; P.O. Box 1614, Mt. Laurel, NJ; Phone: 609-778-5702; http://www.survive.com

## IBM Systems

1. IBM Users Groups (SHARE); Phone: 312-822-0932; http://www.share.org

## Information Security

1. COMPUTER SECURITY INSTITUTE (CSI); 600 Harrison St., San Francisco, CA 94107; Phone: 415-905-2378; http://www.gocsi.com
2. INFORMATION SECURITY FORUM; Plumtree Court (PCG8); London EC4A 4HT, United Kingdom; Phone: Tel: 44-(0)20 7213 1745; Fax: 44-(0)20 7213 4813; http://www.securityforum.org
3. INFORMATION SECURITY INSTITUTE; 310 Wrights Circle - Suite A; Seneca, SC 29678; Phone: 864-882-8666; http://www.misti.com
4. INFORMATION SYSTEMS SECURITY ASSOCIATION (ISSA); ISSA Headquarters, c/o Technical Enterprises, Inc., 7044 S. 13th St., Milwaukee, WI 53154; Phone: 414-768-8000; http://www.issa-intl.org
5. INTERNATIONAL COMPUTER SECURITY ASSOCIATION (ICSA); 1200 Walnut Bottom Road, Carlisle, PA 17013; Phone: 888-627-2281; http://www.icsa.net
6. INTERNATIONAL INFORMATION SYSTEMS SECURITY

CERTIFICATION CONSORTIUM (ISC2), Inc.); Parkview Office Tower –
Suite 100, Worcester, MA 01609; Phone: 508-842-7329; http://www.isc2.org
7. INTERNATIONAL INFORMATION INTEGRITY INSTITUTE (I-4); SRI
International; 333 Ravenswood Avenue; Menlo Park , CA 94025-3493; Phone:
415-859-4729
8. SYSTEM ADMINISTRATION, NETWORKING, AND SECURITY (SANS)
INSTITUTE; 5401 Westbard Ave. – Suite 1501; Bethesda, MD 20816; Phone:
310-951-0102; Fax: 310-951-0140; http://www.sans.org

### Information Systems Auditing
1. INFORMATION SYSTEMS AUDIT & CONTROL ASSOCIATION
(ISACA); ISACA International Headquarters; 3701 Algonquin Road, Suite
1010; Rolling Meadows, IL 60008; Phone: 708-253-1545;
http://www.isaca.org
2. THE INSTITUTE OF INTERNAL AUDITORS (IIA); 249 Maitland Ave.,
Altamonte Springs, FL 32701; Phone: 407-830-7600; http://www.theiia.org
3. MIS TRAINING INSTITUTE; 498 Concord St., Framingham, MA 01702;
Phone: 508-879-7999; http://www.misti.com

### NOVELL NetWare
1. NOVELL USERS INTERNATIONAL; 122 East 1700 South, Provo, UT
84606: 800-453-1267 x-1267;
ttp://www.novell.com/community/nui/index.html

### Records Management
1. ASSOCIATION OF RECORDS MANAGERS & ADMINISTRATORS
(ARMA); ARMA International, 4200 Somerset, Suite 215, Prairie Village, KS
66208; Phone: 913-341-3808; http://www.arma.org

### UNIX-TCP/IP
1. USENIX Association; PO Box 2299; Berkeley, CA 94710; Phone: 510-528-
8649; http://www.usenix.org

# Academic Institutions Offering Information Assurance (Security) Education

This list includes academic institutions known to offer Information Assurance
(Security) Education and having a related web address. It is an ever-growing list
and does not purport to be all inclusive.
1. Florida State University  (COE) http://www.cs.fsu.edu/
2. George Mason University  (COE) http://www.isse.gmu.edu/~csis/index.html

3.  George Washington University
    http://www.gwu.edu/~mastergw/programs/info_security/
4.  Georgia Tech Information Security Center http://www.oit.gatech.edu
5.  Idaho State  (COE) http://bilbo.isu.edu/security/security.html
6.  Information Resources Management College, National Defense University
    (COE) http://www.ndu.edu/irmc/
7.  Iowa State University  (COE) http://www.ISSL.org
8.  James Madison University  (COE) http://www.infosec.jmu.edu
    http://cob.jmu.edu/mba/MBAPgms.htm#TheInformationSecurityMBA
9.  Johns Hopkins University
    http://www.ftp://junix.hcf.jhu.edu/pub/miscellaneous_security_papers/
10. Naval Postgraduate School  (COE) http://www.cisr.nps.navy.mil
11. North Carolina State University http://www.ncsu.edu or
    http://www2.ncsu.edu/eos/info/computer_ethics/www/
12. Princeton http://www.cs.princeton.edu/sip/
13. Purdue University  (COE) http://www.purdue.edu
14. Rutgers University http://www.rutgers.edu or
     http://www.ns.rutgers.edu/www-security/index.html
15. Stanford University  (COE)
    http://www.stanford.edu/group/itss-ccs/security/secinfo.html
    http://Theory.Stanford.EDU/seclab/
16. Stevens Institute of Technology
    http://www.stevens.edu/academic_programs/default.html
17. Towson University http://www.towson.edu/ir/programs.html
18. Western Connecticut State University http://www.wcsu.ctstateu.edu
19. University of California, Davis  (COE) http://www.ucdavis.edu or
    http://seclab.cs.ucdavis.edu/Security.html
20. University of California, Santa Cruz, John Baskin School of Engineering
    http://www.cse.ucsc.edu/~darrell/
21. University of Idaho  (COE) http://www.cs.uidaho.edu
22. University of Illinois, Urbana-Champaign  (COE)
    http://www.cs.uiuc.edu/index.html
23. University of Maryland, Baltimore County http://29.125.144.52/index.html
24. University of New Haven, California http://www.newhaven.edu/california/
25. University of New Mexico http://www.cs.unm.edu/soe/cs/courses/descrip/
26. University of Virginia http://www.cs.virginia.edu

NOTE: (COE) = The academic institution has been recognised by the United States National Security Agency as a "Center of Academic Excellence in Information Systems Security Education"
(http://www.nsa.gov/isso/programs/nietp/corseval.htm)

*Acknowledgement: ISI thanks Allan Berg, Director, Information Security Program, College of Integrated Science and Technology, Department of Computer Science, James Madison University, for his research in contributing the list of academic institutions presented in this section.*

# Appendix G

## Authors' Biographies

### Dr. Andrew J. C. Blyth, Ph.D.

Dr. Andrew Blyth received his Ph.D. from the Computing Laboratory at the University of Newcastle Upon Tyne, UK in 1995. In 1996, he took up an appointment as a senior lecturer at the School of Computing University of Glamorgan, UK.

He is currently the scheme leader of the M.Sc. Information Security and Computer Crime. Dr. Blyth has published several papers in the area of information security and intrusion detection systems. His main research area is: *How do you specify, design, build, deploy, manage and defend trusted information systems within an organisation so as to achieve and maintain a competitive advantage?*

Dr. Blyth also works as a consultant in the area of information security and computer crime and has functioned as an expert witness for the police. He also performs IT security health checks and penetration tests in his spare time.

### Dr. Gerald L. Kovacich, CFE, CPP, CISSP

Dr. Kovacich graduated from the University of Maryland with a bachelor's degree in history and politics; the University of Northern Colorado with a master's degree in social science; Golden Gate University with a master's degree in telecommunications management; the US DoD Language Institute (Chinese Mandarin); and August Vollmer University with a doctorate degree in criminology. He is also a Certified Fraud Examiner, Certified Protection Professional, and a Certified Information Systems Security Professional.

Dr. Kovacich has over 37 years of corporate security, investigations, information systems security, and information warfare experience in the US government as a special agent; in international corporations as a technologist and manager; and as a consultant to United States and foreign government agencies and corporations.

Dr. Kovacich has taught both graduate and undergraduate courses in criminal justice, technology crimes investigations and information systems security for Los Angeles City College, DeAnza College, Golden Gate University, and August Vollmer University. He has also lectured internationally and presented workshops on these topics for national and international conferences; as well as having written numerous, internationally published articles on high-technology crime, information systems security, and information warfare.

He has authored five other books (published by Butterworth-Heinemann). These are:

*Information Systems Security Officer's Guide: Establishing and Managing an Information Protection Program* (May 1998, ISBN 0-7506-9896-9)

*I-Way Robbery: Crime on the Internet,* with Bill Boni (May 1999, ISBN 0-7506-7029-0).

*High-Technology Crime Investigator's Handbook: Working in the Global Information Environment,* with Bill Boni (September 1999; ISBN 0-7506-7086-X).

*Netspionage: The Global Threat to Information,* with Bill Boni (September 2000, ISBN: 0-7506-7257-9).

He is also co-authoring a book tentatively entitled: *Information Warfare: How Businesses, Governments and Others Achieve Global Objectives and Attain a Competitive Advantage*, to be published in June 2002 by Auerbach Publishers; and another book entitled: *The Managers' Handbook for Corporate Security: Establishing and Managing a Successful Assets Protection Program*, to be published in November 2002 by Butterworth-Heinemann.

Dr. Kovacich currently resides on Whidbey Island, Washington, where he continues to conduct research, write, and often lectures nationally and internationally on such topics as: global, nation-state and corporate aspects of information systems security, fraud, corporate security, high-technology crime, information assurance, proprietary information protection; as well as netspionage, economic and industrial espionage, and information warfare. He is also the founder of *ShockwaveWriters.Com*, an informal association of writers, researchers and lecturers who concentrate on the above noted topics. (See http://www.shockwavewriters.com)

# Index